FINANCING EDUCATION
Fiscal and Legal Alternatives

Edited by

Roe L. Johns
Kern Alexander
Forbis Jordan

University of Florida

A Summary of the
National Educational Finance Project

CHARLES E. MERRILL PUBLISHING COMPANY
A Bell & Howell Company
Columbus, Ohio

MERRILL'S SERIES
FOR EDUCATIONAL ADMINISTRATION

Under the Editorship of

LUVERN L. CUNNINGHAM, Dean
College of Education
The Ohio State University

and

H. THOMAS JAMES, President
The Spencer Foundation
Chicago, Illinois

Published by
CHARLES E. MERRILL PUBLISHING COMPANY
A Bell & Howell Company
Columbus, Ohio

International Standard Book Number: 0-675-09071-7

1 2 3 4 5 6 7 8 9 10 / 75 74 73 72

Printed in the United States of America

Contributors

iii

Preface

Financing Education: Fiscal and Legal Alternatives is a com-
ation of key articles taken from the publications of the four-
ir National Educational Finance Project which concluded in
d-1972. Selected chapters of most general interest comprise
is book intended for use by students enrolled in classes in school
ance and general educational administration. It should also be
value to school superintendents, school board members, state
gislators, and many others.

For those not familiar with the project, some background
ight be helpful. This comprehensive, nation-wide research proj-
on school finance was initiated by the United States Office of
ucation to (1) identify the dimensions of educational need in
nation; (2) identify target populations with special educa-
al needs; (3) measure cost differentials among different edu-
ional programs; (4) relate the variations in educational needs
d costs to the ability of school districts, states, and the federal
ernment to support education; (5) analyze economic factors
ecting the financing of education; (6) evaluate present state
d federal programs for the financing of education; and (7) con-
ruct alternative school finance models, both state and federal,
d analyze the consequences of each.

Administered through the Florida State Department of Edu-
tion and the University of Florida at Gainesville, research was
nducted by thirty-six experts in educational finance and eco-
mics employed by twenty universities throughout the United
ates. These specialists were assisted by more than thirty re-
arch associates, and finance specialists from all fifty states co-
erated in providing much vital information.

The findings and recommendations of the project were reported in earlier publications by the central staff of the project; summaries of ten satellite projects were also summarized in these volumes. Of these publications, most of which are now out of print, only the summary monograph, *Future Directions for School Financing*, will be reprinted. Therefore, the central staff has selected chapters from these publications for reprinting in this volume. Charles E. Merrill Publishing is paying customary royalties, but since the editors do not wish to profit personally from the sale of this book, a private, non-profit corporation, The Institute for Educational Finance, has been created to receive the royalties which will be used to carry on research in school finance.

Roe L. Johns

Kern Alexander

K. Forbis Jordan

Contents

vii

Contents

vii

CHAPTER 1

The Development of State Support
for the Public Schools

State support for the public schools has a long history. It probably began in the early part of the nineteenth century. Unfortunately, authentic financial reports are not available from which the evolution of state support during the nineteenth century may be traced. However, by 1890 the states collectively provided $33,987,581 in financial aid for the public schools.[1] This amounted to 23.8 percent of total school revenue in 1890.[2] Undoubtedly, much of the state aid reported was derived from income from sixteenth section land grants from the federal government which could be strictly interpreted as federal aid rather than state aid. In fact, Mort, in the study from which these data are quoted, referred to the revenue as "state and federal"— revenue although the federal government did not make any direct appropriations for the public schools until the Smith-Hughes Bill was enacted into law in 1917.

The sixteenth section land grants, provided in the Ordinance of 1787 and the action of Congress in 1802, continuing the policy of making land grants for public education in all states newly admitted to the Union, undoubtedly stimulated state support. State agencies handled these land grants and distributed funds derived from the land grants. This set a precedent of providing funds for the public schools from the state level. Some of these land grants proved to be valuable and productive of income, and others worthless. The demand was made in some states during the nineteenth century that the state provide funds for the schools in the townships which had happened to receive worthless land grants. This was probably the beginning of the concept of financial equalization for the purpose of equalizing educational opportunity.

Although it was generally conceded that education was a state responsibility under the Tenth Amendment to the federal Constitution, most states during the nineteenth century exercised that responsibility, primarily by authorizing the levy of local school taxes for the support of the public schools. No integrated plans of school finance were developed during the nineteenth century. No conceptual theory of school finance was developed. Such state funds, as were distributed, were generally apportioned on a school census basis with little consideration being given to equalization of educational opportunity or the provision of at least a minimum program of education for all children. In the remainder of this chapter, primary attention will be given to the development of conceptual theories of state support, the development of state support since 1930 and the principal issues of state support.[3]

THE DEVELOPMENT OF THEORIES AND PRINCIPLES OF STATE SUPPORT[4]

All important social movements have had an intellectual leader or leaders. These men, who are almost always theorists, are sometimes considered impractical by the general public. However, it is the theorists who shape social policy and social organization more than any other group in society. Politicians and public officials usually base their policies on theoretical assumptions of some kind. Politicians such as Jefferson, Hamilton, and Madison, who were also theorists, have had a profound effect on governmental policy in the United States.

The early theorists on state school finance were not politicians or holders of public office. All of them were university professors, but they have had a profound influence on political policy in the United States with respect to state school financing. These theorists dealt with some of the crucial values, issues, and

2

problems in American society. Therefore, what they had to say was of great interest to the public. Some of the values and issues involved in determining policies on state school financing follow: Is equalization of educational opportunity a function of a democratic government? What level of education should be guaranteed to everyone in order to promote the general welfare? To what extent should the states exercise control over the public schools? To what extent should "home rule" in school government be encouraged? Are nonproperty state taxes more equitable than local property taxes? What percent of school revenue should be provided from state sources?

The central stream of state school finance theory in the United States originated at Teachers College, Columbia University, at the beginning of the twentieth century. The chief participants in this stream and their principal concepts are discussed in the following sections.

Ellwood P. Cubberley

The development of the theory of state school support began with Cubberley, who was a student at Teachers College, Columbia University, near the beginning of the twentieth century. His famous monograph on *School Funds and Their Apportionment,*[5] a revision of his doctoral dissertation, was published in 1905. It is interesting to note that George D. Strayer, Sr., who is discussed later, also received his doctor's degree at Teachers College in 1905. These two were among the first professors of educational administration. Strayer stayed at Teachers College, and Cubberley went to Stanford University. These two giants were largely responsible for developing the early literature of educational administration. The conceptualizations of school finance developed by these two men, their students, and students of their students have dominated the thinking on educational finance during the twentieth century.

Cubberley's work was so fundamental in formulating the basic concepts of state school financing that several quotations from his original study published in 1905 are set forth below. He studied the historical development of education in the United States, the legal arrangements provided for public education, the effect of the Industrial Revolution on the distribution of wealth, and the inequalities of educational opportunity among the several districts of a state. He then formulated his concept of the

3

state's responsibility for providing educational services as follows:

> The state owes it to itself and to its children, not only to permit of the establishment of schools, but also to require them to be established—even more, to require that these schools, when established, shall be taught by a qualified teacher for a certain minimum period of time each year, and taught under conditions and according to requirements which the state has, from time to time, seen fit to impose. While leaving the way open for all to go beyond these requirements the state must see that none fall below.[6]

He applied his basic concept of state responsibility to the apportionment of state school funds in the following words:

> Theoretically all the children of the state are equally important and are entitled to have the same advantages; practically this can never be quite true. The duty of the state is to secure for all as high a minimum of good instruction as is possible, but not to reduce all to this minimum; to equalize the advantages to all as nearly as can be done with the resources at hand; to place a premium on those local efforts which will enable communities to rise above the legal minimum as far as possible; and to encourage communities to extend their educational energies to new and desirable undertakings.[7]

These concepts were stated by Cubberley in 1905, but they seem quite applicable today. Numerous books, monographs, and articles have been written on state responsibility for education and state school financing, but it is difficult to find in all the literature on this subject a better or clearer statement than Cubberley's conceptualization. It is true, as will be pointed out later in this chapter, that Strayer and Mort at a later date criticized one part of Cubberley's conceptualization; but the differences that arose were on the technology of state distribution of school funds rather than the values or goals. The difference arose over the implementation of the phrase, " . . . to place a premium on those local efforts which will enable communities to rise above the legal minimum as far as possible. . . ."

After formulating his conceptualizations of sound policy in state school financing, Cubberley used them as criteria to evaluate the methods used by the states to distribute school funds at

4

the beginning of the century. As Cubberley's study was the first comprehensive one to be made of state school funds, and as it was made at the very beginning of the twentieth century, his findings provide a valuable benchmark for measuring progress in state school financing. Therefore, some of his principal findings are set forth below:

1. That due to the unequal distribution of wealth, the demands set by the states for maintaining minimum standards cause very unequal burdens. What one community can do with ease is often an excessive burden for another.

2. That the excessive burden of communities, borne in large part for the common good, should be equalized by the state.

3. That a state school tax best equalizes the burdens.

4. That any form of state taxation for schools fails to accomplish the ends for which it was created unless a wise system of distribution is provided.

5. That (judged by Cubberley's criteria) few states (at the beginning of the twentieth century) had as yet evolved a just and equitable plan for distributing the funds they had at hand.

6. That "taxes where paid," property valuation, total population, and school census were all undesirable methods of apportionment.

7. That total enrollment, enrollment for a definite period, average membership, average daily attendance, and aggregate days attendance are each successive improvements over the census basis of apportionment.

8. That any single measure for distributing state funds is defective; but if one is used, the best single measure is the number of teachers employed.

9. That the best basis for distributing state funds is the combination of the teachers actually employed and aggregate days attendance.

10. That special incentive funds shall be provided to encourage communities to provide secondary education, kindergartens, manual training, evening schools, and so forth.

11. That a reserve fund should be established for the relief of those communities which have made the maximum effort allowed by law and yet are unable to meet the minimum demands made by the state.[8]

Harlan Updegraff

Updegraff is not as well known as some of the other theorists in state school financing, but his contributions are important. Although he accepted the concepts of Cubberley for the most part, he did make some important additions to Cubberley's model. Updegraff, a professor of educational administration at the University of Pennsylvania, made a survey of the financial support of rural schools in New York state in 1921 in which he presented some new concepts of state support.[9] These are the principles of state support he proposed:

1. Local support is fundamental.

2. The local units for the support of schools should contain, insofar as practicable, enough property taxable for school purposes to raise that portion of the expenses of the school which it is believed should be borne by the local districts without an undue burden upon the owners of property.

3. Some portion of the support of local schools should come from the state government, the amount being dependent upon certain factors, exact standards for which have not been scientifically determined, but which will vary in the different states.

4. The administration of state aid should be such as to increase the efficient participation of citizens in a democratic form of government.

5. The purpose of state aid should be not only to protect the state from ignorance, to provide intelligent workers in every field of activity, and to educate leaders, but also to guarantee to each child, irrespective of where he happens to live, equal opportunity to that of any other child for the education which will best fit him for life.[10]

Those were the days in which the word efficiency was greatly emphasized in administration. Therefore, it is not surprising that Updegraff presented a set of criteria for determining the efficiency of state support, a summary of which follows:

1. The efficient participation of citizens in the responsibilities of citizenship should be promoted by making the extent of the state's contribution dependent upon local action.

2. The state should neither be timid nor autocratic in withholding state funds because of deficiencies in local action.

6

3. Special grants should be provided to encourage the introduction of new features into the schools.

4. The districts should receive support in inverse proportion to their true valuation per teacher unit.

5. Efficiency in the conduct of schools should be promoted by increasing the state grant whenever the true tax rate is increased and by lowering it whenever the local tax is decreased.

6. The plan of state aid should be so framed that it will measure precisely the elements involved and will respond promptly and surely to any change in the local districts.[11]

Updegraff not only proposed principles and criteria for state support, but he developed techniques for the distribution of general school aid which embodied his ideas. He proposed a sliding scale that provided increased amounts of state aid per teacher unit for each increase of 1/2 mill of school taxes levied ranging from 3 1/2 to 9 mills,[12] but he provided proportionately more state aid for a district with a low true valuation per teacher unit.

Under Updegraff's plan, the state would support variable levels of minimum programs ranging from $840 per teacher unit to $2,160 depending upon the amount of local tax effort. He attempted to incorporate the concepts of equalization of educational opportunity and reward for effort within the same formula. As will be pointed out below, both Strayer and Mort opposed that approach. Updegraff justified his proposals for encouraging additional local effort on the basis of efficiency. Updegraff's ideas fell into disfavor for many years following the emergence of the concepts advanced by Strayer and Mort. However, today Updegraff's concept of a variable level foundation program depending upon the level of local effort is being utilized in some modern state support programs. It is not being justified on the basis of efficiency, but on the basis of providing an incentive for quality education.

Updegraff introduced another idea, the teacher unit, which today is incorporated in many state support programs. He suggested that instead of using teachers employed as a basis of state distribution, standard numbers of pupils per teacher should be fixed for different school levels, for urban and rural districts, and for different types of classes.[13]

7

George D. Strayer, Sr.

Strayer, like Cubberley, was interested in the total area of educational organization and administration, and he made major contributions in every sector. In none, however, did he make a greater contribution than in state school finance for he advanced the theoretical basis of school financing. Strayer first advanced his theories of school finance in Volume I of the Report of the Educational Finance Inquiry Commission which was published in 1923. This volume, *The Financing of Education in the State of New York*[14] by Strayer and Haig, devoted four pages to a theoretical conceptualization of the equalization of educational opportunity which has had a major impact on educational thought and policy.

So important has been the effect of this report that some selected excerpts from it are set forth below. The concept "equalization of educational opportunity" that prevailed at that time was described as follows:

> There exists today and has existed for many years a movement which has come to be known as the "equalization of educational opportunity" or the "equalization of school support." These phrases are interpreted in various ways. In its most extreme form the interpretation is somewhat as follows: The state should insure equal educational facilities to every child within its borders at a uniform effort throughout the state in terms of the burden of taxation; the tax burden of education should throughout the state be uniform in relation to tax-paying ability, and the provision for schools should be uniform in relation to the educable population desiring education. Most of the supporters of this proposition, however, would not preclude any particular community from offering at its own expense a particularly rich and costly educational program. They would insist that there be an adequate minimum offered everywhere, the expense of which should be considered a prior claim on the state's economic resources.[15]

Strayer and Haig stated that to carry into effect the principle of "equalization of educational opportunity" or "equalization of school support," it would be necessary:

> . . . (1) to establish schools or make other arrangements sufficient to furnish the children in every locality within

the state with equal educational opportunities up to some prescribed minimum; (2) to raise the funds necessary for this purpose by local or state taxation adjusted in such manner as to bear upon the people in all localities at the same rate in relation to their tax-paying ability; and (3) to provide adequately either for the supervision and control of all the schools, or for their direct administration by a state department of education.[16]

Strayer and Haig then presented the following conceptual model for formulating a plan of state support which incorporated the principles they had outlined:

(1) A local school tax in support of the satisfactory minimum offering would be levied in each district at a rate which would provide the necessary funds for that purpose in the richest district.

(2) The richest district then might raise all of its school money by means of the local tax, assuming that a satisfactory tax, capable of being locally administered, could be devised.

(3) Every other district could be permitted to levy a local tax at the same rate and apply the proceeds toward the cost of schools, but

(4) since the rate is uniform, this tax would be sufficient to meet the costs only in the richest district and the deficiencies would be made up by state subventions.[17]

It will be noted that Strayer and Haig emphasized the equalization of the tax burden to support schools as well as the equalization of educational opportunity. However, they did not incorporate the reward for effort or incentive concepts in their state support model. They attacked these concepts, which had been advanced by Cubberley and Updegraff, in the following words.

Any formula which attempts to accomplish the double purpose of equalizing resources and rewarding effort must contain elements which are mutually inconsistent. It would appear to be more rational to seek to achieve local adherence to proper educational standards by methods which do not tend to destroy the very uniformity of effort called for by the doctrine of equality of educational opportunity.[18]

9

Paul R. Mort

Mort was one of Strayer's students and later became his colleague at Teachers College, Columbia University. Strayer and Haig referred to a "satisfactory minimum program" to be equalized, but they offered no suggestions concerning how to measure it. Mort assumed the task of defining a satisfactory minimum program as his doctoral problem. His doctoral dissertation, *The Measurement of Educational Need*,[19] was published in 1924.

Mort perhaps should be classified a disseminator and developer,[20] but he was a theorist as well. Although he accepted completely the conceptualization of Strayer and Haig, he somewhat clarified their theories, and he advanced some concepts of his own concerning the formulation of a state minimum program. Therefore, some of the key ideas developed by Mort in his dissertation are presented below.

Mort presented an extremely advanced concept of what should be included in the state-assured minimum program. These are the elements he recommended for inclusion:

(1) An educational activity found in most or all communities throughout the state is acceptable as an element of an equalization program.

(2) Unusual expenditures for meeting the general requirements due to causes over which a local community has little or no control may be recognized as required by the equalization program. If they arise from causes reasonably within the control of the community they cannot be considered as demanded by the equalization program.

(3) Some communities offer more years of schooling or a more costly type of education than is common. If it can be established that unusual conditions require any such additional offerings, they may be recognized as a part of the equalization program.[21]

Mort modestly stated that " . . . it cannot be hoped that these will prove exhaustive as the thinking in this field develops."[22] However, his concepts of the elements to include in a minimum program are as valid today as when they were written. For example, his third element includes compensatory education for the

10

disadvantaged, which is a comparatively recent extension of the educational offering.

Mort defined a satisfactory equalization program as follows:

> A satisfactory equalization program would demand that each community have as many elementary and high school classroom or teacher units, or their equivalent, as is typical for communities having the same number of children to educate. It would demand that each of these classrooms meet certain requirements as to structure and physical environment. It would demand that each of these classrooms be provided with a teacher, course of study, equipment, supervision, and auxiliary activities meeting certain minimum requirements. It would demand that some communities furnish special facilities, such as transportation.[23]

Mort sought objective, equitable measures of educational need that could be used by a state legislature in determining the amount of the state appropriation for equalization. He also wished his measure to be used by officials in the state department of education for apportioning state school funds with a minimum of state control.

Mort used complicated sets of regression equations to estimate on the basis of average practice the typical number of teachers employed in elementary schools that varied in numbers of pupils. He assumed that sparsity of population would make it necessary for some districts to operate certain small schools which would not have the economies of scale provided by larger schools. In other words, he assumed that a greater number of teachers for a given number of pupils would need to be employed in the small schools than in the large schools. His statistical studies, based on average practice in New York State at that time, showed that more teachers were employed per pupil in elementary schools with an average daily attendance of less than 142, but that the average number of teachers per pupil employed for larger elementary schools did not vary substantially. He found that the number of pupils per teacher varied in high schools up to 518 in average daily attendance but did not vary substantially in high schools above that size. He developed separate regression equations for both elementary and high schools. One could take the average daily attendance of any size school, substitute it in the appropriate equation, and compute the number of either typical elementary teachers or typical high school teachers.[24]

Mort's concept of "weighting pupils" was later extended to include weighting pupils enrolled in vocational education, exceptional education and compensatory education in order to provide for the extra costs of these special programs.

Most foundation programs today use some form of the weighted teacher or weighted pupil measure.[25] The weights, of course, have changed, as well as the methods of determining them, but the concept of making allowance for necessary cost variations beyond the control of local boards of education is generally recognized as sound policy.

Mort directed a national study of state support in 1931. The report of this survey entitled *State Support for Public Education* contained a summary of the status of state support at that time. Following is a brief summary of his findings concerning the condition of state support in 1931-32:

1. In all but a few states, the actual minimum status of education was determined by the economic ability of local districts to support schools rather than the social needs for education.

2. The minimum program actually guaranteed was in nearly every state far below the program provided in communities of average wealth.

3. An analysis of the methods used by the different states to measure educational need revealed that no state was using as refined measures as were available. Measures in use were inequitable in one or more of the following respects: treatment for variation of size of school, treatment of districts of the same size, caring for the higher costs of high schools, caring for nonresidence, consideration of costs of living, consideration of transportation and consideration of capital outlays.[26]

Henry C. Morrison

Morrison is sometimes forgotten by those studying the theory of state school financing. He is perhaps more noted for his theories of instruction and curriculum than for his theories in school finance. However, Morrison wrote an important book, *School Revenue*,[27] in which he made some significant contributions to the literature on school finance. He noted the great inequalities of wealth among school districts that caused great inequalities in educational opportunity. He observed that consti-

12

tutionally education was a state function and that local school districts had failed to provide that function efficiently or equitably. He asserted that attempts to provide equal educational opportunities by enlarging school districts, by offering state equalization funds—such as those advocated by Mort—or by offering state subsidies for special purposes had failed. He theorized that those measures would continue to fail to meet educational needs and, at the same time, to provide an equitable system of taxation to support schools. Therefore, Morrison proposed a model of state support whereby all local school districts are abolished and the state itself becomes both the unit for taxation for schools and for administration of public schools. He suggested that the most equitable form of tax for the state to use for the support of schools was the income tax.

Morrison's ideas on state school finance were not well received. At that time, great emphasis was being given to local initiative and local home rule. In fact, local self-government was almost equated to democracy itself in the political thought of Morrison's time. The Cubberley, Updegraff, Strayer, Haig, Mort axis of thought was in the mainstream of American political thought and, therefore, widely accepted.

However, the defects that Morrison saw in local school financing are as evident today as in his time. Furthermore, educational opportunities are far from being equalized among school districts within most states, and there is more complaint about the inequities of local property taxes for schools than ever before. It is interesting to note that in recent years Hawaii has established a state system of education with no local school districts that is similar to the model advocated by Morrison. The federal Elementary and Secondary Education Act of 1965 was enacted by Congress largely for the purposes of remedying some of the defects of the American system of education that Morrison foresaw if the states continued to rely largely on local school districts to perform state functions. Morrison's model for state school financing is not as far outside of the mainstream of American thought today as it was in 1930.

SOME TRENDS IN SCHOOL FINANCING 1890-1930

The first section of this chapter is devoted to a discussion of the development of the basic theories and concepts of state support. Practically all of these theories were developed prior to

13

TABLE 1-1

AMOUNT OF PUBLIC SCHOOL REVENUE DERIVED FROM FEDERAL AND STATE SOURCES, 1890-1930*

State	1890 (1)	1900 (2)	1910 (3)	1920 (4)	1930 (5)
Continental United States	$ 33,987,581	$ 44,317,952	$ 78,701,256	$162,559,399	$372,189,813
Alabama	$ 609,667	$ 907,000	$ 2,125,931	$ 4,381,514	$ 8,076,071
Arizona	1,783	11,100	64,715	966,974	2,207,727
Arkansas	536,112	446,558	1,301,484	1,856,574	3,913,085
California	2,627,471	3,505,268	5,348,316	8,679,325	26,531,318
Colorado	112,702	117,548	134,050	1,211,856	863,418
Connecticut	401,716	474,183	776,377	1,855,244	3,428,103
Delaware	65,263	66,000	195,633	579,740	4,589,880
Florida	116,777	124,449	196,062	454,444	2,764,847
Georgia	576,786	1,323,153	2,328,062	3,968,662	4,806,544
Idaho		205,329	293,850	663,146	827,833
Illinois	1,709,651	1,900,184	1,881,549	5,695,218	4,054,786
Indiana	2,053,172	2,174,062	3,190,713	4,294,196	4,579,763
Iowa	266,338	118,139	991,706	522,328	2,129,137
Kansas	306,982	421,134	502,159	600,181	662,572
Kentucky	1,310,109	1,448,129	3,500,000	2,920,773	5,840,801
Louisiana	302,633	342,409	1,087,733	2,415,615	5,358,745
Maine	407,298	520,019	1,199,383	2,219,083	3,196,175
Maryland	616,205	779,144	1,527,991	2,066,126	3,952,035
Massachusetts	282,081	168,850	424,849	4,459,624	8,224,805
Michigan	791,882	1,020,283	5,707,562	7,147,690	20,199,913
Minnesota	816,688	1,296,466	2,983,898	6,090,635	10,155,250
Mississippi	515,032	810,667	1,617,252	2,097,426	6,202,603
Missouri	1,512,874	1,489,306	2,518,043	3,685,515	5,412,890
Montana			180,824	1,141,140	1,970,414
Nebraska	629,030	693,205	622,786	1,031,224	1,410,607
Nevada	64,611	125,341	200,281	372,969	475,317
New Hampshire	73,596	39,047	111,704	346,973	639,921
New Jersey	2,071,497	2,516,147	3,214,555	13,808,944	21,629,445
New Mexico		402,698	58,694	644,740	1,550,264
New York	3,531,696	3,745,000	5,296,570	12,922,152	89,058,759

North Carolina	558,773	817,309	264,571	3,470,717	6,969,000
North Dakota	127,123	446,626	1,086,792	1,435,620	1,403,183
Ohio	1,982,038	2,028,485	2,610,245	4,279,559	5,701,577
Oklahoma	—	129,653	525,013	1,472,354	3,347,790
Oregon	151,188	203,408	320,272	470,424	454,506
Pennsylvania	1,492,664	5,493,028	7,202,595	11,682,344	23,891,063
Rhode Island	127,972	137,138	196,624	258,423	1,197,749
South Carolina	372,019	533,639	82,244	1,003,075	3,980,838
South Dakota	174,687	253,234	581,256	1,724,548	1,725,780
Tennessee	1,748,133	129,413	706,332	1,575,002	5,366,686
Texas	2,562,773	3,326,492	5,994,297	17,443,152	32,341,298
Utah	163,493	328,455	704,963	2,034,154	3,755,922
Vermont	67,550	139,472	295,859	1,155,001	692,658
Virginia	837,673	1,011,815	1,701,010	4,352,275	6,372,246
Washington	—	918,465	2,625,823	3,669,944	8,497,710
West Virginia	366,639	411,205	750,000	738,040	2,173,777
Wisconsin	785,341	776,132	1,800,710	3,729,441	7,946,581
Wyoming	—	43,265	150,213	750,272	1,658,421

*Adapted from *The National Survey of School Finance-State Support for Public Education* by Paul R. Mort and Staff. Washington, D. C.: The American Council on Education, 1933.

1930.   This section deals with some major trends in school financing between 1890 and 1930.

Mort made a study of trends in state support, 1890-1930.[28] Table 1-1 is adapted from that study.   In that study, Mort did not distinguish between state and federal funds.   But since federal funds, exclusive of sixteenth section funds, comprised only 0.3 percent of total school revenue by 1930, Table 1-1 can be considered as a valid presentation of trends in state funds.   It will be noted that these funds increased from approximately $34,000,000 in 1890 to approximately $372,000,000 in 1930.

Table 1-2 shows trends in percent of revenue from state and federal sources from 1890 to 1930.   It will be noted that state funds (including a negligible amount of federal funds) declined from 23.8 percent of total revenue in 1890 to 17.3 percent in 1930.   This decline in percentage of total revenue was not due to a decline in state revenue but rather due to large increases in local school revenue, especially during the decade following World War I.   The demands for public education, especially for universal secondary education became insistent during that decade.   However, the taxpayer in local school districts provided proportionately more of the school revenue to meet that demand than did state legislatures.

TRENDS IN STATE SUPPORT 1930-1970

In this section trends in total expenditures, trends in revenue by level of government and trends in percent of revenue from state sources by state are presented.

Trends in Total Expenditure

Expenditures for the public schools have increased greatly since 1930 as determined by any valid method of measurement. An analysis of increases in school expenditures since 1930 is presented in Table 1-3.   Column 2 of this table shows that total expenditures for the public schools (uncorrected for the decreased purchasing power of the dollar and increased attendance) increased from $2,307,000,000 to $39,489,000,000 or 1,612 percent between 1930 and 1970.   This is an invalid measure of increases in school cost but it is the figure that frightens taxpayers. Column 3 of Table 1-3 shows that the cost of living increased 114 percent between 1929 and 1969.   When expenditures for all years are

16

TABLE 1-2

PERCENTAGE OF PUBLIC SCHOOL REVENUE DERIVED
FROM FEDERAL AND STATE SOURCES, 1890-1930*

State	1890	1900	1910	1920	1930
Continental United States	23.8	20.3	18.1	16.8	17.3
Alabama	67.7	82.3	74.1	51.3	40.8
Arizona	1.0	4.0	7.4	18.7	19.6
Arkansas	48.9	31.1	35.3	23.7	33.7
California	51.6	48.7	28.1	20.4	25.6
Colorado	5.2	4.0	2.3	9.0	3.2
Connecticut	19.9	15.9	14.0	12.3	8.1
Delaware	26.1	24.0	32.7	35.3	87.9
Florida	22.6	18.3	13.5	7.2	22.8
Georgia	56.5	64.4	53.0	43.5	35.6
Idaho	—	40.4	14.0	9.7	7.7
Illinois	14.3	10.2	5.2	8.7	5.3
Indiana	36.9	29.2	21.0	10.6	5.5
Iowa	3.9	1.4	7.5	1.5	4.3
Kansas	7.2	9.4	6.1	2.3	1.7
Kentucky	59.3	52.6	53.0	37.1	26.1
Louisiana	37.2	30.0	25.3	24.5	26.9
Maine	30.9	29.2	36.5	35.6	28.6
Maryland	34.4	26.5	39.2	41.6	17.7
Massachusetts	3.4	1.2	2.0	12.3	9.5
Michigan	14.0	15.3	41.1	17.1	18.2
Minnesota	18.1	22.7	20.8	19.5	20.6
Mississippi	44.3	59.4	55.2	52.1	33.5
Missouri	18.9	20.8	19.4	11.9	10.6
Montana	—	—	6.7	9.9	14.1
Nebraska	19.2	17.4	8.9	6.6	5.4
Nevada	35.0	55.5	35.0	26.6	19.0
New Hampshire	9.8	3.9	7.0	8.7	9.0
New Jersey	62.3	40.6	17.6	35.6	21.2
New Mexico	—	91.5	7.8	17.6	21.8
New York	19.8	10.9	9.6	12.1	27.6
North Carolina	77.4	82.9	9.0	30.1	16.6
North Dakota	21.1	30.7	20.5	12.1	11.1
Ohio	19.0	15.2	10.2	7.3	4.1
Oklahoma	—	18.1	15.8	7.5	10.6
Oregon	16.4	12.4	6.9	4.8	2.3
Pennsylvania	10.6	22.0	15.6	15.9	13.9
Rhode Island	13.1	9.4	8.6	5.2	8.6
South Carolina	82.7	65.5	3.9	15.8	25.5
South Dakota	14.8	13.7	14.9	16.6	10.1
Tennessee	81.7	7.2	15.9	17.8	24.7
Texas	79.9	75.0	57.2	54.0	42.6
Utah	47.3	28.2	26.8	31.5	33.6
Vermont	9.5	15.7	19.8	33.1	12.2
Virginia	52.7	50.4	39.1	36.7	27.9
Washington	—	43.8	28.4	18.1	28.9
West Virginia	28.2	20.2	19.0	6.4	8.3
Wisconsin	19.5	13.3	15.8	15.6	17.0
Wyoming	—	14.8	19.5	24.3	27.1

*Adapted from *The National Survey of School Finance-State Support for Public Education* by Paul R. Mort and Staff. Washington, D. C.: The American Council on Education, 1933.

17

TABLE 1-3

TRENDS IN TOTAL EXPENDITURES FOR THE PUBLIC SCHOOLS 1930-1970
(Includes All Items for Current Expense, Capital Outlay and Interest on School Indebtedness)

Year Column 1	Expenditures in Current Dollars (Millions) Column 2	Consumer Price Index (1957–59 Prices=100) Column 3	Expenditures in Terms of 1969 Dollars (Millions) Column 4	Average Daily Attendance (Thousands) Column 5	Expenditures Per Pupil In ADA In 1969 Dollars Column 6	Percentage of the Gross National Product Expended for the Public Schools Column 7
1929–30	$ 2,307	59.7	$ 4,935	21,165	$233	2.2
1939–40	2,331	48.4	6,149	22,042	279	2.6
1949–50	5,768	83.0	8,877	22,284	398	2.2
1959–60	15,613	101.5	19,641	32,477	605	3.2
1969–70	39,489	127.7	39,489	42,168	936	4.2
Percent Increase 1929–30 to 1969–60	1,612	114	700	99	302	91

Source: Data on expenditures and average daily attendance from the U. S. Office of Education except for the year 1969–70 which was estimated by the National Education Association. The price index is for the calendar year in which the school year began. Also, the gross national product for the calendar year in which the school year began is used in computing the percentage of the gross national product. Data for the price index were obtained from the *Survey of Current Business.*

converted into the purchasing power of 1969 dollars, it is noted from Column 4 that the total increased 700 percent. But average daily attendance increased 99 percent during this 40 year period and Column 6 shows that the expenditure per pupil in terms of the purchasing power of 1969 dollars increased from $233 to $936 or 302 percent between 1929-30 and 1969-70. This is a fairly valid measure of the increase in school expenditures, however, it does not take into consideration the increases in the types of educational services rendered, some of which, such as vocational education and education for exceptional children are very expensive. Furthermore, this figure does not take into consideration the increase in the quality of the services rendered. It is not possible to measure objectively the cost of providing this increase in the quality of the educational services provided.

Another way of measuring the increase in costs of education is to compare the increase in expenditures for education during the past forty years with the increase in the gross national product. Column 7 of Table 1-3 shows that 2.2 percent of the gross national product was expended for the public schools in 1929-30 and 4.2 percent in 1969-70. This is a substantial increase of 91 percent. The growth of the national economy has made the great increases in expenditures for education possible. However, education has contributed greatly to the growth of the national economy.[29]

Trends in Revenue by Level of Government

Trends in revenue for the public schools from 1929-30 to 1969-70 from federal, state and local sources are presented in Table 1-4. It is noted from this table that school revenues from each level of government have increased substantially during the past forty years but the percentage of the total from each level has changed. The proportion from the federal government increased from 0.3 percent to 6.6 percent; increased from state sources from 17.0 percent to 40.7 percent; and decreased from local sources from 82.7 percent to 52.7 percent. About 98 percent of all local school tax revenue is derived from property taxes. Numerous studies have shown that the property tax in modern times is the most inequitable of all major types of taxes.[30] Although there has been a trend during the past forty years to increase the percentages of school revenue provided from state and

TABLE 1-4

TRENDS IN SOURCES OF SCHOOL REVENUE RECEIPTS
BY LEVEL OF GOVERNMENT
(In Millions of Current Dollars)

Year	Federal Amount	Federal Per-Cent	State Amount	State Per-Cent	Local Amount	Local Per-Cent	Total Amount	Total Per-Cent
1929–30	7	0.3	354	17.0	1,728	82.7	2,089	100.0
1939–40	40	1.8	685	30.3	1,536	67.9	2,261	100.0
1949–50	156	2.9	2,166	39.8	3.155	57.3	5,437	100.0
1959–60	649	4.4	5,766	39.1	8,332	56.5	14,747	100.0
1969–70	2,545	6.6	15,645	40.7	20,286	52.7	38,476	100.0

Source of Data: U. S. Office of Education except for the year 1969–70 which was estimated by the National Education Association.

federal sources, the major portion of school revenue was still obtained from local sources in 1970.

Trends in Revenue from State Sources by State

Table 1-5 shows the amount of revenue provided from state sources by state from 1930 to 1970 by decades. This table shows that the total amount of school revenue for the nation from state sources increased each decade during the past forty years. The total amount of school revenue from state sources in current dollars (uncorrected for differences in the purchasing power of the dollar) increased 77.3 percent between 1930 and 1940; the increase was 228.2 percent between 1940 and 1950; 164.2 percent between 1950 and 1960; and 173.4 percent between 1960 and 1970. The percentage increase in state funds was the greatest in the 1940-1950 decade but the dollar increase was the greatest in the decade 1960-1970. Although a few states did not increase the amount of state funds each decade, all states increased the total amount of state funds for the public schools between 1930 and 1970.

Table 1-6 shows the percent of school revenue provided from state services for each state by decade from 1930 to 1970. It will be noted from this table that the percent of school revenue obtained from state sources increased from 17.3 percent[31] in 1930 to 40.7 percent in 1970. This is a major shift in sources of revenue. However there has been very little change in the percent of revenue from state sources during the past 20 years. In

TABLE 1-5

PUBLIC SCHOOL REVENUE DERIVED FROM STATE SOURCES, 1930-1970
(In thousands)

State	1930	1939–40	1949–50	1959–60	1969–70
U.S. Overall	$372,193	$659,868	$2,165,689	$5,721,937	$16,645,366
Alabama	8,076	11,954	53,527	121,873	257,717
Alaska	—	—	—	—	38,489
Arizona	2,208	2,204	11,546	44,512	165,127
Arkansas	3,913	6,084	26,339	44,209	112,384
California	26,531	78,234	236,753	754,793	1,550,000
Colorado	863	1,179	9,927	32,498	106,000
Connecticut	3,428	2,762	15,376	78,982	210,000
Delaware	4,590	4,124	10,141	42,700	87,900
Florida	2,765	12,402	50,138	194,970	608,727
Georgia	4,807	15,409	51,863	154,046	377,546
Hawaii	—	—	—	—	149,000
Idaho	828	1,108	5,478	15,111	51,000
Illinois	4,055	13,301	58,185	168,739	797,649
Indiana	4,580	18,584	56,484	109,942	360,000
Iowa	2,129	472	18,298	24,981	167,000
Kansas	663	3,316	20,668	38,860	117,404
Kentucky	5,841	10,570	23,992	69,025	235,000
Louisiana	5,359	14,274	73,889	192,809	331,890
Maine	3,196	1,778	7,121	15,665	78,500
Maryland	3,952	5,586	29,747	88,038	300,901
Massachusetts	8,225	7,937	26,750	63,439	200,000
Michigan	20,200	41,902	143,387	327,355	770,000
Minnesota	10,155	16,120	41,104	127,613	365,000
Mississippi	6,203	6,053	18,549	77,541	162,000
Missouri	5,413	17,572	40,687	85,861	255,972
Montana	1,970	944	7,374	16,144	45,000
Nebraska	1,411	180	2,669	6,656	42,378
Nevada	475	439	2,447	15,300	40,500
New Hampshire	640	396	947	2,376	9,400
New Jersey	21,629	6,003	34,656	127,508	429,000
New Mexico	1,550	3,955	28,549	68,812	128,174
New York	89,059	117,508	238,496	653,389	2,071,000
North Carolina	6,969	26,752	91,294	185,917	571,559
North Dakota	1,403	1,342	6,142	14,429	28,500
Ohio	5,702	48,529	81,924	205,483	560,000
Oklahoma	3,348	13,080	46,106	51,182	142,934
Oregon	455	75	20,679	52,962	97,000
Pennsylvania	23,891	36,715	117,279	388,970	1,039,369
Rhode Island	1,198	1,202	4,503	11,485	51,259
South Carolina	3,981	8,126	32,820	95,833	245,000
South Dakota	1,726	1,029	2,838	4,858	14,500
Tennessee	5,367	8,633	53,255	109,708	257,000
Texas	32,341	34,314	170,729	362,849	775,000
Utah	3,756	4,453	15,824	41,021	111,615
Vermont	693	771	3,230	6,830	21,040
Virginia	6,372	8,469	34,692	89,539	300,000
Washington	8,498	18,555	68,652	185,055	400,000
West Virginia	2,174	14,273	45,311	65,350	134,500
Wisconsin	7,947	8,100	20,978	70,290	256,932
Wyoming	1,658	240	6,383	16,931	18,500

Source of Data: United States Office of Education except for the year
1969–70 which was estimated by the National Education
Association.

21

TABLE 1-6

PERCENTAGE OF SCHOOL REVENUE DERIVED
FROM STATE SOURCES, 1930-1970
(In thousands)

State	1930	1940	1950	1960	1970
U.S. Overall	17.3*	29.2	39.8	39.4	40.7
Alabama	40.8	54.1	71.6	65.3	63.0
Alaska	—	—	—	—	43.7
Arizona	19.6	18.8	33.8	34.0	47.5
Arkansas	33.7	43.2	58.1	46.6	45.5
California	25.6	45.9	41.3	40.6	35.0
Colorado	3.2	5.0	20.2	19.5	25.3
Connecticut	8.1	8.7	23.6	34.6	33.1
Delaware	87.9	84.4	83.5	82.5	70.6
Florida	22.8	50.4	50.8	56.5	56.5
Georgia	35.6	56.8	57.4	64.0	58.7
Hawaii	—	—	—	—	87.0
Idaho	7.7	10.7	23.5	27.6	43.2
Illinois	5.3	10.0	16.5	20.6	34.4
Indiana	5.5	32.2	37.4	29.9	34.9
Iowa	4.3	1.1	19.1	12.0	30.1
Kansas	1.7	10.9	24.0	19.2	26.1
Kentucky	26.1	40.0	35.1	45.8	52.6
Louisiana	26.9	52.3	69.6	70.2	58.3
Maine	28.6	15.6	27.8	25.8	44.9
Maryland	17.7	21.6	38.3	34.2	35.2
Massachusetts	9.5	10.0	20.5	20.0	20.0
Michigan	18.2	41.6	53.4	43.2	45.1
Minnesota	20.6	31.7	36.2	39.7	43.4
Mississippi	33.5	37.1	47.8	56.5	51.6
Missouri	10.6	32.1	38.9	31.0	34.5
Montana	14.1	7.2	25.3	23.6	30.9
Nebraska	5.4	1.0	6.2	6.5	20.0
Nevada	19.0	17.0	36.5	51.3	39.2
New Hampshire	9.0	5.1	6.2	6.3	8.5
New Jersey	21.2	5.5	19.0	23.7	28.5
New Mexico	21.8	45.3	86.0	74.4	62.7
New York	27.6	33.1	40.0	39.5	45.4
North Carolina	16.6	65.8	67.5	66.7	70.9
North Dakota	11.1	12.8	27.0	26.4	27.2
Ohio	4.1	35.3	31.4	27.7	31.6
Oklahoma	10.6	34.0	56.5	27.7	40.8
Oregon	2.3	.4	28.6	29.3	20.6
Pennsylvania	13.9	21.0	35.1	45.8	46.9
Rhode Island	8.6	10.3	20.2	23.2	34.5
South Carolina	25.5	48.6	55.2	66.6	61.6
South Dakota	10.1	7.6	12.1	8.9	13.6
Tennessee	24.7	33.3	56.9	58.0	49.3
Texas	42.6	39.4	61.8	50.0	42.8
Utah	33.6	37.3	50.3	44.0	51.4
Vermont	12.2	14.5	27.6	24.8	28.6
Virginia	27.9	31.2	39.6	37.0	36.6
Washington	28.9	57.9	65.6	61.6	58.8
West Virginia	8.3	50.7	62.7	52.9	48.2
Wisconsin	17.0	17.2	17.4	22.6	29.4
Wyoming	27.1	4.3	42.0	47.5	25.4

Source of Data: United States Office of Education except for the year
1970 which was estimated by the National Education
Association.
*Includes 0.3 percent of federal funds.

1949-50 state sources provided 39.8 percent of school revenue which is only 0.9 percent less than the percent provided in 1969-70.

Only three states, New Hampshire, Delaware and Wyoming, provided a lower percent of revenue from state sources in 1969-70 than in 1929-30.

SOME POLITICAL, ECONOMIC AND HISTORICAL FACTORS INFLUENCING STATE SUPPORT[32]

Many of the basic problems and issues of state school finance cannot be separated from the problems and issues of federal and local public school financing. What should public education cost? What percent of the gross national product should be allocated to the public schools? These questions can never be finally answered because conditions are continually changing and, therefore, the answers are continually changing. It is true that less than 2 percent of the gross national product was allocated to the public schools at the beginning of the century and approximately 4.2 percent in 1970. But no governmental authority at the federal, state, or local level ever made any conscious decision concerning what percent of the gross national product should be allocated to the operation of public schools. The 4.2 percent of the gross national product allocated to the public schools in 1970 was merely the summation of the results of thousands of battles for revenue fought in the 18,000 local school districts of the United States, hundreds of battles in the 50 state legislatures, and dozens of battles in Congress. The percent of the gross national product that has been allocated to public education since the beginning of this century has borne only an accidental relationship to school needs.

Perhaps this unplanned method of allocating the gross national product to different sectors of the economy is the natural condition in a mixed private enterprise-government economy such as we have in the United States. In the private sectors of our economy, the gross national product is allocated in the marketplace; in the government sector, it is allocated through political processes.

Political and economic factors and historical events, such as wars, depressions, and threats to national security, all have had some effect on the development of state aid. These same factors also have had some effect on federal aid, which actually is easier to trace. But that is not the task of this chapter. Let us examine briefly, then, some of the effects of these factors and events on state aid.

As has already been pointed out, Cubberley noted at the beginning of the twentieth century that the industrialization of the nation had created great inequalities in wealth among school districts. This same fact was noted by every researcher on state aid, and it was used as a powerful argument for state aid. Advocates of state aid have continuously appealed throughout this century for the extension of state aid programs in order to equalize educational opportunity. Why has it taken so long to develop adequate state aid programs throughout the nation? Why did many states still have inadequate state aid programs as late as 1970? The causes of the successes and failures in the development of state aid programs no doubt have varied greatly from state to state, for they vary greatly in their political liberalism versus their political conservatism. The political liberal considers it the responsibility of central government to equalize educational opportunity by means of adequate programs of state or federal aid. The political conservative fears the control of central governments and is willing to sacrifice the ideal of equalization of educational opportunity in order to preserve "home rule" in government. He considers it socialist doctrine to advocate the taxing of wealth in rich school districts or rich states in order to equalize educational opportunities among school districts and among states.

The conservative point of view with respect to state aid prevailed in most states throughout the first two decades of the twentieth century. Liberal arguments, such as those voiced by Cubberley, fell largely on deaf ears. However, this attitude began to change after World War I, a war we fought "to make the world safe for democracy." We may have failed to make the world safe for democracy, but the war undoubtedly caused us to want more democracy in education in the United States. Young men from all over the United States were brought together in the armed services, and great differences were noted in the education of men from different sections of the nation. A national demand developed to make the opportunity for a high school education universal. The demand for the extension of opportunities for high school education in the years immediately following World War I served as a great stimulus to the development of state aid.

24

World War I also accelerated the rate of change of the United States from an agrarian to an industrial society. The war started the breaking up of the parochialism and the isolation of rural America. The automobile industry, led by the Model T, further promoted the mobility of the population. An industrialized, mobile population needed much more education than an isolated rural population. This fact had long been known to the educational leadership of the states. It began to be recognized by the state political leadership in the decade following World War I. State aid for the public schools more than doubled between 1920 and 1930.

The Great Depression had a profound effect on school financing. In 1930, about 82 percent of school revenue came from local sources, and practically all local school tax revenue was derived from property taxes. During the Depression, property taxes became increasingly onerous as thousands of people lost their homes, farms, and businesses. The injustice of being required to pay property taxes when the taxpayer had no income became a political issue in many states. The opposition to property taxes during this period provided an opportunity for the advocates of state aid to advance their programs.

World War II also had an important effect on school financing, for it accelerated the development of technology nationally, even more than World War I. It became apparent to all informed observers, during and immediately after World War II, that an education was a necessity not only for the benefit of the individual but also for the welfare of society. The demands for an improved quality of education became insistent throughout the nation. Furthermore, inflation was causing a rapid increase in prices that far exceeded any increase in the property tax income of the schools. The problem was further complicated by a "baby boom" starting in 1946 and continuing throughout the 1950's.

Studies were conducted in many states in order to deal with this situation. There was a great demand to find sources of revenue for the public schools that would correspond more closely with price changes and school enrollment than property taxes. Furthermore, the ownership of property was becoming less related to the sources of the income of the people. For example, 58 percent of the national income was derived from compensation of employees in 1929, but this had increased to more than 72 percent in 1969.

FOOTNOTES

1. Paul R. Mort, *The National Survey of School Finance: State Support for Public Education* (Washington, D. C.: The American Council on Education, 1933, p. 24).

2. *Ibid.*, p. 26.

3. In this chapter, the terms "state support" and "state aid" are used interchangeably.

4. This section is abstracted largely from Chapter 4, "State Financing of Elementary and Secondary Schools" by R. L. Johns in *Education in the States: Nationwide Development Since 1900*, Edgar Fuller and Jim B. Pearson, eds. (Washington, D. C.: National Education Association, 1969).

5. Ellwood P. Cubberley, *School Funds and Their Apportionment* (New York: Teachers College, Columbia University, 1905).

6. *Ibid.*, p. 16.

7. *Ibid.*, p. 17.

8. *Ibid.*, adapted from the summary presented on pp. 250-54.

9. Harlan Updegraff, *Rural School Survey of New York State: Financial Support* (Ithaca: By the author, 1922).

10. *Ibid.*, p. 117.

11. *Ibid.*, pp. 117-18.

12. *Ibid.*, pp. 134-35.

13. *Ibid.*, p. 155.

14. George D. Strayer and Robert Murray Haig, *The Financing of Education in the State of New York*, Report of the Educational Finance Inquiry Commission, Vol. I (New York: Macmillan Co., 1923).

15. *Ibid.*, p. 173.

16. *Ibid.*, p. 174.

17. *Ibid.*, pp. 174-75.

18. *Ibid.*, p. 175.

19. Paul R. Mort, *The Measurement of Educational Need* (New York: Teachers College, Columbia University, 1924).

20. See Stephen K. Bailey, et al., *Schoolmen and Politics: A Study of State Aid to Education in the Northeast* (Syracuse, N.Y.: Syracuse University Press, 1962).

21. Mort, *The Measurement of Educational Need*, pp. 6-7.

22. *Ibid.*, p. 7.

23. *Ibid.*, p. 8.

24. In later years, Mort's "typical teacher" came to be known as "weighted teacher" or "weighted instruction unit" in some states.

25. Today the term *foundation program* is more commonly used than the terms *equalization program* or *minimum program*.

26. Paul R. Mort and Research Staff, *State Support for Public Education* (Washington, D. C.: American Council on Education, 1933).

27. Henry C. Morrison, *School Revenue* (Chicago: University of Chicago Press, 1930).

28. Paul R. Mort and Research Staff, *State Support for Public Education* (Washington, D.C.: American Council on Education, 1933).

29. See *Economic Factors Affecting the Financing of Education*, Vol. 2 of the National Educational Finance Project, edited by Roe L. Johns, Irving J. Goffman, Kern Alexander and Dewey Stollar. (Gainesville, Florida, 1212 S.W. 5th Avenue, The Project Office, 1971).

30. *Ibid.*, Chapters 8 and 10.

31. This figure includes 0.3 percent of federal funds.

32. This section is adapted from Chapter 4, "State Financing of Elementary and Secondary Schools" by R. L. Johns in *Education in the States: Nationwide Development Since 1900.* Edgar Fuller and Jim B. Pearson, eds. (Washington, D.C.: National Education Association, 1969).

CHAPTER 2

Classification of State School Funds

No two states finance their public schools in the same way. While each state, except Hawaii, utilizes both state and local tax sources, the amounts contributed by level of government and the methodology used to combine the state and local tax dollars are different in every state.

Many factors, historic, social, economic, geographic, and psychological are undoubtedly responsible for this diversity. For example, the historical development of Hawaii as a territorial government has led to the adoption of a centralized system of finance whereby allocation decisions are made almost totally at the state level. In New England and in some parts of the Midwest, the "town meeting" philosophy still prevails to a large extent, and is reflected in school finance programs which generally depend on local rather than state taxation and decision making. On the other hand, in the Southeast, social and economic conditions have probably worked in concert to form larger school districts, and in some of these states county unit school systems have been legislatively mandated. The reorganization and consolidation of smaller districts in the South may have gained primary impetus from a lack of local fiscal ability, causing creation of larger, more efficient units. In any case, as persons versed in the history of American education can testify, the array of conditions causing educational differences in states are endless. The simple fact of the matter is that each state's educational program has developed in a separate and sovereign state government, and except for federal constitutional and statutory influences, each has developed, more or less independently, its own fiscal and educational structure.

The idiosyncrasies of the states are manifested in variations in governmental levels of support—high and low percentages of state aid, specificity of grants leading to more or less state control of funds, varying degrees of equalization among school districts—and in types of educational programs identified by state legislatures.

The purpose of this chapter is to classify and describe the array of fiscal mechanisms by which states redistribute tax dollars for the public schools. To accomplish this, state school aid programs are classified by method and by purpose.

DESCRIPTION OF STATE SCHOOL FINANCE PROGRAMS

Few attempts have been made to classify and describe the methods by which states allocate funds to local school districts. Over the last quarter of a century, the United States Office of Education has sporadically made reports on the status of school finance in the United States. A few of these studies have focused on the purposes and methods adopted by each state to finance education. Such descriptive studies are, in and of themselves, rather monumental when one considers the problems inherent in attempting to describe over 400 school finance funds in 50 states, with each state having its own vocabulary, information system and reporting techniques.

By reviewing these U. S. Office of Education publications, one can identify two commonly used methods for describing systems of state school finance. One of these methods categorizes the various state school funds into what is called *general* and *special* grants. The *general* grant is usually the large basic state aid program which is non-restrictive and can be used with wide local discretion. The *special* grant is descriptive of what has come to be known as categorical aids which zero in on a particular educational need as identified by the state legislature. The special or categorical subventions tend to limit local administrative prerogative in their use.

The broad classifications of *general* and *special* are then further broken down into *flat* and *equalizing* subcategories. The designation of a fund as a *flat* grant means that it is distributed uniformily on a per pupil or some other unit basis and goes to all districts alike regardless of local school district wealth. The *equalizing* subvention is one which takes local fiscal ability into consideration and theoretically allows greater state funds based on the relative wealth of local school districts. Table 2-1, showing the total of all state school funds, uses this classification technique.

A span of twenty years between 1949-50 and 1968-69 is given in this Table indicating the trends in method of distribution between general and special funds and equalizing and flat distributions. From Table 2-1, one can observe the steady progression toward greater use of equalization programs. In 1949-50, only 44.9 percent of the total dollars were distributed through equalizing formulas, while in 1968-69, 77.5 percent of the funds were distributed on a basis which took the fiscal ability of the school district into account. Accompanying this trend is a tendency for states to allocate resources through the larger general or basic state aid formulas. A certain amount of ebb and flow is apparent in shifts between general and special aid formulas, which indicates a tendency for states to enact one large basic state aid formula and then over a period of years to allow the large basic program to fragment into several smaller special purpose grants. The national totals given in the Table can be greatly influenced by changes taking place in very large states. For example, a partial explanation for the increase in special aid fund allocations between 1962-63 and 1968-69 can be attributed to California which had nine special aid programs in 1962-63 totalling $131,-290,957 or 16.84 percent of the total funds distributed in California, while in 1968-69 this total had increased $414,685,613 and the percentage to 19.5.

Another method used by the U. S. Office of Education to analyze state school funds is a twelve-part typology[1] which provides a more detailed breakdown of method of distribution. Here, funds are analyzed in terms of variation in allotments based on unit weighting or some other need designation, equalization of fiscal capacity, purpose or use of grants, and extent of district participation. This rather complicated classification can be reduced to four descriptive elements, as follows:

30

TABLE 2-1

ESTIMATED AMOUNT AND PERCENT OF STATE GRANTS DISTRIBUTED BY STATE EDUCATION AGENCIES FOR PUBLIC SCHOOL PURPOSES, BY METHOD OF DISTRIBUTION 1949-50, 1957-58, 1962-63 AND 1968-69

Amount in Millions

Distribution	1949-50[a]		1957-58[b]		1962-63[c]		1968-69	
	Amount	Percent	Amount	Percent	Amount	Percent	Amount	Percent
Total Distributions	$ 1,998	100.0	$ 4,480	100.0	$ 6,539	100.0	$12,620	100.0
Flat	1,101	55.1	1,855	41.4	2,506	38.3	2,843	22.5
Equalizing	897	44.9	2,625	58.6	4,033	61.7	9,777	77.5
General Purpose	1,535	76.9	3,687	82.3	5,806	88.8	10,793	85.5
Flat	749	37.5	1,361	30.4	2,027	31.0	1,760	13.9
Equalizing	786	39.4	2,326	51.9	3,779	57.8	9,033	71.6
Special Purpose	463	23.1	793	17.7	733	11.2	1,827	14.5
Flat	352	17.6	494	11.0	479	7.3	1,082	8.6
Equalizing	111	5.5	299	6.7	254	3.9	745	5.9

Sources:
[a]Edgar L. Morphet and Erick L. Lindman, *Public School Finance Programs of the Forty-Eight States*, Federal Security Agency, Office of Education, Circular No. 274, U. S. Government Printing Office, Washington, D. C., 1950, pp. 75–77.
[b]Albert R. Munse and Eugene P. McLoone, *Public School Finance Programs of the United States, 1957–58*, Office of Education, U. S. Government Printing Office, Washington, D. C., 1960, p. 34.
[c]Albert R. Munse, *State Programs for Public School Support*, Office of Education, U. S. Government Printing Office, Washington, D. C., 1965, p. 112. (Amounts given do not include about $120 million in Tennessee which were predominately general purpose equalizing grants.)

(1) *General* and *special purpose*—*General* denotes funds used for non-restrictive general operation while *special* identifies funds of a restricted or categorical nature.

(2) *Variable equalizing*—The fund allocation is adjusted for both educational need variations of children and the fiscal capacity of the local school district. *Nonequalizing* simply means the fiscal capacity of the school district is ignored by the formula.

(3) *Fixed*—Funds are allocated on a standard amount per unit with no modification for local fiscal capacity or educational need differentials.

(4) *Universal* and *limited*—Funds distributed to all districts are *universal,* while funds distributed to only selected districts are classified as *limited.*

Using this typology of state school funds, the year of 1962-63 is contrasted with 1968-69 in Table 2-2. This Table indicates that *variable equalizing* funds have increased substantially over this short period of years in every category except the *limited, special purpose* category. *Limited, special purpose* represented a minute part of the whole in 1962-63 and constituted an even smaller percentage in 1968-69. Table 2-2 supports the conclusion that legislatures are tending to place more emphasis on equalization through the use of adjusted units of educational need and local fiscal ability measures. In keeping with the trend shown in Table 2-1, the *universal, special purpose* category is shown in Table 2-2 to have increased rather significantly during the short period from 1962-63 to 1968-69.

Probably the most noticeable feature of both tables is the total increase in state funds from a little over $6.5 billion in 1962-63 to over $12.6 billion in 1968-69. This reflects a trend by states to increasingly rely on taxes collected at the state level to provide support for the rising costs of education.

NATIONAL EDUCATIONAL FINANCE PROJECT CLASSIFICATION

Although the two techniques described above are quite useful in most circumstances, they each have the inherent limitation of assuming that equalization exists when, in fact, the net effect of the fund may be to provide little or no equalization. State funds having extensive equalizing qualities are classified the same as

32

TABLE 2-2

ESTIMATED AMOUNT AND PERCENT OF STATE DISTRIBUTIONS
BY METHOD OF DISTRIBUTION USING MUNSE'S CLASSIFICATION

Classification	Estimated Amount of Distribution (Millions)[a] 1962–63		Estimated Amount of Distribution (Millions) 1968–69	
	Amount	Percent	Amount	Percent
Total	$ 6,539	100.0	$12,620	100.0
Fixed	2,190	33.5	3,648	28.9
Variable Equalizing	4,034	61.7	8,420	66.8
Variable Non-Equalizing	316	4.8	538	4.3
Universal, General Purpose	5,806	88.8	10,498	83.2
Fixed	2,007	30.7	2,327	18.5
Variable Equalizing	3,779	57.8	8,093	64.2
Variable Non-Equalizing	20	0.3	64	0.5
Universal, Special Purpose	143	2.2	1,860	14.8
Fixed	112	1.7	1,222	9.7
Variable Equalizing	29	0.4	225	1.8
Variable Non-Equalizing	1	—	412	3.3
Limited, General Purpose	88	1.3	136	1.1
Fixed	8	0.1	24	0.2
Variable Equalizing	69	1.1	72	0.6
Variable Non-Equalizing	11	0.2	41	0.3
Limited, Special Purpose	502	7.7	126	1.0
Fixed	63	1.0	75	0.6
Variable Equalizing	156	2.4	30	0.2
Variable Non-Equalizing	283	4.3	21	0.1

[a]Albert Munse, op cit., 1965, p. 46.

state funds possessing only moderate or very weak equalization. Both of these classification methods also separate flat or fixed grants from equalizing grants and, therefore, do not give credit for the equalizing qualities which can be derived from providing a given unit amount to rich and poor alike. Such a situation is illustrated by North Carolina, where a high percentage of all school monies are derived from state level taxation and redistributed back to local school districts without taking local fiscal ability into account. The two previously discussed classification schemes identify North Carolina's funds as non-equalizing, however, the actual impact of this state's funds provides for substantial equalization, since over 70 percent of all the funds are derived from state resources.

In order to avoid misinterpretations of the intent and impact of state school finance funds, the National Educational Finance Project has analyzed all state school funds using three different techniques. First, in this chapter all state funds are classified as to their method and purpose. This classification does not attempt to measure or even identify equalizing features. The second approach is presented in Chapter 3 of Volume 4 of the National Educational Finance Project; a revenue profile has been developed for school districts in each state showing the impact of local state and federal revenues on districts with 1,500 or more pupils. The third view is provided in Chapter 4 of Volume 4; the emphasis is on the equalization aspects of all state and local funds for education. An equalization rating is provided for each state. The first of these classifications, funds by method and purpose, is given below.

Method

The classification of funds by method, as used here, has five categories, they are: circumscribed, uniform, fiscal-modified, client-modified, and fiscal-client-modified. None of the categories reflect equalizing tendencies. Each category is simply descriptive of the type of formula manipulation utilized by the legislature. For example, fiscal-modified indicates that the legislature makes adjustments in the formula for the fiscal ability of the school district; however, there is no attempt to show the degree of correlation with wealth or whether the fund, in fact, fiscally equalizes or disequalizes. Descriptions of the above categories follow.

Type I, Circumscribed. Many states have funds which are allocated on the basis of (a) circumstance of the local school districts, (b) special conditions or imposed restrictions, and (c) discretion or judgment of administrators. This type of fund is limited to certain school districts and, therefore, cannot be considered in the same light as funds with universal distributions.[2] Distributions with formulas based on geography or political organization, such as unorganized territories in Maine, are classified as *circumscribed*. Special legislation which imposes conditions, such as funds to cities with over 100,000 population, are classified as *circumscribed* because of their limited application.

Also included in this category are funds distributed at the discretion of the chief state school officer or other state official. These funds include those allocated to districts for reasons of emergency. (See Column I, Table 2-3.)

Type II, Uniform. Funds distributed on the basis of a given amount per unit (per teacher, per pupil in average daily attendance, per pupil in average daily membership, per pupil enrolled, etc.) are all described as *uniform.* (See Column II, Table 2-3.)

Type III, Fiscal-Modified. If a distribution formula takes the fiscal capacity or wealth of the school district into account then it is designated as having fiscal modification. Fiscal modification can be based on any one of several wealth measures including assessed valuation of property, equalized valuation of property, income or indexes of ability. (See Column III, Table 2-3.)

Type IV, Client-Modified. With the advent of the foundation program concept, the notion that state aid programs should be designed to meet variations in educational needs of children became commonplace. Funds were no longer distributed totally on a uniform per unit allocation. Several states weight pupils based on high cost education programs. Districts containing pupils with mental, physical, social, economic and other handicaps are allowed proportionally more money since it costs more to bring handicapped children to a functional education level. Such provisions in state aid programs are classified as *client-modified.* Sometimes such modifications include adult education courses and teacher training programs in addition to programs for children, hence the use of the term "client" modified instead of "pupil" or "child" modified. (See Column IV, Table 2-3.)

Type V, Fiscal-Client-Modified. Where state programs contain weighting adjustments for both educational needs of the clientele and fiscal ability of school districts, the category is called *fiscal-client-modified.* As will be observed, most *basic* state aid formulas fall within this category. (See Column V, Table 2-3.)

Purpose

State school funds are allocated for a great number of purposes, ranging from general unrestricted aid for current operation to very specific categorical aids such as driver education. It is not always possible to identify all programs financed by a state since in many instances specific educational programs are required by and subsumed in the basic state aid formula. No attempt is made here to ferret out the program benefits of each of the large basic funds; for this reason one should not assume that a state is not providing money for, say, culturally deprived children simply because there is no categorical aid for that specific purpose.

The classification design presented here categorizes all funds for general, nonrestricted elementary and secondary use as *basic multi-program*. Foundation programs, or other large "equalization" aid funds are types of subventions which are classified in the *basic multi-program* category.

Special categorical grants which have separate legislative appropriations are classified as *specific educational programs* according to purpose (early childhood education, compensatory education for culturally deprived, exceptional or handicapped education including programs for gifted, vocational education, adult and continuing education and junior-community college education). It should be emphasized that all the state aid funds considered here are distributed through the state education agency or state department of education in charge of administering the public or common school program. Funds are not included if they are channeled through other state agencies such as separate junior college or vocational education boards or departments.

In addition to the broad programmatic areas listed above, funds for transportation, school housing, textbooks and the like, are classified as *support programs* and listed separately.

OBSERVATIONS ON METHOD AND PURPOSE

Nearly one-half (48.84 percent) of the total $12.6 billion dollars distributed by states in 1968-69 was allocated through formulas which provided adjustments for both the clientele and the fiscal condition of the school district (Table 2-3). Adjustments for clientele (generally pupils) were usually made by weightings for average daily attendance or average daily membership. These weightings were expressed both in terms of pupil units and classroom units. Occasionally, adjustments were made in terms of reimbursement expenditures for the previous year. Allocation formulas with only fiscal modifications were found in $2.36 billion or 18.67 percent of all funds distributed by states (Table 2-3). Where funds were fiscally modified, the states distributed the funds on a standard unit, adjusted for the

TABLE 2-3

CLASSIFICATION OF STATE AID FUNDS BY METHOD OF DISTRIBUTION, 1968-69
(Millions of Dollars)

State	I (Circumscribed)	II (Uniform)	III (Fiscal-Modified)	IV (Client-Modified)	V (Fiscal-Client-Modified)	Total
Alabama	$	$ 21.47	$	$	$ 166.11	$ 187.58
Alaska		22.08	26.00	.23		48.31
Arizona		73.05	12.00		66.00	151.05
Arkansas	1.03	86.59	7.10			94.72
California	24.53	712.61	492.64	109.40		1,339.18
Colorado	.46	41.65	49.87			91.98
Connecticut	.30	127.54		4.50		132.34
Delaware		13.56		63.41		76.97
Florida		83.12			577.75	668.56
Georgia		36.08			291.77	327.85
Hawaii						**
Idaho	0.10				32.86	32.96
Illinois	9.56	37.01	263.81	117.15		427.53
Indiana	0.01	51.20	28.87	5.03	179.85	264.96
Iowa	4.80	52.43		3.50	111.00	171.73
Kansas		5.09	98.40	2.31		105.80
Kentucky		2.60			182.61	185.21
Louisiana	0.31	29.82		1.69	262.53	294.35
Maine	0.89	0.83	40.65	0.65		43.02
Maryland		45.74	192.40			238.14
Massachusetts	1.13	3.69	23.70	24.70	106.04	159.26
Michigan	2.00	3.25	579.76	30.00		615.01
Minnesota	3.13	57.07	0.20		198.59	258.99
Mississippi		28.33			129.30	157.63
Missouri	1.06	185.38	33.02			219.46
Montana		11.26		0.02	23.00	34.28
Nebraska		5.92		1.10	25.00	32.02
Nevada					29.15	29.15

State						
New Hampshire	2.75	1.88		0.45	4.28	9.36
New Jersey	5.31	121.14	95.26			221.71
New Mexico	0.30	22.57	20.00	72.92		115.79
New York	62.00	39.90	41.00		1,817.70	1,960.60
North Carolina		20.94		346.85		367.79
North Dakota		2.87		0.45	22.08	25.40
Ohio	0.28	30.72	33.29	0.30	404.02	468.61
Oklahoma		37.30	54.20			91.50
Oregon	0.62	40.20		57.11		97.93
Pennsylvania	3.40	71.19	32.55	83.68	598.57	789.39
Rhode Island		3.00	39.30			42.30
South Carolina	17.99	34.41		117.02		169.42
South Dakota		2.41			9.13	11.54
Tennessee	3.43	16.15	174.14		365.53	193.72
Texas		277.58			365.53	643.11
Utah	0.18	7.04	5.10	0.24	75.72	88.28
Vermont		7.51			32.99	40.50
Virginia	0.23	98.80		187.28	251.50	286.31
Washington		40.01	13.00		251.50	304.51
West Virginia		49.47		11.07	53.01	113.55
Wisconsin		23.56		16.11	130.31	169.98
Wyoming		3.55			17.13	20.68
Total	$ 153.49 (1.22%)	$ 2,689.57 (21.31%)	$ 2,356.26 (18.67%)	$ 1,257.17 (9.96%)	$ 6,163.53 (48.84%)	$12,620.02 (100.00%)

**State Budget

fiscal ability or inability of school districts. In these programs, the relative needs of children are not taken into account. On the other hand, $1.26 billion, or 9.96 percent, of all funds were distributed on a *client-modified* basis (Table 2-3). Here, no attention was given to the fiscal condition of the school district, and the entire amount was allocated on some basis of legislatively perceived educational need of the clientele.

Uniform or flat grants constituted $2.69 billion (21.31 percent) of all state funds distributed (Table 2-3). As pointed out above, *uniform* distribution provides for no fiscal modification and no educational need or clientele adjustments other than a standard unit designation. With this type of distribution, the wealthy school district receives the same amount of funds per unit as the poor district and no compensation is given for students with high cost educational needs.

The smallest proportion of the funds was distributed through *circumscribed* grants. *Circumscribed* funds accounted for about $153 million or 1.22 percent of the total (Table 2-3). The major portion of the *circumscribed* funds are found in New York where over 50 million dollars are distributed for the aid of the urban education, and in California where *circumscribed* funds are appropriated for compensatory education, special education therapists, local emergency assistance, and grants to teachers for educational advancement.

Regarding purposes of distributions, over $10 billion or 85.53 percent of the total state funds were distributed through basic multi-purpose programs (Table 2-4). These large grants, of course, encompass current operation and sometimes capital outlay and, in many cases have, as in Florida, special unit allotments for exceptional children, kindergarten, vocational and adult education. The funds for these special programs are distributed to the local school district in a lump sum, and no special earmarking or accounting is generally required except that the local school district must staff and provide facilities for the designated program.

Thirty-five of the states have special funds for exceptional and handicapped children and several of the other 15 states, such as Kentucky, New York, and Georgia, have program provisions in their basic state aid formulas (Table 2-4). The largest amount of funds for exceptional and handicapped children is funded by categorical grants in California where over $125 million is provided for such purposes. Pennsylvania, Illinois, Michigan and Washington all make very large categorical grants for exceptional and handicapped children.

The emergence of state grants for compensatory education programs for culturally deprived children is a comparatively recent phenomenon, gaining its impetus from the federal Elementary and Secondary Education Act of 1965. At least thirteen states make special provisions for programs which can be interpreted as being designed to assist culturally deprived children. One fund in New York accounts for $52 million of the total $88.73 million categorized for this purpose.

Vocational education programs are distributed through separate special funds in 36 states (Table 2-4). Once again, as in the case of exceptional and handicapped children, several states include allocations for vocational education in their basic general aid formula. These special funds account for $131.4 million of the vocational educational funds in the United States.

It is quite common for states to allocate funds separately for support programs such as transportation, school housing, driver education and textbooks. Special support grants for transportation were $290.80 million. During the one year of 1968-69, special support grants for school housing constituted $407.56 million dollars. Textbooks claim $121.37 million of the support funds while driver education programs, categorically funded in 23 states, amount to $42.87 million. A detailed breakdown of support programs is found in Table 2-5.

SUMMARY

The classification offered here leaves open the question of equalization (to be treated in later chapters), and considers state aid funds only as to the method of distribution. It is not intended in this presentation that the implication be made that funds classified as *fiscal* or *client-modified* are so modified in the same degree—merely that funds so classified do contain evidence of these considerations.

The apparent trend toward equalizing-type distribution methods, indicated by previous studies, is not denied in this study—in fact, the preponderance of fiscal-client-modified monies for basic multi-program use tends to confirm the trend.

TABLE 2-4

CLASSIFICATION OF STATE AID FUNDS BY PURPOSE FOR
BASIC MULTI-PROGRAM AND SPECIFIC EDUCATIONAL PROGRAMS, 1968-69
(Millions of Dollars)

State	Basic Multi-Program	Specific Educational Programs					
		Early Childhood	Compensatory Education	Special or Exceptional Education	Vocational Education	Adult and Continuing Education	Junior (or Community) College
Alabama	$ 178.11	$	$ 0.10	$ 0.31	$ 7.49	$	$
Alaska	41.67*				1.61		
Arizona	147.76			1.34	1.95		
Arkansas	84.00			0.40	1.03	0.08	
California	1,032.75*	4.11	11.05	125.64	1.03	9.36	91.85
Colorado	82.60*		0.17	4.00			
Connecticut	97.67*		6.18	4.50	1.10	0.25	
Delaware	63.41						
Florida	497.75*			4.03	1.20		90.25
Georgia	291.77				7.28		
Hawaii							
Idaho	32.86				0.10		
Illinois	365.65*			23.77	8.96	3.28	
Indiana	194.66*		3.28	4.18	1.20	0.86	
Iowa	149.58*			3.50	12.00		
Kansas	100.10*			2.31	0.38		2.33
Kentucky	182.61						
Louisiana	270.03*			1.69	1.23	0.51	
Maine	35.54*			0.66	0.70	0.09	
Maryland	141.90*			17.50		0.81	5.50
Massachusetts	106.04			11.37			
Michigan	579.76*		2.00	30.00			
Minnesota	220.19*			8.50			
Mississippi	143.26				9.90		
Missouri	169.75			8.45	5.41		7.31

State	Amount	$4.11	$88.73	$356.50	$131.14	$18.09	$214.44
Montana	32.49				0.45		
Nebraska	30.32*			1.10	0.06		
Nevada	29.15*						
New Hampshire	5.29*			0.52	0.05		
New Jersey	168.57*			8.44	2.63	0.34	
New Mexico	105.34			1.18	1.60		
New York	1,817.70*		52.00	0.45	11.51		
North Carolina	338.24			10.14	0.21		
North Dakota	24.76			0.78	5.79		
Ohio	404.30*		8.81	2.75	1.20	0.12	
Oklahoma	86.85			44.05	0.13		8.32
Oregon	73.90		0.60	1.00	13.40		8.88
Pennsylvania	607.66*		0.03	0.05			
Rhode Island	35.20*				6.09		
South Carolina	128.54					1.61	
South Dakota	11.54*		2.00				
Tennessee	174.80			1.20	3.43		
Texas	625.69		0.80				
Utah	78.06*				0.24		
Vermont	32.99			1.87	0.50	0.12	
Virginia	249.76		1.71	5.86	8.92	0.66	
Washington	251.50*			14.80	3.75		
West Virginia	110.60			0.57	1.46		
Wisconsin	139.53*						
Wyoming	20.68*			9.59	6.86		
Total	$10,792.90	$4.11	$88.73	$356.50	$131.14	$18.09	$214.44

*Includes State Aid for Kindergarten.

Table 2-5

CLASSIFICATION OF STATE AID FUNDS BY PURPOSE FOR SUPPORT PROGRAMS, 1968-69
(Millions of Dollars)

State	Support Programs													Total All Programs Tables 2-4 and 2-5
	Transportation	School Housing	Administration and Supervision	Textbooks	Emergencies and Contingencies	Orphans	Driver Education	Professional and Curriculum Improvement	School Lunch	District Organization	Libraries	Health Service	Other	
Alabama	$ 2.94	$ 1.62	$	$ 1.08	$	$	$ 0.19	$	$ 0.23	$	$	$	$ 0.24	$ 187.58
Alaska														48.31
Arizona														151.05
Arkansas	7.10		0.34	1.51		0.05					0.08		0.13	94.72
California	19.08			21.26		*	11.40						11.65	1,339.18
Colorado	4.75				0.30			0.16						91.98
Connecticut	5.43						1.04				0.17			132.34
Delaware	2.92	16.00												76.97
Florida		10.64		9.60			1.92							668.56
Georgia		63.80												327.85
Hawaii		28.80												**
Idaho														32.96
Illinois	14.57	1.90	2.54			1.11	5.75							427.53
Indiana	14.18	46.60				0.15	1.70							264.96
Iowa		4.75			0.05		0.68							171.73
Kansas														105.80
Kentucky		0.20		2.60					12.35					185.21
Louisiana		4.02	0.03	7.88			0.38						0.08	294.35
Maine							0.12			1.85			0.01	43.02
Maryland	21.20	50.50					0.73							238.14

State														Total
Massachusetts	13.33	23.70				1.13			3.69					159.26
Michigan	19.00		3.25		0.70	0.20			0.50					615.01
Minnesota		6.66												258.99
Mississippi		1.80		2.53				5.18						157.63
Missouri	16.91			8.70		0.07	0.02	1.06						219.46
Montana	1.20					0.10	0.54							34.28
Nebraska														32.02
Nevada														29.15
New Hampshire		2.75	0.30							0.45			0.05	9.36
New Jersey	13.14	28.36		2.30	0.18	0.30								221.71
New Mexico	7.55				0.30									115.79
New York				25.29				10.00	13.01	41.00				1,960.60
North Carolina	2.84			8.61			5.12	0.29						367.79
North Dakota								0.61					0.30	25.40
Ohio	33.29						5.25							468.61
Oklahoma				2.67										91.50
Oregon	6.63	5.00	3.86		0.50	0.60	3.42							97.93
Pennsylvania	32.00	56.08								2.73		12.23		789.39
Rhode Island		4.10	0.20											42.30
South Carolina	10.56	18.01		3.50	0.20	0.30			0.36		0.20			169.42
South Dakota														11.54
Tennessee		10.38	3.91	17.42										193.72
Texas	2.20					0.50		0.07	1.67		0.50			643.11
Utah		4.24				0.49								88.28
Vermont		4.65												40.50
Virginia	8.75		2.85	2.21		0.94		1.88			1.15		2.01	286.31
Washington	18.50	13.00		0.30	0.15									304.51
West Virginia			0.06	2.30	0.03	0.13			0.40					113.55
Wisconsin														169.98
Wyoming	12.73					1.27								20.68
Total	$290.80	$407.56	$13.43	$121.37	$2.18	$9.61	$42.87	$19.25	$32.21	$46.03	$2.10	$12.23	$14.47	$12,620.02

*Negligible.
**State Budget.

TABLE 2-6

FUND CLASSIFICATION BY METHOD OF DISTRIBUTION AND PURPOSE, 1968-69
(Millions of Dollars and Percent)

Purpose	I Circumscribed $	%	II Uniform $	%	III Fiscal-Modified $	%	IV Client-Modified $	%	V Fiscal-Client-Modified $	%	Total $	%
Basic Multi-Program	26.46	17.24	1,733.88	64.47	2,048.23	86.92	951.44	75.69	6,032.89	97.89	10,792.90	85.53
Specific Educational Programs:												
Early Childhood	4.11	2.68									4.11	0.03
Compensatory	54.60	35.56	34.13	1.27							88.73	0.70
Special or Exceptional	9.65	6.29	96.34	3.58	8.45	0.36	206.06	16.39	36.00	0.58	356.50	2.82
Vocational	6.18	4.03	111.32	4.14			13.64	1.08			131.14	1.04
Adult and Continuing	3.30	2.15	11.43	0.42	2.50	0.11	0.86	0.07			18.09	0.14
Junior College			106.31	3.95	43.25	1.84			64.88	1.05	214.44	1.70
Support Programs:												
Transportation	3.70	2.41	187.20	6.96	86.57	3.67	13.33	1.06			290.80	2.30
School Housing	28.04	18.27	176.10	6.55	123.66	5.25	50.00	3.98	29.76	0.48	407.56	3.23
Administration and Supervision	0.03	0.02	13.40	0.50							13.43	0.11
Textbooks			112.76	4.19			8.16	0.68			121.37	0.96
Emergency and Contingency	2.18	1.42									2.18	0.02
Orphans	1.13	0.74	7.71	0.29	0.75	0.03	0.02				9.61	0.08
Driver Education			42.87	1.59							42.87	0.34
Professional and Curriculum Improvement	11.30	7.36	7.95	0.30							19.25	0.15
School Lunch			31.98	1.19			0.23	0.02			32.21	0.26
District Organization	2.73	1.78			42.85	1.82	0.45	0.04			46.03	0.36
Libraries			2.10	0.08							2.10	0.02
Health Services							12.23	0.97			12.23	0.10
Other	0.08	0.05	14.09	0.52			0.30	0.02			14.47	0.11
Total	153.49	100.00	2,689.57	100.00	2,356.26	100.00	1,257.17	100.00	6,163.53	100.00	12,620.02	100.00

If all funds with fiscal modifications are summed, one finds that over 67 percent of all state dollars are distributed, to some degree, with fiscal capacity or wealth of local school districts taken into account.

Similarly, client modifications are found in over 58 percent of the funds. Contrasting client-modified funds with those with fiscal adjustments, it might be said that legislatures give greater attention to variations in fiscal ability of school districts than to variations in the needs of the client population. However, such a conclusion would ignore the fact that economic inadequacies of school districts are, in most cases, symptomatic of educational and cultural deficiencies of the population.

Table 2-6 is a summary of all state aid funds by method of distribution and by purpose, showing dollars and the percentage (within each method) allotted for various purposes. This represents the national picture which has been displayed, by state, in Tables 2-3, 2-4 and 2-5.[3]

FOOTNOTES

1. Albert R. Munse, *State Programs for Public School Support*, Office of Education, U. S. Government Printing Office, Washington, D.C., 1965.

2. *Ibid.*, p. 112.

3. Basic information for these tables was obtained from: Thomas L. Johns, *Public School Finance Programs*, 1968-69, U. S. Government Printing Office, Washington, 1969.

CHAPTER 3

Economics and the Financing
of Education

As education has become an ever larger component of the public budget, particularly at state and local government levels, interest has grown in the short-run and long-run effects on the economy of expenditures for education. This new field of study has acquired the name "economics of education." This phrase did not generally appear in textbooks or discussions on school finance until the late 1950's and is still treated perfunctorily by many educators. However, the economics of education contributes a new and rigorous perspective which may help to improve decisions concerning the way public schools are financed.

Activities associated with what may be thought of as the "education industry" engage a significant portion of the economic resources of the United States. During 1969-70, for example, a total of $66.8 billion was spent by educational institutions in the United States and an estimated six million persons were employed by these institutions.[1] Public elementary and secondary schools alone expended $39.5 billion and employed over three million persons. Thus, by practically any criterion, education is a major user of economic resources. And since the educational industry has accounted for a significant and increasing portion of the gross national product, it has in recent years, attracted the attention of a number of economists as well as professional educators.

In this chapter we shall consider briefly some of the economic aspects of education, drawing heavily upon the material prepared by economists for an earlier publication in the NEFP series,[2] as well as upon the work of others who have written on various aspects of the economics of education. Our discussion will apply primarily to elementary and secondary education. We shall first consider education as an economic good or commodity giving special attention to some of its characteristic attributes. Attention will then be turned to the concept of education as human capital, to the rate of return on investment in education, and to the relationship between education and economic growth. The chapter will be concluded with an examination of some applications of economic analysis which might be employed to achieve more efficient utilization of the resources devoted to education and a discussion of some of the alternatives to existing organizational arrangements for education which have been advanced.

EDUCATION AS AN ECONOMIC GOOD

Economics deals with the allocation and utilization of scarce resources. The notion of scarce resources is basic, for it implies that for such resources there exist alternative uses. The economist is concerned with allocating scarce resources in a manner which maximizes the satisfactions gained by consumers. For the economist, the ultimate in efficiency will be achieved when scarce resources are utilized in such ways that any change in their allocation among alternative uses would reduce the total satisfaction of consumers. Obviously, the resources consumed by education could be devoted to other uses, so the proper allocation of resources to education and the efficient use of the resources which are allocated to education are legitimate concerns of the economist.

Some may question whether education can be regarded as a commodity. The answer is a qualified "yes!," for it has a price and is bought and sold. However, as a commodity education has a number of somewhat unique characteristics—some arising from the fact that it is produced and consumed in a complex sociological matrix and some arising from the nature of education itself.

Demand Versus Need for Education

Since the two terms are used so frequently, it is important that we distinguish between the concept of demand and the concept of need. Demand, as used in economics, refers to a functional relationship between the price of a commodity and the quantity of the commodity which will be purchased. The demand for most commodities is susceptible to objective measurement and can be quantified with considerable precision. Demand is a subjective concept only to the extent that it measures the relative value that consumers place upon a given commodity in comparison with other things for which they could spend their money. Thus, (assuming the demand for it is elastic) as the price of a commodity increases the amount purchased will generally decrease, for other commodities tend to become more attractive. In short, the demand for a commodity usually declines as its price increases and vice versa.

The concept of need, on the other hand, involves an essentially subjective determination of the amount of a given commodity or service that "ought" to be provided. The supply of most public goods and services, for example, highways, police and fire protection, and education, reflects an administrative and/or legislative judgment with respect to the amount of a given good or service that should be provided to best serve the general welfare of society. The judgments of public officials—legislators, executives, or both—rather than the operation of the market, determine the kind and amount of goods and services that will be made available to consumers—whether or not they are willing to pay the cost and, hence, whether or not they "demand" the commodity.

Application of the concept of need to determine the supply of goods and services enables public officials to circumvent one of the great drawbacks of the market. Namely, that individual consumers typically act only in their own self interest, which is not always in the best interests of society. By utilizing the concept of need, public officials can decide upon the kind and amount of education, police and fire protection, highways, and the like which they believe will best serve the general welfare of society. The *need* for educational service for handicapped children, for example, may be far greater than the *demand*. Such services are often quite expensive and the parents of handicapped children often are not in a position to afford them. Public officials may decide that the general welfare of society will best be served by appropriating public funds to provide educational services for handicapped children. It is in this way that the concept of need is employed in determining the supply of public goods and services.

Musgrave has identified two classes of goods which are satisfied through the public sector of the economy, social goods and merit goods.[3] Social goods are those which, by their very nature, cannot be supplied effectively by the market because they are equally available to all persons whether or not they pay for them —for example, national defense and the judicial system. Merit goods are those which could be provided through the market, but which are thought to be so important to the general welfare of society that their provision cannot be left to the vagaries of the marketplace. Education is a prime example of a merit good. The maintenance of an educational system in which all citizens have free access to at least a minimum level of education is thought to be so vital to the maintenance of democratic self-government that education is financed primarily through the public budget.

There is no economic reason which would prevent education from being supplied entirely through the market. Consumers (households) could purchase education for their children from privately operated schools just as they now purchase many other goods and services. It is likely, however, that the amount of education which would be purchased in the market by households would be considerably less than optimal in terms of the general welfare of society. Thus, we have chosen to finance education through the public budget to a large extent. In effect, we subsidize the production of education. The difference between what consumers (households) would spend for education if it could be purchased only in the market at its full cost, and the total amount of money which is expended for education in the private and public sectors combined, may be thought of as a subsidy. The purpose of this subsidy is, of course, to insure that at least a minimal level of education will be made available to each consumer (household).

The nature of the relationship between the price of education and the demand for education is of considerable practical importance, for it will largely determine the size of the subsidy which will be required to make available the desired quantity of education. If supply and demand are relatively unresponsive to price (inelastic) so that a relatively large change in price is required to produce a given change in demand, a rather large subsidy will be required. If, on the other hand, supply and demand are quite responsive to price (elastic) so that a relatively small change in price is required to produce a given change in demand, only a small subsidy will be required. Unfortunately, relatively little is known about the nature of the relationship between the price of education and the demand for education.

Research concerning the relationship between the income level of a household and its expenditure for education (the income elasticity of demand for education) suggests that at subsistence or low income levels an increase in disposable household income will not result in proportionately greater expenditures for education, probably because other necessities of life have a higher priority; at middle income levels an increase in disposable household income will result in proportionately greater expenditures for education; and at high income levels an increase in disposable household income will again result in proportionately lower expenditures for education, probably because the range of feasible expenditures for education is limited.[4] (By proportionately lower, we mean that the percentage increase in expenditure for education will be less than the percentage increase in disposable household income.) These research findings imply that income subsidies to low income households are not likely to increase their propensity to spend (pay taxes) for education, whereas an increase in the income level of middle income families (or an increase in the percentage of middle income families) can be expected to result in a greater inclination to purchase (pay taxes for) education. Thus, a social policy which aims at providing a guaranteed minimum level of income, while it may be laudable on other grounds, will not go far toward solving the problem of financing education.

The Consumers of Education

A second characteristic of education which makes it a somewhat unusual commodity is the great diversity of the consumers of education. (By consumers of education we refer to households—students and their families—the units most directly involved in what is generally termed "formal education.") Consumers of formal education range from the child attending nur-

51

sery school through the adolescent attending secondary school, the young adult attending college or vocational school, the middle-aged person retraining for a new job, to the recent retiree attending classes in which he hopes to learn how to cope with the problems of retirement. One set of questions which is immediately posed by the existence of such a diverse array of consumers relates to their reasons for attending the various formal educational programs. Some students expect to reap immediate financial returns; others seek only personal enjoyment and satisfaction. Some students attend voluntarily; some attend primarily because others (for example, their parents) expect them to do so; and some attend only under compulsion or duress (for example, because of sanctions imposed by compulsory attendance laws).

For those who attend school voluntarily with an expectation of receiving greater financial return, the application of market principles in pricing education poses no great problem. Presumably, they will be willing to pay for their education so long as the anticipated returns are greater than the cost. As a matter of fact, several commercial organizations operating in the private sector do provide job training and other educational services on precisely this basis. The market model is also generally appropriate for situations in which the consumer is interested primarily in personal enjoyment, for example, recreation. However, a case can be made for at least a partial public subsidy if one purpose of the educational activity is to provide safe and wholesome outlets for youthful exuberance, as is often true of recreation programs for children and youth.

In the case of students attending colleges or vocational schools, it often is difficult to delineate clearly between the extent to which an educational program yields a direct economic return to the student, the extent to which it yields purely personal satisfaction to the student, and/or the extent to which society at large, (rather than the immediate consumer) is benefited. If society at large benefits substantially from the education an individual receives, there is some justification for a public subsidy. And even when education yields direct financial benefits to the individual, it can be argued that the public budget should provide credit (for example, through guaranteed loans) for those individuals who are unable to finance their education from personal savings and who are unable to secure credit from existing financial institutions.

A persuasive case for financing education from the public budget can be made when school attendance is essentially involuntary, as, for example, under statutes which make school attendance compulsory for children within a given age range. Such laws place an exceedingly important constraint on the operation of the market, for they eliminate for the individual consumer the alternative of deciding not to attend school. While compulsory school attendance need not eliminate competition in education (the child may attend a private school, for example), it does clearly imply that the state must regulate education to insure protection of the student from unqualified teachers and inadequate curricula since he no longer has the alternative of refusing to purchase education. Compulsory school attendance laws clearly imply the need for a state subsidy of education, for if school attendance is required then the state has at least a moral obligation to see to it that a minimum level of adequate education is available to all who are required to attend school.

Compulsory attendance laws represent only one type of constraint on consumer decisions. An even more direct constraint resides in the fact that most decisions concerning the kind and amount of schooling to be obtained are made by parents and not by the children who are the actual consumers. Parents generally determine what school a child will attend and what course of study he will pursue. For this reason, and because neither parents nor children typically have much knowledge about alternative choices, the consumer preference model has serious shortcomings when applied to education.

The Output of Education

The foregoing considerations inevitably force one to consider the question of what is the product (or output) of education, for the market model implicitly assumes that one's decision concerning whether or not to buy (or to buy more) depends upon what he thinks he is getting for his money. The output of most enterprises, though not all of them, is tangible, concrete, and short-lived; the output of education often is intangible, abstract, and as long-lived as the individual in whom it is embodied. Although some would claim that the output of education is useful knowledge, this answer provides little help in assessing the quantity, much less the quality, of the products of education. It is very difficult to assess the utility of knowledge during the learning process, for the ultimate test is at some point in the future—and in the case of knowledge gained in elementary and secondary schools, in the relatively distant future.

At this juncture it is appropriate to consider some of the problems involved in measuring the output of the educational enterprise. Almost all educational programs have multiple objectives and outputs, and all educational activities contribute in varying degree to the quantity and quality of these outputs. In the absence of tested and proven human learning theory, it is not possible to determine the extent to which a given activity contributes to each component of educational output, much less to a student's gain in total knowledge. One approach to the problem of measuring educational output has been to test for evidence that certain components of knowledge—for example, reading speed and comprehension, English usage, and ability to recall facts and figures—have been "learned." This approach suffers the disadvantage of failing to acknowledge that educational outputs involve both cognitive and affective dimensions. That is, the values, attitudes and behaviors acquired as a result of the educational process may be at least as important as the knowledge measured by standardized tests.

Another approach to the problem of measuring educational output has been to assume that a relationship exists between exposure to and assimilation of knowledge—that is, days or years of school attendance are viewed as proxies for knowledge gained. Neither approach is entirely satisfactory. There is no assurance that the components of knowledge measured in the first approach will prove to be useful in either an economic or a philosophical sense and, perhaps more important, this approach virtually ignores some of the social and behavioral components of knowledge which may be even more useful. In the latter approach the assumption that a positive correlation exists between time spent in learning and the amount and value of knowledge gained is, at best, tenuous and, at worst, fallacious.

Education: A Craft Enterprise

Even the casual observer is struck by the heavy reliance upon labor in the educational enterprise. There has been little substitution of technology for human labor in education, at least when compared with other major industries. In fact, the machines which are used in education are often regarded as "frills." Conventional wisdom asserts that learning is a uniquely personal process which requires extensive interaction between teacher and pupil. Actually, very little is known about the process of human learning. This means that we know little about how greater utilization of technology in education might affect acquisition of knowledge—not to mention acquisition of attitudes.

The heavy emphasis upon labor is directly reflected in school budgets. It is not unusual for 80 to 85 percent of a school's operating budget to be allocated for salaries, with salaries of teachers alone accounting for 60 to 65 percent of current operating costs. It is easy to explain why school costs have grown so rapidly in recent years. The success of teachers' organizations in securing higher salaries for teachers, the effects of a sharply increasing demand for teachers as a consequence of the post-World War II "baby boom," the increased rates of high school completion, and the inroads of inflation all have contributed prominently to the rising cost of education.

Higher wages for workers can be justified on economic grounds if they are paralleled by increases in productivity, i.e., higher output per worker, or if their wages are low in comparison with those of other workers. In most industries higher output per worker has been obtained by utilizing improved technology—by substituting machine for hand production so that a worker can produce more in a given period of time. Since the utilization of improved technology has been a minor factor in education, it is understandable why the output per teacher may not have increased markedly. Admittedly, output in education is difficult to measure, but we do have accurate statistics concerning one aspect of the educational process in the form of pupil-teacher ratios. If pupil-teacher ratios are regarded as a proxy measure of output per worker, then productivity in education has changed very little over the past decade. If anything, it has decreased. However, pupil-teacher ratios are, at best, inadequate measures of output and are not even satisfactory measures of process, for they reveal nothing of the quality of interaction between the teacher and the pupil. In any event, from an economic viewpoint, education, with its limited use of technology and its heavy reliance on labor, does not appear to be an efficient enterprise. In the absence of valid and reliable measures of output, the charge that education is inefficient is difficult to refute.

Entry into the labor market in education is quite closely regulated by the state through its licensure requirements. One must be licensed to teach. This, of course, is not unique to the profession of education. The state licenses practitioners in most professions (medicine, law, dentistry, pharmacy, etc.) and craft unions also effectively control entry into many trades through apprenticeship requirements.

Externalities and Spillovers

Education yields direct benefits to students and their families—for example, the increased earning potential which is associated with increases in the level of schooling completed. These may be termed internal or private benefits, since they accrue to the student or to his family. Education also conveys benefits to other families in the community and to the society at large—for example, by increasing indirectly the productivity of persons other than the student himself. (It also should be noted that additional costs to society may arise from the consequences of lack of education—for example, higher welfare costs.) The benefits that accrue to individuals other than the student or his family may be termed external or social benefits. Externalities arise when goods or services either confer benefits or impose costs on persons other than the consumer or the producer. Education is generally thought to be characterized by substantial externalities because it affects so many people who do not buy it directly, although there is little direct evidence on this point.

The importance of the existence of externalities lies in the fact that private decisions concerning whether or not to purchase education will be made solely on the basis of internal benefits. The resulting level of supply of education will not be economically efficient because the external benefits which accompany education will not be taken into consideration in the individual student-parent decision. Consequently, too few resources will be allocated to education. In other words, the decision of a student or his family to invest in his education will be based on the anticipated direct benefits to the student and will disregard any external benefits which may be conferred on other families or on the community in general.

Some of the external benefits of education are economic in nature; others are social in nature. Among the economic benefits

56

are improvement of the environment in which production takes place, greater flexibility and adaptability of the labor force, and greater ability to develop technical improvements and incorporate them into production processes. Conversely, externalities of a negative nature, such as unemployment and crime, may result from the lack of education.

It is difficult to attach an economic value to the broad social benefits which are associated with education, although they may be far more important than the private benefits over the long haul. There is general agreement, for example, that an educated citizenry is a requisite for democratic self-government. Education also is recognized as a major instrument for promoting equality of opportunity and is probably more effective than any other instrument in compensating for social or economic disadvantages of children.

It is the external benefits associated with education that provide the most persuasive case for subsidizing education with public funds. As we have seen, the externalities are not considered in private investment decisions, and because they are ignored the optimum allocation of resources to education will not be achieved. Financing education primarily from public funds permits the external benefits of education to be given proper consideration in the process of allocating resources.

Closely related to externalities are geographic spillovers. Geographic spillovers refer to the benefits of education which accrue to persons located outside the boundaries of a school district (as distinguished from those benefits which accrue to persons who reside in a school district). The concept of geographic spillovers translates into economic terms the notion that every citizen has an interest in the quantity and quality of the education which is provided in every school district in the nation. Citizens of our large cities, for example, have a vital interest in the education received by persons in remote rural areas, since many of these persons will migrate to urban core cities in search of employment. Geographic spillovers vary with distance. A citizen of Maine, for example, is likely to be more concerned with the educational services provided in Maine than with those in California, since expenditures in Maine are more likely to affect him directly.

The existence of geographic spillovers provides a strong argument for state and federal participation in the financing of education, since only these larger units of government are in a position to levy taxes over an entire state or the nation. Admittedly, there is no practical way to levy taxes in direct proportion to the benefits each taxpayer obtains from geographic spillovers, but state and federal taxing powers do provide a way of spreading taxes over the total population which benefits from them.

EDUCATION AS A FORM OF HUMAN CAPITAL

The notion of human capital is relatively new, having come to the forefront only during the past two decades. It is based on the idea that the skills and knowledge possessed by people are, in fact, resources, and that human resources represent a very important part of the capital available to society. Capital, from an economic viewpoint, is characterized by its ability to generate future satisfactions, or future earnings, or both. Education represents a stock of resources just as surely as does land, industrial plants, or oil wells, for education does have the ability to generate future satisfaction and future income. The economic value of education as a form of capital is a function of the income stream it is able to generate. When education is viewed as a form of capital, decisions with respect to education, whether made by a student, by his family, or by public or private agencies, are viewed as investment decisions and are based on the relative rates of return available to alternative investment opportunities.

Education is but one of several means whereby the stock of human capital can be improved. For example, improved health care which reduces the time lost from work as a result of illness or which lengthens the working life of a person clearly contributes to the productivity of human capital. However, it is generally agreed that education is a major determinant of the value of the stock of human capital.

From the human capital approach, education can be viewed as one component in the total stock of capital and decisions with regard to the level of investment in education should follow the same rules which serve to guide other investment decisions, such as plant expansion or replacement of machinery. Thus, additional investment in education would occur only if the rate of return from that investment would equal or exceed the rate of return available from any other alternative investment. The same investment rules also would apply within the entire field of education. That is, the decision to invest in preschool education, or

58

elementary school education, or graduate school education would depend upon the relative rates of return to investment at these educational levels.

The Present Stock of Educational Capital

As Schultz has noted, "In terms of either years or cost of schooling, the population and labor force of the United States possess more educational capital per person than their counterparts in any other country."[5] As of 1968, 63 percent of the civilian labor force in the United States 18 to 64 years of age had completed at least four years of high school and over 12 percent had completed four or more years of college. Between 1929 and 1957 the annual rate of increase in educational capital in the United States labor force was twice as high as the annual rate of increase of reproducible tangible wealth. There is reason to believe that this rate of increase has continued since 1957. Even though the stock of educational capital has grown at an impressive rate during the past 50 years, one may question whether or not investment in educational capital has been properly directed, whether the existing stock of educational capital has been utilized efficiently, and whether the marginal rate of return has been maintained.

Education, like most forms of capital, pays dividends only when it is used. Unemployment reduces the return on educational capital. Not only is a considerable amount of educational capital idle during times of high unemployment, but also the skills of workers tend to deteriorate when they are idle. This underlines the importance of maintaining a high level of employment, for failure to do so not only substantially reduces the rate of return from investments in educational capital, but causes depreciation of the educational capital itself.

Educational capital is subject to obsolescence. In a rapidly changing, technologically oriented economy, demands for various skills and knowledge will change as new techniques and processes of production are introduced. In general, the more specialized a person's skills, the more rapidly they will become obsolete. It is becoming increasingly clear that education cannot be viewed as a process which terminates upon entry into the work force. Most persons will need to be retrained several times during their productive lives. The rapidity with which highly specialized skills become obsolete suggests that high priority should be given to education directed toward helping people bring to bear knowledge and analytical skills in the solving of problems, as well as toward up-dating existing skills and acquiring new ones.

The Distribution of Educational Capital

Investment in education is weighted rather heavily in favor of youth because most investment in schooling occurs at a relatively early age. This is likely to reduce the value of the educational capital possessed by older persons. Young people who enter the labor force with a greater stock of educational capital and who possess new skills which are in high demand may tend to make the skills of older workers obsolete. The higher level of educational capital embodied in younger members of the labor force which tends to render obsolete the educational capital of older members poses a difficult trade-off problem which has not been recognized adequately and which has further implications for welfare and retirement policies.

A second problem with regard to the distribution of educational capital lies in the relatively inadequate and/or inferior stock of educational capital acquired by most children from lower socioeconomic classes. This maldistribution of investment in educational capital is associated with inequality in the distribution of personal income. Children from low income families generally acquire less educational capital, and that which they do acquire typically is of lower quality, than that acquired by children from middle and high income families. (Schools serving low income areas tend to spend less per pupil and to be staffed with less experienced teachers than schools serving high income areas.) Public schooling is neither free nor equal and there is good reason, purely on investment grounds, for improving both the quality and quantity of educational capital acquired by children from low income households. The long-run economic benefits which may be derived from improving the educational capital of children from low income families may also include lower expenditures for welfare, public housing, medical care and similar items. These potential savings are, of course, in addition to the direct gains in personal income which could be expected as a result of improved education.

As noted earlier, quality in education traditionally has been

60

defined primarily in terms of inputs using such measures as days of school attendance, expenditure per pupil, and pupil-teacher ratios. There is a pressing need for research which will define quality in terms of the outputs of the schools rather than the inputs to them. Even a cursory examination, however, reveals that great differences in both the quality and the quantity of inputs exist in the nation, within individual states, and even within individual school districts. These differences constitute a major reason for believing that our present investment in educational capital is less than optimal.

Inefficiency in the Acquisition and Use of Educational Capital

The primary distinction between educational and other human capital, on the one hand, and physical capital, on the other, lies in the fact that educational capital is inseparable from the person in whom it is embodied. Whereas other forms of capital can be sold or mortgaged, educational capital cannot. Educational capital is subject to all of the value systems, social customs, and legal provisions which govern the rights of persons. This situation poses obvious problems with regard to the sources of funds for investment in educational capital. For example, funds which are loaned for the purchase of tangible property can be secured by obtaining a mortgage on such property. However, one who loans money to a student has no security other than the student's promise to repay the loan. This makes it difficult for students to obtain loans from private sources to finance investment in educational capital unless provisions can be made for guaranteeing repayment of the loans.

Inefficiency also results from the constraints which are related to cultural and/or social expectations. For example, if the head of a household moves to another location to take advantage of an employment opportunity, the entire household usually migrates to the new location whether or not employment opportunities for other members of the household are improved.

Another major source of inefficiency in human capital is discrimination in employment on the basis of race, sex, religion, or the like. Discrimination will cause inefficiency in investment in human capital if those who are subject to discrimination have less economic incentive to acquire the amount and quality of schooling than they would have acquired if they were free from

61

discrimination and/or if they have less motivation to attend and perform well in school than those who are free from discrimination. Considerable evidence shows that discrimination against blacks does exist, both in the job market and in education, and that it becomes more significant economically as the educational level of a person increases. If white students can anticipate a 25 percent rate of return on the additional cost involved in obtaining a high school education and black students can expect a rate of return near zero on this additional cost, black students obviously have little economic incentive to complete high school, hence they are likely to drop out of high school at the first opportunity. For example, one study has shown that blacks who have completed five to seven years of schooling receive $790 less annually than do whites with comparable education and that the difference is $1,950 for those completing twelve years of schooling.[6] Such findings indicate the importance of eliminating discrimination based on race, sex, or religion if maximum returns from investment in educational capital are to be obtained.

Tax laws which do not recognize that educational capital depreciates and becomes obsolete constitute yet another source of inefficiency. In the case of physical capital, both depreciation and obsolescence are taken into account in taxation; in the case of educational capital, they are not. Thus, existing tax laws discriminate against investment in educational capital in comparison with investment in physical capital.

Finally, some economists argue that efficiency in the acquisition of educational capital could be improved if investment decisions were made primarily by students and their families rather than by public bodies. It is argued that reliance on consumer sovereignty would bring about greater competition among schools and would consequently result in a more efficient allocation of resources. Whether greater efficiency would be realized depends primarily upon whether or not the prices charged reflect the real cost of producing the educational services and second, upon whether or not there is widespread availability of accurate information concerning the quality of the educational services available for purchase.

RETURNS TO INVESTMENT IN EDUCATION

Considerable work has been done in recent years concerning the returns to investment in education at various levels. Based upon his own studies and those of other investigators, Schultz has estimated the private rates of return for the United States economy and for investment in education at various levels as follows:[7]

1. For the private domestic economy of the United States, the annual rate of return was estimated to be between 10 and 15 percent before personal taxes.
2. An annual rate of return for investment in elementary education at 35 percent or higher was estimated.
3. An annual rate of return on investment in high school education for white males at 25 percent was estimated. Estimated rates of return to members of minority groups ranged down to near zero for southern rural black males.
4. An annual rate of return on investment to improve the quality of elementary and secondary schooling in the neighborhood of 25 percent was estimated.
5. An annual rate of return on investment in college education in the neighborhood of 15 percent (before personal taxes) was estimated for white males. Estimated rates of return ranged downward from 15 percent for rural males, women, and non-whites.
6. An annual rate of return to investment in graduate education in the neighborhood of 15 percent was estimated when stipends awarded graduate students are treated as earnings.

The above estimates are only part of the total picture, for they are only for private rates of return to investment in education. There also are returns to society for its investment in education. Such returns come, for example, from the increases in knowledge and the reduced lag in the application of knowledge which result from education. It is very difficult to estimate the social rates of return to investment in education but from the studies which have been done it appears that the social rates of return are, in general, similar to the private rates.[8]

Viewing the estimated rates of return, one is struck by the apparent under-investment in elementary education. Data are lacking concerning the possible rates of return to investment in early childhood education, but judging by the rates of return to investment in elementary education, the returns to investment an early childhood education would be equally impressive. Examination of the estimates also suggests that there is considerable under-investment in secondary education and underlines the importance of eliminating discrimination in employment based on race or sex if maximum returns to investment in education are to be achieved.

Substantial differences in the level of investment in elementary education exist among the various school districts in the United States. In communities where the level of personal income is high and parents are well educated, such as the typical high income suburb, the investment in elementary education probably is near (or even beyond) optimum at the present time. In many communities, however, there is underinvestment in elementary education and it is due, in large part, to inadequate local tax bases and inadequate state plans for financial support. Underinvestment in elementary education is especially likely to occur in rural communities, particularly those in the South; in communities that have a substantial non-white population; in economically backward areas, such as Appalachia; and in the ghettos of central cities.

Investments aimed at improving the quality of education at the elementary and secondary school levels also pay handsome dividends. Although quality admittedly is still a somewhat nebulous item in education, the evidence on rates of return to investments to improve educational quality lend strong support to the urgency of developing measures of educational output which can serve to guide investment.

EDUCATION AND ECONOMIC GROWTH

The study of education as a factor in the nation's economic growth is closely related to the study of education as human capital. The desirability of economic growth as a national policy has been affirmed repeatedly by the two major political parties and is generally an important concern of public policy-makers, although a concern for protection of the environment for improving the quality of life has also come to the forefront. The role education plays in economic growth has attracted increased attention during recent years. Interest in the relationship between education and economic growth was stimulated by the discovery of a "residual" of unexplained growth which was equal to well over half of the total economic growth during the postwar years in most western countries. Schultz and Dennison were among the first investigators to attempt to quantify the contribution of education to economic growth.[9] Schultz used essentially the same assumptions and the same data employed in the human capital approach. Basically, the effect of education on the growth of the total economy was estimated by summing the effects of education on the income of all individuals. Using data for nine western nations for the period 1950-62, Dennison found that education accounted for between .4 and .5 of a percentage point of the annual growth in national income in the United States, Belgium, and Italy. The proportion of total growth in national income attributable to education depends in part upon the overall rate of growth in the particular nation. In nations which have low growth rates education makes a relatively large contribution, while in nations which have a high rate of growth the contribution of education is less impressive, percentagewise. The difficulty with these procedures is that there is no independent validation of the contribution of education to economic growth, for it is assumed that whatever residual remains after accounting for all other identifiable inputs may be attributed to education.

More recently, econometric studies of the aggregate production function have been used to get at the relationship between education and economic growth. Summing up the results of these studies, Bowman noted that the education embodied in the labor force contributed to economic growth at a statistically significant level whether one looks at the agricultural sector, the manufacturing sector, or the economy as a whole.[10] However, these studies also indicate that education's contribution to economic growth is probably not as great as was indicated by some of the earlier studies.

While there is substantial evidence that education does contribute to economic growth, the precise ways in which this contribution occurs are not known. Existing evidence is based primarily upon wage rates, which are assumed to reflect differences in the quality of labor, which, in turn, are assumed to reflect differences in the stock of educational capital. The studies lend support to the argument that education has contributed to past economic growth, but they do not demonstrate that additional expenditures for schooling would be an efficient way to encourage future economic growth. Such evidence can come only from studies which will reveal in much greater detail the precise ways in which education is related to economic growth.

More needs to be known about the relationship between the distribution of education in the labor force and the rate of economic growth. We need to know the answer to the question of what is the optimal distribution of education (in terms of years of school completed by various segments of the population) if economic growth is taken as the criterion for investment in education? Answers also are needed to such questions as the following:

1. Why have wage ratios remained relatively stable over a long period of time despite the fact that substantial changes have occurred in the proportion of the population at each level of educational attainment?

2. Do current employment practices reflect the level of education required to perform a particular job, i.e., are the educational qualifications demanded of applicants for certain positions essentially unrelated to the actual knowledge and skill required to perform the job satisfactorily?

3. How is education related to innovation and adaptation, i.e., does education serve primarily to increase the pool of talent available to fill critical positions and to increase the adaptability of workers so that improved technology can be diffused more rapidly? If education does indeed create greater adaptability, what type of education, and what level of education, is most effective in improving the adaptability of the labor force?

Our knowledge of the relationship between education and economic growth does not warrant a prediction that merely making additional expenditures for schooling would be the most efficient way to encourage growth. It is true that the available evidence indicates there has been a relatively high rate of return to investment in secondary education. It is almost certain, however, that these rates of return will vary over time, and that they will be influenced by the proportion of the labor force who are high school graduates. Graduating more high school students may contribute substantially to economic growth when there are relatively few high school graduates, but as the proportion of high school graduates increases their relative wage advantage may decline. Also, as a higher percentage of the school age pop-

66

ulation completes high school there is likely to be negative selection with regard to those who fail to complete high school. When the societal norm is high school graduation, those who fail to complete high school are increasingly likely to be qualitatively inferior, that is, possess less ability or less will to succeed, than those who complete high school. Thus, it would be naive to assume similar rates of return to additional high school graduates if such a situation exists. The available evidence indicates that a fairly large portion of the nation's past economic growth is likely to have been due to increases in the educational capital embodied in the labor force. At the same time, a prediction that further expenditures on schooling in the future would have the same effect on future economic growth is unwarranted. At this point there simply is not enough known about the processes by which education contributes to economic growth to warrant such a prediction.

EFFICIENCY IN EDUCATION

Efficiency is measured by the relationship between input and output in an enterprise. To achieve maximum efficiency a school or school district must obtain the largest possible educational output within the limits of its budget. (From an economic standpoint, efficiency also could be increased by achieving an existing level of output with a lower level of budget.) As noted earlier, little is known about the relationship between the various inputs to the educational enterprise and their effect on educational outputs. In recent years, however, increasing attention has been directed to the task of measuring educational outputs. A number of management tools, for example, systems analysis, operations research and program budgeting, are being sharpened for use in improving the quality of decisions regarding the allocation of resources to the educational enterprise as well as their utilization within the educational enterprise. Several of the emerging management tools have their roots in the discipline of economics and draw heavily upon economic concepts and analyses.

Currently, there is much ado about accountability in education. Accountability has always been stressed in education, but in past years accountability was defined primarily in terms of safeguarding school funds to assure that they were properly expended and that they were not lost or stolen. The recent concern with accountability, however, is more closely related to the economic concept of efficiency. The question being raised today is, "What are we getting in return for the dollars we are spending on education?" Since accountability is primarily an economic concept concerned with input-output relationships, at least as the term is used today, it is appropriate to look to economics for analytical tools which may help answer questions concerning accountability.

Systems Analysis of Education

The first phase in the application of systems analysis to education is that of identifying the objectives to be served by a program and the priority to be attached to each objective. It is preferable that objectives be stated in operational terms so that progress toward their accomplishment may be more easily measured. Virtually all educational programs have multiple objectives and a thorough analysis requires that all objectives be considered. A number of problems must be dealt with at this stage of the process. One, for example, is that educational programs serve both short-run and long-run objectives. This poses the question of which objectives to emphasize as well as the problem of possible conflicts between the achievement of short-run and long-run objectives. Another problem arises in the task of assigning priorities to objectives. In the absence of a market in education, public preferences are difficult to ascertain. The issue is further complicated by the fact that educational programs serve both individual and social objectives; for example, a prime social objective of education is the equalization of opportunity. For individuals, equalization of opportunity may have a low priority relative to more direct benefits, but it may have a very high priority insofar as the social objectives of education are concerned. Thus, the process of establishing priorities involves a balancing of social objectives and individual objectives and inescapably requires that value judgments be made. The analyst should insist that such value judgments be made by others, not by the analyst.

The second phase in the application of systems analysis is that of identifying alternative means for achieving the specified objectives. This phase involves the generation of alternative means of accomplishing objectives as well as the evaluation of such options. The analyst attempts to consider consumer preferences in this aspect of the planning process. For example, an attempt may be made to determine citizen preferences for various educational programs through such devices as citizen participation in program planning, the use of neighborhood schools, and votes cast in school elections. A second method which might be used to assess consumer preferences is the use of fees and user charges. While determining consumer preferences via a price system has some appeal, it has only limited applicability in education because the externalities involved in education and the social objectives of education are not mirrored in the preference patterns of individual consumers. A third possible method of determining consumer preferences would be through the creation of competitive markets. It is argued, for example, that a voucher system would create greater competition in education and permit consumers to select a school in accordance with their preferences. In one sense, the existence of a number of local school districts already provides a competitive market in education, for people can move from one district to another to obtain what they perceive to be a "better" education.

Current educational practice is one fertile source of ideas concerning alternative means of accomplishing specified objectives. The analyst attempts to identify feasible ways of improving output within the context of the present system by using the components presently employed in the system. He may consider, for example, changes in sequence, in level of activity, or in timing. He might ask, "Is it necessary that formal schooling extend over 12 years?", or "Why must baccalaureate degree programs consist of four years of study?", or "Why not have children begin school at age four rather than at age six?"

Another fruitful source of alternatives is knowledge gained from experiments and demonstrations. The analyst may turn to research for evidence concerning alternative ways of accomplishing educational objectives. New ideas or new applications of old ideas are not precluded in the search for alternatives. The objective of the analyst in this phase is to develop a number of program options for consideration by decision makers to insure that choices from among the various options are made consciously rather than programs being continued simply because they exist.

The third phase of the analytical process involves identification of the costs involved in each of the alternative courses of action. Insofar as possible, all cost implications—direct and indirect, capital and operating, short-term and long-term—must be identified. The estimated cost of each program option open to the decision maker is needed. The estimates must include the cost of each program option for a specified period of time, the future cost implications of each program option, and any changes in cost which may be associated with changes in the volume or quality of the services provided under each program option. Attention also must be directed toward any indirect cost items, such as the foregone income of students and the value of the hours of time parents devote to educating their children. The time mothers spend in educational activities with their children does constitute an educational cost, because that time could be devoted to other activities and therefore is not "free." The challenge confronting the analyst at this point is to identify all resources which would be utilized in each program option, to estimate as accurately as possible the cost of such resources, and to project the future cost of each of the program options.

In the fourth and final phase of the process, the analyst attempts to measure the benefits and compare the effectiveness of alternative program options. This task is greatly complicated by the difficulty of separating school-induced gains from gains due to the influence upon the student of other environmental factors (home, community, etc.). Obviously, the measures of benefit (output or achievement) which are chosen must relate directly to the objectives of a program, and ideally they will reflect both long-run and short-run benefits. While the analyst would prefer economic measurements (such as rates of return to investment in various program options), these reflect primarily long-run outcomes and, more importantly, they relate only indirectly to significant objectives which are difficult or impossible to quantify in monetary terms, such as participation in civic activities and use of leisure time.

Achievement tests are the most widely used measures of short term objectives but they fall short of the mark for long-run objectives, primarily because they lack a future time orientation. That is, one must assume that whatever is measured by achievement tests (reading speed and comprehension, verbal ability, mathematical skills, and the like) is directly related to the long-run objectives of an educational program. While some argue that the development of market-oriented organizational arrangements for providing education would enable consumers to apply

70

cost-benefit measures directly, that is a fallacy. In fact, valid objective outcome measures would be extremely important in any market-oriented system in order that consumers could make well-informed decisions when they purchase education for themselves or their children, i.e., when they choose the schools that they or their children will attend.

Planning-Programming-Budgeting (PPB) System

A PPB system may be viewed as an operational application of systems analysis in education. In general, a PPB system attempts to identify the objectives to be served by educational programs; plan programs which will maximize the accomplishment of these objectives by systematic identification of alternatives and comparison of potential benefits and costs; allocate resources, through the budget process, to the program selected for implementation; and monitor progress toward objectives in the programs that are implemented so that the results of evaluation can be fed back to modify and sharpen the programs.

A major contribution of PPB is the focus upon multi-year program and financial plans so that the future cost implications of each program are clear. School budgeting typically has covered only a one-year or perhaps a two-year time frame; under a PPB system the time frame is extended to cover at least five years. A second major contribution of PPB is its output orientation. Rather than focusing upon the array of program inputs, analytic attention is devoted to the output of the program relative to the objectives of the program. A third contribution of PPB is the focus on program accounting rather than fiscal accounting based upon broad functional categories.

Application of a PPB system approach in education is still in its formative stages but experience to date indicates clearly that adaptations of the PPB approach will be required. The Educational Resources Management System developed by the Association of School Business Officials provides one example of the way in which PPB concepts may be adapted for use in education.

One reason for the need to adapt PPB concepts for use in education is that a PPB system tends to be centralizing in its effect upon educational decisions. It also may easily become a mechanistic system with rather intractable operating rules. Education is, above all, a "people oriented" enterprise. Imposition of a

PPB system of educational decision making will be of little avail without the commitment of those who must make the system work. High sounding goals and clearly defined objectives established by a central body may have little impact or even a negative impact in the classrooms where the learning process occurs. Thus, those who view PPB as a panacea for achieving efficiency in education would be well advised to give serious consideration to the human dimension of the educational enterprise.

Educational Production Functions

A production function is employed by economists to identify the maximum amount of output that could be produced from a set (or sets) of specified inputs. An educational production function might take the following form: $A = f\ (B, X_1, X_2, \ldots, X_n)$. In this generalized function, A may represent either a single educational outcome (such as might be measured by an achievement test), or a composite of educational outcomes in which might be combined gains in learning, gains in social and civic participation, and changes in attitudes. It would be preferable to consider A as a measure of the net gain in a specified outcome (or outcomes) achieved within a specified period of time, thus making it analogous to a measure of "value added." Admittedly, there are problems involved in measuring short-run educational gains. Even more serious, however, are the problems of measuring the long-term effects of the educational process—which may be far more important than the short-run effects.

The symbol B in the production function represents the characteristics of the learners who are involved in the educational process. Too frequently students have been regarded as interchangeable units. This is clearly erroneous, for we know that students come to school with different backgrounds, that they vary in ability to acquire knowledge and skill, and that they vary greatly in their attitudes toward learning. Despite our knowledge of individual differences, we have tended to treat students as if they were alike when we know that they are not. It is true that most schools can exercise little control over the nature and quality of their students' input. They can, however, provide educational treatments which accommodate the varying characteristics of individual students. An educational production function which does not consider the effect of characteristics

72

of students upon the outcomes of the learning process is simply not adequate.

The variables X_1 through X_n in the production function represent all of the other human and material resources employed in the educational process to produce the educational outcomes. These inputs include, for example, teachers, administrators, and other educational personnel; books, laboratory equipment, and other instructional materials; classrooms, shops, and other educational facilities; and all of the other resources that are employed to produce educational outcomes. The qualitative characteristics of the inputs as well as the quantity of inputs should be included in the analysis. Thus, the number of teachers may be one input variable, the years of teaching experience may represent another input variable, and the teachers' verbal or quantitative abilities may represent yet a third input variable.

The objective of analysis based on educational production functions is to allocate the available resources in such a way that the additional contribution to educational output from the last dollar expended on each unit of input is the same. It is at this point that output is maximized for a given level of input. The amount of money available to purchase inputs (the school budget) is assumed to be fixed. The task, then, is to determine how to distribute the budget to the various input factors so as to maximize output for the total funds that are available.

Thomas has employed the production function concept to examine three distinct types of input-output relationships.[11] He distinguished between the three types of educational production functions according to the manner in which inputs and outputs are defined and named them for their principal users. In the administrator's production function, outputs are defined as units of specific service (such as student-years or student-hours); inputs include space, equipment, books, materials, etc.; and analyses are concerned with determining the cost of providing a given unit of service. In the psychologist's production function, outputs are defined in terms of behavioral changes in students (such as additions to knowledge or the acquisition of values); inputs include quantitative and qualitative attributes of the inputs to the educational process (such as the time of teachers and pupils and their personal characteristics as well as space, equipment, books, materials, etc.); and analyses are designed to provide information concerning the relationship between inputs and outputs using multivariate statistical procedures. In the economist's production function, outputs are viewed as the additional earnings which accrue from an increment of schooling and inputs are viewed as the cost of that increment. Analyses are designed to reveal whether or not the earnings which are associated with an additional increment of schooling exceed the cost of the increment.

If schools are to operate so as to maximize the output obtained from a given level of spending then educational managers obviously must be given considerable discretion regarding the inputs which are to be purchased and the way in which they are to be organized in the educational process. Second, reliable measures of output—preferably measures of change during a specified period of time—also are needed. Third, a system of incentives which rewards educational managers who operate efficiently would be very helpful.

Unfortunately, these conditions generally do not exist in education. Educational managers typically have relatively little discretion concerning the utilization of school inputs. They are constrained by state law, by contracts with teachers, by accreditation requirements, and by tradition. Although the educational process abounds with tests, there is little systematic measurement of output and such data as do exist often are not available in useful form. Traditional fiscal accounting systems record expenditures for broad functional categories, rather than on the basis of educational programs. It is very difficult to obtain accurate data concerning the inputs to a given program—to say nothing about similar data concerning the outputs of that program. The reward systems which prevail in education typically do not reward efficiency, nor do they penalize inefficiency. Teachers and administrators who are notably successful in achieving desired educational outcomes are treated about the same as those who are abysmally unsuccessful. While educational production functions do represent a potentially useful analytical tool which can contribute to greater efficiency in education, their full potential cannot be realized unless the sources of inefficiency identified above can be remedied.

Economies of Scale

In most economic activities the average cost per unit of output declines as the size of the operation increases until, at some

74

point, the unit cost begins to rise again—perhaps because it is increasingly difficult to administer a large organization efficiently, or perhaps because of higher concentrations of pupils who require more expensive programs. The result is a U-shaped curve. In education, the effect of economies of scale is shown by the fact that at very low enrollment levels the cost per pupil tends to be very high, declines quite rapidly as enrollment increases, then begins to rise after a certain size has been reached. Expenditure per pupil, however, is an input measure. The few studies of economies of scale which have used output data do not indicate that larger districts outperform smaller districts in standardized achievement test scores when variations in student input and school expenditure are accounted for. In fact, when output measures are employed there appear to be substantial diseconomies of scale in large urban school districts—suggesting that the cumbersome bureaucratic structure which exists in large urban school districts may lead to substantial inefficiency in operation.

Although relatively little is known about the relationships between various combinations of resources and educational outputs, a positive and significant relationship between teacher salary levels and student achievement has been found when other influences are held constant. Teacher turnover has been found to be negatively related to student achievement. Certain attributes of teachers also have been found to be related to academic achievement. Teachers' verbal ability scores were found to be related to student achievement in several studies. Teacher experience (within certain limits) also has been found to be related to student achievement, although the training of teachers (as reflected in degree level) has not. In the vast majority of studies, little or no relationship has been found between class size and student achievement.

INSTITUTIONAL ALTERNATIVES FOR EDUCATION

We have made frequent reference in this chapter to the economic principles of efficiency and equity. The proposals for achieving greater efficiency and equity in education which have been advanced by economists fall within two major categories. One category includes those proposals designed to secure greater efficiency within the context of existing organizational arrangements or through modifications of existing organizational arrangements. Economic models for securing greater efficiency in education which were discussed in the preceding section fall within this category. Also falling within this category are proposals for decentralizing decision-making in large urban school systems, and similar proposals aimed at modifying existing organizational arrangements to make them more sensitive and responsive to the needs and demands of the clientele served by the organization.

Proposals which would completely restructure organizational arrangements for education constitute the second major category. Most prominent are the various proposals advocating adoption of some sort of voucher system for financing education. Virtually all economists recognize that the externalities which characterize education require that education be publicly financed or aided. However, public financing of a service does not require that the service be publicly provided. In the area of national defense, for example, the weapons of war typically are purchased by government from firms operating in the private sector. Public school facilities are generally constructed by private contractors. Thus, one who advocates the public financing of education while, at the same time, advocating organizational arrangements which would encourage greater private sector activity in education is not being inconsistent.

Decentralization

Critics claim that large, highly bureaucratized school districts (for the most part synonymous with large urban school districts) are economically inefficient because they are inflexible, offer no incentive for innovation and experimentation, and are insensitive to the needs and wishes of their clients. One remedy proposed by these critics is decentralization of decision-making to permit decisions regarding who will teach and what will be taught to be made at the local school level. Decentralization of this type would appear to offer students and their families a much greater opportunity to influence the nature and type of the school services they receive, although it would not permit them wide latitude in choosing the school they would attend. Experimentation and innovation in instructional practices and procedures would likely be encouraged under decentralization plans, although whether or not this would improve efficiency is subject to question. A key

76

factor in the success or failure of all decentralization plans is access to educational resources. Any plan which decentralizes decisions but which does not permit all operating units within the system to have equal access to the system's educational resources is meaningless. Furthermore, the level of educational resources available in the total system must be adequate to permit meaningful decisions to be made if decentralization is to achieve greater economic and social efficiency.

Voucher Systems

In essence, voucher systems provide for the issuance of vouchers to parents of school age children; the vouchers may be redeemed at any approved school, public or private, for a stated amount of money. Voucher proposals envision, either implicitly or explicitly, a restructuring of organizational arrangements for education by providing a wide choice of schools which children may attend. Advocates of vouchers assume that parents will "shop around" and select the school whose program (and charges) best fit the needs of their child. Whether or not the adoption of a voucher system would provide students and their families with greater choice would depend upon such factors as the amount of the voucher, the extent to which the voucher could be supplemented with private funds, the minimum requirements for certification as an approved school, and the extent to which market choices are, in fact, available. While experimentation and innovation might be encouraged under a voucher plan, it is difficult to perceive a marked advantage for a voucher system over other organizational arrangements in this regard. It is difficult to identify any significant educational innovations which have come from private schools other than those associated with institutions of higher learning.

At the heart of all voucher system proposals is an underlying faith that a competitive market system for providing education would be superior to all other organizational arrangements in achieving economic efficiency. Whether or not this faith is justified has not been tested; however, at least five questions should be raised with regard to this issue.

First, the assumption is made that all consumers (students and their families) have thorough knowledge of the market (the quantity and quality of education available at various schools),

77

that their choices will be based primarily upon this knowledge, and that they will not hesitate to seek other suppliers if they are dissatisfied with their initial choice. One can hardly doubt that at the present time most parents are poorly informed with regard to the quantity and quality of education provided in various schools, whether public or private. Observations and interviews indicate that parental judgments with regard to schools tend to be based largely on what they know about the clientele attending a school rather than knowledge of the nature and quality of the educational program provided by the school. Furthermore, once a student enters a school, it is no easy matter to remove him and place him in a different school. As a practical matter, the realistic range of alternatives is likely to be narrow, for most parents will wish to have their children attend school in reasonable proximity to their home. If they have more than one child, it is likely that few parents will elect different schools for each of their children. Thus, the extent to which a voucher system would result in realistic alternatives in the choice of schools which children might attend is certainly open to question.

Second, education is extremely labor-intensive. It is common knowledge that in recent years teachers have become much more militant and that they have obtained statutory authority to bargain collectively concerning their wages, hours, and conditions of employment in many states. The proponents of voucher systems tend to ignore the latent political and economic power which teachers can wield with regard to matters of educational programming. Large, cohesive teachers' organizations could easily overpower any proposed changes if they bargain with a multitude of small, independent private schools. It is unlikely that merely introducing a voucher system to finance education would alter significantly the educational choices available to parents.

Third, education is heavily weighted with externalities. In fact, these externalities provide the major justification for public financing of education. Clearly, the public interest requires that there be substantial regulation of schools to insure that minimum standards are met by those schools which receive public funds. It is quite conceivable that a bureaucracy at least as intransigent as any existing educational bureaucracy could arise to police the operation of a voucher system.

Fourth, it is very likely that the adoption of a voucher plan would contribute to economic and social inefficiency. One of education's major contributions to economic growth is that of breaking down the barriers between class and caste, thus facilitating social mobility. Adoption of a voucher plan undoubtedly would inhibit social mobility by raising economic, religious, and racial barriers. All religious sects would have a strong incentive to establish their own schools lest some other denomination secure control of the bulk of the nation's educational system. A spate of private schools catering to select groups also could be expected to emerge. For example, adoption of a voucher plan for financing elementary and secondary education would encourage the further development of segregated private schools in the South and in northern cities. If the national goal is to foster the development of more segregated white schools and more sectarian parochial schools of all denominations, then voucher systems can do the job. However, if the national goal is to equalize educational opportunities for all citizens and to promote social mobility by breaking down the barriers between caste and class, then voucher systems have little to recommend them.

Fifth, the creation of a large number of competing schools could lead to substantial diseconomies of scale. This would be especially true in the case of secondary schools where the thrust for many years has been to eliminate small, inefficient high schools. The diseconomies of scale which could arise with many small private and public schools in competition for students could easily reduce their output per dollar expended for education rather than producing greater efficiency in the use of the resources allocated to education.

Performance Contracts

Contracts in which the contractor is paid on the basis of student achievement are a relatively new arrival on the educational scene. School districts have for many years contracted with private sector enterprises for such things as the construction of facilities, the transportation of pupils, and the provision of food services. However, the notion of contracting for the performance of specific instructional activities with the contractor's compensation based on gains in student achievement is quite recent.

Performance contracts may be viewed as a means for modifying existing organizational arrangements, or they may be viewed as a means for implementing entirely new organizational arrangements for education. For example, if the statutes permit it to do so, a school district might contract with a private enterprise to take over the complete operation of a school. It might also negotiate a contract with the teachers and administrators in a given school building under which their compensation would be determined by the extent to which agreed upon objectives were attained.

Private contractors must, of course, make a profit if they are to remain in business. Since they use essentially the same resources that school systems do—teachers, aids, materials, administrators (managers), etc.—private contractors can make a profit only by making more efficient use of these resources. If private contractors can do this, there is no reason why teachers and administrators, given proper incentives, could not also operate more efficiently.

Performance contracts are better suited to the short-run objectives of education that are susceptible to measurement by standardized objective tests. They appear to possess some potential for affording consumers (students and their families) a wider array of choices, although this will depend largely upon how such contracts are used. Performance contracts would certainly provide great incentive for experimentation with innovative instructional practices and procedures.

Performance contracts may have considerable potential for improving efficiency in education, at least in terms of the attainment of short-run objectives. Whether or not performance contracts can be utilized to achieve broad social objectives is less clear. The rapidity with which school districts throughout the country have begun experimenting with performance contracts may be indicative of their potential for improving economic efficiency in education. On the other hand, it may simply be another manifestation of the "bandwagon syndrome" which seems to be so prevalent in American education. In any event, performance contracts cannot be expected to improve equality of educational opportunity unless resources adequate to provide the type of education needed by each child are made available.

FOOTNOTES

1. Research Division, National Educational Association, *Financial Status of the Public Schools*, 1970 (Washington, D. C.: NEA, 1970), pp. 18, 31.
2. *Economic Factors Affecting the Financing of Education*, ed. R. L.

Johns, et al. (Gainesville, Florida: National Educational Finance Project, 1970).

3. Richard A. Musgrave, *The Theory of Public Finance* (New York: McGraw-Hill, 1959), pp. 6-15.

4. Charles S. Benson, *The Economics of Public Education* (Boston: Houghton-Mifflin, 1961), pp. 88-93.

5. Theodore W. Schultz, "The Human Capital Approach to Education" in *Economic Factors Affecting the Financing of Education*, ed. R. L. Johns, et al. (Gainesville, Florida: National Educational Finance Project, 1970), p. 3.

6. Finis Welch, "Labor-Market Discrimination: An Interpretation of Income Differences in the Rural South," *Journal of Political Economy*, 75 (June, 1967), p. 239.

7. Schultz, *op. cit.*, pp. 47-50.

8. *Ibid.*, p. 50.

9. Theodore W. Schultz, "Education and Economic Growth" in *Social Forces Influencing American Education* (Chicago: University of Chicago Press, 1961), pp. 46-88. Edward F. Denison, *The Sources of Economic Growth in the United States and the Alternatives Before Us*, Supplementary Paper No. 13 (New York: Committee for Economic Development, 1962) and Edward F. Denison, *Why Growth Rates Differ* (Washington, D. C.: The Brookings Institution, 1967).

10. Mary Jean Bowman, "Education and Economic Growth," in *Economic Factors Affecting the Financing of Education*, ed. R. L. Johns, et al. (Gainesville, Florida: National Educational Finance Project, 1970), pp. 94-96.

11. J. Alan Thomas, *The Productive School* (New York: John Wiley & Sons, 1971), pp. 11-30.

CHAPTER 4

Variations in Ability and Effort to Support Education

The fact that variations in ability and effort to support education exist among states, regions, and school districts in the United States has been demonstrated so frequently that it hardly needs repeating. However, despite years of effort to develop and put into practice systems of financing education which will reduce the effect of such variations, they remain with us today. Why are such variations a matter of concern? The fact is that equality of educational opportunity is fundamentally a matter of equality of access to financial resources. Wide variations in ability and effort to support education are a major obstacle to the attainment of substantial equality of educational opportunity in the United States. Thus, one important criterion against which school finance programs must be measured is the extent to which variations in the ability of school districts and states to raise revenue for the support of education are permitted to control the level of financial resources available to educate children in the schools.

The terms ability and fiscal capacity will be used interchangeably in this chapter. For our purposes, fiscal capacity is a measure of the fiscal bases which a taxing jurisdiction is taxing, or could tax, to raise revenue for public purposes. Thus, when we refer to the fiscal capacity of a school district or any other unit of government, we are referring to the tax base (or bases) against which that unit of government may levy taxes. Tax effort refers to the extent to which a taxing jurisdiction—for example, a state or a school district—is using its capacity to raise revenue by taxation. Obviously, the amount of revenue which can be raised by a unit of government will depend upon both the size of its tax base and the tax rate which it levies. A district with a very limited tax base can raise relatively little revenue even at confiscatory tax rates, while a district with a large tax base can raise substantial amounts of revenues by levying a very modest tax rate.

TAX SOURCES FOR EDUCATION

Before examining the extent to which variations in fiscal capacity and tax effort exist among states and school districts, it will be useful to consider some of the taxes which might be used to obtain revenue for education, particularly with regard to several generally accepted criteria which may be used to evaluate various taxes and tax structures.

It is generally agreed that a tax should not bring about economic distortions by causing people to alter their economic behavior. For example, a tax should not reduce the output of some goods or services relative to others; it should not affect decisions regarding the location of industrial plants, shopping centers or other economic activities; it should not reduce the efficiency of the production and distribution of goods and services; and it should not reduce the willingness of persons to work.

A second major criterion is that a tax should be equitable. This criterion indicates, for example, that persons who are in the same economic circumstances should be treated equally; that taxes should be distributed on the basis of the taxpayer's ability to pay; and that the overall tax structure should not be regressive relative to the income of taxpayers (i.e., should not take a greater percentage of the income of low income taxpayers than of high income taxpayers).

A third major criterion is that a tax should be collected easily and effectively. This criterion suggests that a tax should be difficult to evade or avoid, that collection procedures should be simple, and that the cost of collecting the tax should be minimal.

A fourth criterion which has gained increasing acceptance in recent years is that the revenue obtained from the tax structure

83

should rise at least in proportion to income. Governmental expenditures tend to rise at least as rapidly as income and unless the revenue obtained from the tax structure increases at the same rate, either frequent adjustments in tax rates or a search for new tax bases are required.

The Property Tax

The property tax traditionally has provided the bulk of the revenue received by local governments in the United States. During fiscal year 1969 local governments in the United States received about 86 percent of their tax revenue from the property tax and school districts received about 98 percent of their tax revenue from this source. During the past decade property tax yields expressed as a percentage of gross national product have remained relatively constant at about 3.4 percent, and current percentages are about the same as they were throughout the period 1870 through 1914.

The property tax is particularly well suited for use by units of local government and frequently units of local government are given no other taxing powers. A major advantage of the tax is that property is not easily moved to escape taxation (in contrast to income, for example). Furthermore, some of the expenditures made by units of local government (such as those for police and fire protection) directly benefit property owners.

On the other side of the ledger, however, the property tax does have some serious limitations. It is likely to cause economic distortions and inefficiency in that it constitutes a heavy tax on housing; it tends to discourage rehabilitation of deteriorating property (improving property generally increases the tax on the property) ; it is likely to affect decisions by business and industry with regard to location (the existence of favorable property tax rates may override all other factors when determining a business location) ; and it does not bear equally on all businesses (favoring those that have a low ratio of property to sales).

The property tax also fares rather poorly on the equity criterion. Because of the inequities which occur in the assessment of property there frequently is unequal treatment of equals. Another serious shortcoming is that property ownership is not closely correlated with either income or net wealth. In other words, in an urban industrialized society the ownership of prop-

84

erty is a rather poor measure of ability to pay taxes. This is seen most clearly, for example, in the case of older persons who own a home but have little current income which can be used to pay the property tax. In most cases a tax on business property is shifted forward to the consumer, i.e., added to the price of the item, although the ease with which the tax may be shifted varies from one business to another. The property tax frequently is criticized as being regressive in relation to income. The evidence on this question is not at all clear, although there is some evidence that persons in the lowest income groups pay a much higher percentage of their income in property taxes than do persons in the highest income groups.[1]

The property tax does not rate well on the criterion of revenue elasticity. Netzer concluded that when national income increases by 1 per cent, property tax revenues will increase by approximately .8 per cent.[2] One reason for this lag is the fact that the rate of increase in the property tax base depends upon action by assessors. Consequently, the property tax base does not increase automatically as business activity expands. Also, the rather low correlation which exists between property and income indicates that the two are not likely to increase at the same rate.

The property tax undoubtedly could be improved substantially by the adoption of more accurate and more uniform assessment practices. Other recommendations for changes aimed at removing some of its deficiencies include exemption of low income groups from the property tax, a freeze in tax rates to encourage new construction and renovation of existing property, and exemption of owner-occupied homes from the property tax. Although the property tax undoubtedly could be improved, increased use of this tax base is difficult to justify. Its inherent disadvantages cannot be removed completely. Furthermore, the property tax is already used so heavily by units of local government that it does not appear to offer much potential for significant increases in local government revenue.

The Sales Tax

The sales tax is a major source of revenue at the state level. Although in most states school districts are not authorized to levy a sales tax, the sales tax nevertheless is a major source of revenue for education because state grants-in-aid to local school districts are financed in part from revenue which the state derives from sales taxes.

In 1970, 45 states containing 98 per cent of the population of the United States levied some type of sales tax. During 1969, sales tax collections by the states totaled $12.3 billion, which represented about 30 per cent of all state tax revenue. Sales tax rates in 1970 ranged from 2 per cent to 6 per cent with the median state sales tax rate being 3 per cent.

The extent to which the sales tax meets the equity criterion depends primarily upon how the tax base is defined. A sales tax on all goods tends to be regressive relative to income. A good bit of the regressivity can be removed, however, by either exempting food from the base of the sales tax or by allowing a credit against income tax liability for the sales tax paid on minimum necessary purchases.

With regard to economic distortions, sales taxes may affect decisions concerning the location of shopping centers and other large retail developments. This is particularly true at the borders of a state if one state levies a sales tax and a neighboring state does not, and in metropolitan areas if local municipalities levy sales taxes at varying rates. Economic distortions also may occur if sales taxes are levied upon goods used in production. Another type of economic distortion may arise if some goods are exempted from the tax, since consumers then have an incentive to increase their consumption of exempt goods in comparison with those which are taxed.

Administration of a sales tax is relatively simple, at least at the state level, for the tax generally is collected by the retailer and remitted to the governmental unit levying the tax. Interstate sales do pose some problems, for a state cannot levy a tax on sales for delivery outside the state and often has difficulty collecting a tax on purchases made by its residents in another state. Problems of administration and compliance are multiplied if there are many exemptions to the tax base since record keeping is made more complicated and audit is made more difficult.

The revenue elasticity of the sales tax will depend upon how the tax base is defined and upon the items which are exempted from the tax. However, the revenue derived from a sales tax tends to increase at about the same rate as income increases.[3]

Personal Income Tax

The personal income tax is the largest single source of revenue of the federal government and also is an important source of revenue for the states. Forty-one states made use of some type of personal income tax in 1970, although it should be noted that state income taxes varied widely both in definition of the tax base and in rate structure. Local income taxes are not widely used, although they do represent a significant source of revenue for units of local government in a few states.[4]

A personal income tax which treats all income uniformly should cause the least economic distortion of any tax. In terms of equity, the personal income tax has the advantage of being directly related to the most generally accepted measure of tax paying capacity, i.e., the income of the taxpayer. Furthermore, the tax can be adjusted to take into account circumstances which affect tax paying capacity. For example, exemptions can be provided for dependents and certain necessary expenditures, such as those for medical care and for payment of state and local taxes, which can be deducted from gross income to arrive at taxable income.

Administration of the personal income tax, although potentially rather complicated, has been greatly aided by adoption of such practices as withholding and payroll deductions. The use of computers and the exchange of information by the federal and state governments has greatly improved administration of the tax as well as making tax evasion more difficult.

The personal income tax ranks the highest of all taxes on the criterion of revenue elasticity, particularly if the rates are progressive, i.e., increase as the individual's personal income increases. When a progressive rate structure is employed the revenue obtained from the income tax increases more rapidly than does personal income, thus tending to keep pace with the growing demand for public services. On the other hand, revenue from the personal income tax will tend to decline at a more rapid rate than personal income declines in periods of economic recession if the rate structure is progressive.

Corporate Income Taxes

In addition to the corporate income tax levied by the federal government, 43 states levied a tax on the income of corporations in 1970. The nature of the corporate income tax varies quite widely among states, as do the tax rates levied on corporate income. During fiscal year 1969, state taxes on corporate income yielded $3.18 billion, which was 7.6 per cent of all state tax collections during that year.

Taxes on corporate income are not likely to cause serious economic distortions if they are relatively uniform from state to state, although a potential for economic distortion does exist. It is often asserted that if a state deviates too far above its neighbors in taxing corporate income it will be at a disadvantage in the competition to attract and/or retain industries. However, the evidence with regard to this claim is far from clear.

Taxes on corporate income generally comply reasonably well with the criterion of equity. A moderately progressive rate structure is found in some states, although proportional tax rates on corporate income are more common at the state level.

In terms of difficulty of administration and compliance, corporate income taxes are comparable to personal income taxes. Revenue elasticity from the corporate income tax is somewhat less than from the personal income tax, but is higher than the revenue elasticity characteristic of nearly all other levies.

Other Taxes

Excise taxes, particularly those levied on motor fuel, liquor, and tobacco products, produce a substantial amount of revenue at the state level—$8.9 billion in fiscal year 1969.[5] Excise taxes are also levied by the federal government but their use by units of local government is quite limited. Excise taxes already are used heavily and do not have the potential to produce significantly greater amounts of revenue in the future.

Estate and inheritance taxes are levied at the state level but they do not produce a great deal of revenue and their potential is rather limited. Severance taxes on natural resources such as petroleum and minerals are levied by some states but generally do not represent a major source of governmental revenue.

There are no major unused taxes. It is true that not all states levy each of the major taxes at the present time. Some states, for example, still do not levy a tax on personal or corporate income and a few states do not tax sales. However, as revenue demands have increased in recent years the states have been forced

88

to search continually for new sources of revenue and it is likely that all states will levy each of the major taxes in the foreseeable future. Thus, it seems more productive to concentrate attention on improving the productivity of existing tax structures rather than searching for new sources of tax revenue.

VARIATIONS AMONG THE STATES IN FISCAL CAPACITY AND EFFORT

The concept that education is a state function has been so firmly established by a long line of court decisions that it is beyond argument. Since education is a state function, responsibility for providing financial support for the operation of public schools rests with the state. A local school district has no inherent power to levy taxes; its power to levy a tax must be expressly conferred upon it by the state. Consequently, we shall first examine variations among the states in fiscal capacity and effort, particularly as such variations affect the financing of education.

There are two general approaches which have been employed in measuring fiscal capacity. The first approach utilizes economic indicators, primarily measures of income, and compares the several states on the basis of such economic indicators. The second approach to measuring fiscal capacity evaluates the tax bases available within a state, estimates the amount of revenue these bases would produce if they were subjected to various rates of taxation, and compares the several states on the basis of these data.

Fiscal Capacity of States Based on Economic Indicators

Personal income expressed on either a per capita or a per household basis is the measure most commonly used for determining the relative ability of the states to raise revenue to finance state and local governmental activities. Total personal income per capita is not the most satisfactory basis for comparisons because it ignores the fact that people must purchase food, clothing, and shelter in order to survive, and that they must pay federal income taxes. A study conducted for the National Educational Finance Project developed estimates of personal income per capita in the 50 states by deducting from total personal income (1) an allowance of $750 per person to cover basic expenditures for

89

food, clothing, and shelter and (2) federal personal income tax paid.[6] The estimates of net personal income per capita and of net personal income as a percentage of personal income per capita for each of the 50 states are shown in Table 4-1.

For the United States, net personal income per capita was estimated to be 69.55 per cent of personal income per capita. The lowest percentage was found for Mississippi, where net personal income was estimated to be only 58.94 per cent of personal income per capita. The highest percentage was for Alaska, where net personal income was estimated to be 74.68 per cent of personal income per capita. Net personal income ranged from a low of $1,292 per capita in Mississippi to a high of $3,369 per capita in Alaska.

Some have proposed that measures related more directly to the demand for education should be used to assess the capacity of states and units of local government to finance education. Such measures as personal income per person age 5-17 or personal income per child in average daily attendance have been suggested. In Table 4-2 are shown estimates of personal income and the rankings of the fifty states on these two measures. (Estimates of personal income per capita are shown in Table 4-1.)

Income per school age child does more accurately reflect the educational "load" of the area in question. It also adjusts for differences in the age distribution of the population of a state. States with a large proportion of persons in the upper age brackets may rank considerably higher when their fiscal capacity is measured on the basis of personal income per school age child. Florida, for example, ranked 28 on the basis of personal income per capita but on the basis of personal income per school age child Florida ranked 15. In Alaska, on the other hand, where the school age population is a much larger percentage of the total population, the state ranked 2 on per capita income but 19 on income per school age child. A comparison of the data contained in Table 4-1 and Table 4-2 indicates that 13 states changed in rank by five or more places when income per school age child was used as the basis for the ranking. Six states (Alaska, Arizona, Minnesota, New Mexico, Utah and Wisconsin) dropped five or more places; seven states (Florida, Maine, Missouri, Oregon, Pennsylvania, Rhode Island and Tennessee) increased in rank by five or more places.

TABLE 4-1
Net Personal Income in 1969 After Deduction of an Allowance for Basic Expenditures ($750/capita) and Federal Income Tax Paid[a]

State	Gross Personal Income Per Capita (Dollars)	Rank	Net Personal Income Per Capita (Dollars)	Rank	Net Personal Income Per Capita as a Percentage of Personal Income Per Capita	Rank
Alabama	$2,566	48	$1,605	48	62.55	48
Alaska	4,511	2	3,369	1	74.68	1
Arizona	3,336	29	2,291	29	67.68	27
Arkansas	2,520	49	1,582	49	62.78	47
California	4,272	7	3,096	5	72.47	2
Colorado	3,568	21	2,492	22	69.84	20
Connecticut	4,537	1	3,209	2	70.73	8
Delaware	4,013	10	2,781	10	69.30	24
Florida	3,427	28	2,338	28	68.22	30
Georgia	3,040	36	2,031	37	66.81	38
Hawaii	3,809	13	2,689	12	70.60	9
Idaho	2,857	42	1,875	42	65.63	43
Illinois	4,310	5	3,077	6	71.39	5
Indiana	3,691	16	2,579	17	69.87	19
Iowa	3,517	24	2,477	23	70.43	11
Kansas	3,532	23	2,493	21	70.58	10
Kentucky	2,850	43	1,871	43	65.65	42
Louisiana	2,781	45	1,784	45	64.15	45
Maine	3,039	37	2,029	38	66.77	39
Maryland	4,095	9	2,864	9	69.94	16
Massachusetts	4,138	8	2,946	8	71.19	6
Michigan	3,944	11	2,767	11	70.16	13
Minnesota	3,608	20	2,538	19	70.34	12
Mississippi	2,192	50	1,292	50	58.94	50
Missouri	3,459	26	2,373	26	68.60	28
Montana	3,124	33	2,127	33	68.09	31
Nebraska	3,643	19	2,580	16	70.82	7
Nevada	4,359	4	3,138	4	71.99	3
New Hampshire	3,474	25	2,365	27	68.08	32
New Jersey	4,278	6	2,992	7	69.94	16
New Mexico	2,893	40	1,909	40	65.99	40
New York	4,421	3	3,170	3	71.70	4
North Carolina	2,890	41	1,907	41	65.99	40
North Dakota	3,011	38	2,049	36	68.05	33
Ohio	3,779	14	2,633	15	69.67	21
Oklahoma	3,065	34	2,056	35	67.08	36
Oregon	3,565	22	2,473	24	69.37	22
Pennsylvania	3,664	17	2,538	19	69.27	25
Rhode Island	3,788	15	2,644	14	69.98	15
South Carolina	2,581	47	1,623	47	62.88	46
South Dakota	3,052	35	2,105	34	68.97	26
Tennessee	2,810	44	1,806	44	64.27	44
Texas	3,254	32	2,191	32	67.33	35
Utah	2,994	39	2,006	39	67.00	37
Vermont	3,267	31	2,239	30	68.53	29
Virginia	3,293	30	2,222	31	67.48	34
Washington	3,835	12	2,686	13	70.04	14
West Virginia	2,610	46	1,628	46	62.38	49
Wisconsin	3,647	18	2,549	18	69.89	18
Wyoming	3,445	27	2,388	25	69.32	23
UNITED STATES	3,675		2,556		69.55	

[a]Adapted from Roe L. Johns and Oscar A. Hamilton, Jr., "Ability and Effort of the States to Support Public Schools" (Gainesville, Fla.: National Educational Finance Project, 1970), 15pp. (Mimeo)

On the other side of the ledger, it must be noted that education is only one of the public services which are financed by states and local governments. Older persons, for example, may not require education but they are likely to require other public services which school age children do not require. Using income per school age child as a measure of fiscal capacity tends to ignore the fact that other public services also must be financed by the states. The use of net income as shown in Table 4-1 tends to adjust for this factor.

Income per child in average daily attendance has also been proposed as an alternative measure of fiscal capacity. It is claimed that this measure reflects the actual educational "load" since it is based on the children actually in school. This measure, of course, markedly affects the apparent fiscal capacity of states or school districts in which a high percentage of the children attend nonpublic schools or which have a substantial number of children who are not in school. Comparing the rankings of the states on income per school age child versus income per child in ADA, it will be noted that 14 states changed in ranking by five or more places. Seven states (California, Florida, Indiana, Maine, Nevada, Oregon and Washington) declined in apparent fiscal capacity by five or more places while the other seven states (Hawaii, Kansas, Kentucky, Louisiana, Missouri, New Hampshire and Wisconsin) increased by five or more places.

Net personal income per child in ADA (or ADM) is a better measure of a state's ability to support education because it reflects the net personal income after deducting $750 per capita for subsistence and federal personal income taxes paid. That measure of ability is also shown in Table 4-2. It will be noted that the use of this measure causes some changes in the ability ranking of the states.

Fiscal Capacity of States Using Various Tax Bases

In Chapter 5 Due has estimated the additional revenue which might be obtained from taxes levied by the states on personal income and corporate income.[7] In 1969 the 50 states received revenue totaling approximately $7.58 billion from taxes on personal income and approximately $3.18 billion from taxes on corporate income. Due estimated that if all states had levied a personal in-

TABLE 4-2

COMPARISON OF PERSONAL INCOME PER SCHOOL AGE CHILD (5-17), AND
PERSONAL INCOME PER CHILD IN AVERAGE DAILY ATTENDANCE, 1969

State	Personal Income Per School Age Child[a]	Rank	Personal Income Per Child in ADA[a]	Rank	Net Income Per Child in ADA	Rank
Alabama	9,526	46	11,731	46	7,210	49
Alaska	13,674	19	17,354	18	14,027	8
Arizona	11,675	34	14,581	30	10,299	30
Arkansas	9,489	47	11,983	45	7,629	45
California	16,695	5	18,032	11	14,231	7
Colorado	13,256	25	15,126	28	10,768	27
Connecticut	18,305	2	23,166	2	16,917	2
Delaware	14,886	12	18,358	9	13,062	13
Florida	14,050	15	17,061	21	11,694	23
Georgia	11,303	35	13,981	33	9,304	35
Hawaii	13,909	17	18,275	10	13,263	11
Idaho	10,495	42	12,324	44	7,890	43
Illinois	16,618	6	22,814	3	16,567	4
Indiana	13,802	18	16,540	24	11,733	22
Iowa	13,248	26	15,806	25	11,085	25
Kansas	13,272	24	17,215	19	12,253	19
Kentucky	10,788	39	14,201	32	9,410	34
Louisiana	9,705	45	13,409	37	8,386	42
Maine	11,714	32	13,174	40	8,990	37
Maryland	15,229	9	18,901	8	13,748	10
Massachusetts	16,757	4	21,355	6	15,488	5
Michigan	14,437	13	17,601	16	12,414	17
Minnesota	13,044	27	15,547	26	11,072	26
Mississippi	7,697	50	9,977	50	5,624	50
Missouri	13,528	20	17,751	15	12,403	18
Montana	11,138	36	13,424	36	9,111	36
Nebraska	13,514	22	16,645	22	11,870	21
Nevada	16,296	7	17,960	12	13,132	12
New Hampshire	13,527	21	17,762	14	12,649	14
New Jersey	17,087	3	22,470	4	16,654	3
New Mexico	9,025	49	10,777	49	7,224	48
New York	18,547	1	25,976	1	18,772	1
North Carolina	10,979	37	13,610	35	8,926	39
North Dakota	10,523	41	13,046	41	8,932	38
Ohio	14,061	14	17,872	13	12,637	15
Oklahoma	12,227	30	13,948	34	9,502	32
Oregon	14,017	16	16,626	23	11,662	24
Pennsylvania	14,937	11	19,797	7	13,861	9
Rhode Island	15,905	8	21,537	5	15,223	6
South Carolina	9,259	48	11,691	47	7,242	47
South Dakota	10,612	40	12,461	43	8,834	40
Tennessee	10,937	38	13,384	38	8,617	41
Texas	11,700	33	14,988	29	10,250	31
Utah	9,788	44	10,898	48	7,351	46
Vermont	12,509	29	14,565	31	10,489	29
Virginia	12,667	28	15,395	27	10,598	28
Washington	15,049	10	17,121	20	12,052	20
West Virginia	10,453	43	12,758	42	7,785	44
Wisconsin	13,359	23	17,432	17	12,566	16
Wyoming	11,791	31	13,199	39	9,453	33
U. S.	14,013		17,615		12,400	

[a]Adapted from Research Division, National Education Association, *Rankings of the States, 1971.* Research Report 1971-R1 (Washington, D. C. the Association, 1971), p. 32.

come tax with a rate progression of from 4 to 10 per cent and with an exemption of $600 per person, (the Oregon model), an additional $12.47 billion of revenue could have been obtained in 1969. He also estimated that if all states had levied a corporate income tax at a 7 percent rate, they would have obtained an additional $2.43 billion in revenue in 1969.

Due also developed estimates of the potential revenue which could be obtained from a sales tax in each state.[8] Whereas the 50 states received a total of $12.29 billion from sales taxes in 1969, Due estimated that if a sales tax had been levied in each state at a rate of 5 percent, additional revenue totaling $6.35 billion would be obtained; that a levy on consumer services at a 5 percent rate would have produced an additional $1.66 billion in revenue; and that eliminating exemptions from the sales tax base would have produced an additional $2.39 billion in revenue.

Using Due's estimates of the potential yield of personal and corporate income taxes and sales taxes in the various states, the staff of the National Educational Finance Project developed estimates of the total potential yield and the estimated per capita yield of the three taxes for each state. These estimates are shown in Table 4-3. A personal income tax levied at the Oregon rates by all states would have produced over $20 billion in revenue in 1969—compared with the $7.58 billion which was actually obtained from state taxes on personal income. If corporate income taxes had been levied by all states at a 7 percent rate they would have produced approximately $5.6 billion of revenue in 1969, compared with the $3.18 billion actually obtained by the states from corporate income taxes in 1969. A sale tax levied in each state at a 5 percent rate with no exemptions would have produced $22.575 billion of revenue, compared with the $12.296 billion obtained from sales taxes in 1969. The total estimated potential yield of the three taxes was $48.241 billion.

The estimated per capita yield of the three taxes provides an indication of the variations in fiscal capacity which exist among the 50 states. The estimated potential per capita yield of the three taxes for the United States as a whole was $240. The lowest estimated potential yield was $148 per capita in West Virginia; the highest estimated potential yield was $368 per capita for Nevada. Thus, if Nevada were to levy a personal income tax at the Oregon rates, a corporate income tax at a 7 percent rate, and a sales tax at a 5 percent rate with no exemptions, it would

94

TABLE 4-3

ESTIMATED POTENTIAL YIELD OF STATE TAXES ON PERSONAL INCOME, CORPORATE INCOME AND SALES, 1969[a]

State	Personal Income Tax at Oregon Rates[b] (Millions of Dollars)	Corporate Income Tax at 7%[b] (Millions of Dollars)	Sales Tax at 5%—No Exemptions[b] (Millions of Dollars)	Total Estimated Yield of Three Taxes (Millions of Dollars)	Total Population (Thousands)	Estimated Per Capita Yield of Three Taxes (Dollars)	Rank
Alabama	249	62	270	581	3,531	165	49
Alaska	33	5	40	78	282	277	7
Arizona	150	30	270	450	1,693	266	11
Arkansas	138	42	190	370	1,995	185	46
California	2,297	593	2,835	5,725	19,443	294	3
Colorado	204	45	225	474	2,100	226	29
Connecticut	378	86	335	799	3,000	266	11
Delaware	61	18	65	144	540	267	10
Florida	588	196	965	1,749	6,354	275	8
Georgia	381	85	565	1,031	4,641	222	30
Hawaii	87	16	170	273	794	344	2
Idaho	56	11	70	137	718	191	43
Illinois	1,313	437	1,285	3,035	11,047	275	8
Indiana	519	173	550	1,242	5,118	243	15
Iowa	280	42	345	667	2,781	240	17
Kansas	227	65	255	547	2,321	236	19
Kentucky	256	69	275	600	3,232	186	45
Louisiana	294	62	420	776	3,745	207	37
Maine	83	27	105	215	978	220	32
Maryland	420	55	440	915	3,765	243	15
Massachusetts	640	185	380	1,205	5,467	220	32
Michigan	567	272	1,095	1,934	8,766	221	31
Minnesota	336	83	395	844	3,700	228	28
Mississippi	146	68	220	434	2,360	184	47
Missouri	453	94	545	1,092	4,651	235	21
Montana	61	9	65	135	694	195	41
Nebraska	140	23	190	353	1,449	244	14
Nevada	53	15	100	168	457	368	1
New Hampshire	69	20	75	164	717	229	26
New Jersey	840	247	595	1,682	7,148	235	21
New Mexico	80	7	145	232	994	233	24
New York	2,250	610	2,290	5,150	18,321	281	6
North Carolina	408	132	440	980	5,205	188	44
North Dakota	51	5	70	126	615	205	39
Ohio	1,113	370	1,050	2,533	10,740	236	19
Oklahoma	218	57	290	565	2,568	220	32
Oregon	204	44	220	468	2,032	230	25
Pennsylvania	1,203	284	1,055	2,542	11,803	215	35
Rhode Island	96	28	100	224	911	246	13
South Carolina	190	48	255	493	2,692	183	48
South Dakota	59	13	85	155	659	235	21
Tennessee	306	86	420	812	3,985	204	40
Texas	996	330	1,235	2,561	11,187	229	26
Utah	87	18	115	220	1,045	211	36
Vermont	39	7	45	91	439	207	37
Virginia	423	95	385	903	4,669	193	42
Washington	363	110	520	993	3,402	292	4
West Virginia	135	5	130	270	1,819	148	50
Wisconsin	462	221	335	1,018	4,233	240	17
Wyoming	30	8	55	93	320	291	5
TOTAL U. S.	20,056	5,610	22,575	48,241	201,123	240	

[a]SOURCE: R. L. Johns and Oscar A. Hamilton, Jr., "Ability and Effort of the States to Support Education" (Gainesville, Fla.: National Educational Finance Project, 1970), 15 pp. (Mimeo)

[b]Calculated from data in John Due, "Alternative Tax Sources for Education", in *Economic Factors Affecting the Financing of Education* (Gainesville, Fla.: National Educational Finance Project, 1971), Tables 10-2 and 10-5.

realize nearly 2.5 times as much revenue as West Virginia would realize if it were to levy the same taxes at the same rates. However, if one takes the sixth ranking state (New York) and the 45th ranking state (Kentucky), the gap is narrowed considerably. The estimated potential per capita revenue for New York was $281 compared with $186 for Kentucky. Thus, on this particular set of measures the sixth ranking state had approximately 1.52 times as much fiscal capacity as the 45th ranking state.

The NEFP staff used several measures to examine the extent of the effort being made by the various states to support state and local governmental functions in relation to their fiscal capacity. The results of their analyses are shown in Table 4-4. In 1969 the general revenue available to state and local governments from their own tax sources totaled $95.011 billion. Over one-third of this amount, $32.069 billion, consisted of state and local revenue for elementary and secondary education. When expressed as a percentage of net personal income, the general revenue of state and local government accounted for nearly 18.5 percent of net personal income, with 6.24 percent of net personal income being allocated for elementary and secondary education. The percentage of net personal income devoted to elementary and secondary education ranged from a high of 8.9 percent in New Mexico to a low of 5.0 percent in Nebraska. It was found that 33.75 percent of the general revenue of state and local governments consisted of revenue for elementary and secondary education. The percentages ranged from a high of 39.73 percent in Utah to a low of 25.51 percent in Wyoming.

The data concerning fiscal capacity and tax effort of the 50 states contained in the preceding tables are summarized in Table 4-5 and the contrasts between the five states which ranked highest and lowest on each measure are emphasized. The five highest states had 1.76 times as much personal income per capita as did the five lowest states. The five states with the highest estimated potential yield from personal income, corporate income, and sales taxes would have obtained 1.72 times as much revenue from these levies as would the five lowest states. The five highest ranking states in terms of tax effort devoted 1.63 times as great a percentage of their net personal income to state and local taxes as did the five lowest ranking states. The five highest ranking states devoted 1.56 times as great a percentage of their net personal income to elementary and secondary education as did the five lowest

96

TABLE 4-4

Efforts of the States To Support State and Local Governmental Functions In Relation To Their Fiscal Capacity, 1969[a]

State	Net Personal Income ($ Millions)	General Revenue of State and Local Governments From Own Sources[b] ($ Millions)	State and Local Revenue for Elementary and Secondary Education[c] ($ Millions)	General Revenue of State and Local Governments as a Percentage of Net Personal Income	Elementary and Secondary Education as a Percentage of Net Personal Income	State and Local Revenue for Elementary and Secondary Education as a Percentage of General Revenue of State and Local Governments From Own Sources
Alabama	5,669	1,122	312	19.79 (22)	5.50 (43)	27.81 (47)
Alaska	950	183	59	19.26 (27)	6.21 (30)	32.24 (32)
Arizona	3,879	826	299	21.29 (11)	7.71 (6)	36.20 (16)
Arkansas	3,157	584	194	18.50 (30)	6.15 (31)	33.22 (27)
California	60,198	12,822	3,900	21.30 (10)	6.48 (23)	30.42 (40)
Colorado	5,233	1,052	346	20.10 (20)	6.61 (19)	32.89 (28)
Connecticut	9,626	1,394	543	14.48 (49)	5.64 (41)	38.95 (4)
Delaware	1,502	281	108	18.71 (28)	7.19 (11)	38.43 (7)
Florida	14,857	2,740	941	18.44 (31)	6.33 (27)	34.34 (24)
Georgia	9,425	1,685	541	17.88 (34)	5.74 (38)	32.11 (34)
Hawaii	2,135	466	136	21.83 (7)	6.37 (26)	29.18 (45)
Idaho	1,346	299	96	22.21 (6)	7.13 (13)	32.11 (34)
Illinois	33,992	4,898	1,831	14.41 (50)	5.39 (45)	37.38 (10)
Indiana	13,197	2,179	864	16.51 (43)	6.55 (21)	39.65 (2)
Iowa	6,889	1,352	484	19.63 (23)	7.03 (14)	35.80 (17)
Kansas	5,787	1,034	386	17.87 (35)	6.67 (17)	37.33 (12)
Kentucky	6,046	1,171	347	19.37 (24)	5.74 (38)	29.63 (42)
Louisiana	6,681	1,547	498	23.16 (5)	7.45 (9)	32.19 (33)
Maine	1,984	359	128	18.09 (32)	6.45 (24)	35.65 (20)
Maryland	10,784	1,879	729	17.42 (38)	6.76 (16)	38.80 (6)
Massachusetts	16,107	2,841	840	17.64 (37)	5.22 (48)	29.57 (43)
Michigan	24,258	4,694	1,563	19.35 (26)	6.44 (25)	33.30 (26)
Minnesota	9,391	1,954	691	20.81 (15)	7.36 (10)	35.36 (21)
Mississippi	3,048	763	239	25.03 (3)	7.84 (5)	31.32 (37)

TABLE 4-4 (CONTINUED)

Missouri	11,036	1,758	609	15.93 (44)	5.52 (42)	34.64 (22)
Montana	1,476	312	119	21.14 (12)	8.06 (3)	38.14 (8)
Nebraska	3,739	693	187	18.53 (29)	5.00 (50)	26.98 (49)
Nevada	1,434	285	85	19.87 (21)	5.93 (33)	29.82 (41)
New Hampshire	1,696	263	91	15.51 (47)	5.37 (46)	34.60 (23)
New Jersey	21,834	3,406	1,248	15.60 (46)	5.72 (39)	36.64 (14)
New Mexico	1,898	473	169	24.92 (4)	8.90 (1)	35.73 (18)
New York	58,080	12,472	4,057	21.47 (9)	6.99 (15)	32.53 (31)
North Carolina	9,924	1,721	585	17.34 (39)	5.89 (35)	33.99 (25)
North Dakota	1,260	322	90	25.56 (2)	7.14 (12)	27.95 (46)
Ohio	28,278	4,196	1,499	14.84 (48)	5.30 (47)	35.72 (19)
Oklahoma	5,280	1,022	299	19.36 (25)	5.66 (40)	29.26 (44)
Oregon	5,025	1,025	403	20.40 (16)	8.02 (4)	39.32 (3)
Pennsylvania	29,954	4,739	1,842	15.82 (45)	6.15 (31)	38.87 (5)
Rhode Island	2,409	403	124	16.73 (41)	5.15 (49)	30.77 (39)
South Carolina	4,370	786	291	17.99 (33)	6.66 (18)	37.02 (13)
South Dakota	1,387	302	82	21.77 (8)	5.91 (34)	27.15 (48)
Tennessee	7,196	1,284	422	17.84 (36)	5.86 (36)	32.87 (29)
Texas	24,513	4,086	1,331	16.67 (42)	5.43 (44)	32.57 (30)
Utah	2,096	443	176	21.14 (12)	8.40 (2)	38.73 (1)
Vermont	983	198	74	20.14 (19)	7.53 (8)	37.37 (11)
Virginia	10,374	1,796	652	17.31 (40)	6.28 (28)	36.30 (15)
Washington	9,137	1,845	571	20.19 (18)	6.25 (29)	30.95 (38)
West Virginia	2,961	602	226	20.33 (17)	7.63 (7)	37.54 (9)
Wisconsin	10,792	2,262	713	20.96 (14)	6.61 (19)	31.52 (36)
Wyoming	764	196	50	25.65 (1)	6.54 (22)	25.51 (50)
TOTAL U. S.	514,043	95,011	32,069	18.48	6.24	33.75

[a]SOURCE: R. L. Johns and Oscar A. Hamilton, Jr., "Ability and Effort of the States to Support Education" (Gainesville, Fla.: National Educational Finance Project, 1970), 15 pp. (Mimeo)

[b]U. S. Department of Commerce, Bureau of the Census, *Governmental Finances in 1968-69*, G.F. 69, No. 5.

[c]National Education Association, Research Division, Research Report 1969 R-15, *Estimates of School Statistics, 1969-70.*

SUMMARY OF DATA CONCERNING FISCAL CAPACITY AND TAX EFFORT OF THE STATES

	Personal Income Per Capita (Table 4-1)	Net Personal Income Per Capita (Table 4-1)	Estimated Yield of Three Taxes Per Capita (Table 4-2)	General Revenue of State and Local Governments From Own Sources as a Percentage of Net Personal Income (Table 4-3)	State and Local Revenue for Elementary and Secondary Education as a Percentage of Net Personal Income (Table 4-3)	State and Local Revenue for Elementary and Secondary Education as a Percentage of General Revenue of State and Local Governments From Own Sources (Table 4-3)
U.S. Total or Avg.	$ 3,675	$ 2,556	$ 240	18.48	6.24	33.75
High State Amount	Conn. 4,537	Alaska 3,369	Nevada 368	Wyo. 25.65	N. Mex. 8.90	Utah 39.73
Low State Amount	Miss. 2,192	Miss. 1,292	W. Va. 148	Ill. 14.41	Neb. 5.00	Wyo. 25.51
Ratio High-Low	2.07/1.00	2.61/1.00	2.49/1.00	1.78/1.00	1.78/1.00	1.56/1.00
Five Highest States	Conn. Alaska N. York Nevada Ill.	Alaska Conn. N. York Nevada Calif.	Nevada Hawaii Calif. Wash. Wyo.	Wyo. N. Dak. Miss. N. Mex. La.	N. Mex. Utah Mont. Ore. Miss.	Utah Ind. Ore. Conn. Pa.
Weighted Avg., Five Highest	$ 4,394	$ 3,139	$ 297	24.18	8.17	39.14
Five Lowest States	Miss. Ark. S. Car. Ala. W. Va.	Miss. Ark. Ala. S. Car. W. Va.	W. Va. Ala. S. Car. Miss. Ark.	Ill. Conn. Ohio N.H. N.J.	Nebr. R.I. Mass. Ohio N.H.	Wyo. Nebr. S. Dak. Ala. N. Dak.
Weighted Avg., Five Lowest	2,497	1,549	173	14.84	5.25	27.36
Ratio Highest to Lowest Weighted Avg.	1.76/1.00	2.03/1.00	1.72/1.00	1.63/1.00	1.56/1.00	1.43/1.00

SOURCE: R. L. Johns and Oscar A. Hamilton, Jr., "Ability and Effort of the States to Support Education" (Gainesville, Fla.: National Educational Finance Project, 1970), 15 PP. (Mimeo)

ranking states. The percentage of general revenue devoted to elementary and secondary education was 1.43 times as great in the five highest ranking states as it was in the five lowest ranking states.

It is clear from these data that considerable variation does exist among the states—both with regard to their fiscal capacity as measured by three major tax bases and with regard to their effort to raise revenue to support state and local governmental functions, including education. A correlation of −.29 was found between percent of net income allocated to revenue for the public schools (state effort to support education) and per capita net income. While this is a relatively low correlation, it does indicate that the less wealthy states were exerting a somewhat greater effort to support education than were the wealthier states.

Studies by the Advisory Commission on Intergovernmental Relations

The Advisory Commission on Intergovernmental Relations (ACIR) regularly conducts studies of state and local fiscal capacity and effort. The Commission's landmark study published in 1962[9] has recently been augmented by an even more comprehensive study based on data for 1966-67.[10] In the latter study ACIR used an "average financing system" approach to measuring fiscal capacity. In this approach the fiscal capacity of any area is defined as "the total amount of revenue that would result by applying, within the area, the national average rate of each of the numerous kinds of state-local revenue sources."[11] The sources of revenue included tax revenue, fees and charges collected in connection with governmental services (such as tuition fees at colleges and charges at public hospitals), interest earned on financial assets, and nontax revenue such as money obtained from the operation of state liquor stores or public utilities.

In Table 4-6 are shown the revenue capacity, the actual revenue received by state and local governments, and the personal income per capita in each of the 50 states for 1968-69. The estimated revenue capacity is the total amount of revenue which could be raised if a state levied all taxes at the average national rate and received nontax revenue at the average national rate. The index measures indicate the extent to which a state is actually using its revenue capacity in comparison with the national

100

TABLE 4-6
MEASURES OF STATE-LOCAL TAX CAPACITY AND TAX EFFORT FOR STATES: 1968–69

State	Per capita amounts			Index measures (per capita) amounts as % of U.S. averages)			
	Tax capacity	Tax revenue	Personal income (1968)	Tax Capacity	Tax revenue	Personal income (1968)	Relative tax effort
U.S.	386	386	3,421	100	100	100	100
Alabama	270	227	2,337	70	59	68	84
Alaska	403	399	4,146	104	103	121	99
Arizona	381	393	3,027	99	102	88	103
Arkansas	299	222	2,322	77	58	68	74
California	472	547	3,968	122	142	116	116
Colorado	398	392	3,340	103	102	98	98
Connecticut	451	397	4,256	117	103	124	88
Delaware	465	377	3,795	120	98	111	81
Dist. of Columbia	465	426	4,464	120	110	130	92
Florida	419	338	3,191	109	88	93	81
Georgia	314	273	2,781	81	71	81	87
Hawaii	381	492	3,513	99	127	103	129
Idaho	338	340	2,668	88	88	78	100
Illinois	431	376	3,981	112	97	116	87
Indiana	375	338	3,412	97	88	100	90
Iowa	385	395	3,265	100	102	95	103
Kansas	405	351	3,303	105	91	97	87
Kentucky	312	278	2,645	81	72	77	89
Louisiana	364	301	2,634	94	78	77	83
Maine	316	321	2,824	82	83	83	102
Maryland	398	416	3,742	103	108	109	105
Massachusetts	382	455	3,835	99	118	112	119
Michigan	404	439	3,675	105	114	107	109
Minnesota	367	413	3,341	95	107	98	112
Mississippi	252	245	2,081	65	63	61	98
Missouri	373	304	3,257	97	79	95	81
Montana	391	356	2,942	101	92	86	91
Nebraska	416	361	3,239	108	94	95	87
Nevada	669	475	3,957	173	123	116	71
New Hampshire	422	325	3,259	109	84	95	77
New Jersey	410	411	3,954	106	106	116	100
New Mexico	355	324	2,651	92	84	77	91
New York	418	580	4,151	108	150	121	139
North Carolina	308	267	2,664	80	69	78	87
North Dakota	352	333	2,730	91	86	80	95
Ohio	387	318	3,509	100	82	103	82
Oklahoma	392	290	2,880	102	75	84	74
Oregon	401	406	3,317	104	105	97	101
Pennsylvania	350	346	3,419	91	90	100	99
Rhode Island	355	380	3,549	92	98	104	107
South Carolina	254	227	2,380	66	59	70	89
South Dakota	349	353	2,876	90	91	84	101
Tennessee	302	254	2,579	78	66	75	84
Texas	388	280	3,029	101	73	89	72
Utah	326	337	2,790	84	87	82	104
Vermont	339	394	3,072	88	102	90	116
Virginia	337	323	3,068	87	84	90	96
Washington	424	434	3,688	110	112	108	102
West Virginia	284	269	2,470	74	70	72	95
Wisconsin	358	441	3,363	93	114	98	123
Wyoming	530	413	3,190	137	107	93	78

Source: Adapted from Advisory Commission on Intergovernmental Relations, *Measuring the Fiscal Capacity and Effort of State and Local Areas* (Washington, D.C.: Government Printing Office, 1971), Table G-14.

average. In 24 states the income index differed from the revenue capacity index substantially. For example, in Wyoming, personal income was only 93 percent of the national average and tax capacity 135 percent; in Florida, personal income was 93 percent and tax capacity 109 percent; and in Nevada, personal income was 116 percent and tax capacity was 173 percent.

Conversely, in Rhode Island, personal income was 104 percent of the national average and tax capacity, 92 percent; in Alaska, personal income was 121 percent and tax capacity, 104 percent; and in Massachusetts, personal income was 112 percent and tax capacity, 99 percent.

Space does not permit the reproduction of other significant tables produced by the Advisory Commission on Intergovernmental Relations. Following are the observations made by the Commission with regard to the relative revenue capacity and effort of states and local governments:[12]

1. A 2.6 to 1 range existed in revenue capacity of the 50 states (from $670 per capita in Nevada to $259 per capita in South Carolina).

2. Greater interstate variation existed in revenue capacity than existed in per capita personal income, where the range from the highest to lowest state was 2.1 to 1 in 1966.

3. Regional factors are important. The seven lowest ranking states all were located in the South; the five highest capacity states all were located in the West.

4. In 29 states per capita personal income *understated* relative fiscal capacity as measured by the average financing system method by at least 2 percent. In 19 states per capita personal income *overstated* relative fiscal capacity by at least 2 percent.

5. In states where mining or tourism are important elements of the economy the revenue raising capacity of the state is likely to be greater than the per capita personal income of its residents would suggest.

6. Most of the states with less revenue raising capability than per capita personal income would suggest were located in the northeastern or north central regions of the country, are generally quite heavily urban in character, and have had population growth less rapid than the national average in recent years.

102

7. Regional patterns were less evident for revenue effort than they are for revenue capacity. The four highest states (Hawaii, New York, Vermont and Wisconsin) and the four lowest states (Illinois, Nevada, New Hampshire and Texas) are widely scattered geographically.

8. The southern states, when compared with those in other regions of the country, tended to exhibit (1) a lower level of per capita revenue capacity, (2) somewhat less overall tax effort but greater-than-average use of nontax revenue capacity, (3) less reliance on property taxation, and (4) a lower level of effort with regard to taxes on business.

9. A correlation of .633 was found between per capita estimated revenue capacity and per capita personal income of the states, and a correlation of .833 was found between per capita estimated revenue capacity and a composite measure in which property tax yield and personal income were weighted equally. Thus, for areas as large as states the three approaches to measuring fiscal capacity produced rather similar results.

Implications

It is clear from the data which have been presented that substantial variations in fiscal capacity and effort do exist among the 50 states. Whether one uses a single measure of fiscal capacity (such as personal income per capita), or an index of fiscal capacity which employs a composite of several techniques, it has been shown consistently that a large part of the differences in school expenditure levels among these states can be explained by variations in their fiscal capacity.

The variation in fiscal capacity which occurs among the states is, for the most part, beyond the control of the individual states. Much of the variation is the result of differences in the natural resources of the states. Differences in the relative tax paying capacity of the states seem to be declining over time, but the rate of decline is not rapid. Although some states apparently have succeeded in increasing their taxable wealth over time through policies designed to attract and hold human and fiscal resources, there is no quick and easy way in which a state can increase its wealth relative to other states.

Differences in the fiscal capacity of the states inevitably lead to variations in expenditure levels and variations in tax burdens. A state with limited revenue capacity will be able to match the expenditure levels of wealthier states only if it is willing to exert a substantially higher-than-average tax effort. It is much more common to find a relatively low level of governmental services (as evidenced by low expenditure levels) in states which have relatively low fiscal capacity. Since there is little that a state itself can do to alter its revenue potential, at least in the short run, it would appear that only the federal government is in a position to take action to reduce the variations in fiscal capacity which exist among the states. Although virtually any federal aid would tend to reduce differences in revenue capacity among the states to some degree, it should be noted that fewer federal dollars would be required to reduce variations in revenue capacity if equalization factors were incorporated into federal aid programs.

VARIATIONS IN FISCAL CAPACITY AND EFFORT AMONG SCHOOL DISTRICTS AND OTHER UNITS OF LOCAL GOVERNMENT

Variations in fiscal capacity among school districts and other units of local government typically are greater than the variations in fiscal capacity which exist among states. Most studies dealing with the fiscal capacity and effort of units of local government have dealt with variation within a state, primarily because of the difficulties involved in securing comparable data for units of local government located in several states. Recently, however, studies have been completed utilizing data obtained from the Census of Governments which is conducted every five years by the U.S. Bureau of the Census. Of particular interest in this regard are a study of metropolitan areas and counties reported by the Advisory Commission on Intergovernmental Relations (ACIR) and a study of the fiscal capacity of school districts undertaken as a part of the National Educational Finance Project.

Fiscal Capacity and Effort of Standard Metropolitan Statistical Areas

The ACIR study utilized data for 215 standard metropolitan statistical areas (SMSA's) as defined by the Bureau of the Census. The revenue capacity of local governments ranged from a

104

high of $343 per capita to a low of less than $100 per capita. Fiscal effort by local governments also showed considerable variation with a high of 46 percent above the national average and a low of 40 percent below the national average.

Table 4-7 provides a summary of comparative measures of state and local government revenue capacity and revenue effort for the 215 SMSA's categorized by location and population size. In commenting upon these data, ACIR noted:

● Southern SMSA's average lower than those elsewhere not only in revenue capacity and actual revenue per capita, but also in relative revenue effort. . . .

● Southern SMSA's generally resemble those elsewhere in the proportions of their local government capacity represented by the various revenue components shown in the table, with one exception: because public operation of municipal utilities is somewhat more common in the South than elsewhere, potential utility surpluses make up a larger revenue component in Southern SMSA's. . . .

● The 30 largest SMSA's—those with a million inhabitants or more—stand out conspicuously above the others in per capita revenue capacity and actual revenue. Their relative revenue effort also averages higher than that of any other size group, though not dramatically so.

● The four SMSA groups of less than a half-million population resemble one another in state-local revenue capacity per capita, but less populous areas show less actual revenue and, therefore, a generally lower level of revenue effort. . . . Except for the SMSA's of under 100,000, each size group shows local property tax effort above the national average, with the highest index reported for the areas of 200,000 to 300,000 population.

● Some material differences appear among the several size-groups of SMSA's in the composition of local revenue capacity: with decreasing population size of area, the share contributed by farm property taxes moves up consistently, while the (far larger) proportion contributed by taxation of nonfarm residential property drops off. Perhaps rather surprisingly, the business property tax share of the local revenue base averages about the same for each of the size groups of areas.[13]

105

Fiscal Capacity and Effort of Counties

The ACIR study also examined revenue capacity and effort for 666 selected county areas in the United States. Data summarizing the revenue capacity of these selected counties (on a state-by-state basis) are shown in Table 4-8 and indexes of revenue effort are shown in Table 4-9. For local government sources only (counties in this instance) per capita revenue capacity exhibited a range of 11 to 1—from $420 per capita in Washoe County, Nevada to $38 per capita in Berkeley County, South Carolina. The range in the county revenue effort was 4.9 to 1, with a range of 7 to 1 on the property tax effort of county governments. It should be noted, of course, that these comparisons were for entire counties and revealed nothing about the variations in revenue capacity and effort which may occur for smaller areas within these counties.

Fiscal Capacity and Effort of School Districts

Most studies of the fiscal capacity and effort of school districts have employed the value of property per pupil in average daily attendance (or average daily membership) as the criterion of fiscal capacity and the property tax rate as the criterion of fiscal effort. This procedure is understandable, since very few school districts have authority to levy a tax on any base other than property. In addition, it has been very difficult to conduct studies of the fiscal capacity of school districts based on income because of the difficulty of obtaining reasonably accurate estimates of income for school districts. It has frequently been shown, however, that property value per pupil or per capita is not closely related to income although presumably all taxes must eventually be paid from income.

In a study conducted for the National Educational Finance Project, Rossmiller, Hale and Frohreich utilized a sample of 223 school districts drawn from eight states to study the fiscal capacity and effort of school districts.[14] The study included representation from seven categories of school districts: major urban core cities, minor urban core cities, independent cities, established suburbs, developing suburbs, small cities, and small towns. Data concerning revenues and expenditures of school districts, as well as data concerning market value of property, personal income and retail sales in each of the school districts were obtained

106

TABLE 4-7

SUMMARY COMPARATIVE MEASURES OF STATE AND LOCAL GOVERNMENT REVENUE, REVENUE CAPACITY, AND REVENUE EFFORT FOR 215 METROPOLITAN AREAS, BY LOCATION AND POPULATION-SIZE: 1966-67

Index measures for SMSA's (unweighted mean ratios; related U.S. averages=100)

Item	U.S. average[a]	All population sizes of SMSA's			Area population, 1966 (000)					
		Total	South[b]	Non-south	1,000-plus	500-999	300-499	200-299	100-199	Under 100
Number of areas	—	215	81	134	30	36	28	45	56	20
Per capita revenue capacity (on U.S.-average-rate basis):										
State and local sources	$396	100	95	104	113	103	99	96	97	97
State government sources	$195	104	102	106	112	104	102	101	103	109
Local government sources	$201	96	88	102	115	101	96	92	91	85
Per capita actual revenue:										
State and local governments	$396	97	88	103	113	101	96	94	92	89
Local governments only	$201	92	76	101	117	99	90	86	84	78
Relative revenue effort (with capacity estimated on U.S.-average-rate basis):										
State and local governments	100%	97	93	99	100	98	97	95	95	91
Local governments only	100%	95	87	99	102	98	93	93	92	91
Relative revenue effort of local governments (with capacity estimated on State-adjusted basis):										
All local revenue sources	100%	97	94	99	100	99	98	99	95	89
Local property taxes	100%	103	103	104	104	105	104	109	101	95
Local nonproperty taxes	100%	66	65	67	86	71	74	67	54	49
Charges and miscellaneous general revenue	100%	98	92	101	98	98	102	96	97	95
Utility surpluses	100%	105	103	106	100	103	115	107	104	101

107

TABLE 4-7 (CONTINUED)

		All population sizes of SMSA's			Area population, 1966 (000)					
Item	U.S. average[a]	Total	South[b]	Non-south	1,000-plus	500-999	300-499	200-299	100-199	Under 100
Proportion of revenue capacity of local governments represented by:										
Property taxation of—										
Nonfarm residential property	30.2%	98	92	102	105	105	98	98	96	83
Business property	25.3%	107	110	105	109	106	107	105	105	116
Farm property	5.2%	77	78	76	36	38	77	59	112	146
Other local taxes	12.8%	111	116	107	101	107	113	113	112	120
Charges and miscellaneous general revenue sources	22.8%	94	93	94	100	94	94	98	91	86
Utility surpluses	3.7%	100	118	89	82	122	89	106	103	84

[a]Averages shown pertain to the entire U.S., rather than relating only to areas reported here.
[b]SMSA's in 14 Southern States.

Source: Advisory Commission on Intergovernmental Relations *Measuring the Fiscal Capacity and Effort of State and Local Areas* (Washington, D.C.: Government Printing Office, 1971), Table 11.

TABLE 4-8

INDEXES OF PER CAPITA REVENUE CAPACITY (ON STATE-ADJUSTED BASIS), FOR 666 SELECTED COUNTY AREAS, BY STATES: 1966-67 (U.S. AVERAGE PER CAPITA AMOUNTS=100)

State	Areas reported		State and local government sources				Local government sources			
	Number	Percent of State population (1966)	Average[a]	Highest	Lowest	Ratio of high to low (=1)	Average[a]	Highest	Lowest	Ratio of high to low (=1)
U.S.	666	76	92	208	31	6.7	87	209	19	11.0
Alabama	18	64	73	90	48	1.9	59	80	35	2.3
Alaska	—	—	—	—	—	—	—	—	—	—
Arizona	5	83	99	111	94	1.2	90	106	78	1.4
Arkansas	10	40	78	105	53	2.0	53	77	32	2.4
California	32	93	110	143	85	1.7	127	180	91	2.0
Colorado	10	81	98	145	69	2.1	101	145	66	2.2
Connecticut	7	97	102	120	81	1.5	102	132	70	1.9
Delaware	3	100	102	135	85	1.6	57	80	42	1.9
District of Columbia	1	100	116	116	116	—	97	97	97	—
Florida	22	85	97	124	67	1.9	107	134	76	1.8
Georgia	14	52	82	118	54	2.2	76	104	45	2.3
Hawaii	2	90	103	105	102	1.0	62	68	56	1.2
Idaho	3	30	87	95	79	1.2	67	80	57	1.4
Illinois	27	85	103	155	76	2.0	116	176	82	2.1
Indiana	32	73	92	117	71	1.6	89	122	64	1.9
Iowa	9	39	105	120	92	1.3	103	113	88	1.3
Kansas	7	46	103	120	57	2.1	108	144	53	2.7
Kentucky	11	44	91	114	47	2.4	69	94	27	3.5
Louisiana	16	65	109	176	63	2.8	66	102	33	3.1
Maine	3	42	87	94	80	1.2	74	84	64	1.3
Maryland	13	92	93	118	75	1.6	88	138	67	2.1
Massachusetts	7	68	88	133	69	1.9	90	129	66	2.0
Michigan	25	86	98	126	73	1.7	91	128	68	1.9
Minnesota	9	57	95	134	63	2.1	96	136	54	2.5
Mississippi	9	34	79	110	54	2.0	66	96	43	2.2

TABLE 4-8 (CONTINUED)

State	Areas reported		State and local government sources				Local government sources			
	Number	Percent of State population (1966)	Average[a]	Highest	Lowest	Ratio of high to low (=1)	Average[a]	Highest	Lowest	Ratio of high to low (=1)
Missouri	12	64	91	130	59	2.2	94	145	62	2.3
Montana	3	31	111	127	95	1.3	114	141	84	1.7
Nebraska	4	41	109	130	78	1.7	138	166	109	1.5
Nevada	2	79	176	193	160	1.2	189	209	170	1.2
New Hampshire	3	48	100	107	89	1.2	113	120	104	1.2
New Jersey	21	100	101	144	73	2.0	124	195	81	2.4
New Mexico	5	51	115	188	87	2.2	65	109	44	2.5
New York	38	95	89	133	63	2.1	91	143	59	2.4
North Carolina	35	69	77	119	52	2.3	53	96	23	4.2
North Dakota	3	31	129	167	105	1.6	99	135	80	1.7
Ohio	47	87	86	119	58	2.1	97	144	62	2.3
Oklahoma	10	52	93	142	57	2.5	74	111	36	3.1
Oregon	10	74	102	143	82	1.7	100	131	84	1.6
Pennsylvania	41	91	79	112	59	1.9	75	110	48	2.3
Rhode Island	5	100	80	97	71	1.4	75	86	65	1.3
South Carolina	15	66	66	88	31	2.8	40	53	19	2.8
South Dakota	1	14	112	112	112	—	116	116	116	—
Tennessee	13	58	85	113	59	1.9	81	110	48	2.3
Texas	40	73	92	208	54	3.9	90	154	49	3.1
Utah	4	77	83	104	67	1.6	70	87	59	1.5
Vermont	—	—	—	—	—	—	—	—	—	—
Virginia	12	56	90	130	62	2.1	74	112	52	2.2
Washington	12	83	112	155	82	1.9	89	158	55	2.9
West Virginia	16	63	78	123	42	2.9	53	107	27	4.0
Wisconsin	18	66	93	115	81	1.4	76	97	54	1.8
Wyoming	1	19	121	121	121	—	109	109	109	—

ᵃUnweighted mean of indexes computed for individual areas.

Source: Advisory Commission on Intergovernmental Relations, *Measuring the Fiscal Capacity and Effort of State and Local Areas* (Washington, D. C.: GPO, 1971), Table 14.

TABLE 4-9

INDEXES OF REVENUE EFFORT (ACTUAL REVENUE AS PERCENT OF REVENUE CAPACITY) FOR 666 SELECTED COUNTY AREAS, BY STATES: 1966–67

State	State and local governments				Local governments— all revenue sources				Local property taxes only			
	Aver-age[a]	High-est	Low-est	Ratio of high to low (=1)	Aver-age[a]	High-est	Low-est	Ratio of high to low (=1)	Aver-age[a]	High-est	Low-est	Ratio of high to low (=1)
U.S.	97	140	56	2.5	96	171	35	4.9	103	195	28	7.0
Alabama	97	112	85	1.3	95	127	64	2.0	112	195	44	4.4
Alaska	112	121	108	1.1	117	140	108	1.3	—	—	—	—
Arizona	90	121	108	1.1	117	140	108	1.3	134	162	112	1.4
Arkansas	110	100	81	1.2	94	127	69	1.8	116	162	70	2.3
California	110	133	90	1.5	114	154	81	1.9	119	178	78	2.3
Colorado	92	122	99	1.2	113	136	92	1.5	117	151	88	1.7
Connecticut	99	98	89	1.1	91	103	85	1.2	98	117	91	1.3
Delaware	85	103	95	1.1	92	106	75	1.4	100	135	59	2.3
District of Columbia	91	85	85	—	85	85	85	—	85	85	85	—
Florida	98	101	75	1.3	90	107	64	1.7	89	124	65	1.9
Georgia	123	111	92	1.2	98	125	85	1.5	121	195	80	2.4
Hawaii	110	125	120	1.0	120	128	111	1.2	107	137	78	1.8
Idaho	86	114	105	1.1	115	127	102	1.2	107	129	92	1.4
Illinois	99	94	71	1.3	86	100	61	1.6	91	114	69	1.7
Indiana	102	119	88	1.4	101	139	80	1.7	108	164	76	2.2
Iowa	97	109	90	1.2	99	114	76	1.5	101	118	72	1.6
Kansas	93	113	89	1.3	99	131	84	1.6	109	168	83	2.0
Kentucky	91	99	84	1.2	92	107	66	1.6	103	128	66	1.9
Louisiana	99	100	86	1.2	90	115	72	1.6	99	154	39	3.9
Maine	97	103	97	1.1	96	106	90	1.2	102	111	95	1.2
Maryland	119	111	84	1.3	92	122	64	1.9	95	130	66	2.0
Massachusetts	98	131	99	1.3	126	149	90	1.7	152	195	94	2.1
Michigan	116	118	84	1.4	95	140	70	2.0	96	166	64	2.6
Minnesota	99	140	108	1.3	118	171	101	1.7	120	192	95	2.0
Mississippi	99	106	87	1.2	94	110	66	1.7	114	154	81	1.9

TABLE 4-9 (CONTINUED)

State	State and local governments				Local governments—all revenue sources				Local property taxes only			
	Average[a]	Highest	Lowest	Ratio of high to low (=1)	Average[a]	Highest	Lowest	Ratio of high to low (=1)	Average[a]	Highest	Lowest	Ratio of high to low (=1)
Missouri	89	94	83	1.1	88	98	75	1.3	96	108	85	1.3
Montana	94	99	85	1.2	94	103	78	1.3	107	130	80	1.6
Nebraska	79	88	57	1.5	76	89	45	2.0	88	110	48	2.3
Nevada	78	80	77	1.0	79	82	77	1.1	79	85	72	1.2
New Hampshire	84	87	78	1.1	83	89	73	1.2	82	92	71	1.3
New Jersey	94	110	84	1.3	95	122	79	1.5	94	135	75	1.8
New Mexico	97	101	86	1.2	100	115	64	1.8	110	146	41	3.6
New York	117	131	96	1.4	109	136	71	1.9	136	182	84	2.2
North Carolina	95	105	87	1.2	91	118	65	1.8	98	163	59	2.8
North Dakota	97	98	96	1.0	102	104	101	1.0	101	102	98	1.0
Ohio	85	97	70	1.4	84	106	59	1.8	85	111	59	1.9
Oklahoma	88	100	76	1.3	87	115	61	1.9	95	124	64	1.9
Oregon	99	104	89	1.2	97	108	79	1.4	96	106	73	1.5
Pennsylvania	95	108	87	1.2	90	118	74	1.6	86	121	66	1.8
Rhode Island	101	103	98	1.1	102	106	96	1.1	110	116	103	1.1
South Carolina	99	107	91	1.2	96	118	71	1.7	111	149	65	2.3
South Dakota	97	97	97	—	90	90	90	—	93	93	93	—
Tennessee	86	97	72	1.3	83	105	56	1.9	78	110	46	2.4
Texas	84	101	56	1.8	84	119	35	3.4	91	151	28	5.4
Utah	106	107	103	1.0	101	104	95	1.1	102	112	96	1.2
Vermont												
Virginia	96	110	84	1.3	96	129	58	2.2	112	174	63	2.8
Washington	100	104	93	1.1	97	108	82	1.3	96	119	71	1.7
West Virginia	100	113	85	1.3	101	144	67	2.1	123	188	75	2.5
Wisconsin	114	133	92	1.4	114	166	71	2.3	115	178	59	3.0
Wyoming	83	83	83	—	80	80	80	—	73	73	73	—

[a] Unweighted means of ratios computed for individual areas.

Source: Advisory Commission on Intergovernmental Relations, *Measuring the Fiscal Capacity and Effort of State and Local Areas* (Washington, D.C.: GPO, 1971), Table 14.

for the 1961-62 and 1966-67 school years. Table 4-10 provides a summary of data for each of the five variables used as measures of fiscal capacity—property value per pupil in average daily membership (ADM), retail sales per capita, retail sales per household, effective buying income per capita, and effective buying income per household.

It was found that both retail sales and effective buying income were correlated negatively with market value of property per pupil in average daily membership, whether these measures were expressed on a per capita or a per household basis. The negative correlations were rather low, ranging from −.095 for retail sales per capita to −.125 for effective buying income per household. From these correlations it would appear that, for all practical purposes, no relationship existed between the market value of property per pupil in average daily membership and the other two measures of fiscal capacity. Effective buying income per household and effective buying income per capita were closely related, with a correlation of .958. The correlation between retail sales per capita and retail sales per household was .640, while the correlations between retail sales per capita and effective buying income per capita and per household were .622 and .589, respectively.

When the data concerning sources of revenue of the various categories of school districts were subjected to multivariate analyses of variance, in every instance it was found that the differences in fiscal capacity between the school district categories increased between 1962 and 1967. In no instance, however, did the market value of property contribute to the significant differences which were found. Effective buying income, measured on either a per capita or a per household basis, was the major source of variation in fiscal capacity among the seven categories of school districts.

In Table 4-11 are shown the mean school property tax rates for each of the seven categories of school districts for the school years 1961-62 and 1966-67. During the 1961-62 school year, the mean tax rate on true market value of property for the 220 school districts in the sample was 10.247 mills and ranged from a low of 7.768 mills in the major urban core city category to a high of 12.647 in the developing suburb category. The mean school tax rates in the two suburb categories were considerably higher than those in the other five categories. A one-way analysis of variance

113

TABLE 4-10

MEANS OF FIVE VARIABLES USED AS MEASURES OF THE FISCAL CAPACITY OF VARIOUS CATEGORIES OF SCHOOL DISTRICTS FOR THE SCHOOL YEARS 1961-62 AND 1966-67

Measure of Fiscal Capacity	Category A		Category B		Category C		Category D		Category E		Category F		Category G	
	'61-62	'66-67	'61-62	'66-67	'61-62	'66-67	'61-62	'66-67	'61-62	'66-67	'61-62	'66-67	'61-62	'66-67
Market Value of pupil in ADM	$30,999	$32,946	$24,827	$28,077	$24,253	$27,497	$26,965	$30,691	$25,911	$29,967	$22,397	$27,228	$21,648	$26,308
Retail sales/capita	1,697	1,828	1,723	1,962	1,856	2,093	1,393	1,679	1,542	1,455	1,922	2,243	1,453	1,509
Retail sales/household	5,314	5,651	5,684	7,263	6,008	6,680	4,827	5,863	5,386	5,272	6,230	7,293	6,280	5,116
Effective buying income/capita	2,080	2,653	1,938	2,447	1,985	2,614	2,258	2,884	2,572	2,746	1,908	2,419	1,504	2,020
Effective buying income/household	6,567	8,223	6,435	8,128	6,468	8,379	7,784	9,997	9,001	9,913	6,231	8,039	5,339	6,940
Number in sample	13		34		35		35		34		35		35	

Category A = Major Urban Core City
Category B = Minor Urban Core City
Category C = Independent City
Category D = Established Suburb
Category E = Developing Suburb
Category F = Small City
Category G = Small town or agriculture service center

Source: Richard A. Rossmiller, James A. Hale and Lloyd E. Frohreich. *Fiscal Capacity and Educational Finance*, National Educational Finance Project Special Study No. 10 (Madison, Wis.: The University of Wisconsin, 1970), Tables 3.15 and 3.40.

114

TABLE 4-11

	1961–62		1966–67	
Category	N	Mean	N	Mean
Major urban core city	13	7.768	13	8.971
Minor urban core city	35	10.103	35	11.596
Independent city	35	9.383	35	10.910
Established suburb	35	12.496	35	13.604
Developing suburb	32	12.647	34	13.892
Small city	35	8.870	35	9.890
Small town	35	9.174	35	9.984
Grand Mean =		10.257		11.479

Source: Richard A. Rossmiller, James A. Hale and Lloyd E. Frohreich, *Fiscal Capacity and Educational Finance*, National Educational Finance Project Special Study No. 10 (Madison, Wis.: The University of Wisconsin, 1970), Tables 3.22 and 3.47.

indicated that the differences in property tax rates among the seven types of districts were statistically significant—that is, they were not likely to have occurred by chance.

For the 1966-67 school year, the mean school tax rate on market value of property for the 222 districts included in the sample was 11.479 mills and ranged from a low of 9.871 mills in the major urban core city category to a high of 13.892 mills in the developing suburb category. The mean school tax rate in each of the two suburb categories again was considerably higher than it was in any of the other five district categories. A one-way analysis of variance indicated that in 1966-67 the differences between district categories were not statistically significant, i.e., they could be expected to occur by chance.

It will be noted from Table 4-10 that the major urban core city category had the highest mean true market value of property per pupil in ADM in both school years and that the mean value increased from $30,999 per pupil in 1961-62 to $32,946 per pupil in 1966-67. The small town category had the lowest mean value of property per pupil in ADM in both years, but showed a gain from $21,648 per pupil in 1961-62 to $26,308 per pupil in 1966-67. The established suburb category ranked second in property value per pupil in ADM and the developing suburb category ranked third in each of the two years.

In retail sales per capita, the small city category ranked first in both 1961-62 and 1966-67 with $1,922 and $2,243 per capita respectively, and was followed by the independent city category and the minor urban core city category in each of the two years. Retail sales per capita were lowest in two suburb categories and in the small town category in each of the two years.

In effective buying income per capita the rankings were practically identical in each of the two years. The two suburb categories ranked either first or second, the major urban core city ranked third, and the small town category ranked last.

Although three measures of the fiscal capacity of school districts have been discussed, it cannot be emphasized too strongly that, as a practical matter, school districts are virtually limited to the property tax. In many states school districts have no authority to tax anything other than property. And in the 22 states which authorized the use of nonproperty taxes by school districts in 1969, the amount of revenue derived from such taxes was generally small and the expense of collecting the taxes was relatively large.

Of even greater concern, however, is the fact that NEFP research indicates that revenue from nonproperty taxes levied by school districts does not have an equalizing effect.[15] In fact, nonproperty taxes are disequalizing in that those districts which have the greatest fiscal capacity as measured by their property tax base almost invariably obtain the largest amount of revenue from nonproperty taxes. Thus, the use of local nonproperty tax levies tends to *increase* the revenue disparities among school districts rather than to equalize their fiscal capacity.

In Table 4-12 are shown the mean amounts of revenue per pupil in ADM received by school districts in each of seven categories during the 1961-62 and 1966-67 school years. It is worth noting that the established suburb, developing suburb, and small town categories fared substantially better than did the four city categories in the amount of revenue per pupil they obtained from state sources during both school years. In mean revenue per pupil from the local property tax the two suburb categories again ranked highest but here the small town category ranked lowest. School districts in the small town category raised only about one-half as much revenue per pupil from the local property tax as did school districts in the established suburb category. Revenue from state sources and revenue from local property tax consti-

TABLE 4-12

SOURCES OF REVENUE PER PUPIL IN AVERAGE DAILY MEMBERSHIP OF SEVEN CATEGORIES OF SCHOOL DISTRICTS IN A RANDOM SAMPLE OF DISTRICTS FROM EIGHT STATES*

1961–62 School Year

Revenue Source	Category A Mean	A S.D.	Category B Mean	B S.D.	Category C Mean	C S.D.	Category D Mean	D S.D.	Category E Mean	E S.D.	Category F Mean	F S.D.	Category G Mean	G S.D.	All Districts Mean	All S.D.
1. State	156	9	177	14	167	9	246	7	240	6	182	11	254	7	208	9
2. Federal	40	11	48	30	73	13	111	12	111	9	72	28	104	8	94	18
3. Other governmental agencies	4	12	6	22	15	24	13	34	5	21	17	39	17	39	12	31
4. Property tax	238	96	207	96	223	103	280	149	252	158	170	100	146	89	215	124
5. Other local taxes	13	24	3	8	2	7	5	16	8	19	4	17	5	13	5	15
6. All other sources	10	7	8	6	12	15	14	15	21	45	15	28	10	12	13	23

1966–67 School Year

Revenue Source	Category A Mean	A S.D.	Category B Mean	B S.D.	Category C Mean	C S.D.	Category D Mean	D S.D.	Category E Mean	E S.D.	Category F Mean	F S.D.	Category G Mean	G S.D.	All Districts Mean	All S.D.
1. State	216	63	239	54	244	50	391	28	374	33	245	50	337	50	301	46
2. Federal	83	36	91	32	141	50	196	21	186	41	149	41	167	40	165	39
3. Other governmental agencies	15	44	11	32	10	19	13	40	4	11	21	51	27	56	15	40
4. Property tax	308	174	264	109	287	135	368	203	342	196	229	125	188	112	282	162
5. Other local taxes	22	42	3	9	3	8	7	21	12	25	7	18	6	13	7	19
6. All other sources	18	17	17	37	8	8	16	10	18	20	11	12	8	12	14	19
	N = 13		N = 34		N = 35		N = 35		N = 34		N = 35		N = 35		N = 221	

Category A = Major Urban Core City
Category B = Minor Urban Core City
Category C = Independent City
Category D = Established Suburb
Category E = Developing Suburb
Category F = Small City
Category G = Small town or agriculture service center

*Florida, Kentucky, New York, North Dakota, Oregon, Texas, Utah and Wisconsin
Source: Richard A. Rossmiller, James A. Hale and Lloyd E. Frohreich, *Fiscal Capacity and Educational Finance*, National Educational Finance Project Special Study No. 10 (Madison, Wis.: The University of Wisconsin, 1970), Tables 3.1 and 3.26.

tuted by far the most important sources of revenue for school districts in all seven categories.

With regard to changes which occurred between 1962 and 1967, it will be noted that revenue from the state displaced revenue from the local property tax as the largest source of revenue for the total sample of districts. The increase in revenue from the state (from $208 to $301 per pupil in ADM) represented an increase of 45 percent during this five-year period. Small towns and suburbs fared best in terms of mean revenue per pupil from state sources. The small town category received the largest amount per pupil from state sources in 1962 ($254) and the two suburb categories received the largest amount per pupil from state sources in 1967 ($391 and $374). In both 1961-62 and 1966-67 the mean revenue per pupil from state sources received by school districts in the major urban core city category was only about one-half the mean revenue per pupil received by school districts in the two suburb categories.

The local property tax ranked first as a source of revenue in 1962 and second as a source of revenue in 1967. Mean revenue from the local property tax for the total sample of districts increased from $215 per pupil to $282 per pupil, an increase of 31 percent during the five-year period. In both years mean revenue per pupil from the local property tax was highest in the two suburb categories and in the major urban core city category. Revenue from federal sources moved from the fifth ranking source in 1962 to third ranking in 1967, increasing by over 400 percent (from $9 per pupil to $46 per pupil). Mean revenue per pupil from federal sources increased seven-fold in both the major urban core city and the small town categories and increased four-fold or more in the two suburb categories.

A number of statistically significant differences were found when the data with regard to sources of revenue of the seven categories of school districts were submitted to multivariate analyses of variance. Specifically, a significant difference was found between school districts in the minor urban core and independent city categories, the independent city and established suburb categories, and the developing suburb and small city categories. However, no significant differences were found between school districts in the major and minor urban core city categories, in the established and developing suburb categories, and in the small city and small town categories. Where a significant difference

118

with regard to sources of revenue did exist, the difference was due primarily to either revenue from state sources or revenue from property taxes.

Education is only one of the many public services financed by units of local government and much has been heard in recent years about the problem of "municipal overburden." Consequently, analyses were made of the combined sources of revenue of school districts, and the municipality and county most closely associated with each school district, for the fiscal years 1962 and 1967. Six revenue sources were identified—state sources, intergovernmental sources, property taxes, other local taxes, other local sources, and utilities—and all revenues received by these three units of local government were combined and expressed on a per capita basis. The results of the analysis are shown in Table 4-13.

During 1962 revenue from property taxes was the leading source of revenue in each of the seven categories, ranging from a high of $124 per capita in the major urban core city category to a low of $83 per capita in the small city category. Revenue from the state was the second ranking revenue source in each category, ranging from a high of $71 per capita in the developing suburb category to a low of $41 per capita in the minor urban core city category. The relative importance of the other four revenue sources differed considerably from one category to another. For example, revenue from other governmental sources ranked sixth in importance in the major urban core city; fifth in the minor urban core city, independent city and small city categories; and third in the established suburb, developing suburb, and small town categories.

During 1967 revenue from property taxes again was the most important revenue source in each category, and revenue from the state again ranked second in importance in each category. Mean revenue from property taxes ranged from high of $178 per capita in the developing suburb category to a low of $106 per capita in the small city category. Mean revenue for the state ranged from a high of $110 per capita in the developing suburb category to a low of $55 per capita in the minor urban core city category.

No change occurred between 1962 and 1967 in the relative importance of the two major revenue sources—revenue from property taxes and revenue from the state. A substantial up-

TABLE 4-13

SOURCES OF PER CAPITA REVENUE OF A RANDOM SAMPLE OF SEVEN CATEGORIES OF SCHOOL DISTRICTS AND THE MUNICIPALITY AND COUNTY ASSOCIATED WITH EACH SCHOOL DISTRICT, 1961–62 AND 1966–67

1961–62

Revenue Source	Category A Mean	S.D.	Category B Mean	S.D.	Category C Mean	S.D.	Category D Mean	S.D.	Category E Mean	S.D.	Category F Mean	S.D.	Category G Mean	S.D.
1. State	44	27	41	20	51	24	58	24	71	26	43	18	64	25
2. Intergovernmental	18	17	21	24	26	20	31	50	30	51	25	25	29	25
3. Property taxes	124	55	106	79	114	51	117	60	124	55	83	42	91	77
4. Other local taxes	19	21	9	11	10	10	4	5	5	5	6	8	7	8
5. Other local sources	33	12	28	18	35	19	19	11	20	16	29	22	24	10
6. Utilities	23	21	32	45	35	34	14	16	12	8	40	53	15	5

1966–67

Revenue Source	Category A Mean	S.D.	Category B Mean	S.D.	Category C Mean	S.D.	Category D Mean	S.D.	Category E Mean	S.D.	Category F Mean	S.D.	Category G Mean	S.D.
1. State	72	71	55	34	74	38	89	36	110	49	56	30	86	42
2. Intergovernmental	47	44	36	34	43	25	39	20	46	35	41	34	51	30
3. Property taxes	152	81	127	95	140	65	154	75	178	110	106	60	126	110
4. Other local taxes	25	31	14	24	12	13	4	5	7	7	9	12	8	10
5. Other local sources	47	23	41	25	46	24	30	18	27	10	32	16	35	15
6. Utilities	28	24	41	58	45	48	19	21	18	14	46	58	28	13

NOTE: Expenditure for education includes capital outlay reported by school district; expenditure for all municipal and county functions are exclusive of capital outlay.

Category A = Major Urban Core City
Category B = Minor Urban Core City
Category C = Independent City
Category D = Established Suburb
Category E = Developing Suburb
Category F = Small City
Category G = Small Town

Source: Richard R. Rossmiller, James A. Hale and Lloyd E. Frohreich, *Fiscal Capacity and Educational Finance*, National Educational Finance Project Special Study No. 10 (Madison, Wis.: The University of Wisconsin, 1970), Tables 6.1 and 6.15.

ward change did occur, however, in the *amount* of revenue per capita obtained from each source. Revenue from other governmental sources became a more important source of revenue in 1967, especially in the major urban core city category. The relative importance of the other three revenue sources changed relatively little between 1962 and 1967, although the amount of revenue per capita obtained from each of them did increase rather substantially.

When the data regarding the combined sources of revenue of school districts, municipalities and counties were subjected to multivariate analyses of variance, the only instance in which a statistically significant difference in sources of revenue was not found was the comparison involving the established and the developing suburb categories. Revenue from state sources was the variable which most frequently contributed to the variation between the categories.

A similar analysis of purposes of expenditure by school districts and the municipality and county most closely associated with each school district revealed that expenditure for education was the largest component of expenditures in each of the seven categories in both 1962 and 1967. Mean per capita expenditures for such purposes as sewerage and welfare were generally quite similar in each category. Mean expenditure per capita for police protection was highest in the three large city categories, while mean expenditure per capita for highways was considerably higher in the suburb, small city and small town categories.

With regard to municipal overburden, it was found that the cities were spending somewhat more per capita for police and fire protection, parks, and housing and urban renewal than were the suburbs and small cities, but were spending somewhat less per capita for highways and education. No persuasive evidence of the existence of a general problem of "municipal overburden" was uncovered. Similarly, the large cities did not appear to have less fiscal capacity than the other categories, although their relative advantage in per capita fiscal capacity declined between 1962 and 1967.

The results of the NEFP studies suggest that if measures related to the market value of property per pupil in ADM are regarded as the proper criteria for judging a school district's fiscal capacity to support education, one is tempted to conclude that

121

a fair amount of equity does exist between various categories of school districts, at least if the sample of school districts employed in the study is representative of the national picture. Rossmiller and his colleagues found no significant variation between the seven categories of school districts they studied when fiscal capacity was measured by the market value of property per pupil in average daily membership. Similarly, the variance in property tax rates between the categories was barely significant in 1962 and was not significant in 1967. In both 1962 and 1967, mean property tax rates were surprisingly similar in all district categories except the established suburb and the developing suburb, where they were about two mills higher than the next highest category. Revenue from property taxes per pupil in ADM was not a major contributor to the variations between the categories of school districts except in the comparison of school districts in the developing suburb category with those in the small city category. Revenue per capita from property taxes varied significantly only in the comparison of the independent city category with the established suburb category. When all sources of revenue of school districts, municipalities, and counties were combined and analyzed, revenue from property taxes varied significantly only in the comparison of the developing suburb and the small city categories. Thus, extraordinary fiscal inequities were not found between the categories of school districts compared if market value of property, property tax rates, or revenue from property taxes are used as criteria for determining whether or not equity in fiscal capacity and effort exists.

However, if indices of consumption and income—such as retail sales or effective buying income—are applied as the criteria for judging fiscal equity, then it is noteworthy that marked differences were found between several of the categories of school districts with regard to both their fiscal capacity and their sources of revenue. Effective buying income, expressed on either a per capita or a per household basis, was the major source of variation between the categories of school districts. Retail sales per capita also was an important source of variation between categories in several instances. Revenue from state sources was a major contributor to the variation between the school district categories as well as to the variation between categories in the analyses based on the combined sources of revenue of school districts, municipalities, and counties.

122

Implications

A number of studies have established beyond dispute the causes of differences in fiscal capacity among the school districts of a state. Property, income and retail sales tend to be distributed somewhat unevenly within a state and, as we have noted, income and sales tend to be distributed more unevenly than does property. If one accepts the argument that all taxes ultimately must be paid from income, then heavy reliance on property taxes levied by local school districts to finance education inevitably will result in inequities in the fiscal capacity and effort of such districts because, as we have seen, there is not a close relationship between fiscal capacity as measured by property value per pupil in daily membership and fiscal capacity as measured by income per capita or per household.

The fact that education is a state function has been so well established by the courts that it is beyond argument. The state creates local school districts and delegates to them authority to operate educational programs and to levy taxes for the support of these programs. The delegation of taxing authority to smaller units of government almost inevitably will result in creating differences in fiscal capacity among such units of government. In general, the smaller the taxing units and the greater the taxing authority delegated to them, the more likely it is that variations in fiscal capacity will occur among such units.

As evidenced by the data presented in the studies cited in this chapter, the provision of some state grants-in-aid to local school districts (and other units of local government) may tend to perpetuate, or even aggravate, the existing inequities. A state aid system which recognizes only those variations in fiscal capacity which arise from the distribution of property within a state and ignores the variations in fiscal capacity which arise from the distribution of income within a state has virtually guaranteed the continuance of inequities in fiscal capacity and tax effort at the local level.

The states must recognize that they created local school districts and delegated to them taxing authority. Thus, the state is directly responsible for the inequities in fiscal capacity which exist among school districts. Furthermore, the state has it within its power to remove such inequities. The state created local school districts and it has full power to reorganize them in a manner which will mitigate or alleviate fiscal inequities. The state granted school districts taxing authority and this too can be modified. Even if a state chooses to retain its existing organizational arrangements for education, the state can reduce or remove inequities in fiscal capacity and effort among school districts by distributing state school aids in a manner which will offset the inequities which arise because of the existing organizational structure and taxing authority.

The obvious consequence of permitting the continued existence of marked disparities in fiscal capacity and effort among the school districts of a state is the continued existence of disparities in educational opportunity among districts. A district of limited fiscal capacity can match the educational programs provided by its more fortunate neighbors only if its citizens are willing to tax themselves at an extraordinarily high rate. Even then, such a district will do well to approach the state average. This situation is intolerable if one believes in equality of educational opportunity and if one recognizes the legal fact that education is, indeed, a state function. Only by tapping the total fiscal capacity of the state with a tax structure and allocation plan which integrates state and local efforts in a manner which assures to all school districts of the state reasonable equality of access to the total financial resources of the state can equity in fiscal capacity and effort for the support of education be attained.

Inequities in fiscal capacity and effort among the school districts of a state are a problem which can be solved by that state. However, inequities in fiscal capacity and effort among the states will require action by a larger taxing jurisdiction, for example, the federal government, if such disparities are to be reduced or eliminated.

FOOTNOTES

1. Dick Netzer, *Economics of the Property Tax* (Washington, D.C.: Brookings, 1966), Chapter III.

2. *Ibid.*, p. 189.

3. Advisory Commission on Intergovernmental Relations, *State and Local Finances* (Washington, D. C.: GPO, 1969), p. 64.

4. Advisory Commission on Intergovernmental Relations, *State and Local Finances and Suggested Legislation* (Washington, D. C.: GPO, 1970), pp. 100-103.

5. *Ibid.*, p. 6.

6. Roe L. Johns and Oscar A. Hamilton, Jr., "Ability and Effort of the

States to Support the Public Schools," (Gainesville, Fla.: National Educational Finance Project, 1970), 15pp. (Mimeo)

7. John Due, "Alternative Tax Sources for Education," in *Economic Factors Affecting the Financing of Education*, eds. R. L. Johns, et al. (Gainesville, Florida: National Educational Finance Project, 1970), pp. 317-318.

8. *Ibid.*, pp. 307-308.

9. Advisory Commission on Intergovernmental Relations, *Measures of State and Local Fiscal Capacity and Tax Effort* (Washington, D. C., GPO, 1962).

10. Advisory Commission on Intergovernmental Relations, *Measuring the Fiscal Capacity and Effort of State and Local Areas* (Washington, D. C.: GPO, 1971).

11. *Ibid.*, p. 7.

12. *Ibid.*, pp. 10-20.

13. *Ibid.*, p. 24.

14. Richard A. Rossmiller, James A. Hale and Lloyd E. Frohreich, *Fiscal Capacity and Educational Finance: Variations Among States, School Districts and Municipalities*, NEFP Special Study No. 10 (Madison, Wis.: Department of Educational Administration, the University of Wisconsin, 1970).

15. Duane O. Moore, "Local Nonproperty Taxes for Schools", in *Status and Impact of Educational Finance Programs*, eds. R. L. Johns, Kern Alexander and Dewey H. Stollar (Gainesville, Fla.: National Educational Finance Project, 1971), pp. 209-221.

125

CHAPTER 5

Alternative Tax Sources For Education

Almost certainly additional funds will be required for the financing of education in the coming decade. At the same time education must compete with other growing activities of government as, for example, control of air and water pollution and elimination of poverty, which are likely to receive high priority. It is the purpose of this chapter to consider various alternative sources for additional funds and possible improvement in present sources that will make them more acceptable.

While consideration will be given to the relative effectiveness of different taxes at various levels of government, the chapter will not be concerned specifically with the appropriate relative role of various levels of government in financing education, in view of the coverage of this question in another chapter.

SUMMARY OF CRITERIA FOR EVALUATION OF TAXES

Several criteria have come to be generally accepted for use in evaluating tax structures. These criteria are not derived by scientific analysis, but merely reflect widespread popular attitudes, in conformity with generally accepted objectives of contemporary society. While consensus on the criteria is strong, interpretations of their meaning in particular circumstances vary widely.

Economic Distortions

A major criterion is the establishment of tax structures in such a fashion as to minimize distorting effects upon the functioning of the economy—that is, effects that cause persons to alter economic behavior in a fashion contrary to the objectives of the society. Such alterations in behavior result in "excess burdens"—in the sense of reduced real income of society not offset by governmental output.

Distortions take several forms. Taxes may reduce the output of some commodities relative to others and cause a loss in satisfaction on the part of those persons with high preferences for the goods whose relative output is reduced. Deliberate changes, sought, for example because excessive use of the product (e.g., liquor) causes losses for society, may be defended. It is the unintended type of change that reduces economic well being of the society. Secondly, taxes may interfere with efficiency in the conduct of production and physical distribution of goods, by altering decisions about the selection of methods of organization and operation utilized. If taxes cause a firm to use a method of production other than the most efficient, output from given resources is reduced below the potential level and society suffers a loss; total real income is less than the potential.

A specific type of distortion important in the sphere of state and local taxation involves decisions relative to location. Tax differentials among areas may cause firms to select locations other than those that are optimal from the standpoint of efficiency.

A further type of distortion is interference, in an undesired fashion, with decisions about work; taxes may cause some persons to drop out of the labor market or seek to work fewer hours. Similar considerations apply to owners of other resources used in production and particularly the willingness to undertake risk. If taxes reduce the willingness of persons to work, to accept more responsible positions, to gain education necessary for professional work, or take risk, society suffers a loss in the form of reduced output.

Finally, distortions that reduce the rate of economic growth are regarded as objectionable. Not only do distortions reduce the extent to which the economy attains the goals of society, but they also reduce governmental revenue from a given tax structure and require higher overall tax rates. Any tax that causes

persons to change behavior to escape it will produce less revenue
than could be obtained from the given tax rates if behavior
were not altered.

Equity

Taxes are compulsory payments imposed upon individuals by
government to distribute the costs of governmental activities
among the various members of society. The rule that governmental costs be distributed in a fashion regarded by contemporary society as equitable is generally accepted. What constitutes equity, however, is strictly a value judgment and there
are wide differences of opinion. Usually equity is considered to
require:

a. Equal treatment of equals. Persons regarded as being in
the same relevant circumstances should be taxed the same
amount.
b. Distribution of the overall tax burden on the basis of ability to pay, as measured by income, by wealth, by consumption.
c. Exclusion from tax of persons in the lowest income
groups, on the grounds that they have no taxpaying capacity.
d. A progressive overall distribution of tax relative to income, on the basis that tax capacity rises more rapidly than
income. This requirement is less generally accepted than the
others. There is general agreement that the structure should
be at least proportional to income.

Unless a tax structure meets to an acceptable degree the
current attitudes on equity, it will not attain general tolerance.
If many persons regard a particular tax as inequitable, there
will be continuous complaint and political pressure to modify
the structure.

Compliance and Administration

Attainment of the objectives of society requires that taxes
be collectable to a high degree of effectiveness with minimum
real costs (money and nuisance) to the taxpayers and reasonable
cost to the government for collection. Inability to enforce a tax
effectively at tolerable costs will cause loss of both revenue and
equity. If some persons are meeting their liabilities while others

128

are not, discrimination results and economic distortion will arise from the efforts of others to escape tax. Easy compliance is important if taxpayers are to accept the tax and to meet their obligations, with minimum use of resources for the purpose.

Revenue Elasticity

Governmental expenditures tend to rise at least in proportion to national income even if programs are not increased. If tax revenues do not keep pace at given tax rates, constant rate changes are required. Experience suggests that legislative bodies are slow to make these changes and the changes may have disruptive effects on the economy. As a consequence revenues tend to lag behind expenditures.

These criteria serve as the basis for evaluation of the various major sources for the financing of education.

THE PROPERTY TAX

The traditional support for the financing of education and other local government activities in the United States has been the property tax. In the 1969 fiscal year, local governments received about $30 billion or 86 percent of their tax revenue from the property tax despite expansion of local nonproperty taxes in recent years, and the school districts received 99 percent of their tax revenue from this source. Property tax yields expressed as a percentage of GNP have remained roughly constant in the last decade at about 3.4 percent. Current percentages are about the same as they were throughout the period 1870-1914.[1]

The property tax applies to a variety of types of property, but to an increasing extent to real property.[2] Currently, about 44 percent of the tax is collected from households in the form of tax on real property and some personal property, about 43 percent from nonfarm business property, about 9 percent from farm property, and the remainder from miscellaneous types.[3] The portion on business property is in part shifted forward . through price increases to the consumers of the products, and a portion of the tax on farm property may be shifted in the same fashion.

General Evaluation

The dominance of the property tax in local finance is a

product primarily of the limited potential of other local tax revenues. School districts usually have no other taxing powers and those of other local units are severely limited. As subsequently explained, even if the local governments had broader powers, there would be significant administrative and economic obstacles to collecting large sums of money from these other sources. Most property cannot escape from local jurisdictions and can be discovered by local authorities—to a greater extent than other tax bases. In part, admittedly, the dominance of the property tax is a matter of tradition rather than necessity. Local governments were given the power to levy the tax when income and sales taxes were virtually unknown. They came to rely highly on them; other levels of government came to dominate sales and income tax fields.

In addition to revenue productivity, there are certain specific advantages to the property tax. Some local government expenditures directly benefit property owners and thus the taxes are regarded in part as a form of user charge. This reasoning, however, does not apply to education. A portion of the tax rests upon land, in a sense an ideal base for taxation since the supply is fixed and since landowners benefit from economic growth whether they make a contribution to it or not. A large portion of the tax rests upon business property. Business taxation is always politically popular, even if it has little support on more rational grounds. This is particularly true with large corporate holdings whose stockholders live outside the taxing jurisdiction. Especially in earlier years of the country's development, ownership or rental of expensive homes was a reasonably good measure of taxpaying ability not then reached directly by income taxation.

The property tax, however, suffers from several inherent limitations which restrict its ability to finance additional expenditures for education or other local activities. These limitations are reflected in part in political resistance to further property tax increases. Even without this political reaction, there are significant economic and equity considerations that dictate restrictions on increases in the tax.

Economic Effects

It is difficult to quantify the economic effects of the property tax. But studies suggest three areas in which there is almost certain to be some adverse effects, one of which is related to the most pressing current economic and social problems of the nation. In the first place, the tax constitutes a very heavy "excise" tax on housing. Nearly half of the tax rests directly upon housing facilities and is for the most part borne by those owning or renting the facilities. While the precise elasticity of demand for housing is not known, it is certainly not zero and the property tax inevitably creates excess burden by deterring expenditures on improving housing. From the viewpoint of social policy, it may be argued that this is a particularly undesirable consequence: that modern society is relatively short of quality housing compared to other goods.

Much more serious—given the concerns of contemporary society—is the adverse effect the property tax has upon rehabilitation of the deteriorating central city portions of metropolitan areas. Part of the impact is direct and immediate. If property is improved by replacing slum dwellings or old store buildings by modern facilities, the property tax may rise so drastically as to render the change unprofitable. But also important is the common tax differential pattern in metropolitan areas: the tax rates in the central city are often higher than those in portions of the surrounding areas.[4] Thus investors have incentive to locate outside the central city—whether for apartment or office buildings, industrial or other developments— instead of in the older areas. Therefore the depressed areas become more depressed.

Apart from the central city, property tax differentials can affect other location decisions within metropolitan areas— although they are unlikely to have much effect on decisions among widely dispersed locations.[5] Since other locational factors may be comparable within a metropolitan area, property tax rate differentials may be the key element in the decision. Particularly attractive are "industrial enclaves"—cities with a large industrial property base and few people to serve and few children to educate. Vernon in Los Angeles county and Emeryville in the San Francisco-Oakland area are classic examples.

Finally, the property tax places a relatively heavier burden, per dollar of sales, on industries that use disproportionate amounts of real property relative to total sales. To the extent that the tax reflects higher costs of local government for which the particular industries are responsible (e.g., fire protection) the differential burden may be regarded as warranted. But for

131

financing education the differential is not acceptable, relative to most efficient use of resources. Netzer in his recent study of the property tax concludes that of all industries the railroads are most seriously affected by the property tax because their ability to compete with motor transport, not subject to equivalent burdens, is reduced.[6]

Equity

On several counts the property tax fails to meet accepted standards of equity:

1. *Unequal Treatment of Equals.* Because of uneven assessment, lack of uniformity of valuation results in different tax burdens on persons owning equivalent amounts of property. Innumerable studies have shown the dispersion in assessments, even when efforts are made by assessors to do a careful job.[7] The difficulty is in part inherent in the tax. Other levies are imposed on flows—on income or sales. Since the property tax is imposed on the value as of a particular time, constructive valuation is required. This is not difficult with some property but is very troublesome with others. In addition, as is well known, the approach to assessment has often been unscientific. This defect can be corrected, but the inherent difficulty of the task will remain.

2. *Inequity from Varying Ratios of Taxable Property to Total Wealth and Total Income.* Income is typically regarded as the best measure of taxable capacity, and total net wealth as a secondary acceptable measure. But the property tax is not closely correlated with either. The portion of the property tax on homes distributes the tax burden on the basis of the gross value of one particular kind of property. Since there is a wide dispersion in ratios of such property to income or net wealth, there is substantial departure from accepted criteria of equity. Specifically, the tax places a disproportionate burden on persons owning their homes but having little current income, and on those having relatively high portions of their total wealth in taxable form. The effect is a severe burden on older persons owning their homes, on families with incomes temporarily reduced, and on persons who prefer to spend relatively high percentages of their incomes on housing.

Much of the remainder of the tax has direct impact on business property. There will be a tendency for this to shift forward to the consumers of the products—but in uneven fashion since the ratio of tax to selling prices will vary. Any firm having high property tax relative to sales volume will find complete shifting impossible and the owners will bear a portion of the cost for a time. Farmers selling in perfectly competitive markets will be unable to shift until market supply falls in response to the higher cost and presumably cannot shift tax on land at all. The distributional pattern of the shifted portion is similar to that of a sales tax, but with uneven burden on various goods arising from the varying ratios of real property to sales in different lines of production. Thus persons with relatively strong preferences for high-tax goods will bear disproportionate amounts of the overall tax burden.

3. *Regressive Distribution of Burden.* The property tax is usually characterized as highly regressive relative to income. The question has been studied extensively in recent years and the evidence is by no means clear cut.[8] Part of the regressivity has been attributed to the tendency to assess less valuable property closer to full value than more valuable property. On this question the evidence is conflicting. The tendency appears in some areas but not in others.[9] The second source is the tendency of housing expenditures to rise less rapidly than income. Because of this tendency, the lowest income groups, homeowners or tenants, pay much more in property taxes as a percentage of income than do persons in the highest income groups.[10] But, apart from the lowest groups, the tendency is by no means general. Nevertheless the heavy absolute burden on the lowest income groups is a significant limitation to the tax on equity grounds—in addition to the wide dispersion noted in the preceding section.

Revenue Elasticity

The elasticity of property tax revenue at a given tax rate is dependent upon (1) the relationship of increases in property values to increases in national income, and (2) the relationship of changes in assessed values to changes in sales values. The former relationship is undoubtedly high although uneven. The behavior of assessed valuation is controlled by the reassessment patterns. Unlike other taxes, the base does not rise automatically with expansion of business activity, since increase depends

133

upon action by assessors. The time lag is often very substantial, particularly in states in which actual reappraisal takes place at intervals as long as 10 years or more. The behavior of actual property tax yields in recent years relative to national income has not been bad; Netzer concludes that a .8 relationship is a reasonable estimate.[11] That is, if national income rises 1 percent, property tax revenues rise .8 percent. But this record is not nearly as good as that of other major taxes, and in some areas the record has been poor.

Reforms

Endless suggestions for changes in the property tax have been made. Further improvements in administration—particularly in the use of professional techniques of assessment—can reduce inequity and increase potential yield. More far reaching changes, such as exemption of property of low income groups and of various types of new construction involving rehabilitation or urban areas, can make the tax somewhat more tolerable. But these changes reduce the revenue obtainable. The property tax is certain to continue to play a major role in the financing of education. But it does not offer potentialities for significant increases in revenue. The objectionable features are sufficiently serious that the case for increased use is difficult to defend. The objections voiced by many groups make continued increases progressively more difficult politically. Other fields of taxation offer much greater potentiality for additional revenue for education.

THE SALES TAX

While sales taxes are not used directly by school districts, with minor exceptions, the sales tax has indirectly become a major source of funds for the financing of education through state grants to school districts and offers potential for still greater support.

Present Use

As of July 1, 1970, the sales tax is employed by 45 states containing 98 percent of the population of the United States and is used extensively by the local governments in a forty-sixth, Alaska (Table 5-1). In only four states, Montana, New Hamp-

134

TABLE 5-1
STATE SALES TAXATION, JULY 1, 1970

State	State Sales Tax Rate (%)	Sales Tax Revenue as % of Total State Tax Revenue, 1969	Sales Tax Revenue as % of Personal Income, 1969	Food exemption
Alabama	4	34.3	2.4	
Arizona	3	35.9	2.9	
Arkansas	3	32.7	2.2	
California	4	32.1	2.2	X
Colorado	3	30.2	1.8	
Connecticut	5	32.2	1.4	X
Florida	4	45.2	2.9	X
Georgia	3	37.2	2.4	
Hawaii	4	47.4	5.1	
Idaho	3	25.5	2.0	
Illinois	4	51.4	2.3	
Indiana	2	22.6	1.2	
Iowa	3	35.1	2.3	
Kansas	3	35.7	1.8	
Kentucky	5	37.8	2.9	
Louisiana	2	20.6	1.6	
Maine	5	44.5	2.6	X
Maryland	4	17.7	1.2	X
Massachusetts	3	12.8	.8	X
Michigan	4	35.3	2.5	
Minnesota	3	19.0	1.4	X
Mississippi	5	43.3	3.6	
Missouri	3	41.6	2.0	
Nebraska	2.5	32.4	1.5	
Nevada	3	35.2	2.5	
New Jersey	5	22.4	1.0	X
New Mexico	4	34.8	3.1	
New York	3	13.1	.9	X
North Carolina	3	23.7	1.8	
North Dakota	4	33.8	2.1	
Ohio	4	40.3	1.7	X
Oklahoma	2	18.4	1.2	
Pennsylvania	6	39.3	2.2	X
Rhode Island	5	36.3	2.2	X
South Carolina	4	29.6	2.2	
South Dakota	4	37.8	1.8	
Tennessee	3	35.4	2.2	
Texas	3.25	25.8	1.3	X
Utah	4	32.1	2.3	
Vermont[1]	3	------	----	X
Virginia	3	20.0	1.3	
Washington[1]	4.5	43.2	3.5	
West Virginia[2]	3	19.5	1.5	
Wisconsin	4	10.7	.8	X
Wyoming	3	37.9	3.0	

[1]Not in operation 1969.
[2]Excluding gross receipts tax.
Source of revenue data: U.S. Bureau of the Census, *State Tax Collections in 1969.*

135

shire, Delaware, and Oregon, three of which have population less than a million, is the sales tax not employed. The sales tax yields about 30 percent of total state tax reveune and about 4 percent of local government tax revenue (1969 fiscal year). The states collected $12.3 billion from sales taxes in 1969, the local governments $1.2 billion.

In that year the sales tax yielded over half the tax revenue of Illinois,[12] and, including gross receipts taxes, of Washington and West Virginia. In eight states the yield exceeded 40 percent of state tax revenue. On the other hand, the tax yielded less than 15 percent in three (Massachusetts, New York, and Wisconsin). The tax collections ranged downward from 5.1 percent of total personal income in Hawaii to .8 percent in Wisconsin.

Summarization of the use of the tax at the local level, usually city and/or county, is more difficult. Roughly, the picture is as follows (1970):

1. In seven states the municipal tax is universal or almost so (in terms of population) and is state collected: California, Illinois, Oklahoma, Tennessee, Texas, Utah, and Virginia. Most of these use 1 percent rates. A universal mandatory county tax in Nevada is regarded as a state levy.

2. In Alaska, with no state levy, the tax is widely used at the local level, with rates as high as 5 percent. In five states local sales taxes are widespread but less universal, with purely local collection (Arizona, Louisiana), partly state, partly local (Alabama, Colorado), or, in one (New York) entirely state. The rates are less uniform; figures range from 1 percent to 3 percent.

3. Limited use of the tax is made in ten states, in a few of these in only one local jurisdiction. Collection may be state (Arkansas, Missouri, Nevada, New Mexico, North Carolina, Nebraska, Ohio, South Dakota, Washington) or local (Minnesota). The local taxes differ in one very important respect. In some states, such as Illinois, liability for tax depends upon location of the vendor; in others liability is determined by place of delivery and thus typically place of residence on delivery sales.

The median state sales tax rate is 3 percent with range from 2 percent in three states to 6 percent in Pennsylvania. The median will almost certainly become 4 percent in the next few years. Fifteen states have figures of 4 or 5 percent and six have 5 percent figures. If the maximum local rates are added to the state rates, the range is changed only slightly (high of 6.5 per-

136

cent) but the median is now 4 percent with 6 percent in three and 5 percent in ten. The thirteen states with rates of 5 percent to 6 percent contain 40 percent of the population of the country.

The exemptions vary somewhat among the states. Fifteen states, primarily ones introducing the tax since 1948, exempt all food, and North Dakota exempts limited categories. Many exempt prescription drugs. Six states provide credit against income tax liability for sales tax paid on prescribed minimum necessary expenditures, and a seventh (Idaho) does to a restricted extent.

Evaluation—Equity

Despite the importance that sales taxes now play in state-local tax structures, virtually never have they been introduced as measures to reform the structures; they have been established as emergency financial measures, to meet expenditure needs in the face of lagging yields from other taxes. The reluctance of legislators to enact them or voters to approve them, coupled with their tendency to remain once they have been introduced, suggest that there are significant arguments on both sides.

Sales taxes may meet equity requirements more satisfactorily then property taxes. Under the assumption that they are shifted forward, they are distributed in relation to consumer spending on taxed goods, rather than to outlay on housing, and thus on a much broader and presumably more equitable base. Nevertheless, most of the opposition to them has been based on equity grounds. First, if they apply to all goods they place a substantial absolute burden on the lowest income groups, ones that may be considered to have no tax capacity. Second, the overall distribution of burden tends to be regressive relative to income, if all goods are taxed. This has been demonstrated empirically a number of times.[13] Expenditures on nontaxable services and savings tend to rise as a percentage of income as income rises, and therefore expenditures on taxable goods tend to fall. Third, the tax affects various families in a somewhat haphazard way, placing a heavier burden on those families whose circumstances (such as number of children) compel them to spend relatively high percentages of their incomes. Likewise, no adjustment of tax burden on the basis of circumstances affecting taxpaying ability (e.g., heavy medical expenses) is possible.

The first two basic defects, and, in large measure, the third as well, can be eliminated much more easily than equivalent ones of the property tax. One alternative, the most widely used, is the exemption of food from the base of the sales tax. Much of the burden (but not all) is removed from the lowest income groups, which concentrate their expenditures very heavily for food, and the tax is, according to various empirical studies, made more or less proportional instead of regressive.[14] Much of the penalty on large families is removed. Food exemption, however, suffers from several defects, and an alternative approach, the provision of a credit against income tax liability for sales tax paid on minimum necessary purchases, is a much more satisfactory solution, as discussed below.

With this type of adjustment, the sales tax may be regarded as reasonably in accord with usually accepted standards of equity. It cannot effectively be made progressive, however. Accordingly, under the assumption that progression is desired in the tax structure as a whole, the role of the sales tax must be restricted relative to that of income taxation.

Economic Distortions

The most significant potential distortions of state and local sales taxes are those upon location, especially of retailing. With rates of any magnitude, shoppers have an incentive to shop in a low tax area, and shopping centers and other large store developments have incentive to locate in the low tax areas. How important these effects are is difficult to assess. Since stores must be located close to their customers, the effect is only on the precise site within a metropolitan area, and local sales taxes therefore offer much greater potential hazard than do state sales taxes. The danger from the state levies has become less serious as the levies have spread, since now the opportunity to buy tax free over-the-counter is limited to a very few areas. With many purchases it is not worthwhile to have the goods shipped across a state line to escape tax.

Empirical studies in recent years have concluded that there are measurable effects on sales when a jurisdiction using a sales tax has populated areas close to a border of a jurisdiction not using the tax. Harry McAllister discovered significant effects on sales in border cities in Washington state,[15] and W. Hamovitch concluded that New York City retailers lost substantial revenue to nearby states when the latter did not have sales taxes.[16] On the other hand he concluded that Alabama, with little of its population located close to borders and with taxes in the neighboring states, suffered little loss. An econometric study by John Mikesell concluded that municipal sales taxes cause significant loss of sales to nontax areas.[17] On the whole the dangers of locational influences are most significant for local sales taxes that are not uniform throughout a trading area.

A second type of distortion with a retail sales tax arises from the application of the tax to some producers goods, such as industrial machinery and equipment, building materials, office supplies, fuel, etc. A few states make a strong effort to exclude major classes of producers goods, but most do not, except for sales for resale, including goods becoming physical ingredients of articles produced for sale. Taxation of producers goods may affect location decisions of business firms and may affect choice of methods of production, since some methods will result in greater tax burden than others. As sales taxes increase in rate, exclusion of producers goods becomes increasingly important but this type of change in the tax structure has little political appeal and reduces revenue. Administrative considerations make complete exclusion of all producers goods difficult, since all purchases for business use cannot be identified at time of sales, but major classes can be excluded from tax.

A third type of distortion arises from nonuniform coverage. If some goods are exempted, or as is customary, few services are taxed, consumers are encouraged to buy more of the exempt goods and fewer taxable goods, thus distorting choice away from the optimum and potentially producing excess burden. Taxation of producers goods has some effect of this type also, since this portion of the tax will be more significant relative to final selling prices for some consumer goods than for others.

Despite these effects the overall distorting effects of a sales tax appear to be minor compared to those of property taxes, and they can be minimized by (1) avoiding consumer goods exemptions except when there is strong justification, (2) excluding major categories of producers goods from tax, and (3) avoiding geographic rate differentials within metropolitan areas.

Administration and Compliance

The sales tax is basically an easier tax to operate than a property tax since no constructive valuations are needed (with minor exceptions), the tax rate being applied to actual sales figures. So long as the tax structure is kept simple, the task of the retailer is not a difficult one, requiring merely the addition of the tax at the cash register and determination of tax liability each month by applying the tax rate to the figure of taxable sales. An audit program involving examination of vendors' accounts is necessary, but the cost of audit is seldom in excess of 1 percent of revenue gained from the tax. The task of the retailer is made unnecessarily difficult in some states by the nature of the tax. A number of exemptions, with fine lines of distinction between taxable and exempt goods, is perhaps the major source of difficulty. Incorrect application of tax by clerks results, and the task of record keeping is complicated, with a new avenue opened for evasion. Audit is made more difficult and costly. Minor provisions of the acts sometimes cause retailers unnecessary headaches, such as the rule that the retailer pay the state the exact sum collected in tax from customers.

The chief administrative difficulty arises with interstate sales. A state cannot tax sales made for delivery outside the state; the state of the purchaser can apply the use tax but cannot effectively reach the purchaser except on automobiles and a few other goods. Only by requiring the out-of-state vendor to collect and remit tax can the states be assured of their revenue. But the courts have restricted the powers of the states to enforce collection from out-of-state vendors, and proposed Federal legislation would restrict the powers still more drastically. Even if the states had the power, they would not be able to enforce tax effectively against out-of-state firms selling only by mail to numerous customers in the state.

Serious complications are created for compliance and enforcement when local sales taxes are applied on the basis of location of the purchaser, with local use taxes imposed on purchases made in other local jurisdictions in the state. The vendor must collect tax on the basis of place of delivery, the task of applying and reporting tax is greatly complicated, and, with local collection, many local units are not actually able to enforce tax against outside vendors selling into the area. Record keeping and audit are greatly complicated. When local sales taxes are locally collected, as in a few states, complications for the vendor are multiplied still further, particularly if the bases of the tax are different. Unnecessary nuisance is created through the need for filing more than one tax return. Audit by the local govern-

140

ments—if any—duplicates state audit. Probably no greater mistake was ever made by the states in the tax field than allowing local governments to impose and collect their own sales taxes, with liability dependent upon place of delivery and a tax base different from that of the state levy.

Revenue Elasticity

While presumably consumption of taxable goods rises less rapidly than income, the differential does not appear to be great. Estimates of revenue elasticity of the tax range from .9 to 1.05.[18]

Additional Revenue from the Sales Tax

There are several ways in which the states can gain additional revenue for education from the sales tax:

1. *Introduction of the Tax in the Five States Not Using It.* This change has little impact on the national picture, but is of great importance for the five states. Introduction in Alaska, except to replace the present local taxes by a simpler statewide tax, is less important, as substantial revenues are already being obtained from the tax at the local level.

2. *Rate Increases.* The experience of states with 5 percent rates suggests that this figure causes no measurable economic disturbances (except minor ones arising out of interstate complications), and with proper adjustment of the tax causes no serious inequity. Table 5-2 indicates the additional revenue available to the states from raising the state rate to 5 percent.

Increasing the sales tax rate to 5 percent in all states would increase the yield from the tax by about $6.4 billion a year, with the assumption that sales volumes are relatively insensitive to increase in the sales tax rate. Each additional 1 percent increase would bring in an additional $3.7 billion, or, with the broader base noted below, $4.5 billion— again with the given assumption about demand elasticity. Figures by state are given in Table 5-2 and in summary fashion in Table 5-3. A state rate of 5 percent would run the combined state-local rate above 5 percent in the states in which local taxes are imposed, to a figure of 8 percent in some jurisdictions. If all local sales taxes were eliminated when the state rate was raised to 5 percent, the net gain would be about $5.1 billion instead of $6.4 billion. These are 1969 figures; for 1971, the estimates should be increased by at least 10 percent.

TABLE 5-2
PRESENT AND POTENTIAL SALES TAX REVENUES, BY STATE

	Tax Rate 1969	Revenue, 1969	Per 1% of Tax Rate Present Taxes[1]	Additional Revenue			
				From Raising Rates to 5%	From Including Consumer Services at 5% Rate	From Eliminating Consumer Exemptions	Per 1% of Tax With Broader Base
Alabama	4	197	49	50	25		54
Alaska	—	0	7	35	4		8
Arizona	3	148	49	100	25		54
Arkansas	3	104	35	70	17		38
California	4	1684	421	421	210	520	567
Colorado	3	123	41	82	20		45
Connecticut	3½[3]	174	50	75	25	63	67
Delaware	—	0	12	60	6		13
Florida	4	574	143	143	72	180	193
Georgia	3	308	103	206	51		113
Hawaii	4	137	34	34			34
Idaho	3	38	13	26	5		14
Illinois	4¼[3]	996	234	174	107		257
Indiana	2	199	100	300	50		110
Iowa	3	208	69	138			69
Kansas	3	137	46	92	23		51
Kentucky	5	248	50		25	19	55
Louisiana	2	160	80	240	20	82	84
Maine	4½[3]	70	15	7	8	88	21
Maryland	3[3]	197	66	132	33		88
Massachusetts	3	158	53	106	26		76
Michigan	4	795	199	200	100	75	219
Minnesota	3	174	58	116	30		79
Mississippi	4[3]	174	44	44			44
Missouri	3	296	99	200	50		109
Montana	—	0	12	60	6		13
Nebraska	2[3]	70	35	105	17		38
Nevada	2[3]	44	15	30	11		20

TABLE 5-2 (Cont.)

| | Tax Rate 1969 | Revenue, 1969 | Per 1% of Tax Rate Present Taxes[1] | From Raising Rates to 5%[1] | Additional Revenue | | Per 1% of Tax With Broader Base |
					From Including Consumer Services at 5% Rate	From Eliminating Consumer Exemptions	
New Hampshire	—	—	—	70	7		15
New Jersey	3[3]	265	88	176	25	130	119
New Mexico	3[3]	87	29	58	100		29
New York	2[3]	699	350	1050	40	440	458
North Carolina	3	240	80	160			88
North Dakota	3[3]	36	12	24	6		14
Ohio	4	621	155	155	78	200	210
Oklahoma	2	104	52	156	26		58
Oregon	—	0	40	200			44
Pennsylvania	6	891	148		90	225	211
Rhode Island	5	72	14		7	18	20
South Carolina	3[3]	138	46	92	23		51
South Dakota	3[3]	46	15	30	7		17
Tennessee	3	229	76	152	38		84
Texas	2[3]	538+	179	360	90	250	247
Utah	3[3]	65	22	44	5		23
Vermont	3	0	8	40	4		9
Virginia	3	211	70	140	35		77
Washington	4½	425	94	47	47		104
West Virginia	3	77	26	52			26
Wisconsin	3[3]	117	39	78	10	100	67
Wyoming	3	29	10	20	5		11
Total		12,296	3,790	6,350	1,669	2,390	4,515

From U.S. Bureau of the Census, *State Tax Collections in 1969*, adjusted to exclude Washington and West Virginia gross receipts business taxes and Indiana gross income tax, and to include separately imposed taxes on hotel-motel service and sale of automobiles that are essentially portions of sales tax structures.

[1] For the states not using the sales tax in 1969, revenues are estimated.

[2] 3% if the mandatory 1% local sales tax is included.

[3] By July 1, 1970, rates had been changed as follows: Connecticut to 5%; Illinois to 4%; Maine to 5%; Maryland to 4%; Mississippi to 5%; New Jersey to 5%; Nebraska to 2½%; New Mexico to 2½%; New York to 3%; South Carolina to 4%; South Dakota to 4%; Texas to 3¼%; Utah to 4%; Wisconsin to 4%.

There are good reasons for restricting the rates to 5 percent, at least in the immediate future, in view of the interstate problem, the difficulty of complete exclusion of producers goods from tax, and the failure of the sales tax designed to contribute toward progressivity.

Some states sacrifice revenue needlessly by applying lower rates to automobiles. These include, with respective motor vehicle and general rates: Alabama, 1.5 percent and 4 percent; Florida, 3 percent and 4 percent; Mississippi, 3 percent and 5 percent; North Carolina, 2 percent with $120 maximum and 3 percent; New Mexico, 2 percent and 4 percent; South Dakota, 3 percent and 4 percent; Texas, 3 percent and 3.25 percent; Virginia, 2 percent and 3 percent. This differentiation makes no sense whatever, given the relationship of automobile purchases to incomes; it makes the taxes more regressive and sacrifices substantial revenue.

The suggestion is sometimes made that higher than basic rates might be applied to luxury goods. Such a system is hard to implement because of the tasks created for vendors in applying more than one rate and discriminates among consumers on the basis of individual preferences. Uniformity of rate, with progression provided by incomes taxes, is greatly preferable.

TABLE 5-3
SUMMARY OF ESTIMATED ADDITIONAL REVENUE FROM SALES TAXES

	Millions of Dollars
Total Sales Tax Revenue, 1969 Fiscal Year	$12,296
Additional Revenue:	
From increases in state rates to 5%	6,350
From extention of tax to consumer services	1,600
From elimination of food and clothing exemptions	2,390
Total	10,340
Additional Gain from Each 1% of Tax Revenue:	
With existing coverage	3,700
With elimination of food and clothing and	
taxation of consumer services	4,500
Possible Offsets:	
Elimination of local sales taxes	1,300
Establishment of credit for sales tax paid on minimum expenditures against income tax liability, at $10 person, limited to lower incomes	250

SOURCE: Based on data in U. S. Bureau of the Census, *State Tax Collections in 1969,* with adjustments as noted in TABLE 5-3

Improved Structure of the Taxes

The structures of the sales taxes have often been designed without careful attention to the criteria. There are several ways in which redesign could increase revenue and simplify operations:

1. *Exemptions.* Exemptions of various classes of consumption goods from sales taxes are objectionable in several ways. Revenue is sacrificed; exemption of food, for example, reduces the yield by 20 to 25 percent. Some exemptions pave the way for demand for additional ones. All exemptions complicate the application of the tax. Merchants must distinguish between exempt and taxable sales; questions of interpretations arise; additional opportunities are created for evasion; record keeping is complicated; and audit by the state is made much more difficult. Any exemption inevitably favors those persons whose preferences for the taxed goods are relatively high.

The most common of the major exemptions is that of food, provided now in 15 states[19] (and to a limited extent in a sixteenth, North Dakota). This exemption does reduce both the absolute burden on the poor and the regressivity; a sales tax with food exempt is more or less proportional, except at the high income levels. But food exemption is far less satisfactory in accomplishing the objectives than is the system of providing a credit against income tax representing sales tax paid on a minimum necessary level of expenditures, with cash refund to those having no income tax liability. This system removes the tax burden completely from the lowest income groups, whereas food exemption does not. At the same time, it avoids a large unnecessary loss in revenue on food purchases in the middle and higher income groups. Since food expenditures rise with income the exemption is greater at the higher income levels. Many food expenditures are in no sense necessary; the exemption favors those families concentrating luxury spending on expensive and exotic foods. Food exemption significantly complicates the tasks of the retailers in applying the tax and keeping records, makes audit more difficult, and increases evasion. The income tax credit increases somewhat the number of no-tax income tax returns, but these can be handled easily and inexpensively with modern computer equipment, as demonstrated by the experience of states such as Indiana that use the system. Elimination of food exemption in the states now providing it would increase tax yields by about $2 billion—whereas a $10 tax credit per person would cost these states less than $1 billion, even if provided to all taxpayers, and much less, perhaps $250 million, if granted only to persons with lower incomes.

Similar reasoning applies to exemption of drugs and medicine, although with less force; there is greater justification for allowing specific exemption of prescription drugs than food, because expenditures on drugs are unevenly distributed among families at given income levels. By their nature these drugs do not attract voluntary luxury. Exemption should, for control purposes, be confined to items sold on prescription.

The argument applied to food exemption is valid with even greater strength for other exemptions, such as clothing, as provided by several states. Recent studies show that a clothing exemption does not lessen regressivity[20] All of these exemptions complicate the tax and reduce rather than increase equity in many respects. Likewise the exemption of cigarettes and motor fuel is objectionable; it is far simpler to apply tax to these goods than to exclude them, even though separate excises are also applied. Motor fuel tax revenue is almost always restricted to highway finance; there is no reason why consumers of motor fuel should not also make a contribution to financing of education and other state activities as well.

The same arguments do not apply to exclusion from tax of various producers goods—although these exclusions do complicate operation of the tax.

2. *Services.* The sales taxes initially applied only to sales of intangible personal property. It has long been recognized that there is no logic in taxing commodities alone, and gradually a number of states have applied the tax to a limited range of services. If the tax is confined to those of a type typically rendered by commercial (as distinguished from professional or personal service) establishments to individual consumers, there is a strong case for taxation. Most of these firms, such as repair shops, are registered taxpaying vendors anyway, and it is far simpler to tax them on their entire charges than on charges for materials only. Broadening the base in this fashion would increase revenue—although by no more than 10 percent. The principal activities covered would be fabrication and installation of all forms of tangible personal property in real property (but

146

not real property contracts), repair, cleaning, and all related activity; laundry and dry cleaning; hotel and motel service; rental of tangible personal property; and similar activities. Barber shop and beauty parlor service can justifiably be included, but doing so adds to administrative costs, since there are large numbers of small barber shops, many are not registered vendors, and control is somewhat difficult.

Some states have considered much broader coverage of services, to include all professional services, transport, and other activities.[21] Such proposals, however, encounter serious difficulties and objections and are not recommended. First, many of these professional services are of such character that taxation is not regarded as desirable on grounds of equity and social policy. Medical, dental, hospital, and educational services are examples. Many of the other services are rendered primarily to business firms, and taxation of them is objectionable on the same basis as is taxation of any producers goods. Taxation of these services offers strong incentive to firms to produce the services within the firm. For example, firms are encouraged to ship goods on their own trucks rather than by public carrier if freight is taxed.

3. *Gross Receipts Taxes.* Similar arguments apply to the gross receipts taxes of the Hawaii, West Virginia, and Washington varieties. These apply in part to nonretail businesses, thus discouraging the location of wholesaling and manufacturing in the states. Frequently they have multiple-application features, applying to the receipts from each transaction through which a commodity passes, encouraging integration in production and distribution channels, and discriminating against the small nonintegrated firms. As sales taxes they are highly objectionable on economic-distortion and equity grounds; as business occupation levies they are inferior to net income taxes or value added taxes subsequently noted. Some elements in these structures, such as severance taxes, may be justified in particular instances.

Improved Administration

Study of sales tax operation suggests that no mass evasion of sales tax is occurring. But it is also obvious that most states have not extended their audit programs far enough to maximize revenue from the taxes. California, with the most effective audit

147

program, has roughly 1 auditor to every 550 accounts; in most states the figure is 1 per 1,000 to 2,000 as shown in Table 5-4. The high productivity of dollars spent on audit—usually several times—suggests that further expansion is warranted in virtually all states. Higher salaries to attract and retain competent auditors are also necessary; in some states the level of competence is not high. It is unlikely that any state can increase its revenue more than 5 percent by this means—but this gain is not negligible. Equity among vendors is also increased by more effective enforcement. Some states lose revenue by failing to take adequate and speedy measures against delinquent vendors.

TABLE 5-4

NUMBER OF SALES TAX VENDORS PER AUDITOR, SELECTED STATES, 1969-70[a]

	Vendors	Auditors	Vendors Per Auditor
Alabama	46,000	100	460
California	363,000	667	544
Connecticut	61,000	50	1,220
Florida	208,000	100	2,080
Georgia	75,000	85	882
Hawaii	50,000	32	1,562
Iowa	78,927	51	1,547
Kansas	53,000	20	2,650
Kentucky	67,000	25	2,680
Louisiana	60,000	30	2,000
Maine	30,000	28	1,071
Maryland	48,000	77	623
Michigan	110,000	300	366
Mississippi	57,000	60	950
North Carolina	95,461	96	994
Ohio	211,000	209	1,009
Oklahoma	49,200	36	1,366
Pennsylvania	215,000	170	1,265
Rhode Island	18,000	37	486
South Carolina	53,000	48	1,104
Tennessee	75,000	80	937
Wisconsin	78,400	33	2,370

[a]Data supplied by states. Where auditors handle income taxes as well, time is allocated between the two types of work.

The weak link in operation of state sales taxes is the control of interstate transactions. Legally the states can require the instate purchaser to pay use tax, but this power is effective only on automobiles and a few other expensive items, and on purchases by registered vendors whose accounts are audited. Tax

148

cannot be collected from individuals making small purchases. Effective collection requires the ability to require the out-of-state vendor to collect and remit use tax. The states can do this if the out-of-state firm has a place of business in the state, as do the large mail order houses. But the mere making of delivery into the state or solicitation of business by catalogs does not enable the state to enforce collection, and pending Federal legislation would weaken the powers of the states still more. There is urgent need for effective Federal legislation that would enable the states to enforce payment without placing an intolerable burden on firms making large numbers of small sales into a number of states. The most effective approach is one that would require the vendor to remit tax either to his home state or to the customer state on interstate sales. This is not a perfect solution, but it would eliminate most of the present leakage without injury to interstate sellers.

Local, State, and Federal Use of the Sales Tax

The sales tax is most appropriately employed at the state level. As noted above, local sales taxes have given rise to several difficulties. If they are universal throughout the state at a uniform rate and are state collected, they are tolerable, at least from standpoints of administration and location effects. But disproportionate revenue goes to the local units that have extensive sales volume relative to population and inadequate amounts to ones with large population and little retailing. For example, in Los Angeles County, local sales tax per capita ranges from .04 cents in Hidden Hills to the fantastic figure of $12,051.78 in Vernon; the Los Angeles city figure was $20.55.[22] A much more satisfactory alternative is an increase in the state rate, with the funds returned to the local governments on some basis other than point of collection. By this means, also, there is much greater chance that the funds will be available, in part, for education rather than exclusively for other purposes. In 1969 Mississippi and New Mexico (except for county taxes) took the step of eliminating the local taxes and increasing the state rate.

If local taxes are not uniform, the tasks of the vendors are greatly complicated and location decisions may be influenced. In some states, such as New York, Alabama, and, to a lesser extent, Colorado, the tasks for all concerned have been greatly increased unnecessarily by the variety of local taxes. These

149

states would particularly benefit from a shift toward a uniform state rate with distribution of funds to the local governments.

At the other extreme, it may be argued that Federal use of the tax in lieu of the states would be advantageous in eliminating the interstate enforcement problem and avoiding adverse locational effects. But this is true of virtually all taxes. The complications arising out of state rather than Federal use of the taxes are not of great overall significance and could be alleviated by Federal legislation relating to interstate commerce. If the Federal system is to be preserved the states must retain autonomous revenue sources—and this is the most productive levy that they can operate with minimum difficulty.

To add a Federal sales tax on top of the state levy would seriously impair ability of the states to raise revenue from the tax and lessen their financial autonomy; it would also create all of the evils noted above of sharp increases in the state taxes and lessen the total amount of money available for education. Since the Federal government can easily raise its required revenue via the income tax, there is no need for it to infringe upon the major state revenue source. Some writers in recent years have stressed the value added tax as the appropriate form of tax for us at the Federal level. Actually this form of sales tax has no significant advantages in a country such as the United States over the usual retail sales tax and would complicate the tax structure unnecessarily.

EXCISE TAXES

State excise taxes are confined, with minor exceptions, to three categories: motor fuel, liquor, and tobacco products. Taxes on motor fuel are appropriately assigned for highway purposes and are not suitable as levies for financing of education (although sales tax should apply to the sale of motor fuel). During the 1968-69 fiscal year, taxes on cigarettes plus minor levies on other tobacco products yielded $2.1 billion or 5 percent of state tax revenue, while levies on alcoholic beverages yielded $1.2 billion, or 3 percent of total tax revenues. The tax on cigarettes ranged from 2 cents to 18 cents a package, with a median figure of 10 cents, in contrast to a median of 3 cents in 1950. Taxes on distilled spirits ranged from $1.20 per gallon to $4.00 per gallon, with a median of $2.25 (1969).

Liquor and tobacco taxes offer the advantage of substantial

productivity, widespread popular acceptance, and minimal danger to economic development. But they have limited justification beyond some compensation for social costs for which use of the products may be responsible and the principle that use can appropriately be penalized. The tax on cigarettes is highly regressive, more so than any other major levy. Declining cigarette consumption will likewise limit future productivity of the tax. States that are well below the median could gain additional revenue with little harm by moving to the median, but these levies generally offer little in the way of long range additional contributions to the financing of education. Their revenue elasticity is particularly low—.6 for liquor, .4 for cigarettes.[23]

PERSONAL INCOME TAXES

The inherent advantages of personal income taxation are so well known that only a brief summary is required. Income taxes alone are directly related to the most generally accepted measure of tax capacity and are adjustable on the basis of circumstances affecting tax capacity at given income levels, such as numbers of dependents, medical expenses, and the like. Only the income tax can provide effective progression in the overall tax structure. A properly designed income tax should have minimum distorting effect on the economy, provided all income is treated in a uniform fashion. While progression increases the danger of distortions, particularly of factor supplies, the high Federal income tax rates of the last two decades have produced little evidence of significant adverse effects upon the economy.[24] The Treasury studies of the late sixties showed that the overall progression was much less than the tax rate table suggests, with a substantial degree of inequality of treatment. But these consequences resulted from defects in the Federal income tax structure, not from the use of the income basis for taxation. Responses of revenue to increases in national income is greater than that of any other tax, estimated in the range of 1.5 to 1.8 at the state level.

The personal income tax, by its inherent nature, is of course the mainstay of the Federal tax structure, and with very good justification, partly because of its potential use as an instrument of fiscal policy. Unlike most other taxes the rates can be varied from time to time in light of changing business conditions and inflationary pressures.

151

TABLE 5-5
STATE INCOME TAX REVENUES AND POTENTIALS
(FISCAL YEAR)

	Personal Income Tax Revenue 1969 (Millions of $)	1-1-70 Range of Tax Rates	Exemption, Family of 4 ($)	Potential Additional Revenue (Millions of $) Oregon Rates	Corporate Income Tax Yield (Millions of $)	Corporate Income Tax Rate, 1-1-70	Potential Additional Revenue Corporate Income Tax 7% Rate (Millions of $)
Alabama	74.9	1.5-5	2600	174	29.0	5[11]	33
Alaska	25.2	16% of Fed.	2400	8	4.3	5.4-9.36	1
Arizona	52.7	2-8	3200	97	18.1	2-8[11]	12
Arkansas	37.7	1-5	[7]	100	22.4	1-6	20
California	1086.9	1-10	[7]	1210	592.5	7	
Colorado	103.5	3-8	3000	100	32.0	5	13
Connecticut				378	86.2	8	
Delaware	61.4	1.5-11	2400		15.1	6	3
Florida				588		6	196
Georgia	139.2	1-6	4200	242	73.0	6	12
Hawaii	86.5	1.25-11	2400		13.7	5.85-6.435	2
Idaho	38.5[1]	2.5-9	2400	17	10.0	6	1
Illinois		2.5	4000	1313	[1]	4	437
Indiana	181.5	2.	3000	337	8.8[8]	2	164
Iowa	106.9	.75-5.25	[7]	173	24.1	4-8[11]	18
Kansas	72.4	2.-6.5	2400	155	20.1	4.5[11]	45
Kentucky	107.6	2-6	[7]	148	39.4	5-7[11]	30
Louisiana	44.5	2-6	5800	249	34.6	4	27
Maine		1-6	4000	83		4[11]	27
Maryland	365.8	2-5	3200	54	54.7	7	
Massachusetts	452.6	4	3800	187	185.1	7½	55
Michigan	390.2	2.6	4800	177	216.8	5.6	
Minnesota	304.2	1.5-12	[7]	62	82.6	11.33[11]	35
Mississippi	20.4[2]	3-4	6000	126	33.3	3-4	75
Missouri	118.2	1-4	3200	335	18.5	2[11]	
Montana	31.2	2-11	2400	30	8.1	6.25	1
Nebraska	36.6	10% of Fed.	2400	103	6.9	2	16

State	Personal Income Tax Revenue 1969 (Millions of $)	1-1-70 Range of Tax Rates	Exemption, Family of 4, ($)	Potential Additional Revenue (Millions of $), Oregon Rates	Corporate Income Tax Yield (Millions of $)	Corporate Income Tax Rate, 1-1-70	Potential Additional Revenue; Corporate Income Tax 7% Rate (Millions of $)
Nevada	—	—	—	53	—	—	15
New Hampshire	2.9[2]	4.25	600	66	—	—	20
New Jersey	14.5[3]	2-14	2400	825	156.6	4.25	90
New Mexico	19.6	1-9	2400	60	5.1[8]	5	2
New York	2151.6	2-14	2400	98	610.3	7	—
North Carolina	239.6	3-7	3200	168	112.5	6	19
North Dakota	14.0	1-11	2700	37	2.2	3-6[11]	3
Ohio	—	—	—	1113	—	—	370
Oklahoma	47.8	1-6	3000	170	22.1	4[11]	35
Oregon	204.3	4-10	2400	—	37.5	6	6
Pennsylvania	—[1]	10[4]	—	1203	284.0	7.5	—
Rhode Island	—	—	—	96	28.1	7	—
South Carolina	84.4	2-7	3200	105	40.5	6	7
South Dakota	—	—	—	57	.6	5.5	12
Tennessee	11.4	5[5]	—	295	61.6	5	24
Texas	—	—	—	996	—	—	330
Utah	50.9	2-6.5	2400	36	10.6	6[11]	7
Vermont	34.0	25% of Fed.[6]	2400	5	5.6	6	1
Virginia	273.4	2-5	2600	150	67.5	5	27
Washington	—	—	—	363	[9]	—	110
West Virginia	31.0	1.5-5.5	2400	104	4.1[10]	6	1
Wisconsin	461.9	2.7-10	[7]	—	101.0	2-7[11]	120
Wyoming	—	—	—	30	—	—	8
Total	7,579.8			12,476	3179.6		2430

[1] Not in operation 1969 fiscal year.
[2] High exemption.
[3] From New York sources only.
[4] Income from capital only.
[5] Limited scope.
[6] +15% surcharge.
[7] Tax credit in lieu of exemption.
[8] Plus $150 million gross income tax.
[9] $98.6 million gross receipts tax.
[10] Plus $89.6 million gross receipts tax.
[11] Federal tax deductible from income.

Source of Basic Data: U.S. Bureau of the Census, State Tax Collection in 1969, ACIR, State and Local Finance, 1967-1970.

State-Local Use

At the state level, the income tax offers the general advantages of income taxation, providing greater equity for the state tax structures, lessening the absolute burden on the lowest income groups encountered with other taxes, providing at least a limited degree of progression, and ensuring greater response of state revenue to increases in personal income. Given the resistance to other taxes, a state can gain greater revenue with an income tax in the tax structure than otherwise. Table 5-5 summarizes the income tax picture by state, with yields for the 1969 fiscal year and rates and exemptions as of January, 1970. As of January 1, 1970, 41 states were using the tax; the exceptions were Connecticut, Florida, Nevada, Ohio, Pennsylvania, South Dakota, Texas, Washington, and Wyoming. However, the taxes in Rhode Island, New Hampshire, New Jersey, and Tennessee are of very restricted coverage. In fact, therefore, only 37 states make effective use of the tax.

Unlike the sales taxes, which are basically very similar, the income taxes vary widely. The Mississippi levy, for example, applies only to married persons with incomes in excess of $6,000, whereas in 13 states the figure is $1,200. Initial rates range from .75 percent to 4 percent, top rates from 2 percent to 14 percent. Three states with general levies have proportional rates. Three states base their liability on that of the Federal tax; the Vermont tax is 25 percent of the Federal tax liability, plus a 15 percent surcharge. One of the best measures of the height of the taxes is the ratio of state income tax to total adjusted gross income as reported for Federal income tax; these range from .4 percent (Mississippi) to 3.8 percent (Wisconsin).[25] Table 5-5 gives some indication of the degree of diversity.

Local income taxes are significant in seven states and used in one city in an eighth (Alabama); these taxes are summarized below:

State	Rate	Usage
Kentucky	1% typical; 2% high	20 cities, including large ones plus one county
Maryland	20% to 50% of state tax	Baltimore city, plus 22 counties
Michigan	1%	10 cities, including Detroit
Missouri	.5%; 1%	St. Louis, Kansas City

154

New York	.4 to 2%	New York City only
Ohio	25 to 1%	Most cities and villages, large and small
Pennsylvania	.5 to 2%; many 1%	About 3,000 local governments, including 1,000 school districts

All of these taxes are locally collected; two of the states in which use is most widespread (Ohio and Pennsylvania) do not have state income taxes. Outside of Michigan and Maryland, the local taxes usually apply only to wage and salary income, rather than to all forms.

Evaluation

State use of income taxation is strongly justified, for reasons suggested above. Interstate problems with personal income taxes are not serious; as the state of residence normally allows credit for tax paid the state where the income is earned, there is little double taxation. Likewise there is little escape from taxation. States rely heavily on IRS information and audit for control of income taxes. There are practical limits, however, to the potential revenue, given the relatively high Federal income taxes. To the taxpayer the combined rate is the significant element, and the Federal tax is—as it should be—sufficiently high that the margins for the states are limited. A number of the taxes are extremely low, however. If the Oregon levy is taken as a model, with rates from 4 to 10 percent and exemption of $600 per person, the states as a whole would obtain $20.1 billion from the tax instead of the present $7.6 billion, on the basis of rough expansion on the basis of total personal income. Estimates by state are given in Table 5-5. Because of variations in per capita incomes by state, these estimates are only very rough. Low income states will not be able to raise as much as indicated and high income states can raise more.

A few features of the structure warrant attention. Progression in rates is much less important than might be expected; deductibility of state income tax liability in determining Federal income tax greatly reduces the significance of progression in rates. The exemption provides a considerable degree of progression. On the other hand the Federal experience of recent years suggests the need for a broad definition of income, including full taxation of capital gains (in view of the limited progression)

155

and minimization or perhaps complete elimination of all personal deductions except the exemption for the taxpayer and each dependent. Theoretically deductions should improve the equity of the tax, but the Federal experience has not been encouraging. The practice in three states of defining tax liability as a percentage of Federal liability has the merit of simplicity but opens the state levies to the defects of the Federal and makes the state yield vary with changes in Federal rates unless offset by state legislation. Using the Federal adjusted gross income figure with deduction of a specified personal exemption for each taxpayer is a preferable alternative.

Use of the income tax at the local level is much more questionable. Separate collection of a local income tax, as is the common policy, compounds the nuisance to the taxpayer. A large portion of income is interjurisdictional, earned in one local area by a resident of another. As a consequence, opportunities for multiple taxation are substantial and control is made much more difficult. Local governments are not in a position to audit income tax returns independently; all they can do is to rely on information in state and Federal returns. But these returns do not localize income sufficiently for local income tax purposes. In practice most of the local income taxes are confined to wage and salary income, thus discriminating against this form relative to others. Given the small size of local units, distortion of location may be significant. If liability depends upon residence, persons have incentive to select those cities in a metropolitan area that do not use the tax. With liability on the basis of place of earning and withholding, business firms are given an incentive to locate plants in jurisdictions not having the tax. But regardless of locational impact, the nuisance factor alone suggests the need to avoid local income taxes except in unusual circumstances and to distribute a portion of state income tax yield to local governments, including school districts.

So far as the Federal government is concerned, given the usually accepted criteria of taxation and the importance of sales taxation at the state level, there is strong justification for primary Federal reliance on the income tax. There is obvious need for further reform of the Federal tax beyond that provided by 1969 legislation, if the tax is to accomplish its objectives in the desired fashion. Discussion of reform of the Federal income tax, however, is outside the scope of this paper.

GENERAL LEVY ON CORPORATIONS

Most states have some form of general levy on corporations. In part these are regarded as supplements to the personal income tax (although four states have a corporate tax but no personal tax). But primarily the taxes are a means for ensuring that the state in which the business operates receives some compensation for the services it renders to the firm.

Currently, the general levy takes the form of corporation income tax in 42 states and partially in another (Indiana). Washington, and in part Indiana, use gross receipts taxes as general business taxes, distinct from their sales taxes, and West Virginia does so in addition to the corporate income tax. Two of the other states have corporate franchise taxes based on capital stock that are relatively productive of revenue. The other four states—Florida, Nevada, New Hampshire, and Wyoming—have no effective general corporate levy. The median rate of the corporate income tax is 5.7 percent (January, 1970), with a range from 1 percent (Missouri) to 12 percent (Pennsylvania.) Some of the states have a limited amount of progression; the remainder use proportional rates. Interstate income is usually allocated on the basis of a formula. The corporate income tax currently yields $3.2 billion, 7.6 percent of state tax collections (1969 fiscal year).

The state corporate income taxes can be justified as desirable elements in the tax structure on the bases suggested above. They provide a means on a current basis of reaching income earned by corporations and an effective means of obtaining revenue from corporations owned outside of the state yet benefiting from state services. Revenue elasticity, 1.2 to 1.3, is higher than that of other levies except the personal income tax.[26] While the final distributional effects of the taxes are not clear, they appear to accord reasonably well with accepted standards of equity. Administration is simple because of the ability to rely on Federal returns and Federal audits as the primary basis of control. Interstate problems are minor so long as uniform formulas are employed for allocation of interstate income, although some nonuniformity still exists. The taxes are not likely to have distorting effects upon location decisions so long as they are more or less uniform among states. Even with the nonuniformity that has prevailed (one major midwest industrial state, Ohio, does not yet use the tax, and Illinois and Michigan have commenced to do so only in recent years) there is no measurable effect on location of industry. If the differentials became too great, however, particularly within metropolitan areas extending over state lines, there would inevitably be some influence. A state cannot safely go too far out of line from its neighbors.[27] As a political matter, corporate income taxes are usually essential if voters are to accept personal income taxes. The chief obstacle to substantial increases in the state corporate income taxes—apart from interstate differentials—is the high level of the Federal tax. With Federal rates in the neighborhood of 50 percent, there is a limit to the amount the states can impose without strong resistance by business groups and possible adverse effects upon economic development. If all states used a 7 percent rate, however, total yield would be about $5.4 billion instead of the present $3.2 billion.

The gross receipts basis used for general business levies by a few states (and as supplements to the retail sales tax in a few others) are objectionable on many grounds. To the extent that they are shifted they have distributional effects comparable to those of sales taxes. In practice shifting is likely to be difficult for many firms because of interstate differences, and the taxes rest on the owners in a highly capricious fashion. Because of their cumulative nature they distort business methods, encouraging integration and leading firms to produce goods and services themselves instead of acquiring them from other firms. Under no circumstances should states not now employing them turn to them. Capital stock taxes are equally capricious in their effects, being tolerable only because the rates are low.

In some states the proposal has been advanced to replace gross receipts taxes or corporate income taxes by a tax on value added, and Michigan used this form of tax for its general business levy for a time. The primary argument is along benefit lines: corporations benefit from state services and should pay accordingly for this "input" into the production process. The best measure of the benefits received by any firm is the value it adds to the materials and other goods it buys—the difference between its receipts and the cost of goods it purchases from other firms. This approach ensures that all firms pay for the inputs of state services whether the firms are profitable or not, whereas the corporate income tax does not. Value added is a much better measure of benefits received than gross receipts, and the value added tax avoids the economic distortions created by a gross receipts tax.

It is obvious that a value added tax is preferable on several grounds to a gross receipts tax. But its advantage over a corporate income tax is not clear. The latter complements the personal tax much more effectively than a value added tax; there are fewer interstate complications; and it may be argued that net earnings is a better basis for taxation than value added, certainly in terms of distributional effects. At any rate, given the widespread use of the corporate income basis, it is more satisfactory from the standpoint of any one state than the value added tax and general change to the latter is most unlikely.

In general, therefore, the most suitable approach for additional revenue in this field includes the following:

1. Establishment of the corporate income tax in those states not now using it, replacing capital stock and gross receipts taxes where these are used.

2. Use of a rate of perhaps 7 percent in those states now using lower figures. These two changes would add about $2.5 billion to state tax revenue (Table 5-5).

3. Greater uniformity in allocation of interstate income, to minimize the compliance tasks and the danger of double taxation, and restrictive federal legislation.

At the Federal level, the corporate income tax is the second most productive tax, yielding $37 billion in the 1969-70 fiscal year, or 18 percent of total tax revenue. It is certain to remain a major source of Federal revenue despite serious questions about distributional effects. The question of whether the corporate income tax is reflected in higher prices or not has been subject to extensive debate and to a number of empirical studies, which show conflicting results. It is impossible at present to be certain as to the shifting of the tax. Further exploration of the tax and of possible reforms is beyond the scope of this paper.

OTHER POSSIBLE SOURCES OF REVENUE

At the state level, there are no major potentials for tax revenues beyond those noted. A few states are able to gain substantial revenue from severance taxes on the output of petroleum and minerals, and others could undoubtedly gain additional money from this source. Estate and inheritance taxes are not

159

productive of substantial amounts. They could be made more effective than they are, but the overall potential is not great relative to other major sources. Other state levies, such as those on public utility or insurance companies, are essentially supplements to sales or income taxes. There is no major avenue to which the local governments and the states can turn for large sums of revenue.

The same considerations apply at the Federal level; there are no new major untapped taxes. The argument for a Federal value added tax often advanced in recent years is merely a disguised argument for a Federal sales tax. The Federal government can raise all revenue needed from the current pattern of income taxes, with some modifications in structure; the sales tax can be left to the states as the major source of state finance for education and other purposes.

SUMMARY

By generally accepted standards of taxation, additional funds for the financing of education cannot, on any significant scale, be found in the local property tax, or in expansion of local non-property taxes, but from expanded state use of sales and income taxes, plus reliance on Federal income taxation for Federal grants. More specifically:

1. Most states can make more effective use of sales taxation, by increasing the rate to at least 5 percent and ultimately beyond, and by broadening the structure to eliminate most exemptions of consumption goods and to include some services. At the same time, to alleviate burden on the lowest income groups and lessen opposition to the tax, credit should be given against state income tax for an amount representing sales tax payments on basic necessary expenditures, with cash refund when the person has no income tax liability.

2. Most states can make more effective use of income taxation, in some by lowering exemptions, in many states by broadening the coverage of the tax by reducing deductions and including tax free income, and by the use of higher rates.

3. The corporate income tax should be the primary general business levy, replacing gross receipts and capital stock taxes where these are still used. Many states can gain substantial revenue by raising the rate to the median figure.

160

4. Local sales taxes and, to an even greater extent, local income taxes are objectionable in a number of respects and should be integrated into the state levies, except in unusual circumstances when one or a few cities require much more revenue than others.

5. The Federal government should continue to rely on personal and corporate income taxes, with some revision in structure, as the primary source of funds for educational and other purposes.

The additional revenue potential for 1970, as compared with 1969, is as follows, on the basis of very rough estimates:

Sales Tax:

	Billions of Dollars
Increase in rate to 5% in all states	7.0
Extension to consumer services	1.8
Elimination of food and clothing exemptions	2.5
Total	11.3
Less: Elimination of local sales taxes	1.5
Credit against income tax	.3
Net gain, with 5% rate	9.5
Additional revenue per 1% of rate	5.0
Personal Income Tax:	
Increase to Oregon level	12.0
Corporate Income Tax:	
Increase to 7%	2.5
Total, with sales tax at 5%	24.0
with sales tax at 6%	28.5

These estimates are subject to one major limitation: the higher income taxes and the higher sales tax rates will reduce the base of the sales tax and thus the additional revenue will be somewhat less than the estimate. The magnitude of this effect has been measured by Legler and Shapiro, but not with sufficient predictive accuracy to warrant acceptance.[28]

FOOTNOTES

1. Yield data from U.S. Bureau of the Census, *Quarterly Summary of State and Local Tax Revenue*, April-June 1969, and *State Tax Collections in 1969*, and D. Netzer, *Economics of the Property Tax* (Washington: Brookings, 1966).

2. From 1956 to 1966 the ratio of real property assessments to total assessments rose from 74% to 78%. U.S. Bureau of the Census, *Trends*

161

in Assessed Valuations and Sales Ratios 1956-1966 (Washington: Government Printing Office, 1970).

3. Netzer, pp. 21-22.

4. Advisory Commission on Intergovernmental Relations (ACIR), *State and Local Finances* (Washington: Government Printing Office, 1969), p. 68.

5. Advisory Commission on Intergovernmental Relations, *State-Local Taxation and Industrial Location* (Washington: Government Printing Office, 1967).

6. Netzer, pp. 72-73.

7. *Ibid.*, pp. 173-83.

8. *Ibid.*, Ch. 3.

9. *Ibid.*

10. *Ibid.*

11. *Ibid.*, p. 189.

12. This will not be true in the future because of the introduction of a state income tax.

13. Most recently by J. M. Schaefer, "Sales Tax Regressivity under Alternative Tax Bases and Income Concepts," *National Tax Journal*, 22 (December, 1969), 516-27.

14. *Ibid.*

15. "The Border Tax Problem in Washington," *National Tax Journal*, 14 (December, 1961), 361-75.

16. "Sales Taxation: An Analysis of the Effects of Rate Increases in Two Contrasting Cases," *National Tax Journal*, 19 (December, 1966), 411-20.

17. "An Analysis of Municipal Sales Taxation," Ph.D. dissertation, University of Illinois, 1969.

18. ACIR, *State and Local Finances*, p. 64.

19. California, Connecticut, Florida, Maine, Maryland, Massachusetts, Minnesota, New Jersey, New York, Ohio, Pennsylvania, Rhode Island, Texas, Vermont, Wisconsin.

20. Schaefer.

21. The taxes in Hawaii and New Mexico apply to these services.

22. R. C. Brown, "Observations on the Distribution of Local Sales Taxes in California," *Proceedings of the National Tax Association for 1968*, pp. 27-39.

23. ACIR, *State and Local Finances*, p. 64.

24. R. Barlow, H. E. Brazer, and J. N. Morgan, *Economic Behavior of the Affluent* (Washington: Brookings, 1969).

25. ACIR, *State and Local Finances*, pp. 111-12.

26. *Ibid.*, p. 64.

27. A detailed discussion is found in Advisory Commission on Intergovernmental Relations, *State-Local Taxation and Industrial Location* (Washington: Government Printing Office, 1967).

28. J. B. Legler and P. Shapiro, "The Responsiveness of State Tax Revenues to Economic Growth," *National Tax Journal*, 21 (March, 1968), 48-56.

SELECTED BIBLIOGRAPHY

Advisory Commission on Intergovernmental Relations. *State and Local Finances: Significant Features 1967 to 1970.* Washington: Government Printing Office, 1969.

———— *State-Local Taxation and Industrial Location.* Washington: Government Printing Office, 1967.

———-— *New Proposals for 1969: ACIR State Legislative Program* Washington: Government Printing Office, 1969.

Ecker-Racz, L. L., *The Politics and Economics of State-Local Finance,* Englewood Cliffs, N.J.: Prentice-Hall, 1970.

Maxwell, James A. *Financing State and Local Governments.* Rev. ed. Washington: Brookings, 1970.

Myers, W. S. "Measures for Making the State and Local Revenue Systems More Productive and More Equitable." *Proceedings of the National Tax Association for 1968*, pp. 441-54.

Netzer, D. *Economics of the Property Tax*, Washington: Brookings, 1966.

CHAPTER 6

School District Organization

Effective operation of a system of public education in a nation as large as the United States requires some type of structural or administrative arrangement. Instead of being superimposed through an educational bureaucracy from the state or federal levels of government, the responsibility for public education initially was placed upon interested citizens in local communities. As the nation expanded and citizens moved westward portions of land were set aside for school purposes, and the opening of schools became an integral part of the settling process.

Interest in state systems of education began to emerge when attention was drawn to the inequalities of educational opportunity within states and the variations in fiscal capacity among districts in a state. Graduation from high school replaced completion of the common school as the social norm, and school operation became too complex for local communities to continue without external assistance. These conditions contributed to the development of the great variety of governmental structures under which the public schools are currently operating.

The relative merits of the structure of the educational system in the United States are often a subject of controversy and debate, but the absence of any mention of education in the Federal Constitution has resulted in education becoming primarily the responsibility of the individual states. In practice, operational

164

responsibility has been decentralized even further through the establishment of local school districts in 49 of the 50 states. Hawaii is the only state which has adopted a wholly state administered school system.

LOCAL SCHOOL DISTRICTS

In their efforts to decentralize authority and responsibility for the operation of schools, the states have fostered the emergence of a wide variety of legally authorized and designated units. The local school district is the basic administrative unit most commonly established by the states to operate local schools. Under this arrangement a single administrative agency is responsible to the state government for designated educational functions. In a few states one local school district may be responsible for elementary schools, another for secondary schools, and yet another for junior or community college education—with a fourth agency having over-arching responsibility for other aspects of higher education. However, the crucial point is that the governing body of each local administrative unit is legally independent of each of the others, but the interdependence and need for communication and cooperation among them is self-evident. The creation of dual districts to operate elementary and secondary schools permits dual tax levies for operation and dual bonding power for school facilities, but it also contributes to duplication of services and increases the problems of communication and articulation. Statutes could be amended to encourage the merger of these dual districts into unit districts.

The differences among local school districts stagger the imagination of any observer. In terms of square miles in individual school districts, the area varies from less than one square mile to several thousand, and in terms of student population the number varies in size from less than ten students in some of the sparsely populated states to approximately one million students in New York City. The complexities are further evidenced by the concentration of a large number of students in a relatively few school districts; for example, the 150 school districts with enrollments exceeding 25,000 students enroll over 12 million students, which comprise over 30 percent of the total public school enrollment for the nation.

The post World War II years from 1950 to 1970 were marked

by considerable interest in school district reorganization and consolidation. The effects of this trend are shown in the reduction in the number of school districts from 95,000 in 1948 to 40,000 in 1960 to less than 18,000 in 1970.[1]

The current interest in decentralization of large urban school districts may contribute to the emergence of another type of school district in the continuing quest for some structural arrangement which will provide a fiscal base adequate to support the schools, which has enrollment sufficient to provide both operational efficiency and quality in the educational program, and which will still permit parents a voice in operational decisions. Evidence that these are continuing concerns is provided by the town meetings in New England and later by the multiplicity of districts which were created in a number of states throughout the country.

Variations in governmental patterns among states are even more obvious when one considers that Illinois had about 12,000 school districts in 1940, but had reduced that number to about 1200 by 1970. Between 1948 and 1970 the number of school districts in Iowa was reduced from over 4700 to less than 500. Ohio had slightly less than 1600 districts in 1948, and had reduced the number to slightly over 600 by 1970. During the same period of time no appreciable reduction in the number of school districts was accomplished in the New England states; in fact, a net increase occurred in Connecticut, Massachusetts, and Rhode Island. The greatest amount of school district consolidation or reorganization occurred in the states comprising the old Northwest Territory.[2]

In 1948, 23 states had in excess of 1,000 school districts, 16 had in excess of 2,000 districts, and 7 had over 5,000 districts. By 1970, only 4 states had over 1,000 districts and none had over 2,000 districts. Over this 20 year period the number of school districts decreased in 34 states, increased in 9 states, and did not change in 5 states. This reduction is even more striking when one notes that the net loss was over 8,000 in one state, but that the highest net gain in any state was less than 60.[3]

Any consideration of the governance of American public education must recognize the basic differences between administrative units and attendance centers. An administrative unit exists for purposes of governance and usually encompasses one or more attendance centers while the term "attendance center" refers to the actual school. Not all administrative units operate schools within their boundaries; some of them transport students to another district which operates an attendance center or a school. Those administrative units which do not operate schools should be merged with an operating unit, for school districts have no educational reason to exist if they do not operate schools. This type of school district reorganization can take place without affecting existing attendance centers. Administrative units may be reorganized, merged, or subdivided, and the former schools may continue to operate in much the same fashion. Similarly, attendance centers may be consolidated, altered, or subdivided without altering the geographic boundaries of administrative units.

Traditionally, citizens have cherished the belief that schools were operating under "local control" when, in fact, the amount of local control and leeway that could be exercised was extremely limited. Local control has become virtually a myth with the proliferation of state statutes and regulations relating to curricular offerings, textbooks, certification of teachers, budgeting and accounting procedures, controls with regard to the expenditure of funds, and limitations on local tax levies. In practice, control of schools is local only to the extent that state legislatures and agencies choose to permit. The courts have been crystal clear in referring to local school districts as arms of the state, creatures of the state, or agencies with limited responsibilities and functions which exercise a portion of the power of the state.

The Board of Education

Local boards of education serve two diverse functions in the American system of education. First, they have responsibility for adoption of policies under which the schools are to operate. This responsibility assures some balance in educational planning and decision-making and provides a means to broaden the participation of citizens in educational governance. Second, boards serve as arms or agents of the state with responsibility for carrying out legislative mandates in the operation of schools, but this role is further complicated by the additional responsibility to represent the educational interests of the local community.

In local school districts boards are normally composed of laymen elected by popular vote. The continuation of this historical

167

pattern illustrates the American commitment to the concept that the people have the ability to manage their own schools and also is evidence of the public's continuing interest in assuming this responsibility. In the nineteenth century local boards were heavily involved in administrative functions, but as the operation of schools became more complex and time-demanding, school boards became less involved in routine operational concerns and moved toward the present pattern of relying upon the superintendent of schools to serve as the board's executive officer and be responsible for school operation. At the present time the contention is that the board of education should assume responsibility for policy making and legislative functions within the framework of state law and regulations, and should assign responsibility for executive functions to the superintendent of schools and his staff. In actual practice, however, this suggested allocation of functional responsibility is somewhat unrealistic, for sharp delineations cannot be drawn between legislative, policy making, and executive functions. For example, statutory requirements in some states dictate that the board must approve each expenditure of funds even after a detailed budget has been formally adopted.

Boards of education are found in nearly all local, intermediate, and state educational agencies. In each instance their functions and responsibilities are limited to those prescribed by statute and related implied and necessary powers, but the method of selection is very diverse. Popular election is the method most often used to select members of local boards of education, but this method of selecting board members is less well established for intermediate units or the state education agency. There is, however, general acceptance of the concept that there is the need and an appropriate role for this legislative and policy making body.

INTERMEDIATE UNITS

As the second major structural component in the governance of education, intermediate units vary extensively among the several states and take on a variety of forms and functions. They range from the midwest's county superintendency where the function is largely record keeping and communication to the cooperative service agency which may encompass one or more counties and which is oriented toward providing certain educational services and programs more efficiently and economically than they can be provided by local school districts. Governing bodies for these agencies may be selected in a variety of ways, but the crucial issue may well be whether the agency is primarily responsible or responsive to the interests of the state educational agency or to the local districts located within its geographic area. The state education agency or the group of local districts upon which the intermediate agency is most dependent for resources or direction is likely to emerge as a stronger entity as a result of the activities of the intermediate agency.

The threat that an intermediate agency will replace the local school district is perceived differently in various states, for local school districts in several states are currently organized on a county unit basis which provides the pattern for the intermediate unit in other states. When the intermediate unit assumes responsibility for those functions normally assigned to the local district, it then in effect becomes the local school district, possibly providing impetus for further evolution through the formation of multi-county intermediate units to provide an even wider range of services and programs.

In some areas of the nation, the intermediate unit provides administrative and/or instructional services. For example, payroll accounting, maintenance of pupil records, curriculum development activities, employment of specialized personnel, and purchasing of supplies and equipment often can be provided more economically and efficiently by an intermediate unit, which serves several districts, than by the individual districts. However, intermediate districts should not be established by the legislature merely to prop up inadequate and inefficient local districts. Such districts should be merged or dissolved without delay or subterfuge. In the same fashion, politically powerful intermediate units should not be permitted to thwart progress in school district reorganization because their continued existence is threatened.

STATE EDUCATION AGENCIES

Increased public interest in education and the shift in the base of financial support from the local to the state and federal levels have contributed, in recent years, to the growth of the state education agencies. These agencies provide various combinations of leadership, control, and service depending upon one's perspective, aspirations, and relationship to the agency. During the decade of the 1960's, substantial amounts of federal funds were appropriated to strengthen state educational agencies and these agencies were given responsibility for administering even larger federal appropriations which were to be expended by local school districts. Inevitable outgrowths of this increased flow of funds have been an enlargement of staff and an expansion of the operational functions being performed by state education agencies.

This third, and potentially most powerful, of the various administrative units for education is searching for its appropriate role in many states. As the state agency expands and moves from a disbursement and service orientation to a leadership and planning orientation, conflicts and problems inevitably will emerge as power bases shift and the focal points for educational policy decisions change. Legislative enactments mandating a statewide planning-programming-budgeting system and proposals for federal revenue sharing are but two examples of developments that could result in additional responsibilities being thrust upon state education agencies.

STATE FINANCE PROGRAMS AND SCHOOL DISTRICT ORGANIZATION

Assessment of the interrelationships between state finance programs and school district organization requires a study of the relationships between equalization and school district size, wealth, tax rates, expenditures, and foundation program support. An analysis of these five factors revealed that wealth was the most significant element in predicting expenditures, with school tax rates being the next most significant. Size of school district and amount of foundation program aid did not appear to exert a significant influence upon expenditure patterns.[4]

Variations in expenditures were found in all states, and the existence of high or low level of expenditure per pupil did not necessarily result in a high or low level of equalization. A more detailed analysis did reveal that in seven states the foundation program was contributing additional revenues to districts with a low valuation of property per pupil. The importance of this pattern was directly related to the level of support provided through the foundation aid program.

In the same vein, one of the most disturbing findings of stud-

170

ies conducted by the NEFP is the failure of state financial support systems in their efforts to equalize the resources available to local districts. Low levels of equalization (in terms of the percentage that the foundation program is of total current expenditures) and the proliferation of categorical and special purpose aids have contributed to a situation in which local district wealth emerges as the primary factor in determining the level of expenditures in a local district.[5]

By forming regional education agencies or intermediate units, local districts can bring together a sufficient number of pupils so that it is feasible to provide specialized educational services for them. Various arrangements for intermediate units have been tried, but the objective has often been to seek an arrangement which will provide an adequate fiscal base, sufficient pupils, and some rationale for existence. The last reason is obviously the least defensible, and the first two may not be complementary. Hooker and Mueller have proposed the use of economic planning regions as logical geographical areas for intermediate units,[6] but the sheer size of these areas may require that they be subdivided in order to implement various educational services or programs.

OBJECTIVES OF SCHOOL DISTRICT ORGANIZATION

When a state undertakes a comprehensive review of its governmental structure for education, consideration must be given to the existing situation and to the historical development of the current pattern of school district organization in that state. In many of the southeastern states, the county unit of civil government has also served as the primary reference point in the organization of schools; in the midwestern states the civil township was the primary unit, with the county functioning as an intermediate unit.

Various efforts have been made to state objectives or goals in school district organization, one of the more recent being The Great Plains School District Organization Project.[7] Previous research and writings on the subject of school district organization provided for support for the following five statements:

1. Each student should have the opportunity to participate in an educational program that will fully meet his educational needs.

171

2. The educational structure of the state should be organized in a manner that will provide an equalization of the expenditures for education throughout the state.

3. The educational structure of the state should be organized in a manner that will provide students with well-trained classroom teachers.

4. The educational structure of the state should be organized in a manner that will utilize efficiently the specialized and technical school personnel in the state.

5. The educational structure of the state should be organized in a manner that will provide the best use of funds expended for education.

Educational Opportunity

The concept of educational opportunity is somewhat illusive, but various research studies and observations have indicated that access to educational programs and services is directly related to the size of the school district and the attendance unit which serve the student. For that reason the bulk of the following discussion will relate to organizational matters and to minimal and optimal student enrollment in school district attendance centers and administrative units.

The various attempts to arrive at a minimum acceptable size for attendance centers have resulted in some common agreement that elementary schools should have at least one section or classroom per grade and that secondary schools should have a graduating class of at least 100 students. Optimum sizes for elementary schools usually approximate 60-100 students per grade with secondary school optimums ranging from 700-1,500 students in a three- or four-year high school, depending upon the concentration of the population and the comprehensiveness of the educational program.[8]

Authorities generally agree that a school district should provide an educational program encompassing both elementary and secondary schools. The dual arrangements with separate elementary and high school districts are not considered desirable because of the duplicated administrative and service staffs and the communication and coordination problems between the elementary and secondary educational programs. Effective educational programs should not be restricted by multiple levels of adminis-

172

tration which result in unnecessary complications for students, patrons, and school staff members.

Although many viewpoints have been expressed concerning the ideal size for a school district or an administrative unit, research has revealed that reasonable economies of scale cannot be secured until districts have at least 10,000 students. These same studies suggest that enrollments of 4,000-5,000 students might be defensible in sparsely populated areas. Even though these sizes may seem large in terms of the enrollments of some school districts, they should be construed as minimal rather than as optimal. Recommendations relating to optimal size often range from 20,000 to 50,000 pupils per administrative unit.[9]

The desirability of school district reorganization to eliminate the small unit is reasonably well accepted and is deemed justified on both educational and fiscal grounds. Workable solutions for resolving operational problems in very large school districts seem to be more evasive, but there is general agreement that constructive action is needed to reduce the communications problems and tensions which characterize these districts, as well as to provide for greater flexibility and diversification in instructional programs. Typical administrative arrangements may be used in efforts to resolve the former problems, but resolution of the latter will depend upon the ability of the district to recognize and respond to the need for differentiated instructional programs to serve subgroups of the total student population.

The number of students needed for an efficient school district operation is dependent upon the functions and services which are provided through the local administrative unit. In the absence of intermediate units, local districts must provide certain services and programs which in other settings could be furnished by an intermediate unit. The individual components of a state school system are interdependent and are in an intricate and sensitive balance as the various units interact to provide a full range of educational services and programs. If the role and responsibility of one component should be altered, that decision will have an impact upon each of the others. If a new level of educational agency (such as an intermediate unit) is introduced, the role, responsibilities, and functions of the local district and the state educational agency will be altered.

Recommendations relating to minimal desirable enrollment for all intermediate units will depend upon the relative sparsity of population in the area to be served, the extent to which local districts have been consolidated or reorganized, and the expectations which the state and local education agencies have for the unit. State statutes concerning minimum size have varied from 5,000 to 100,000 students.[10] Instead of using a minimum enrollment level as the criterion for forming an intermediate unit, a more logical approach would be to give first attention to the programs and services which are to be provided and then to develop an organizational pattern which will facilitate the provision of adequate sevices for all school districts in a given state. As was noted earlier, one of the primary considerations is whether the intermediate units are to be considered extensions of the state education agency or cooperative endeavors fostered by and for local school districts. If they are viewed as arms of the state educational agency, the size criterion will be of lesser importance than such factors as proximity to local districts and capacity to fulfill the designated functions. If they are cooperatives formed by local districts, efficiency criteria similar to those used in determining minimal and optimal sizes for local districts should be considered. However, primary attention should be given to the factors affecting the services and functions to be performed rather than to the number of students who happen to attend schools within the geographical area that constitutes a potential intermediate unit. In those states with large local districts, such as county units, intermediate units typically are not found. This experience suggests that roles and functions for intermediate units must be radically altered from traditional patterns if these units are to be feasible after the state has reorganized local school districts into adequate administrative units.

Equalization of Expenditures and Resources

Inequalities in wealth among school districts and concentrations of fiscal resources within states serve to emphasize the futility of making precise statements relating to optimum district size in terms of either square miles or population. State support programs do make some headway in redressing this inequity, but their efforts typically have focused on equalizing at a minimum level rather than at an optimum or a maximum level. As the percentage of state aid increases, the relative importance of disparities in wealth decreases, but the resources available to some districts still will only support a minimal program.

174

Although there is increasing support for area financing on a multi-district basis, this may be only an intermediate step toward complete state support of local schools. The tax base could be coterminous with a standard metropolitan area, an economic planning unit, or a grouping of counties, whichever appears logical within a given state. Those states which have made significant strides in reducing the number of school districts have found that the wide disparities in available fiscal resources generally are reduced as the number of school districts within a state is reduced. The same result would occur if several operating districts were grouped into an area taxing unit, but retained their operational independence.

Well-Trained Classroom Teachers

Research evidence supports the contention that districts of adequate size usually have teachers with higher levels of training, have these teachers assigned in their major areas of professional preparation, and have a higher rate of staff retention. The number of students is not the only factor which produces this staffing pattern. Increased curricular offerings, availability of instructional supplies and materials, and more favorable working conditions also are factors which contribute to a better staffing situation.

Utilization of Specialized Personnel

The current supply and demand situation relative to teachers and other educational personnel does not reduce the need to strive for more effective utilization of available personnel. Studies of staff utilization have revealed excessively low numbers of pupils per teacher in small school districts. Smaller districts also have difficulty making the best use of the specialized training of teachers and other instructional personnel. A sufficient number of students must be available to justify the employment of specialized personnel, but there is the additional need for a professional team of sufficient size to provide a challenging and satisfying working environment and also permit a teacher to specialize in his professional field of interest.

175

Efficient Expenditure of Funds

Cost per pupil cannot be considered independent of the educational program and the objectives of the school district. With two-thirds or more of the typical school budget being expended for salaries, differences in pupil-teacher ratios, in the experience and training of teachers, and in the availability of specialized support personnel can easily contribute to wide differences in educational expenditures among local school districts. However, the research and literature in the field of school district organization indicates that small school districts and small schools, when compared with larger districts, are more costly to operate. State-wide analyses of the costs of educational programs have continued to support this contention.[11]

In suburbs and in areas with normal concentrations of population there seems to be little justification for a proliferation of small districts. In some of the sparsely populated states some adjustment in the minimum standards for pupil enrollment may be merited, with intermediate units assuming additional functions and responsibilities which can be shifted from the local district.

GUIDELINES FOR REORGANIZATION AND SCHOOL FINANCE

Rather than relying upon one statute or several isolated statutes to expedite school district reorganization, a better approach is to develop a total legislative program or "package" which includes a sound reorganization procedure and financial incentives to encourage positive action by local districts. The following guidelines should be considered by state legislatures in their efforts to encourage school district reorganization:[12]

1. Current statutes and codes should be examined thoroughly to determine their effect upon school district reorganization. Only minor modification may be required, but those provisions should be repealed which retard or discourage reorganization or have become obsolete.

2. State and local reorganization committees should be established to provide organization and leadership for the reorganization process. Duties and responsibilities of these agencies and other groups or persons should be specifically defined in the statutes.

176

3. State-wide studies should be undertaken to determine the extent of the need for reorganization. Following this study, a master plan should be developed which gives consideration to state and local needs.

4. Legislation should be clear and easily understood by lay and professional people and should be easy to implement.

5. Regulations and criteria should be clearly defined. Criteria and minimum standards should be understood by all citizens and uniformly enforced.

6. On both the local and state level, maximum citizen involvement should be sought in the development of plans, criteria for reorganization, and proposed legislation.

7. Equitable voting procedures should be established with each person in the proposed unit having an equal vote. No group of voters should be discriminated against. The principle of "one-man-one vote" should prevail.

8. Reorganization should result in an equalization of fiscal resources insofar as this is geographically feasible.

9. The following fiscal provisions should be avoided if the goal is to encourage school district reorganization:

a. Non-resident tuition aid which enables non-operating districts to send students to an operating district and levy a low local tax rate to operate their own schools.

b. Aid to financially distressed districts in an amount sufficient to permit them to maintain school when they probably should be merged with another district.

c. Minimum standards which are not enforced.

d. Features which allow inadequate districts to circumvent the law and still receive state aid.

e. Sparsity correction factors which perpetuate small, inadequate school districts.

10. The following incentives can be used to encourage school district reorganization:

a. Optional provision for the new district to assume bonded debt and receive state support for retiring the debt incurred by component districts before reorganization.

b. State aid for debt incurred for school construction needed as a result of reorganization.

c. Aid to distressed districts which are viable, but financially troubled because of reorganization.

d. Bonus aid for reorganized districts on a per-pupil basis.

e. Transportation aid designed to cover a high percentage of actual costs or to encourage a specific type or reorganization.

f. Provisions that guarantee aid from the foundation program and other state programs at a level no less than the total amount which would have been received by the component districts if they had remained independent.

11. State officials should exert pressure to see that impacted area funds are distributed through regular state aid channels. This would reduce the distortion in school district structure and provide for more effective operation of state equalization plans.

12. Incentive features should be maintained at a support level high enough to encourage reorganization. Dollar amounts should be based on realistic cost figures and should be increased as the economy demands.

13. Regional taxing units should not be used as a substitute for an appropriate level of state support; the purpose of regional taxing units is to achieve equality in local tax rates and available fiscal resources.

ALTERNATIVE STRUCTURAL ARRANGEMENTS

The traditional patterns for administering schools have come under serious attack in recent years because of the changes in society associated with the myriad of social and cultural developments. Established institutions have a tendency to become rigid and unresponsive to external stimuli; this is counter to the general societal thrust for increased citizen involvement and participation, as well as to the movement toward greater utilization of scientific and technological developments. In the following discussion, several alternative structures are discussed as means for expanding and improving educational opportunities and programs.

Regional Service Units

Improvements in transportation and communication have negated most of the need for the county intermediate units which are still found in several states. The increased demand for educational services suggests the need to form other types of intermediate units which could provide such services as data processing for business and pupil personnel functions, or could operate vocational and technical schools. This type of intermediate unit does not have supervisory responsibilities; it focuses on providing needed services to constituent school districts. A second and related option is for the state education agency to decentralize its activities and establish satellite agencies on a regional basis so that its personnel and services will be more accessible.

An intriguing alternative involves five different settings for educational action—the classroom, the school building, the local school district, the intermediate unit, and the state education agency. Functions could be grouped under the broad categories of operational, developmental, and planning; this design calls for decisions relating to a specific function to be made as close to the point of performance as possible. The key considerations are that (1) a function is to be located at the level at which it can best be performed and (2) responsibility for the performance of a function may shift to another level as conditions change. The incidence, need, and availability of resources are the primary factors to be considered in determining which level would assume responsibility for performing a given function. Recognizing the differences which exist among school districts and the changes which are taking place in society, this "open system" approach recognizes that some local districts should assume responsibility for performing certain functions and that other districts might more appropriately rely upon an intermediate agency or even the state agency for performance of the same function. Fiscal economies should accrue through shared information and also through decisions that certain activities would only be performed at a limited number of sites in a given state. An underlying theme is the built-in emphasis on increased statewide coordination and leadership in decision-making.

Urban Metropolitan Districts

The rapid growth of suburban areas around large cities has focused attention on the inequities associated with concentrations of wealth in one area and concentrations of pupils in another. The geographic configurations of both suburban and urban school districts often predate any consideration of population growth patterns or concentrations of taxable wealth. In many urban areas educational planning is unnecessarily hampered by the proliferation of districts. In an effort to correct some of these

179

inequities, a metropolitan governmental structure for schools has been adopted in some places. One of the earliest experiences with metropolitan government was in Toronto. The formation of that program has spurred interest in the United States.

In the metropolitan areas of most American cities, the logistical and political problems associated with forming a metropolitan governmental structure would be most formidable because of the proliferation of school districts in the suburbs and the multistate character of many metropolitan areas. Notable exceptions are found in those states where the pattern for local districts involves county units; in these states the transition undoubtedly would be easier because a smaller number of agencies would be affected. The situation is further enhanced because of the reduced diversity in social and economic characteristics resulting from the larger unit. Cultural differences within the core city and within the large suburb will, in all likelihood, be greater than the "mean" differences between the city and its suburbs.

Recognizing reasonable size limits in terms of population and square miles, the rationale for the formation of urban metropolitan districts is at least three fold. Educational planning for the area is made easier by the consolidation of school districts, for it can be focused on the entire area rather than being unduly influenced by minor shifts in the population. Through this type of merger, school sites can be selected more objectively because of the elimination of district lines and the increased availability of land. Transportation problems should also be reduced because of the greater flexibility in determining the attendance boundaries for individual schools.

Specialized educational personnel and services can be made available to the entire area rather than being restricted to the wealthy or very large school districts. The critical mass of students will permit the district to provide both human and technological services at a higher level of economic efficiency.

Under this structural arrangement, students in the metropolitan area will have access to the same relative quality of educational program. They will not be short-changed because of the large variations in fiscal resources among districts which result from concentrations of commercial and/or industrial activity in one district and concentrations of students in another. The increased educational expenditures associated with rapid growth in one small area can be spread over the total area rather than im-

180

posing a very heavy tax burden upon the growing area. Racial integration could be accelerated through the use of busing to reduce *de facto* segregation. However, likelihood of a mass movement toward formation of urban metropolitan districts is minimal because of the problems associated with administering large school districts and because of the legal complications related to a school district with territory in more than one state.

Decentralized Administration in Urban Districts

The same districts which embrace the concept of forming an urban metropolitan school district in an attempt to solve their fiscal and planning problems will, in all likelihood, find themselves confronted with equally perplexing operational problems. The interactive impact of teacher militancy, citizen interest in involvement in educational decisions, and questions concerning the efficacy of current educational practices has generated considerable interest in some type of decentralized approach to the administration of urban school districts. When student enrollments exceed 50,000 and result in the need to operate several senior high schools, communication problems seem to mount and the need for divergence in educational programs among schools becomes evident.

Decentralization of operational responsibility in urban schools is complicated by the degree to which commensurate authority can also be decentralized. Master contracts with teachers' organizations often contain clauses pertaining to teacher transfers and to a multitude of working conditions. In effect, teachers might have a centralized contract in a decentralized setting; the potential for conflict is self-evident. Concern is often expressed that staffing practices will tend toward one of two extremes—paternalism and patronage or the unrestricted freedom of decentralized boards to hire and fire at will.

A number of benefits can accrue through decentralization if educational program variations are permitted on a sub-district basis and if administration of the budget also is decentralized. The most obvious benefits are the shortened lines of communication and the reduction of the feeling of isolation which characterizes many of the schools or attendance units in large urban school districts.

The discussion, thus far, has focused on the role of the admin-

181

istrator in the sub-district, but citizens in many sub-district settings are seeking ways in which they can participate actively in decision-making. Typically, their initial interests are in decisions concerning personnel matters and the educational program. The problems associated with their participation in these decisions are evident when one considers the state laws and regulations concerning educational programs and the restrictions on personnel decisions imposed through master contracts with teachers. However, the legitimacy of the push for increased lay involvement in large urban districts is obvious when one considers the fact that the number of students in some urban school districts exceeds the total number found in some states, or even in several states. The challenges are (1) to develop an appropriate definition of the scope of authority granted to the sub-district lay advisory groups or sub-district boards and (2) to provide some means through which opportunities for responsible citizen participation can be assured in the selection of members of such bodies. The potential benefits of greater citizen involvement may be overshadowed by problems if these two goals are not achieved.

Fiscal equalization for the school districts within a state is facilitated by the existence of the larger unit, but the need for internal fiscal equalization may be neglected because of a desire to provide "unequals with equal treatment." Programmatic requirements will vary significantly among the schools because of the different educational needs of students in various attendance units. This potential problem can be resolved through the use of a decentralized budgeting system which will make it possible for one school to receive more funds per pupil or more personnel than another school because of its demonstrated need for a different type of educational program.

Administrative procedures in large urban school districts can be decentralized to provide for a distribution of operational authority and responsibility. A constellation of schools would provide the basis for the sub-district; one or more high schools with their associated elementary and middle schools or junior high schools could comprise the unit. This feeder school system would facilitate the development of close working relationships in curriculum development and the resolution of operational problems. The number of decisions made at the sub-district level should be minimal, for the primary responsibility for determination of op-

182

erational procedures would reside at the school level. Central responsibilities would include establishing district-wide policies, evaluating the progress and needs of the district, obtaining and allocating fiscal resources for operation, stimulating research and development activities on a sub-district and district basis, representing and coordinating district interests with other governmental agencies, reviewing appeals from sub-districts, and protecting the employment rights of employees.

Other potential gains under this type of decentralized arrangement would encompass greater citizen involvement in determination of operational policies, allocation of decision-making powers to personnel who actually conduct the operations, and increased opportunities for parent and citizen participation in decisions affecting the schools serving their area, increased opportunities for school employees to exercise professional judgment in educational decisions, and greater potential for development of innovative and cooperative educational programs.

Inter-District Cooperation

Possibilities for cooperative action by local school districts are many and varied, but the limited powers of governing boards may preclude activities which could be undertaken through legal entities such as intermediate units or regional service units. Through the informal sharing of information and materials or through joint membership in school study councils, districts have the opportunity to work together. More formal cooperative action may be taken through joint purchasing or even joint employment of personnel. Such arrangements may not be satisfactory over an extended period of time because of their heavy dependence upon the informal relationships between the school officials in the participating districts, but they may provide an opportunity for exploratory activities which can be formalized at a later date.

Contracted Services

Local school districts have a long history of contracting with private agencies for various supporting services; one of the most obvious examples is in the field of public transportation. In rural districts there often are multiple contracts with individual owners and drivers of single buses; in suburban and urban districts the contract may be with a single firm which operates a fleet of buses and provides complete transportation services. Local districts have also entered into contracts for custodial services, maintenance services, and food services.

These examples illustrate the precedent for local districts entering into performance contracts with private firms which agree to provide instruction to pupils. The major difference between this recent activity and the previous contracts is that the earlier contractors agreed to provide various support services rather than provide actual instruction. In the scattered districts which have entered into performance contracts, the trend appears to be that the contractor will be paid only if the pupils progress at a predetermined rate. The impact that performance contracts will have upon the organizational structure of the public schools is a matter of lively discussion in many quarters, but at the present time most statements are pure conjecture because of the limited experience with these programs. If performance contracts should become the rule rather than the exception, traditional state controls will need to be reviewed and possibly revised, and modifications in some state support programs will be required to accommodate the diversity of staffing patterns found in these programs.

INTERACTIVE EFFECT OF FUNDING ARRANGEMENTS

The historical contention in school finance has been that the principal locus of financial support will also be the principal locus of control over schools. Research has not validated this contention, but funding decisions will alter the roles to be assumed by the various levels of educational governance. In the following discussion illustrations will be presented of the way that various funding decisions may affect the role of different agencies.

Federal Aid

For the purposes of this discussion, it is assumed that the federal government will continue to perform its traditional data gathering, initiation and development of special programs, and dissemination roles and that these roles will not change appreciably irrespective of the level of federal support for education. The possibility of an expansion of these roles is inherent, but it

184

is assumed that these decisions will be made independent of those relating to support for school operation. In the subsequent discussion in this section, federal aid has been grouped into two broad classifications—general aid and categorical aid.

General Aid. Under a federal support program involving federal aid, the principal role of the federal agency would be disbursement with state and local agencies having the responsibility for expending the funds in accordance with approved state plans. The policing or regulatory function should be minimal provided that decentralized decision-making is maintained.

In view of the state's legal responsibility for education, the state education agency undoubtedly would be actively involved in administration of a general program of federal aid. A federal block grant or general aid program could be administered through the state with a minimum of federal control through guidelines, regulations, and approved state plans. However, each of these administrative devices can also be used as a means to "control" the manner in which funds are expended in the local school district. The question of control or lack of control will only be answered through the statutes which authorize the expenditure of funds and the procedures used to administer the program.

Categorical Aid. Under a categorical aid program, the federal policing or regulatory responsibility will, in all likelihood, be greater because of the increased detail of the regulations and guidelines which must be prepared to protect the specific purpose of the funding. Even though the program may be intended to achieve a high degree of decentralization, the typical decision to create a staff to administer each "category" will contribute to the emergence of a specialized administrative agency. Rather than being cast in the role of a policy-maker, as in the previous example, a federal program of categorical aid is likely to result in the state serving more as transmitter and interpreter of federal guidelines and regulations with a significant reduction in its discretionary power.

State Aid

Various regulatory responsibilities are a direct consequence of state authority and responsibility for education; therefore, the task of isolating those directly related to school finance is virtually impossible. Statutes and regulations vary considerably among the several states, but most states have some legal mechanism through which school budgets are reviewed and fiscal accountability is assured by audits of expenditures. As a result of the adoption of standardized accounting procedures, comparable data are available at the state level for research and dissemination purposes.

As state funds increase in quantity, typically the relative differences among local districts in available fiscal resources will be reduced. Poorer districts will have additional fiscal resources, and richer districts may find that their relative financial advantage has decreased, but access to financial resources will have become more equal among the districts in the state. The relative latitude of local school officials will be increased if an adequate amount of state funds are distributed through general aid channels which recognize differences among districts in unit costs of education as well as taxpaying ability. In Chapter 9 of this volume various models of state general aid are analyzed. Some of those models are far more satisfactory than others.

Categorical grants should be held to a minimum because they increase the difficulties of budgeting and accounting and may also distort educational priorities.

Full state funding. The lack of extensive experience with full state funding of local school operations complicates the task of projecting the problems which might be associated with administration of such a program; however, certain types of problems can be predicted to be associated with this approach.

One of the principal problems resulting from full state funding would appear to be the lack of budgetary flexibility in terms of the ability to project contingencies or unanticipated emergencies and the capacity to accommodate necessary differences in funds required to support educational programs both within and among school attendance units. Emergencies could be resolved by maintaining a contingency fund at the state level which would be under the control of the state board of education and administered through the state education agency. Routine maintenance activities could be scheduled in a normal budget cycle, but permitting each district to maintain a contingency fund adequate for all emergencies would be fiscally unsound. Reasonably accurate predictions could be made concerning the size of the contingency fund which would be required for the entire state over a given period of time.

If a full state funding program should be adopted, a major challenge would be to develop an equitable budgeting system which would recognize the differences in costs associated with various educational programs and services as well as with different areas of the state. Allocation of funds on a flat per pupil basis would have a depressing effect upon educational programs. The budgeting and allocation process should recognize the costs associated with various educational programs, such as vocational education, compensatory education and special education, as well as the unique costs associated with sparsity of population and similar demographic factors. Considerable progress could be made toward the alleviation of these problems through the use of either a cost differential approach or programmatic budgeting in the allocation of funds.

A second problem associated with full state funding is related to the fiscal and budgetary controls which would be required to assure that local school operating units expend funds in accordance with their approved budgets. This problem would not be severe in those states which have established agencies with responsibility for approving budgets and conducting fiscal audits. The likelihood of mismanagement would be reduced if local officials were declared personally responsible for mismanagement or misapplication of funds.

Many observers contend that one of the great strengths of American public education has been the financial and programmatic leeway accorded local districts. Other observers contend that a major defect of this policy is that it disequalizes educational opportunity. Full state funding would obviously require a program approximately uniform in equality throughout the state. Local school districts could be permitted with supplementary state funding to develop innovative or experimental educational programs on a trial basis, but they could not be permitted to levy taxes to obtain revenues beyond the "state program" for this would be in direct contradiction to the basic intent of the program. Chapters 9 and 11 of this volume present some evidence that indicates it would be sound public policy to provide 75 to 90 percent of public school revenue from state and federal sources. However, it seems that innovation and desirable change would be promoted if school districts are left with some local tax leeway. Perhaps the best policy would be to provide sufficient local leeway to permit needed local experimentation without substantially disequalizing educational opportunity and also to provide some supplementary state funds for research and development.

Local Support

Irrespective of the source of funds, current trends indicate that responsibility for operating schools will continue to reside at the local level. In large cities the concept of "local" may mean decentralization to provide for increased citizen involvement at a level closer to the local school, for current thought in both practice and theory supports the view that operational decisions should be made as close to their point of implementation as possible.

Public reaction to the property tax and the general resistance to locally levied income and sales taxes suggest that the relative amount of financial support provided by the local school district will not increase significantly. As the percentage of funds coming from the state and federal levels increases, the relative disparity in fiscal flexibility among local districts will undoubtedly decrease. In the district with above average wealth, the challenge to plan for effective utilization of funds will remain, but the opportunity to call for additional resources will not be available. In the district with average or below average wealth, financial flexibility in terms of available resources will remain constant or be increased.

Rather than being expressed in a fiscal fashion, local support might more appropriately be expressed in terms of human and conceptual capital. Planning, management, and implementation skills may become the primary resources which will be provided by the local school district.

FEDERAL-STATE-LOCAL LEADERSHIP BALANCE

Traditional concepts relative to strict allocation of powers and responsibilities to various levels of government appear to be outdated in terms of the contemporary challenges and opportunities which confront educational institutions. Efforts to expand the role of state and federal educational agencies have often been op-

188

posed on the grounds that only a fixed amount of power existed, and thus the reallocation would result in a reduction of the power of the local school district. Experience with federally supported programs designed to deal with social and economic deprivation has demonstrated that the increased involvement of the federal government has contributed to an increase in power of the state and local governmental units to deal with these problems. Under this concept, rather than being viewed as encroachment, federal interest in an educational problem area would be welcomed, for federal intervention should also enhance the power and the opportunities available to state and local units as they deal with the problems. The problem entailed in full acceptance of this concept is that the federal interest has not always coincided completely with state and local interests, resulting in either a diversion of state and local interests and effort or a rejection of the federal program when the three levels of government are not in agreement.

The challenge is for each of the three levels of governance to develop a strong, well-staffed, and capable educational agency so that the three levels may interact in a triad. This would maximize the opportunities for desirable changes and innovation, and also would encourage the further professional growth and development of the staffs at each of the three levels.

Rather than being viewed as a local and/or state responsibility, the financing of education has come to be viewed as a local-state-federal partnership. The level of federal participation has increased significantly since the enactment of the National Defense Education Act in 1958, and the level of participation must continue to increase if local districts are to have an adequate level of fiscal resources without an unequal tax burden. A state legislature cannot abrogate its responsibility for financing education, for each state, through its constitution, has assumed responsibility for establishing and maintaining an educational system. State legislatures have considerable leeway in making decisions relative to the type of tax and level of government at which the tax is to be levied and collected, but responsibility for providing revenues for school operation still resides with the state legislature.

Even though the federal government has restricted its role in supporting educational programs to a variety of categorical aids, the federal government does have an interest in seeing to it that equal educational opportunities are provided to all students. The relative importance of this role has been enhanced with the increasing urbanization and mobility of the American society. Only the federal government, unhampered by state boundaries and local jurisdictions, possesses the taxing flexibility and resources needed to provide an equitable distribution of funds among the several states and their operating school districts.

Federal Responsibilities

The challenge for the federal government is to move beyond its historical programs of research and development activities, data gathering and dissemination, and such narrow programs as aid for "impacted areas" and operation of Indian schools. A more worthy program is for the federal government to pursue the goal of guaranteeing equal educational opportunity. This goal encompasses the assumption of a national leadership role, stimulation of research and innovation, promotion of expanded professional experiences at the state and local levels, and guaranteed provision of equal access to educational programs and fiscal resources.

A long-term issue in intergovernmental relations in education is the relative balance between state and federal roles in such areas as educational goal setting and the control or actual operation of public schools and related agencies.

State Responsibilities

Plenary responsibility for all aspects of education resides with the state, and the state through the legislature and various state agencies is responsible for the operation of educational programs within the state. Functional responsibility for the day-to-day operation of schools may be decentralized to the local districts, but ultimate accountability still resides at the state level.

State educational agencies typically have some degree of executive, judicial, and legislative powers. Although this may appear to contradict the traditional separation of powers, state legislatures have continued to treat the state education agency as an entity independent of the executive branch of government. Rather than placing state education agencies in the executive branch under the governor, the trend has been to create semi-independent agencies with their own boards which exercise the power to approve or advise on rule-making and administrative procedures.

190

The potential power of the state education agency and the importance of the role of the state board cannot be overemphasized, for a state system of education is so complex that the legislature cannot prescribe in detail all of the policies and procedures which will be required to operate schools.

In enacting statutes pertaining to the fiscal support of schools, state legislatures have a three fold responsibility: (1) to assure that each district has sufficient funds to operate an educational program that adequately meets its educational needs, (2) to develop the state financing program so that the tax burden is equalized among districts, and (3) to provide local districts with some incentive to search for ways to improve the process of education. In addition, sufficient funds must be provided to staff and maintain an effective state education agency.

Beyond the responsibility to provide adequate finances for local schools, the state has primary responsibility for administrative, regulatory, and leadership functions such as the following:

1. Administrative functions
   a. Collect operational data and information from local districts.
   b. Disburse funds.
   c. Issue teacher certificates.
2. Regulatory functions
   a. Develop and enforce minimum standards for schools.
   b. Visit and evaluate operating programs in local schools.
   c. Inspect schools to assure a healthy environment.
   d. Audit school financial and pupil personnel records to assure compliance with regulations.
3. Leadership functions
   a. Coordinate the operations of state and local educational agencies.
   b. Implement planning activities focusing on state and local educational needs.
   c. Develop and implement a defensible plan for school district organization in the state.
   d. Involve representative groups and individuals in planning activities.
   e. Design and implement a research program to support the state's planning activities and to assist local school districts.

191

f. Encourage research and experimentation in local school districts.
g. Promote and evaluate educational innovations.
h. Develop and coordinate a consultative service program utilizing resource personnel from the state education agency, intermediate units, local school districts, and institutions of higher learning.
i. Implement a communications program to keep the public informed about education and to encourage a free exchange of information and communication about areas of concern.
j. Provide assistance to local school districts in planning, conducting, and evaluating in-service programs for their personnel.

Intermediate Unit Responsibilities

A detailed list of responsibilities for intermediate units or regional service agencies will not be presented, for the role of these agencies is truly evolutionary in terms of the tasks and functions being performed by local districts and the state educational agency and in terms of the statutes which provide for the creation of an intermediate unit. In some states existing intermediate units can no longer be justified because of progress in school district reorganization. They must be reconceptualized on the basis of administrative convenience or efficiency to provide services needed by local school districts or the state education agency.

Local Responsibilities

Local school districts serve as arms of the state legislature in the structural organization for school operation in all states except Hawaii. Patterns of school organization vary extensively among states, and a constant process of evolution has kept districts in a state of change as schools have been consolidated or districts have been reorganized. However, the challenge to develop and conduct educational programs has continued to be the responsibility of the local school district. Placing major responsibility for this function at the local district level does not suggest an abdication of state responsibility, but permits flexibility in terms of local situations and also casts the federal and state agencies in a leadership and service role.

192

As the basic operational unit for schools, local school districts must look beyond day-to-day operational concerns and address themselves to long-range planning in terms of the educational program as well as related fiscal matters. The complexity of governmental units and services points to the necessity for cooperation and joint planning among various governmental units. A diverse group of services and activities have become an integral and vital part of a sound educational program; the challenge to local school officials is to identify those which can best be provided by local districts.

From the local district must also come the basic information used in assessment and accountability efforts. Through the analysis of these data alternative delivery systems or processes may be identified which contribute to improved educational opportunities and greater efficiency in the use of the resources devoted to education.

FOOTNOTES

1. Clifford P. Hooker and Van D. Mueller, *The Relationship of School District Reorganization to State Aid Distribution Systems, Part II*, National Educational Finance Project, Special Study No. 11, Minneapolis, Minnesota, 1970, pp. 11-60; *Estimates of School Statistics*, Research Division-National Education Association, Research Report 1970-R15, Washington, D. C., 1970, p. 26.

2. Hooker and Mueller, *op. cit.*

3. *Ibid., Estimates of School Statistics, op. cit.*

4. Hooker and Mueller, *op. cit.*, pp. 177-9.

5. *Ibid.*, p. 178.

6. *Ibid.*, p. 183.

7. William E. Inman, "Size and District Organization" in *Planning for School District Organization*, Selected Position Papers, The Great Plains School District Organization Project, Lincoln, Nebraska; The State Department of Education, 1968, pp. 160-5.

8. *Ibid.*, pp. 171-2.

9. *Ibid.*, p. 173; Ralph D. Purdy, *Guidelines for School District Organization*, A Project Report, Lincoln, Nebraska: The State Department of Education, 1968, pp. 124-5.

10. Inman, *op. cit.*, pp. 173-4.

11. *Ibid.*, pp. 163-5.

12. Hooker and Mueller, *op. cit.*, pp. 184-6.

CHAPTER 7

Measuring Educational Needs and Costs

The first quarter of this century was noted for the development of budgeting procedures for two major categories of expenditures (1) current operating expenses and (2) capital outlay and debt service expenses. The cost-unit concept, based on the pupil and the teacher, emerged slowly in conjunction with the idea of equalization of educational opportunity.

By mid-century a widely adopted procedure for implementing the equalization concept was the encompassing pupil (and instructional) unit, weighted for demographic factors associated with population sparsity. In a few states the beginnings of the present-day approach to program cost analysis appeared in methods that broke down cost units into broad programs and service components.

State and federal categorical aids grew in number and in the proportion of total funds. These aids had two purposes: (1) to stimulate the development of special programs requiring extra costs to meet specific needs and (2) to assure high priority of these programs in the educational milieu.

Capital outlay has received spotty consideration in state aid plans. Even today, only a few states have developed a plan of financing that reflects the principle of integral relationship between the educational program and the necessary capital facilities.

194

After World War II the problems of financing education have been accentuated by mass migrations, increased social malaise and discontent, and high concentrations of youth with serious educational handicaps in the cities. The declining population in the rural areas has had an inflationary effect on per capita costs of education for those remaining. All of these factors have added to the difficulties in keeping up-to-date in the measurement of educational and financial needs in every state.

This study presents a method of measuring the financial inputs of designated program categories. The term *program* is used broadly to classify instructional and service activities into groups with distinctive characteristics. Programs can be described in terms of comparable work or service of the employed staff members, the target population served, essential materials and facilities, and relationships to other programs.

The total educational process can be broken down into programs as functional components which can be related to pupils, their needs and development. The pattern or configuration of programs with distributions of pupils may vary from one local school district to another. However, there are commonalities to provide norms of practice within each state for estimating needs.

The taxonomy of programs in this study includes those in current use. These may be modified in the future as the needs of pupils dictate. The procedure is designed to identify the target population through diagnosis of pupil needs rather than using indirect methods of estimation such as counting the number of children from low income families.

The categories of programs for which measures of differential costs have been developed include the following: (1) Early Childhood Education, (2) Basic Elementary and Secondary Education, (3) Special Education, (4) Compensatory Education, and (5) Vocational Education.

The following programs have been studied, with each one requiring a special procedure for measurement of need: (1) Adult and Continuing Education, (2) Food Services, (3) Transportation, (4) Capital Outlay, and (5) Community Junior College Education.

The findings of special studies on these programs give a picture of the distribution of inputs among samples of school districts throughout the country. Exemplary programs are described; i.e., programs that most nearly represent the best practice we know today. Estimates of pupils in need of these programs, cost differentials among programs, and projected costs for the year 1980 are presented.

EARLY CHILDHOOD EDUCATION

There is not complete agreement among educators on the age range of children to include in the field of early childhood education. Some persons prefer to include children up to about age nine, thereby including the primary or first three grades of elementary school. The most general classification appears to be age five and below, including kindergarten, nursery school, and infants. This study has adopted the latter definition in order to focus on the lack of universality of kindergarten attendance (about 76 percent of 5-year-olds in attendance in 1968-69), and the very limited nature of nursery schools and other programs for children under five years of age.

The acceptance of this definition in no way argues against a program for children beginning at age three and extending through the first two or three years of the elementary school. All evidence reported in this study strongly supports the proposition that early childhood programs should be an integral part of the elementary school. But the definition used in this study helps to focus attention on how best to organize programs that meet the needs of children in their early years.

The researchers for this study found formal schooling for children organized as nursery schools for ages three and four, and kindergarten for five-year-olds. Very few programs for infants under age three were found; and these were limited largely to experimental programs in universities. Most leading scholars argue that formal education outside the home should not be established for children under three years of age until there is more knowledge about the needs of these children and their development.[1]

Parent Education

There is sufficient knowledge from research and experimentation to justify parent education programs for children under three years of age. Parents can follow prescribed programs of activity that will have a profound effect on the development of infants. The special assistance that parents need can be pro-

196

vided by the public school system. These programs include conferences, seminars, and other activities for parents to develop their skills and to plan specific activities with children in the home. Parents are "teachers" of their children. Their effectiveness can be improved immensely. Some investment in parents may yield greater educational dividends than comparable amounts spent directly on the respective children.

Day-Care Program

The day-care program has as its primary objective the care of young children whose mothers are away from home during the day for work, illness, and emergencies. Activities consist primarily of custodial care and supervision of meaningful play, recreation, lunch service, and rest.

To be most effective this program should be carefully planned in conjunction with, or as an extension of, an instructional program. The child's day should be organized to provide a combination of an educational program for part of the time and homelike care for the remainder. The least effective program consists of unskilled supervision which may provide combinations of activities that produce deleterious effects on young children.

There is some reason to believe that the time has come for public school systems to introduce day-care programs for at least the children of most needy families. In addition the public school system should be given responsibility to provide general supervision and technical services to private day-care centers to ensure reasonable standards.

Nursery School: 3-4 Years

Children of three and four years of age need a formal educational program with an appropriate environment that provides an opportunity for a natural and well-rounded development. According to the findings of this study, the model program to be highly effective should be organized into instructional units of about 15 to 20 children with a staff consisting of a teacher and two aides, supplemented by participation of the mothers on a part-time basis. These instructional personnel must be augmented by a supportive staff consisting of administrators, psychologists, media specialists, and others. The school day should be about 2 1/2 to 3 hours. The teacher should devote her time to only one instructional group and to the parents of the children. She should not have two groups, or sessions, each day as is customary for many kindergarten teachers.

The physical environment is extremely important for the staff to operate an effective program of varied activities. Indoor space of about 100 square feet per pupil is essential, with proper arrangement and furnishings for the learning activities. In addition auxiliary space is needed for toilets and for storage of clothing and supplies. Outdoor space with appropriate equipment for play is equally essential. These are the characteristics on which cost estimates of inputs are based in this study.

Kindergarten

The kindergarten is an extension of the nursery school program, primarily for five-year-old children. This program places emphasis on the total development of the child in areas such as speech, language, articulation, problem solving, self-image, and other cognitive qualities. In addition the program includes attention to social and physical development of children.

The characteristics of a model, or effective, kindergarten are as follows: instructional units of 20 to 25 children; a staff consisting of a teacher, a teacher intern, an aide, and a part-time volunteer mother; indoor space of about 100 square feet per pupil properly equipped, augmented by auxiliary storage and other space; and outdoor space with appropriate arrangement and equipment.

The length of the school day should be about 3 to 3 1/2 hours, with the teacher having only one group (session) and conducting a program for parents of the children. Most kindergartens are operated on double sessions with severely limited staff and facilities. The needed changes in the decade of the 1970's are: a conversion to single sessions, increase in inputs of staff and facilities, and establishment of programs for the total 5-year-old population. These changes provide the bases in this study for estimates of needed inputs.

BASIC ELEMENTARY EDUCATION

Since some school districts do not operate kindergartens and other programs below first grade, the elementary grades one through six are defined in this study as a base of reference for

198

analysis of costs. By definition basic education is the residual or great mass of educational activity for most pupils, after netting out the pupils with unique learning difficulties for whom special programs are provided. In elementary school the special programs are defined in this study as (1) special education and (2) compensatory education.

A new image of the elementary school may become widely established by 1980. Knowledge about the development of children suggests that elementary education will be reorganized so as to phase early childhood programs with grades one through five. The sixth, seventh, and eighth grades, or equivalent terms to describe an intermediate developmental level, will probably become the predominant grouping for a middle school between the elementary school and the high school.

The emerging characteristics of basic elementary education may be classified as follows:[2]

1. The program will be planned with clearer objectives for child development.
2. The scope of learning activities (curricula) will be broader than those in contemporary schools.
3. Instruction will be organized with greater collaboration of staff members, a greater variety and flexibility in grouping.
4. Pupils with special needs will have access to a greater number of staff members with varied talents for assistance.
5. Traditional libraries will be expanded into complex resource centers, including all types of learning materials.
6. The physical environment will be designed to accommodate changes in learning activities through such arrangements as more clustering of areas for collaboration of teachers, and special rooms for various groups and types of activities.
7. Schools will have a greater variety of instructional equipment and supplies than at present.
8. Schools will have a proportionately greater staff component for non-teaching services than at present, e.g.: teaching assistants, psychologists, counselors, health personnel, social workers, research and media specialists.

BASIC SECONDARY EDUCATION

For purposes of cost analysis the grades seven through twelve are designated as the base for secondary education.[3]

Middle Schools

Recently middle schools have been organized with grades six, seven, and eight. These grades encompass a desirable combination for the physical, emotional, social, and intellectual development of most youth. The fundamental characteristics of staff, services, and physical resources are similar to the elementary level. Yet, fields of instruction show the beginnings of specialization which become more distinct in high school. There is somewhat more differentiation of staff because of slightly more specialization in fields of knowledge.

The most unique substantive change in the middle grades is the introduction of some learning activities which formerly were deferred to the high school. There are no sound psychological or pedagogical reasons to defer opportunities that begin the development of basic skills in a variety of fields such as practical arts, the fine arts, and science.

Pupils are ready to learn the use of simple power tools, business office equipment, micro analysis in science, music, painting, ceramics, and others at a more sophisticated level of achievement than the typical junior high school has afforded in the past. Some of these basic skills are essential for introductory vocational study that twenty percent or more of the youth need by the time they reach the eighth grade.

High Schools

Basic secondary education in high schools is defined as the residual after netting out special programs and vocational education requiring proportionately high inputs per student.

Like the preceding grade levels, high schools are undergoing changes. Their holding power is increasing due to various social and technological pressures for a minimum achievement—high school graduation. They are being challenged to offer broader and richer opportunities, requiring both a reordering and an increase of inputs.

The exemplars observed in this study may be the forerunners of the typical schools in 1980. Some of their unique characteristics are: expanding breadth of program; greater flexibility in the instructional process, with greater variety and sizes of groups; greater incentive for individual achievement; more specialization, division of labor, and collaborative work among staff members; and more extensive physical resources. In common with exemplary elementary and middle schools, the exemplary high school of today may be the typical school of 1980.

SPECIAL EDUCATION

Special education is a program that was established originally for the extremely deviate pupils with mental and physical handicaps that required separation into groups for special instruction.[4] The incidence of children with severe handicaps averages about three percent of the total school population. However, there is much variation in the incidence among communities because of the mobility of families. Many families choose their place of residence on the basis of the availability of programs to accommodate a handicapped child.

Children with severe handicaps occur most frequently in the six to twelve age range. This is due largely to better identification because of compulsory school attendance and the validity of diagnostic procedures for children of six or seven years as compared with younger ages.

The lower incidence in the middle and high schools can be attributed mainly to inability of many handicapped pupils to progress beyond the curriculum of the elementary grades. A slight effect may be due to lower life expectancy than normal children.

The children in this category have personal needs that require special instruction. Some of them have to be in separate groups, while some do better in regular classes for part of their work and in separate classes for the remainder. The school system, however, needs teachers with special knowledge and skills and nonteaching specialists to accommodate these children.

COMPENSATORY EDUCATION

This category is used to define tutorial and remedial programs for young children and older youth with serious learning difficulties, emotional problems, and general social maladjustments.[5] The source of learning difficulties for these pupils may be impoverished home environment, unwholesome neighborhood, hypertension, emotional illness, and lower than average mental ability (but not as low as children classified in special education programs).

Most programs for youth with these characteristics are in relatively early stages of development. There is much variation among districts in the nature of resources and organization of programs to work with these children. In some districts separate administrative departments have been organized to operate these programs, leading to some fragmenting of professional groups with overlapping, and sometimes competing, roles. In others, the specialized staff has been organized to deal with the total range of deviate needs. This latter pattern appears to be the more adequate one for future development of the total field of special programs.

Current compensatory programs for young children warrant specific mention. About two-thirds of enrollments of children under five in early childhood programs are of short-term compensatory nature. This, however, reflects an experimental stage in the development of compensatory programs rather than the fundamental nature of early childhood programs. The exemplary nursery and kindergarten programs as described earlier are totally adaptive and accommodative for all children of these ages except the severely handicapped ones who may have to be separated into special groups along with older elementary school age children with like difficulties.

For purposes of this study compensatory programs have been divided into two groups by ages of pupils: (1) grades six and below, and (2) seven through twelve.[6] These divisions provide comparisons of inputs and costs of programs that correspond to the respective grade levels of basic or regular programs.

Unavoidably, there is a large overlap in the classification of pupils in special programs among school districts. Some pupils are classified in compensatory programs because of supplementary federal funds. Other pupils with very similar learning difficulties may be classified in special education programs because of definitions that conform to requirements of other sources of supplementary funds. The problems of classification and cost analysis are simplified by defining two groups of severe difficulties: (1) those commonly classified in special education with severe mental and physical handicaps (described in the preceding section); and (2) those with severe social and emotional problems requiring detention or institutionalizing for extended periods of time. The latter group includes those emotionally ill, delinquents, home and hospital bound, unmarried pregnant girls, and some dropouts.

A special group of institutionalized students consists of disoriented dropouts. These are individuals who have become so disorganized that they cannot function in the regular school environment. They exhibit a variety of characteristics: hypersensitivity, social isolation, loss of purpose, and extreme insecurity. These students should be served in so-called continuation schools which are organized for therapy and rehabilitation. Some pupils can be restored to the regular school, others need part-time jobs to help them regain self-confidence and develop skills for making a living. Costs are estimated to be about equivalent to the detention schools for delinquents and emotionally disturbed pupils.

The largest group of pupils classified in the compensatory category are those with a wide range of learning difficulties but of less severity than the two groups of very severe difficulties described above. The treatment which the school provides for this largest group includes instruction in regular groups, additional tutoring, small group instruction, extensive counseling services, and other special attention.

This procedure of diagnosing pupils and developing instructional and remedial services to meet individual needs avoids many problems encountered in using proxy methods such as identifying pupils from family income and other characteristics.

In addition to these special programs, at least part of the time of some special teachers and nonteaching specialists is needed for the majority of pupils who never become identified with any special program. These pupils, too, need the help of counselors, librarians, and even perhaps an infrequent conference with a psychologist. The fundamental distinction between the *special* and the *basic* programs,[7] at least for measuring the cost of inputs, lies not only in the formal organization for instruction but also in the amount of special staff time and resources per pupil.

VOCATIONAL EDUCATION

Vocational education has a long history as a special component of secondary education.[8] The federal government has played a dominant role in stimulating the establishment of programs and fostering new vocational education concepts since the Smith-

Hughes Act of 1917. That act provided funds to support vocational courses of instruction to develop skills exclusively for specific occupations.

By the mid 1930's social and economic changes led to a broadening of the concept of vocational education, bringing the definition closer to the general goal of all education for well-rounded development of the individual.

The federal Vocational Education Acts of 1963 and 1968, and the stated goals in many state plans to implement these acts, express objectives in such terms as the following: "development of the individual as well as meeting the needs of the labor market," "to develop within the individual the personal-social traits which will help him in relating well to other people, both on and off the job, and in making him a good citizen and one who can enjoy and appreciate the finer things in life," "to assist in the development of skills in personal, social, and civic relationships needed for full participation in society as a worker, family member and citizen," and "a common purpose of occupational training and education in general must be a development of students' ability to evaluate their own aptitudes, interests, and abilities in relation to the multitude of occupational opportunities in the modern economy, and to make appropriate educational and occupational decisions on the basis of this self-evaluation."

While these phrases emphasize the learning of salable skills, they also recognize the necessity for total development of the individual. Furthermore, there is the recognition that vocational competence is a function of other personal attributes commonly referred to as general competence.

Despite these declarations of purpose, enrollments in vocational programs in public schools have remained relatively low over the years. Studies of attitudes suggest that many pupils do not perceive the experiences in the vocational programs as contributing to fulfilling the general educational goals. The trends of enrollments, when coupled with other occupational data, provide bases for estimating the needs for vocational education in the public schools.

ADULT AND CONTINUING EDUCATION

Continuing education for adults of all ages may rank close behind early childhood education in the need for development in the immediate years ahead.[9]

204

Enrollments of older adults in programs offered by public school systems vary widely. In a sample of 28 districts[10] in one of the special studies of this project, the adult enrollment in one district during the year equals 23 percent of the regular day school enrollment. The next highest is 11 percent. Most are below 5 percent. Several are one percent or fewer. About three-fourths of the adults are taking work equivalent to postsecondary education offered in most junior colleges. In some states, junior colleges have developed extensive adult programs in recent years which have attracted individuals away from the programs in the public schools.

A heavy demand for programs in the public schools still persists according to the views of educational leaders.[11] The demand appears in two major forms: One is the private demand of young adults and persons of low income for programs to increase their income. High-income adults seek programs primarily for leisure and non-income activities. The other demand is found in the programs that are mandated for apprenticeship and licenses.

Financial support of adult programs from tax revenue ranges from substantial to none. The typical middle to large size school district provides space for instruction, utilities, custodial service, and a staff member to serve as director or general supervisor. Expenses for teachers and instructional materials are provided from fees charged the students. Most programs consist of an ad hoc collection of short-term courses arranged as teachers can be found and as interest is manifested. A few programs consist of firm curricula that possess the qualities of depth and sequence that many adults desire.

One particularly fruitful area for public school involvement is with a group of dropouts in need of continuing education on a part-time basis within a new institutional environment. The public schools are attracting very few of them back into evening programs.

FOOD SERVICES

In 1968-69 about 37 percent of pupils enrolled in the public schools participated in the National School Lunch Program.[12] Some schools serve close to 100 percent of the pupils, while others serve none. Nearly 20 percent of the pupils were in schools with no food service. About 15 percent of all lunches were served to

205

children from needy families. This figure is estimated to be 25 percent in 1971.

Cities with population of 250,000 or more serve the lowest percent of pupils because of crowded conditions, lack of facilities, and the tradition of "home food service" in neighborhood schools. In 36 of 57 large cities reporting in this study there were 1,883 schools attended by 1,083,263 pupils with no food service in the schools.

Sources of Funds

Estimates of expenditures by sources for food services in public and private schools in 1968-69 are as follows:[13]

Federal Government	$ 564 Million—	26.7%
State and Local Governments	180 Million—	8.6
Other Local Contributions		
(Nontax Revenue)	320 Million—	15.1
Children's Payments	1,049 Million—	49.6
Total	$2,113 Million—	100.0%

This total figure was about 5 percent of all expenditures for public and private elementary and secondary schools in 1968-69. About half of the federal government's contribution was in the form of commodities and the remainder in cash.

Organization of Program

Many educators and laymen have argued that food service programs provide an excellent opportunity for instruction in nutrition. Findings in this study indicate that instruction in nutrition occurs in various areas of the curriculum rather than under the management of food service. Most educators do not accept the view that these two functions can be unified effectively. The school cafeteria provides an environment for learning the social norms of dining. Courses in science and homemaking provide the most appropriate environment for systematic study of the knowledge of nutrition.

The food service program entails responsibility at the state level to expedite the federal and state contributions, and provide assistance to local school districts for the most educationally effective and economical operation of food services.

206

Four patterns of food service management have developed in local school districts:

1. Self-contained school cafeteria,
2. Central processing—satellite serving units,
3. Vending systems for complete meals, and
4. Automated vending systems for "convenience" items.

Most children are served by the first two methods.

The trend in the future may be toward central processing supplemented with vending systems. These methods of administration may best serve crowded schools in cities and also meet the rising cost of labor in the processing of food. Large school systems and regional cooperatives of small districts can organize personnel for food service on a competitive basis with private vendors.

Projections of Food Service Needs to 1980

At a maximum participation rate of 95 percent, some 50,250,-000 pupils will be served school lunches in public and private schools in 1980. Estimating the cost of lunches at 66.8 cents each the total cost would be approximately $6,040,000,000. It is estimated that cost of breakfast for needy pupils would be approximately $320,000,000 making a grand total of $6,360,000,000 in 1968-69 dollars. How much of this amount will be financed from public funds and how much by parents paying for children's lunches is unknown. This will be determined by Congress, 50 state legislatures and some 17,000 boards of education. If the same proportion of this total is provided from taxation in 1980 as in 1968-69, approximately $2,245,000,000 would be supplied by the federal, state and local governments. Since these estimates are based on 1968-69 dollars, the actual amount would be considerably greater, assuming that inflationary trends will continue.

TRANSPORTATION

Transportation serves two fundamental functions: (1) a commuting service from home to school and return and (2) an instructional service to expand the learning environment beyond the classroom.[14] The commuting service meets a variety of needs: transporting pupils beyond reasonable walking distance to school and even within walking distance under conditions hazardous to children when walking; facilitating the operation of flexible programs such as kindergarten, special instructional centers for handicapped pupils, regional programs of vocational education; and providing for the integration of ethnic and socioeconomic groups.

The scope of these functions is subject to change during the next decade, increasing the existing complexity of measuring inputs. In the past the problem of measurement centered primarily on the daily commuting to and from home for the purpose of computing the amount of state funds due the local district under the prevailing state policy.

There are several determinants of transportation cost which have been either ignored or treated inadequately in the finance plans of some states. The degree of population sparsity is a major one. Basically the average distance per pupil transported is the most fundamental variable. Road conditions once made a difference, but not much today. The degree of school consolidation in sparse areas is still a variable of substantial effect on aggregate transportation cost, but somewhat less on cost per pupil.

The incidence of pupils in special programs is another variable of importance. These programs call for some custom-type equipment and special scheduling. Children in nursery school and kindergarten have short sessions and must be taken home ahead of other pupils. Regional instructional centers for special programs serving the constituent population of more than one school require secondary scheduling and routing. These variables can have large impacts in sparse areas where distances are great as compared with more populous areas.

In areas of great sparsity the transportation cost increases with consolidation of schools. However, part of the increase is offset in economies achieved through larger size schools. Overall expenditures for consolidated schools may not decline, however, because consolidation often is accompanied by an expansion of the educational program, thus obscuring the inherent economies of scale.

In areas of greater density the relative number of children to be transported because of unreasonable walking distance may be small compared with the sparse areas. However, the costs for pupils in special programs may be relatively larger because of the higher incidence rates of pupils qualified for the programs. Furthermore, the minimum distance set for transporting regular

208

pupils is difficult to maintain. Thus, the aggregate cost is increased by a small percent of spillover at the margins of transportation boundaries.

In all cities and urban areas traffic and other safety hazards justify the transportation of many children, especially young ones, who otherwise could walk to school. Many older students, especially those attending special instructional centers, may have access to public transportation, with some savings in cost. In heavily congested areas the time required per pupil mile of travel is greater than in sparse areas. Though fuel consumption may be less the time of the driver is greater. Another variable whose added impact is not yet known for lack of sufficient data is transportation to achieve balanced socioeconomic-ethnic groups.

Transportation to extend the classroom learning environment could increase sharply if this service were extended to more teachers.

Projected Needs of Transportation for 1980

Little increase in the total number of pupils of school age 5-17 is expected by 1980. There will be changes within local districts with variable impacts on transportation costs. If early childhood programs expand to meet the low demand estimates of this project, additional transportation will be needed. Expansion of these programs will have the greatest effect on transportation cost in small towns and rural areas where these programs are least developed.

New policies on establishing social balance among schools can add substantially to the cost of transportation. If such policies result in educational improvement, the additional transportation cost could be classified as compensatory education expense.

A large factor to affect transportation expense, as other costs, is inflation. Further school consolidation and suburban growth may be expected in the 1970's, perhaps at a rate equal to the rate of the 1960's. During that period the number of pupils transported increased about 50 percent. In the 1970's an annual inflation of 3 percent plus an overall increase in number of pupils transported from a low of 10 percent to a high of 25 percent would result in a total increase from a low of 50 percent to a high of 65 percent above the $900 million national expenditure in 1968-69.

CAPITAL OUTLAY

Capital outlay is perhaps the most capriciously financed element of educational costs.[15] In 1968-69 only 26 states provided state-collected revenues to aid local school districts in the financing of capital facilities. In the other 24 states the districts provided the total cost of these facilities through issuance of local bonds, payment of rentals, and repayment of state loans from local tax revenue.

The legal procedures in most states to provide revenues for capital outlay appear more like ingenious devices to constrain the use of public monies than measures to ensure the flow of funds where needed. In 1968 the public school districts spent a total of $4,461 million for capital outlay and $1,104 million for interest on bonded indebtedness. In that year the sum of these amounted to 19.1 percent of the current operating expenditures for public elementary and secondary schools. Only 11 percent of the capital expenditures were obtained from state funds. The corresponding percentages for 1969-70 and 1970-71 are 14.1 and 13.2, respectively. The percentages may decline further in the future unless methods of financing these facilities are changed.

Beginning in 1949 the percentage of total educational expenditure devoted to capital facilities rose from 22.6 percent to 29.3 percent in 1953-54. Thereafter this proportion declined gradually to the figure of 13.2 percent in the year 1970-71. Why? The principal reasons were a heavy inventory of obsolete facilities around 1950, a reasonably expansive property tax base in the decade of the 1950's, and a growth spurt in the school population. Some states used surplus funds accumulated during the war years, and others authorized a few dramatic bond issues. Only a very few set out to establish a system of funding that was designed to keep up with increases in enrollments, to eliminate the inventory of obsolete facilities, and to establish an adequate replacement schedule of buildings and facilities within a reasonable time.

This historical practice of placing most of the fiscal and administrative responsibility on the local school district to provide the capital facilities has become fiscally and educationally bankrupt. What is the present state of affairs?

There are no reliable data to provide a dependable measure of needs. Mere tabulations of buildings, classrooms, and other space, classified as to date of construction, need of renovation, or other vague descriptors provide only rudimentary facts. The regular information systems do not provide the kinds of data for measurement purposes. Space, equipment, and materials are neither quantified for general comprehension nor for showing relations to the programs and to the pupils who are served. Thus, a dependable picture of the capital needs even in a single school district requires an intensive survey, a procedure of impossible scope for the nation as a whole.

The samplings of districts throughout the nation in this finance project have given some leads on the dimensions of needs for buildings and equipment. Some of the most valuable insights about these future needs come from analyzing the characteristics of selected groups of highly innovative schools; elementary, middle, and high school. The sample consists of thirty schools which clearly are exemplars of 1980. The most striking feature about them is the interdependence of the capital facilities and the programs or processes of learning and instruction. Without exception these schools have adequate facilities for their programs. Space is planned to suit the educational activities. Shops and laboratories are not cramped, they have equipment to accomplish challenging purposes. Gymnasiums are designed for physical education as well as sports. Resource centers bear little resemblance to the libraries of the earlier school. Any worthwhile interest in society, born of the arts and sciences and humanities, finds a place in these schools.

These schools will not be obsolete in five years, or ten years, or even thirty years. They can be adapted to accommodate changes in purposes and programs. The buildings are arranged in campus style with flexibility in usage that a single, compact three-story structure does not possess. Many schools constructed in recent years have much built-in obsolescence that will clamor for renovation before the end of this decade.

No survey exists to indicate the distribution of capital facilities including buildings, sites, and equipment. Despite the lack of this type of information, a number of observers have made estimates based on trend lines extended from the past decade with adjustments for the anticipated leveling off of pupil enrollments.

These methods leave much to be desired as realistic projections. For example, a low demand for development of early childhood programs will call for housing 2,866,000 of 3- and

4-year-old children, 950,000 of 5-year-old children not now in kindergarten, and 1,867,000 additional 5-year-old children in kindergarten if increases in population occur as projected by the Bureau of the Census. These developments alone would call for 255,000 additional classrooms by 1980.[16]

Many obsolete buildings are in need of replacement. In addition, at least 12,000 school districts are in serious need of reorganization, a result which would then facilitate effective planning and consideration of many obsolete schools. Many other schools with a high degree of obsolescence will require extensive renovation. Some schools that appear deceptively good, especially to those who have become attached to them, in truth mask the high cost of inefficiencies in instruction and learning resulting from poor facilities.

Investment in adequate capital facilities appears to offer great returns for expenditures. There is evidence in the exemplary schools observed in this study that the investment in capital facilities designed and planned to serve innovative programs increased the performance of teachers and pupils immeasurably.

Projections of Capital Needs

Conservative estimates indicate that the annual rate of investment in recent peak years of 70 to 80 thousand classroom units should increase markedly to accommodate new programs, expansions in present programs and services, and to replace seriously obsolescent facilities by 1980. The estimates range from a low of 60 percent to 100 percent increase in recent annual investments at 1968-69 prices. The higher rate is more probable in view of capital costs in the exemplary schools observed in this study. These schools with reasonably adequate buildings, equipment, and site development averaged about $4,000 per pupil at 1968-69 prices, or $80,000 per classroom unit.[17] The average for the national expenditures in those same years was close to $60,-000 per classroom unit or $3,000 per pupil.[18] These differences show up in the exemplary schools in a number of ways: larger classrooms, more special rooms for greater variety of instructional activities, better designed laboratories and shops, and others.

Methods of Measuring Capital Needs

In the past the following methods have been used in measuring the costs of capital facilities: (1) costs of approved construc-

212

tion projects, including land and site development, buildings and equipment, (2) a fixed cost per pupil or classroom unit, (3) a fixed cost per pupil or classroom with weightings for variable land prices, costs of construction, and size of the school population, and (4) depreciation schedules based on the useful life of the facilities.

Each of these methods must be applied under conditions of defined educational objectives and the programs to be operated. Also, they must be subject to adjustments for changes in price indexes from year to year. Since these measures are expressed in aggregates or in aggregate unit amounts they must be derived from components of some type. Usually these components consist of classifications such as grounds; buildings divided into types of space such as classrooms, service areas, large mass areas such as auditoriums and gymnasiums; plant equipment such as heating and air conditioning facilities; and instructional equipment such as furniture, scientific apparatus, shop tools, and library resources.

In recent years, some studies using the method of program cost analysis for operating expenses indicate that a similar approach may be feasible for capital facilities. Standards of adequacy for capital facilities of the various programs would be used to estimate the needs for target groups of pupils. Thus, the module of need would be the pupil-learning unit or the classroom unit. For example the standard of space for adequate instructional-learning activity in nursery schools is estimated in this project at about 100 square feet per child. In grades 1-6 the average is 80 square feet. In high school, laboratories for vocational courses require an average of about 150 square feet per pupil, compared with 125 square feet in the basic or regular classes.

In addition there are central service areas for administration, counseling, health, resource learning centers, and food that are functionally related to the aggregate of classroom space and facilities. Also, there are facilities such as gymnasiums, auditoriums, and outdoor playgrounds that are related to the program structure and the number of pupils in the school.

Measures of needs for capital facilities must be designed to obtain an aggregate of the various components of each school, starting with the instructional programs for designated pupil needs as the basic modules.

COMMUNITY JUNIOR COLLEGE

The community junior college has come through a transitional period of nearly 50 years, changing from the early conception as an extension of the high school to an integral part of higher education.[19] There have been extended debates over these two concepts. In some states the development of the junior colleges has been delayed because opposing views have not been reconciled.

In some states the public junior colleges still operate under the jurisdiction of the public school system. In other states these institutions are now organized as a special system within the broad system of higher education.

In some states as junior colleges have been removed from the jurisdiction of public school systems to systems of their own within the framework of higher education they have retained some of the earlier purposes as well as methods of financial support. Their purpose is to serve three major functions: (1) programs for youth who plan to continue higher education and transfer to degree programs in senior institutions, (2) programs in specialized occupational work requiring less than four years of postsecondary training, and (3) continuing education for adults.

Target Population of the Junior College

The target population is not fixed, it is dynamic and changing. Its composition changes as the institution develops in response to perceived demands. A description of this population in a few exemplary institutions that have comprehensive programs, an image of prestige, and acknowledged standards of excellence may indicate the trend of general development in the 1970's.

First, as the name implies, the institution is a community college, serving primarily clientele of the local area. The population is primarily a commuting group. Most students live at home and commute to campus daily. Many of them hold part-time jobs as a condition of earning part of their costs. Some prefer this style of life instead of residing on campus. Second, adults may pursue part-time study and continue in full-time employment. Unemployed adults, like others, can pursue training without relocating their families. Third, the institution may serve students in residence who live beyond reasonable commuting dis-

214

tance or who are attracted because of the educational opportunity.

The age distribution is another important characteristic of the target population. The pattern varies according to the extent to which the institution anticipates the needs of prospective students and provides programs for them. Among the well-established comprehensive colleges the following distributions are common: (1) under 22 years—60 percent, (2) 23 to 29 years—25 percent, and (3) over 30 years—15 percent.

Data are not available on distributions of student age by programs. General observations indicate that increasing proportions of students under age 22 are pursuing college parallel programs to transfer to senior institutions. Substantial numbers are pursuing terminal associate degree programs of two to three years. Most of those over age 23 are pursuing the latter programs.

Financial Support of the Junior College

There is little commonality among the states in the patterns of support for either operating expenses or capital costs of junior colleges. State contributions for operating expenses vary from about 4 percent to 100 percent. Half of the states provide less than 50 percent of these expenses from state taxes. Student fees constitute from 20 to 30 percent of the operating expenses.

The support of capital facilities is divided between local taxes and state taxes, supplemented by some federal funds in recent years. Data are too recent to indicate any trends. Considering the burdens on local tax bases for the public schools and other local government, some states are moving toward major support of operating expense and total support of capital facilities from state sources. Most students of educational finance believe that complete support from state and federal sources is inevitable. The principal hindrances to this development appear to be general reluctance to make the concomitant changes in governance and taxation.

Program Cost Differentials in Junior Colleges

State leaders in higher education are interested in cost differentials among programs for the implications on fiscal policies. Manpower needs require that the state should have policies to offer programs to meet the needs in all occupational fields. Some occupations have relatively few workers as compared with others, and the requisite training programs are expensive. Bio-engineering technology and dental technology are examples which cost twice as much per student as some programs such as business accounting and general college transfer programs.

Every junior college must make a selection of programs among a wide range of potential offerings. These decisions may be affected by the costs of the programs. Moreover, the allocations to other programs within an institution may be affected if the variations are not accommodated reasonably well by the prime funding source.

As uniform program accounting practices develop it will be possible to establish cost norms on the course components of programs. Since courses are the instructional-learning modules of programs, their combinations provide the most accurate method of determining comparative costs applicable to registrations of students in the respective programs. An example of program cost ratios based on the combinations of component courses in one large comprehensive junior college is as follows: Liberal Arts, 1.00; Secretarial Science, 1.14; Business Administration, 1.01; Data Processing, 1.21; Chemical Technology, 1.86; Electrical Technology, 1.54; Commercial Art, 1.44; Medical Assistant, 1.38.

Projections of Junior Colleges to 1980

These projections are based on a careful study of fifteen comprehensive community junior colleges in seven states.[20] The groups of students to be served are the following:

1. High school graduates preparing for transfer to four-year institutions.
2. Youth preparing for specified occupations requiring two years of training beyond high school.
3. Youth who are undecided on their careers.
4. Youth preparing for job-related skills.
5. Talented youth who graduated from high school early.
6. Adults who desire further education for personal, social, and other reasons.
7. Adults requiring vocational upgrading.

216

8. Adults requiring change in occupation.
9. Adults wanting "refresher" courses.

From a third to a half of the students in junior colleges by 1980 may be over 22 years of age. In the fall of 1970 about 2,500,000 students were enrolled in these institutions. If the proportion of the total population enrolled in the fifteen exemplary institutions covered in this study is a guide, the junior college enrollments in the nation will double by 1980. Growth of this magnitude will depend on development of these institutions in more than half of the states.

THE MEASURE OF PROGRAM COST DIFFERENTIALS

In this chapter the measurement of program cost differentials is limited to current operating expenses of the public elementary and secondary schools. Community junior colleges are not included because they are separate operational entities which have more in common with other higher educational institutions than with the secondary schools. The procedures described below show how certain unit cost differentials for important program areas of the elementary and secondary schools may be computed.

The procedures of measurement are based upon definitions of programs to serve pupils with differential needs. The aggregate measure of costs for current operating expenses of day schools is illustrated for three districts in Tables 7-1, 7-2, and 7-3. The participating districts chosen for illustrative purposes are a central city, an independent (nonmetropolitan) district and a suburban district. The central city is typical of others with high concentrations of migrants, impoverished families, and multiethnic groups with bilingual difficulties. The independent district has three ethnic groups, about 60 percent Indian-American, 20 percent Anglo-American, and 20 percent Spanish-American. The suburban district has a high social homogeneity of middle to upper income families.

These measures of costs are based primarily on norms of operating expenditures in the sample of districts studied by McLure and Pence.[21] These norms will, of course, vary for different samples of districts. However, regardless of variations in numerical ratios, high cost pupils in one sample will also be found to be relatively high cost pupils in other samples.

TABLE 7-1

AGGREGATE MEASURE OF PROGRAM COST DIFFERENTIALS

CENTRAL CITY
1968–69

Program (1)	Number Pupils Enrolled (Head Count) (2)	Total Need (Estimated Number in Need of Program) (3)	Average Per Pupil Cost Differential (4)	Number Weighted Pupil Units in Present Programs Col. 2 × Col. 4 (5)	Number Weighted Pupil Units for Total Need in Programs Col. 3 × Col. 4 (6)
Early Childhood and Elementary Education					
1. Parent Education Program	0[a]	12,419[a]	1.40	0	17,387
2. Nursery School 3- & 4-year-olds	1,981	82,795	1.40	2,773	115,913
3. Kindergarten	53,992	81,800	1.30	70,190	106,340
I. Subtotal	55,973	177,014		72,963	239,640
4. Extended Day-Care Program	—	—	1.30	—	—
5. Special Education: Severely Handicapped Mentally & Physically (Grades: 6 and below)	7,509	13,161	2.55	19,148	33,561

[a]One FTE pupil enrollee equals 10 parents. Total parent need equals 1.5 times estimated nursery school enrollment.

TABLE 7-1 (Cont.)

Program (1)	Number Pupils Enrolled (Head Count) (2)	Total Need (Estimated Number in Need of Program) (3)	Average Per Pupil Cost Differential (4)	Number Weighted Pupil Units in Present Programs Col. 2 × Col. 4 (5)	Number Weighted Pupil Units for Total Need in Programs Col. 3 × Col. 4 (6)
6. Detention Schools: Severely Maladjusted Socially and Emotionally (Grades: 6 and below)	637	1,064	2.95	1,879	3,139
7. Compensatory Programs: Remediation for emotional educational difficulties (Grades: 6 and below)	41,778	102,025	1.68	70,187	171,402
8. Basic Education (Grades: 1-6)	242,059	176,728	1.00	242,059	176,728
II. Subtotal	291,983	292,978		333,273	384,830
Secondary Education					
9. Special Education: Severely Handicapped Mentally & Physically (Grades: 7-12)	4,386	8,790	2.03	8,904	17,844

219

TABLE 7-1 (Cont.)

Program (1)	Number Pupils Enrolled (Head Count) (2)	Total Need (Estimated Number in Need of Program) (3)	Average Per Pupil Cost Differential (4)	Number Weighted Pupil Units in Present Programs Col. 2 × Col. 4 (5)	Number Weighted Pupil Units for Total Need in Programs Col. 3 × Col. 4 (6)
10. Detention Schools: Severely Maladjusted Socially and Emotionally (Grades: 7-12)	333	704	2.66	886	1,873
11. Compensatory Programs: Remediation for emotional educational difficulties (Grades: 7-12)	40,104	58,701	1.83	73,390	107,423
12. Vocational Education[b] (Grades: 7-12)	21,578	46,960	1.52[c]	32,799	71,379
13. Basic Education (Grades: 7-12)	168,401	119,647	1.28	215,553	153,148
III. Subtotal	234,802	234,802		331,532	351,667
IV. Grand Total	582,758	704,794		737,768	976,137
V. Total	1.00	1.00		1.27	1.38

[b] Average enrollment equals 0.45 FTE in vocational courses and 0.55 FTE in basic courses.
[c] This would be 1.81 for equivalent full time enrollment in vocational education.

220

TABLE 7-2

AGGREGATE MEASURE OF PROGRAM COST DIFFERENTIALS
INDEPENDENT DISTRICT
1968–69

Program (1)	Number Pupils Enrolled (Head Count) (2)	Total Need (Estimated Number in Need of Program) (3)	Average Per Pupil Cost Differential (4)	Number Weighted Pupil Units in Present Programs Col. 2 × Col. 4 (5)	Number Weighted Pupil Units for Total Need in Programs Col. 3 × Col. 4 (6)
Early Childhood and Elementary Education					
1. Parent Education Program[a]	0[a]	160[a]	1.40	0	224
2. Nursery School 3- & 4-year-olds	0	1,068	1.40	0	1,495
3. Kindergarten	678	1,068	1.30	881	1,388
I. Subtotal	678	2,296	1.30	881	3,107
4. Extended Day-Care Program	—	—	1.30	—	—
5. Special Education: Severely Handicapped Mentally & Physically (Grades: 6 and below)	42	139	2.55	107	354

[a]One FTE pupil enrollee equals 10 parents. Total parent needs equal 1.5 times estimated nursery school enrollment.

TABLE 7-2 (Cont.)

Program (1)	Number Pupils Enrolled (Head Count) (2)	Total Need (Estimated Number in Need of Program) (3)	Average Per Pupil Cost Differential (4)	Number Weighted Pupil Units in Present Programs Col. 2 × Col. 4 (5)	Number Weighted Pupil Units for Total Need in Programs Col. 3 × Col. 4 (6)
6. Detention Schools: Severely Maladjusted Socially and Emotionally Grades: 6 and below)	0	6	2.95	0	18
7. Compensatory Programs: Remediation for emotional educational difficulties (Grades: 6 and below)	1,449	3,205	1.68	2,468	5,384
8. Basic Education (Grades: 1-6)	4,898	3,134	1.00	4,898	3,134
II. Subtotal	6,409	6,484		7,473	8,890
Secondary Education					
9. Special Education: Severely Handicapped Mentally & Physically (Grades: 7-12)	28	92	2.03	57	187

TABLE 7-2 (Cont.)

Program (1)	Number Pupils Enrolled (Head Count) (2)	Total Need (Estimated Number in Need of Program) (3)	Average Per Pupil Cost Differential (4)	Number Weighted Pupil Units in Present Programs Col. 2 × Col. 4 (5)	Number Weighted Pupil Units for Total Need in Programs Col. 3 × Col. 4 (6)
10. Detention Schools: Severely Maladjusted Socially and Emotionally (Grades: 7-12)	0	4	2.66	0	11
11. Compensatory Programs: Remediation for emotional educational difficulties (Grades: 7-12)	594	1,682	1.83	1,087	3,078
12. Vocational Education[b] (Grades: 7-12)	924	1,262	1.52[c]	1,404	1,918
13. Basic Education (Grades: 7-12)	2,659	1,390	1.28	3,404	1,779
III. Subtotal	4,205	4,430		5,952	6,973
IV. Grand Total	11,292	13,210		14,304	18,970
V. Ratio	1.00	1.00		1.27	1.44

[b]Average enrollment equals 0.45 FTE in vocational courses and 0.55 FTE in basic courses.
[c]This would be 1.81 for equivalent full time enrollment in vocational education.

223

TABLE 7-3
AGGREGATE MEASURE OF PROGRAM COST DIFFERENTIALS
SUBURBAN DISTRICT
1968–69

Program (1)	Number Pupils Enrolled (Head Count) (2)	Total Need (Estimated Number in Need of Program) (3)	Average Per Pupil Cost Differential (4)	Number Weighted Pupil Units in Present Programs Col. 2 × Col. 4 (5)	Number Weighted Pupil Units for Total Need in Programs Col. 3 × Col. 4 (6)
Early Childhood and Elementary Education					
1. Parent Education Program[a]	0[a]	775[a]	1.40	0	1,057
2. Nursery School 3- & 4-year-olds	0	5,030	1.40	0	7,042
3. Kindergarten	4,842	5,030	1.30	6,295	6,539
I. Subtotal	4,842	10,815		6,295	14,638
4. Extended Day Care Program	—	—	1.30	—	—
5. Special Education: Severely Handicapped Mentally & Physically (Grades: 6 and below)	432	573	2.55	1,102	1,461

[a]One FTE pupil enrollee equals 10 parents. Total parent need equals 1.5 times estimated nursery school enrollment.

TABLE 7-3 (Cont.)

Program (1)	Number Pupils Enrolled (Head Count) (2)	Total Need (Estimated Number in Need of Program) (3)	Average Per Pupil Cost Differential (4)	Number Weighted Pupil Units in Present Programs Col. 2 × Col. 4 (5)	Number Weighted Pupil Units for Total Need in Programs Col. 3 × Col. 4 (6)
6. Detention Schools: Severely Maladjusted Socially and Emotionally (Grades: 6 and below)	10	30	2.95	30	89
7. Compensatory Programs: Remediation for emotional educational difficulties (Grades: 6 and below)	77	4,527	1.68	129	7,605
8. Basic Education (Grades: 1-6)	29,661	26,746	1.00	29,661	26,746
II. Subtotal	30,180	31,876		30,922	35,901
Secondary Education					
9. Special Education: Severely Handicapped Mentally & Physically (Grades: 7-12)	240	491	2.03	487	997

TABLE 7-3 (Cont.)

Program (1)	Number Pupils Enrolled (Head Count) (2)	Total Need (Estimated Number in Need of Program) (3)	Average Per Pupil Cost Differential (4)	Number Weighted Pupil Units in Present Programs Col. 2 × Col. 4 (5)	Number Weighted Pupil Units for Total Need in Programs Col. 3 × Col. 4 (6)
10. Detention Schools: Severely Maladjusted Socially and Emotionally (Grades. 7-12)	0	26	2.66	0	69
11. Compensatory Programs: Remediation for emotional educational difficulties (Grades: 7-12)	92	2,583	1.83	168	4,727
12. Vocational Education[b] (Grades: 7-12)	1,480	2,583	1.52[c]	2,250	3,926
13. Basic Education (Grades: 7-12)	24,015	20,643	1.28	30,739	26,423
III. Subtotal	25,827	26,326		33,644	36,142
IV. Grand Total	60,849	69,107		70,861	86,681
V. Ratio	1.00	1.00		1.16	1.25

[b] Average enrollment equals 0.45 FTE in vocational courses and 0.55 FTE in basic courses.
[c] This would be 1.81 for equivalent full time enrollment in vocational education.

Column 4 of each table shows the index of average expenditure per pupil in each program in the districts included in this study. The unit value 1.00 is assigned to basic education in grades 1-6. This amount in the sample of districts was $750 per pupil. All pupils except those in vocational education are counted full time in the respective program.

In the vocational program, the pupils in the sample districts spend an average of 0.45 of their total course credit load in vocational courses and 0.55 in the basic courses. In effect the typical vocational curriculum in these schools is composed of 45 percent vocational work and 55 percent basic or general education. In comparing the average cost of pupils in the vocational program with those in the basic secondary program the index is computed as follows: $.45 \times 1.81 + .55 \times 1.28 = 1.52$. This index relates to the unit value of 1.00 for basic elementary grades 1-6. To compare average expenditure on vocational pupils with basic secondary pupils divide 1.52 by 1.28. The quotient 1.18 is the comparative index. The average expenditure per pupil in basic programs in grades 1-6 is $750; basic grades 7-12, $960; and vocational grades 7-12, $1,140. Thus the norm of excess cost per pupil enrolled in vocational programs above the basic secondary program in the sample districts is $180 per pupil.

Other indexes may be translated into excess costs in a similar manner. For example, the index of 1.40 for nursery school may be expressed as an extra or excess cost per pupil as .40 times the average expenditure per regular elementary pupil in grades 1-6. The amount is .40 times $750, or $300.

The detailed procedure for developing these cost indexes is shown in Early Childhood and Basic Elementary and Secondary Education, Special Study Number 1 of this project.[22] This procedure may be used as a guide in developing norms in any state.

The analysis of the three districts illustrated here is based on the categorization of the pupil population into broad educational program components. Two examples, the central city and the independent (isolated) district have relatively larger numbers of pupils with learning difficulties than the suburban district—based on diagnostic standards that could be applied throughout a state.

Thus, this analysis reveals differences among districts in the distribution of pupils among programs that are designed to meet

227

the needs of all individuals. The aggregate index of need relative to the total pupil enrollment, expressed in cost units, is 1.27 for the central city, 1.27 for the independent district, and 1.16 for the suburban district.

These indexes represent the relationship of existing programs one to another and not the true measure of need. The estimates of total need are shown for each district in columns 3 and 6, where specific assumptions are made as to reasonable goals for operation by 1980. For example, in early childhood education, it is assumed that school districts will have: (1) parent programs with enrollments of parents of young children not in school equal to 1.5 times the pupil enrollment in nursery school, (2) nursery school enrollment equal to one-half the kindergarten enrollment, and (3) kindergarten enrollment equal to all 5-year-old children. The estimates of need for the other programs are based on the judgments of educational officials and diagnostic data in the sample of districts in this project.

The aggregate index of total estimated need in pupil units is greater in each case than the actual one in operation. The respective increases are: the central city from 1.27 to 1.38; the independent from 1.27 to 1.44; and the suburban from 1.16 to 1.25. These increases in the aggregate indexes give a measure of the gap between present programs and full accommodation of all pupils in the respective categories.

Detailed procedures for applying cost differentials to alternative state support models are set forth in Chapter 10 of this volume.

PROJECTIONS OF NEEDS TO 1980

Educational activities have been classified in this study into broad program categories and other components for purposes of estimating current needs and also projected to 1980. The projections to 1980 are in reality the current needs with additional estimates to accommodate changes in the school population.

The projections are based on judgments of a wide sampling of educational leaders and other citizens, and the findings of research and experimentation in recent decades, concerning expanding educational objectives and needs of individuals in America. They should provide useful information for broad state and national policies and allocative decisions on education.

228

TABLE 7-4

PROJECTIONS OF NEEDS FOR INCREASED CURRENT OPERATING EXPENSES OF
PUBLIC ELEMENTARY AND SECONDARY SCHOOLS FROM 1968–69 TO 1979–80

Program	Estimated Increase in Percent of National Current Expenditure of $29 Billion
1. Parent Education (For 3 million children: between 1/4 and 1/3 of all parents with children under 3 years of age)	.93%
2. Day-Care Programs (4.49% of population under 6 years of age in 1980)	2.32
3. Nursery School: Children 3 and 4 years of age. —High Demand—18.20% —Medium Demand—14.06 —Low Demand	8.38
4. Kindergarten —To change present programs from double session to single session day—3.80% —To enroll 950,000 5-year-olds not in kindergarten in 1968–69—2.94% —To enroll all 5-year old population increase from 1968-69 to 1979-80—5.79%	12.53
5. Special programs for mentally and physically handicapped (Based on 100% increase in enrollments by 1980)	2.30
6. Special programs for pupils with severe social and emotional maladjustment (Based on serving twice as many pupils in 1980 as served in 1969)	2.00
7. Special remedial and compensatory instruction for pupils with abnormal learning difficulties (Estimated needs as percent increase over number served in 1969; Cities 300%; Suburbs 15%; Independents 85%)	4.91
8. Vocational programs (Based on estimated enrollments of three times the number of pupils in 1969)	6.00
9. Correction of imbalance for states below the national average expenditure per pupil in 1968–69 (8% using USOE data and 9% using NEA revised data)	9.00
10. Improvements in basic programs	10.00
11. Inservice programs for staff members to counteract professional obsolescence (Equivalent to 1/2 year leave with pay for each 6 years of service)	4.00
TOTAL	62.37%

Source: McLure, William P. and Pence, Audra May. *Early Childhood and Basic Elementary and Secondary Education: Needs, Programs, Demands, Costs.* Special Study No. 1 of the National Educational Finance Project. Urbana, Illinois: Bureau of Educational Research, College of Education, University of Illinois, 1970. Pp. 118-20.

Note: These estimates are based on 1968–69 prices and operating expenditures in that year. They do not include estimates for inflation or deflation.

TABLE 7-5

PROJECTED CURRENT OPERATING EXPENDITURES OF PUBLIC
ELEMENTARY AND SECONDARY SCHOOLS BY 1979–80[a]

	Base Year 1968–1969	Levels of Early Childhood Programs					
		Minimum Demand			High Demand		
		1969 Prices	2% Inflation	4% Inflation	1969 Prices	2% Inflation	4% Inflation
1. Amount in Billions	$29	$47	$57	$69	$50	$60	$73
2. Cumulative Percent Increase Above 1968–69		62%	98%	138%	72%	107%	152%

[a]Inflation is compounded annually.

A summary[23] of projections by programs and other components of need is shown in Table 7-4. These estimates include adjustments for projected school age population. The total minimum estimate of current operating expenditures would increase 62 percent above the $29 billion[24] in 1968-69 to $49 billion at 1969 prices in 1979-80. The top increase would be 72 percent assuming a high demand for nursery education (3- and 4-year-old children). The estimated high demand would accommodate 6 million pupils of these ages rather than 2.8 million assumed for the minimum. This low demand would represent an increase from 8 percent of the 3-year-olds and 23 percent of the 4-year-olds enrolled in nursery school in 1968-69 to 27 percent and 41 percent respectively in 1969-70. The high demand would increase the 3-year-old enrollments to 52 percent of that age group and 77 percent of the 4-year-old children.

These estimates represent an absolute increase in the current operating expenses in 1968-69. Inflation will further increase the estimates. Table 7-5 shows how these estimates would be increased at two rates of inflation cumulative annually, one at 2 percent and another at 4 percent.

The data presented in Table 7-5 do not include estimates of costs for capital outlay or increases in the cost of transportation, adult education and the school food service program. If these items are included and if inflation continues at a rate of from 3 to 4 percent, it is possible that total school expenditures will be $70 to $75 billion by 1980 even with an average demand for educational services.

SUMMARY

Adequate financing of education requires a structure of programs and other component parts that are functional in relation to the instructional and learning activities in the system.

This chapter presents a method of measuring differential cost of designated instructional programs in early childhood, elementary, and secondary school levels. The structure of program categories is compatible with sound principles of organizing instructional and learning activities. This method of program cost analysis has the following advantages: (1) provides a useful structure for officials in the local school district to evaluate programs, alternative options, and needs, (2) provides a basis for improving the equity in the distribution of state and federal funds to local school districts, and (3) provides an improvement in present procedures for interpreting the achievements and needs of the public schools to the citizens at large.

In addition to the operating costs of designated programs, there are supplementary related costs that must be treated adequately as special entities in a state finance plan. These include capital outlay, food service, transportation, correction for size of operational scale in extremely sparse areas, cost of living variation, and adult and continuing education.

The measurement of costs in this study is based on two considerations: (1) to improve the rationality in such a complex enterprise as public education, and (2) to provide methods for achieving the goal of equal educational opportunity for every child in America.

FOOTNOTES

1. William P. McClure and Audra May Pence. *Early Childhood and Basic Elementary and Secondary Education—Needs, Programs, Demands, Costs.* National Educational Finance Project, Special Study No. 1. Urbana, Illinois: Bureau of Educational Research, College of Education, University of Illinois. 1970.

2. *Ibid.,* Ch. 3.

3. *Ibid.,* Ch. 4.

4. Richard A. Rossmiller, James A. Hale, and Lloyd E. Frohreich. *Educational Programs for Exceptional Children—Resource Configurations and Costs.* National Educational Finance Project, Special Study No. 2. Madison, Wisconsin: Department of Educational Administration, The University of Wisconsin. August 1970.

5. Arvid J. Burke, James A. Kelly, and Walter I. Garms. *Educational Programs for the Culturally Deprived.* National Educational Finance Project, Special Study No. 3. Albany, N. Y.: State University of New York at Albany, School of Education. 1970.

6. *Op. cit.,* McLure and Pence, Ch. 5.

7. *Ibid.,* pp. 98-100.

8. Erick L. Lindman. *Financing Vocational Education in The Public Schools.* National Educational Finance Project, Special Study No. 4. Los Angeles, California: Graduate School of Education, University of California. 1970.

9. J. Alan Thomas and William S. Griffith. *Adult and Continuing Education.* National Educational Finance Project, Special Study No. 5. Chicago: Midwest Administration Center, The University of Chicago. 1970.

10. *Op. cit.,* McLure and Pence, pp. 105-06.

11. *Op. cit.,* Thomas and Griffith.

12. Robert J. Garvue, Thelma G. Flanagan, and William H. Castine. *School Food Service and Nutrition.* National Educational Finance Project, Special Study No. 8.

13. *Ibid.,* Garvue, *et al.,* p. 222.

14. Dewey Stollar, Pupil Transportation. Chapter 9 in *Planning to Finance Education,* Volume 3. Gainesville, Florida: National Educational Finance Project. 1971.

15. W. Monfort Barr, K. Forbis Jordan, C. Cale Hudson, Weldell J. Peterson, and William R. Wilkerson. *Financing Public Elementary and Secondary School Facilities in the United States.* National Educational Finance Project, Special Study No. 7. Bloomington, Indiana: Bureau of Surveys and Administrative Services, School of Education, Indiana University. June, 1970.

16. For these estimates see McLure and Pence, pp. 118-19.

17. See McLure and Pence, p. 144.

18. *Op. cit.,* Barr, *et al.*

19. James L. Wattenbarger, Bob N. Cage, and L. H. Arney. *The Community Junior College: Target Population, Program Costs, and Cost Differentials.* National Educational Finance Project, Special Study No. 6. Gainesville, Florida: Institute for Higher Education, University of Florida. June 1970.

20. *Ibid.,* Wattenbarger, *et al.*

21. *Op. cit.,* McLure and Pence, Ch. 5.

22. *Ibid.,* McLure and Pence, Ch. 6.

23. Richard H. Barr and Betty J. Foster. *Fall 1968 Statistics of Public Elementary and Secondary Day Schools.* Washington, D. C.: U. S. Department of Health, Education, and Welfare, Office of Education. March 1969. OE-20007-68, and National Education Association Research Division. *Estimates of School Statistics: 1969-70.* Research Report 1969-R15. Washington, D. C.: National Education Association.

Note: For current operating expenses in 1968-69, the USOE document reports $29,842,077. The revised figure $29,040,075, reported by the NEA is used for purposes of projections.

232

Economic Analysis of Institutional Alternatives for Providing Education (Public, Private Sector)

The decade of the 1960's was a time for experimenting with technology of educational processes. Some of the pieces of this "technological revolution" were (1) ungraded primary programs, (2) instructional television, (3) team teaching, (4) language laboratories, and (5) computer-assisted instruction. That technological revolution left American educational institutions largely undisturbed. In contrast, the decade of the 1970's is likely to see a great deal of structural experimentation, i.e., examination and testing of alternative schemes for financing, managing, and controlling schools and various other educational institutions. It is possible that the "structural revolution" will produce fundamental changes in flows of educational and training services and in the distribution of those services among households.

Before we consider the sorts of structural changes that are most widely being discussed, let us consider some of the pressures that have led people to demand new arrangements. In the main, these (somewhat related) pressures can be described in three categories: (1) dissatisfaction with the operations of large public bureaucracies; (2) concern with rising costs in both public and private institutions; and (3) dislike for the manner in which services are rationed among competing households. All three pressures reflect the way in which we have organized production and distribution of social sector goods during that time when we were becoming a highly urbanized nation.[1]

PRESSURES FOR CHANGE IN EDUCATION STRUCTURES

In more detail, let us consider how changes that formerly were unthinkable have now become probable.

Dissatisfaction with Large Education Bureaucracies

This is a problem of economic efficiency, in that it is claimed public school systems are failing to produce those bundles of outputs that are most highly valued by consumers. The problem is found most notably in large metropolitan areas. Big cities have socially heterogeneous populations—fortunately, one may say, unless we have decided we should all be confined in ghettos. At present, big cities seem to be unable to provide school services in sufficient variety and quality to meet the divergent consumer demands of their heterogeneous populations.[2]

Take the rich first. Common observation tells us that rich parents expect their children to receive high-grade instruction in recognized academic fields, to benefit from the help and advice of a high school placement officer who knows—and is known to—admission officers in well-regarded colleges and universities, and to have the pleasures of good sports and activities programs. These are special, albeit reasonable, demands, and in earlier times big cities met them. They met them, on the one hand, by running school systems that in general were superior to rural (and even suburban) systems and, on the other, by operating a set of elite secondary schools, which schools were characterized by college preparatory programs of academic excellence. These schools were protected by careful selection of students and faculty. It is difficult for big cities to maintain elite schools today. Egalitarian pressures, reinforced by a general sense of urban malaise, are inimical to them. Many academically minded teachers appear to find working conditions to be better in the suburbs than in big cities. And in the meantime the rich have opted either to live in the suburbs—probably there to continue to use public schools—or to stay in the city and pay for tuition for their children in private schools.

234

Since students are embodiments of various amounts of education capital—and this is so even when they enter school for the first time—withdrawal of the rich is likely to produce a decline in the productivity of central city schools, unless non-student resources can be provided in sufficient amount to offset.[3] Given that education appears to be forcefully subject to external economies of production, which is to say that the ceiling of academic performance in a classroom is "inexorably" set by the previous learnings, interests and motivations, of, say, the top quartile of students, it is unlikely that the cities can so offset the loss of educational capital of students from upper-(and upper-middle)-class homes, even if we look aside from the cities' claims of municipal overburden and financial crisis.[4,5]

But the real tragedy is the fact that big city schools are no longer regarded as generally superior. This is uniquely an American tragedy, for in most of the rest of the world, the best schools, in the main, are found in large cities. The rich might have held on in public education in the cities even while giving up their elite high schools if the city systems were thought to be generally better than suburban ones. The cities failed to exploit economies of scale that lay within their grasp. The process of deterioration has proceeded to the point where halting and reversing the decline will be difficult at best and especially so under the conventional bureaucracy of the large-city school district.[6] As it is, our youth from well-educated homes are growing up almost exclusively in socially homogeneous suburbs, isolated both from the interest that comes from getting to know people who have come from quite different backgrounds and from easy, first-hand contact with higher reaches of aesthetic life. Most painters, artists, actors, poets, playwriters, novelists, and musicians, after all, still live and work in the big cities— they are their natural environment and the natural showcase for the creative mind.

Next, take the middle class. Middle class families appear to prefer schools that are businesslike, that stress fundamentals of reading, mathematics, and science, that are not encumbered with "frills," and that have strict discipline.[7] Such objectives run somewhat counter, however, to what many poor families see that *they need*: teachers who are both warm and determined to see their students make progress, teachers who can help a child from a slum neighborhood overcome hostility toward the adult world (and toward learning in particular), and his feelings of helplessness and apathy. The response by middle class families, including a small but growing number of black families, to dissatisfaction with big-city *public* schools is to use the parochial.[8] There, learning of fundamentals seems to go along at a better rate and dicipline is stronger. But the poor, alas, have no *major* alternative, except in rejection of the aims of the public school and in a kind of mental withdrawal.[9]

The fact that families, whether rich, middle, or poor, are failing to get what they want in educational services from centralized, large-city districts has led to the demand that "consumers" of educational services be allowed to exercise a greater degree of choice in their purchase.[10] All of the measures proposed imply decentralization in the management and control of educational institutions. Some advocates of change would see it sufficient to break up big-city administrations of public schools into smaller units, adding possibly the proviso that parents' councils might exercise some administrative control over schools in their neighborhoods. Others see it necessary to "privatize" education by giving parents "vouchers," with which they may enter the open market for purchase of educational services. "Family power equalizing" and the use of contracts (all these proposals will be discussed in detail below) are two other non exclusive variants of administrative reorganizations.[11] Basic to the whole discussion is the idea that many families feel strongly about the kind of education their children receive and about its quality; hence, they should be allowed better means to choose for themselves what they are to have.

Stated this way, we can see that the drive for a greater amount of consumer choice may draw strength from parents generally, not just from those who live in the biggest cities. Further, families that are rich enough to exercise choice presently, in the sense that they have enrolled their children in non-public schools, might find proposals such as the voucher plan (though not necessarily family power equalizing) appealing, because those families would receive financial relief toward costs of private tuition.

Resistance to Rising Costs

Dissatisfaction with our present structure of education has roots in the visibly rising costs of services. Between 1963 and 1968, expenditures of state and local governments on elementary

236

and secondary education rose at an average annual rate of 10.2 percent.[12] This was roughly twice the rate of increase in Gross National Product and three times the rate of increase in national income per capita. Ever since World War II, public educational expenditures have risen more rapidly than household incomes.

The reasons are several. One is simply that many households place a high value on education, both as a good thing in itself and also as a means to help their children get ahead in a competitive world that progressively rewards brain power more and physical labor less. Another reason for rising costs is that education has proved, intractably, to be a labor-intensive activity.[13] The possibilities of substituting (possibly) cheap capital goods for dear labor in educational processes have turned out to be extremely limited, so far. Moreover, labor in education has become dear, first, as enrollment increases outran increases in numbers of newly trained teachers and, second, as teachers have succeeded in organizing themselves into powerful bargaining units.[14]

Money is no longer forthcoming easily in many school districts, with middle size cities, a few very large cities, and districts where school tax rates are already at very high levels being hardest hit. In late 1969, the situation was described as follows: "Kingston, Ohio, taxpayers allowed their public schools to remain closed from Thanksgiving, 1968, to January, 1969. The Philadelphia Board of Education thought it might run out of funds. School systems from Chicago to St. Albans, Vermont, worried about school deficits for which no relief was in sight. For example, neither the governor of Illinois nor Mayor Richard Daley could produce the 10 million dollars needed to balance the current Chicago school budget. Everyone's funds were 'already committed.'"[15] People feel that schools—in spite of the difficulties under which they may operate—must find ways to improve their technological efficiency, i.e., to produce a larger volume of outputs for a given size of budget.

Fiscal constraint is not confined to the public sector. Parochial schools, faced with the requirement to employ lay teachers in rising proportions, to reduce class sizes, and to purchase new forms of instructional materials, are suffering budgetary deficits. This is especially the case in large cities. In New York, where the state government is already providing $40 million annually for sectarian schools, the Governor held in early March, 1970, that the financial plight of parochial schools required emergency action.[16] Five states now allow generalized aid to non-public schools (Connecticut, Hawaii, Ohio, Pennsylvania, and Rhode Island) ; legislation toward this end is under consideration in a number of other states, such as Illinois, Iowa, Massachusetts, Michigan, and Wisconsin. Aside from rescuing parochial schools in order to preserve sectarian education (though public funds, of course, are in support of secular instruction only), these actions of the states could be viewed as an attempt to obtain low-cost education in larger proportion, since parochial schools operate at a dollar cost roughly one-half to one-quarter as high as public.

Structural changes to improve technological efficiency take several forms. Privatization of education through, say, the adoption of voucher plans stresses the beneficial effects of competition among education institutions. The "invisible hand" of the market will serve to bring increased trade to those institutions that become more technologically efficient, while those that are inefficient will be pushed to the wall. Similarly, if educational services are to be purchased to a larger extent than at present under contract, and if contractors receive full payment only when they meet pre-arranged specifications about students achievement, then market forces could produce a kind of "survival of the fittest" among firms that provide instruction. Under Assembly Bill 2118 (considered in the 1969 Session of the California Legislature), it was provided that "urban self-determination schools" might be established with public support. Ad hoc governing bodies would staff and operate schools in disadvantaged areas, free of most regulations on certification of teachers and employment of noncertificated instructional staff. This would be one way to test the willingness of organized teachers to experiment with different patterns of staff specialization, including such practices as the assignment of routine duties to junior persons and the part-time employment of students to teach basic skills to younger students.

Another approach to the cost problem stresses not so much changes in technological efficiency as it does a more equitable sharing of the burden. The family-power-equalizing plan would have the amount paid by a household for school services a function of its income *and* of the quality of services it wishes to purchase.[17] Accordingly, user charges would be introduced in such a manner that the general taxpayer might no longer be called upon to foot the local costs for above-average or special-quality provision—in any case, he would find beneficiary households sharing the burden with him.[18] The voucher plan, on the other hand, would lift at least some of the costs of secular education from the shoulders of parents whose children attend parochial schools, as well as other private schools, and place them on the general taxpayer.[19]

Concern About Improper Rationing of Educational Services

Some of those who advocate change in structure of the educational system base their case on improper rationing of education services.[20] They feel that services are rationed in *too great* a degree on the basis of parental income and in *too small* a degree on such other factors as parental concern for the intellectual development of their offspring, "true" (as distinct from the "measured") ability of students, and interests and motivations of students. The problem arises in the first instance because most of our state governments delegate to local districts very substantial responsibilities for provision of school services, at the same time that states have drawn—or allowed to be drawn—a set of district boundaries under which taxable wealth per student varies enormously from one district to the next. While allowing for numerous exceptions, caused mainly by the unequal distribution of nonhousehold taxable wealth (industrial plants, public utilities, office buildings, etc.), it can be said as a general rule that rich households live in school districts where taxable wealth per student is high and poor households live in districts where taxable wealth per student is moderate or low.[21] Various state subvention plans seek to "equalize" expenditure capacities of local districts, but these schemes almost universally fall far short of the mark. Regarding local school tax rates as a "price" for educational services, it follows that rich households are likely to receive expensive services (well-trained teachers, small classes, extracurricular programs, etc.) at low prices (tax rates), while at the same time poor households are taxed heavily (i.e., pay high prices) to provide themselves with meager services.

For example, in 1965-66, within one county of California (Los Angeles), El Rancho, a relatively poor district, had a school tax rate of $4.50 per $100 of assessed valuation and received school services valued at $548 per student. El Segundo, a richer district, had a tax rate of $1.82 and received school services costing $753 per student.[22] Two things may be noted: (1) property valuations are fairly uniform within counties of California, so such an inverse relationship between tax rate and expenditures per student cannot be accounted for by variations in assessment practice; (2) as compared with such states as South Carolina and Illinois, California is commonly regarded as having a relatively well-developed set of "equalizing" state grants for district support of schools. A third point is that in the two districts noted, student achievement, as measured by state-wide tests, stood in a direct relationship to expenditure per student and inversely to tax rates. This kind of situation is by no means unusual in the United States.[23]

One makes of it what one will. Some would see the present state-local system as yielding a proper, not improper, rationing of school services. By and large, high-quality services are laid before students who have grown up in households where the parents are relatively well educated. It might be held that these are the very students who can and will make best use of opportunities provided them by their superior teachers, etc.

Others, including the author, feel that the rationing process, as it is working at present, is evil. "Education is the only planned, continuing, and universal relation with the state. Of all the state's benefits, therefore, it represents both the largest opportunity for and the most significant danger to the individual caught in its maternal embrace."[24] Society has determined that education shall be compulsory. Many households have little choice about where they live, residence not infrequently being determined by the nature and location of a man's work. If the children of a given household are to attend public school—which in many places is in effect required by law, since private schools are not universally available nor can all families afford them in any case—they must do so within the district of residence and in that single school chosen by district authorities. Taking account of these various requirements and practices, the question has recently been raised whether existing systems of educational finance meet constitutional guarantees with respect either to equal protection or to minimum protection of citizens.[25] Insofar as violation of constitutional rights can be proved, the present structure might be said to suffer from "social inefficiency."

ADDITIONAL FORCES FOR STRUCTURAL CHANGE

So far, we have indicated that the existing, basic structure

240

under which educational services are provided is under attack on grounds of economic inefficiency (in failing to see that the character of school services fits well with parental aspirations and desires), of technological inefficiency (in failing to provide a greater degree of cost-effectiveness in its operations), and of social inefficiency (in allowing school services to be rationed substantially on the basis of a criterion largely irrelevant: parental income). There are other sources of unhappiness in our society which turn people against schools as they are now run, though some of them cannot be laid wholly or even partly at the doorstep of educational institutions themselves. Student unrest (which can be attributed only partly to school operations) and racial antagonism are two examples. Likewise, teachers' strikes provoke the public. To a degree, strikes may be a result of poor school management, but they are also manifestly a single element of rising worker militancy in the public sector generally.

Lastly, schools have unfortunately been the victim of false expectations. Note that unemployment is unevenly distributed in our country and that it is concentrated among minority members who have poor school records. Concentration of unemployment, in turn is associated with perpetration of ghetto life, with social disengagement and dependency, with neighborhood violence and crime, with broken homes and the passing along of education failure to the next generation. In the mid-sixties, it was thought that with the help of $1 billion annually of federal money, the schools could practically eliminate social class concentration of education failures, thus playing a major role in breaking the poverty syndrome and yielding a more even distribution of unemployment by social class. This could not be done quickly and it probably cannot ever be done without better planning and preparation than was available in the first attempt. The President's Special Message to Congress on Education Reform, March 4, 1970, stated: "We must stop letting wishes color our judgments about the educational effectiveness of many special compensatory programs, when—despite some dramatic and encouraging exceptions—there is growing evidence that most of them are not yet measurably improving the success of poor children in school." If much was expected and little provided, pressure mounts for structural change, however blameful or blameless most teachers may be.

241

MAJOR APPROACHES TO STRUCTURAL REVISION

Let us now consider major proposals for structural revision: decentralization, voucher plan, family-power-equalizing, contracting, etc. Some will be discussed at greater length than others, reflecting degrees of complexity, novelty, and economic interest.

Decentralization of Large Districts

The seminal document is the Report of the Mayor's Advisory Panel of Decentralization of the New York City Schools, *Reconnection for Learning* (1967), commonly called the "Bundy Report."[26] Though prepared obviously for New York City, the plan is relevant for other large cities of the country. New York had been engaged in a process of decentralization and had established local school boards before the Bundy Report was published. It continues to move toward a more effective decentralization of powers. From the time of presentation of the report, it was known that the Board of Education was opposed to the fast time-table recommended therein. Efforts to implement some of the central suggestions in the report led to a prolonged teachers' strike in 1968-69.[27] None of this background, however, detracts from the report as the major statement of the aims and means of achieving *bona fide* decentralization of powers.

The central shortcoming of New York schools, according to the Bundy Report, was that they were allowing too many students to fall below minimum standards of achievement. "In a 1965 statewide pupil evaluation conducted by the State Education Department, 55 percent of the students found to be below levels the State Testing Service defined as 'minimum competence' were New York City public school students, although the city's enrollment comprises only 35 percent of the state's total."[28] Moreover, ". . . one out of three pupils in the city's schools was a year or more behind youngsters in the nation as a whole in reading and arithmetic."[29]

The report stated that decentralization so far achieved was not "effective."[30] Martin Mayer, himself a former local school board member, was quoted as follows: ". . . there was almost nothing I could do for the people who called me, and little of substance came out of our meetings . . . This giant empire is almost completely insulated from public control."[31] It was said that the local boards could not hold anyone responsible for the

242

performance of the schools in their districts, since insufficient powers had been delegated to the district superintendents.

The proposals made in the Bundy Report centered on the establishment of community school districts (intended to be of size 12,000 to 40,000 students) and on the relations of the community school districts to professional staff.[32] The new districts were to have powers to recruit and hire teachers and to petition the State Commissioner of Education for alternative means of certifying teachers. They would have the power to award tenure and to make assignments of teachers to individual schools. The districts would be responsible for in-service training and staff development.

It was thought that the following benefits would flow from these new arrangements: (1) there should be better cooperation among teachers, parents, other community residents and institutions because of closer community participation in school affairs, (2) a wider pool of professional talent would be available for service in the "less desirable" schools, (3) districts populated mainly by minority groups could hire a higher proportion of teachers sensitive to and sympathetic with the environment of the students than presently are serving in the affeced schools, (4) district schools would have more latitude and flexibility for innovation and experimentation than now exist.

Granted that effective decentralization might, indeed, produce these benefits, how well does this particular kind of structural change meet the problems of economic, technological, and social inefficiencies noted above? No one can say precisely, but the following points may be made:

Economic Efficiency. Unfortunately for the decentralization proposal, there is really no substitute for giving households a choice about which schools their children attend. The decentralization proposal does not do this, as one's specific place of residence still would determine the public school a child is allow to enter. Recall that economic inefficiency occurs (1) when urban consumers are not receiving these school services they value most highly and (2) when choice to rectify the situation is constrained. Under the decentralization proposal, choice remains constrained.

It is true that interested parents in large cities would have a greater chance to influence educational policy under decentralization than they do now, but the substitution of a set of smaller bureaucracies for a single large one does not mean that changes in school environemnt can be made very thoroughly in a short time. Further, even within a given school's attendance area, different parents have different desires for school services; indeed, within a single family, certain services may be sought for one child and other kinds of services for a second.

Imagine a man being chairman of the governing board of the school his child is attending and being a member also of the community school district board (as hypothetical of parental influence). Does he have the means to exercise as much choice about his child's education as he would if he could select to enroll his child in one of, say, six schools, each offering different curricular emphasis, staffing patterns, and expenditure levels? It would seem not. As long as attendance in a given school is determined strictly by specific place of residence, school programs must be more alike than different, because that program must not offend any parent sufficiently to represent violation of constitutional rights. Such bland uniformity is not the way to provide economic efficiency.

Of course, the decentralization plan might specify that the parent may seek to place his child in any school of the district, i.e., it may call for "open enrollments."[33] This forestalls districts from establishing racial or social class balance in school by prerogative of the administrative authorities. Also, a system of open enrollment could better approach both economic and social efficiency by "family-power-equalizing" (to be discussed below).

Technological Efficiency. It appears likely that decentralization would allow a greater amount of innovation and experimentation to take place. The channels for approval of schemes would be shortened and the number of persons who might act to delay approval or to veto schemes would be reduced. Ordinarily, decentralization plans do not call for the abolition of the central district administration (though that administration is expected to hand over most of its powers with respect to professional staff to local boards), and whatever influence the central administration formerly wielded to promote innovation and experimentation could still be wielded. On the net, exploration of new ways of doing things would probably increase, so decentralization could possible help in achieving greater technological efficiency.

244

It is not clear, however, how much gain in technological efficiency is to be achieved by innovation and experiment. On the other hand, it is plain that efficiency would be raised if teachers and students made up their minds to work hard. It is difficult to see how incentives to work hard are materially increased by decentralization. Suppose, however, that as part of the decentralization package it was decreed that (1) school enrollments were to be open; (2) students were to be admitted to schools of their choice on the basis of competitive examinations; (3) school principals were to be judged for merit increases and promotions on the basis of the length of the waiting lines of students to study in their schools and of teachers to work in them, and (4) teachers were to be judged for merit increases and promotions on the progress students made (not on their absolute levels of achievement) during the time they were in the given teacher's classroom. Then it could be said that some incentives had been established. Of course, these same incentives could be laid out before educators and students in a centralized system, but, taking account of racial strife and class antagonisms, they probably could not be accepted in big cities, except as provided under a decentralized system of control, if then.

Social Efficiency. Social efficiency is increased as parental income comes to play a lesser role in determining how educational resources are shared among students. How would decentralization of large city districts affect the relation between parental income and distribution of educational resources? First, decentralization would affect financial relationships *within* the boundaries of big city school districts. It would not attack the problems caused by the fact that some suburban systems can claim an undue amount of public sector resources because (1) they have vast amounts of taxable wealth per student and (2) at the same time they are free of "municipal overburden," i.e., extra heavy costs associated with density of population uncompensated for by having extra taxable resources. Second, let us recognize that at present public schools attended by poor youth in big cities often have larger dollar expenditures per student than do middle class schools in those same cities. Would this differential in favor of the poor be preserved under decentralization? It does not seem likely, if the aims of decentralization are taken seriously. That is, if local groups in the city are to have power with respect to their schools, they must control the school budgets. Such control implies that part of their dollar resources be drawn from local taxation. It is probable that poor neighborhoods will have less taxable wealth per student than middle class neighbors, though efforts could be made to ameliorate this problem by the judicious drawing of local district boundaries. However, say that some such discrepancies remain and that they are to the disfavor of the poor. Past experience indicates that state grants are unlikely to equalize the taxable resources of the separate districts. Hence, schools attended by students from poor households would have less general support per student than they do now, relative to other districts. Third, and on the other hand, decentralization would allow a better targeting of federal monies for disadvantaged youth, so schools in poor neighborhoods might receive more money in the form of special federal aids than they now do. Fourth, it is quite possible, moreover, that money would be more effectively spent in schools of poor neighborhoods under a decentralized rather than a centralized administration. Fewer dollars might buy more effective services, especially if the local districts really could hire teachers who were more understanding of the requirements of deprived young people. Taking it all together, decentralization would probably have a marginal effect toward improving social efficiency.

Summary. Bigness of administrative unit does not necessarily imply low quality of education. Recognition of the historical excellence of big city schools in the United States and of the continuing excellence of schools in the large cities of Europe should dispel such a notion. However, in this time of racial strife and class antagonism, decentralization of authority appears to make sense. This step would go some way toward improving economic and technological efficiency — and perhaps social efficiency as well, depending on the details of the decentralization plan. But the question is whether decentralization would do enough, taking account of the pressures for structural change that we described earlier. Indeed, the main result might be to take the heat off of the establishment and allow it to place the blame for educational failures on the "local community." We turn to some more radical proposals.

Friedman Vouchers

The proposal was made by Professor Milton Friedman, University of Chicago, in 1955, and it continues to draw attention up to the present time.[34] Professor Friedman indicated (1) that maintenance of a minimum standard of education for the whole population and (2) financing of education (in substantial part) by the state could each be justified by the existence of external economies of consumption of school services. On the other hand, he could find no overriding justification for administration of schools by the state, though he recognized that complete, sudden decentralization of education might make it difficult to attain a common core of values (a religious problem) and a mixing of different social classes (a secular problem); further, he foresaw that fragmentation of school services in sparsely populated areas would be technologically inefficient (natural monopoly argument).

Accordingly, we have Friedman I and Friedman II. Friedman I was stated as follows: "Governments could require a minimum level of education which they could finance by giving parents vouchers redeemable for a specified maximum sum per child per year if spent on approved educational services. Parents would then be free to spend this sum *and any additional sum* on purchasing educational services from an 'approved' institution of their choice. The educational services could be rendered by private enterprise operated for profit or by nonprofit institutions of various kinds. The role of the government would be limited to assuring that the schools met certain minimum standards such as the inclusion of a minimum common content in the programs . . ."[35] (italics added).

Friedman II, a milder version of denationalization, was stated in this way: ". . . government would continue to administer some schools but parents who chose to send their children to other schools would be paid a sum equal to the estimated costs of educating a child in a government school, provided that *at least this sum* was spent on education in an approved school. This arrangement would meet the valid features of the 'natural monopoly' argument, while at the same time it would permit competition to develop where it could."[36] (italics added). It may be noted that both Friedman I and Friedman II allow parents to "add on" money to the value of vouchers they receive, to combine or meld the state's contribution for education, that is, with their own private contributions. This cannot conveniently be done now, except in the purchase of piano lessons, ballet lessons, swimming, music camps, etc. Also, Friedman II provides that the value of vouchers be determined by expenditure on elementary and secondary education in the existing local districts. We shall argue later that both of these power-oriented features violate too much the criterion of social efficiency.

Friedman claimed a number of advantages for his proposals. (1) It was held that parental choice with respect to type and quality of education would be increased. The options would be greater than those now available in most states: a single local public school (with entrance to some other public school requiring a change of residence) or a private school (which receives no public subsidy, requiring parents to meet tuition costs from their own pockets or to send their child to a school that is subsidized by religious bodies). (2) Market forces would raise the level of technological efficiency in education, in that schools which failed to provide good services at reasonable rates of tuition would lose trade and go out of business, while those that were efficient would survive and expand (up to the enrollment that represents minimum cost per student of operation). (3) Salaries of school teachers would become responsive to market forces. (4) Parents who wished to use private schools would no longer have to "pay twice" for educational services.

It is interesting that a similar plan was proposed in England in 1926 by Cardinal Bourne.[37] The Cardinal's plan would have provided that parents of children of school age (5-14) receive an annual warrant to admit their children in any recognized school in their neighborhood. The value of the warrant would have been determined by dividing total annual public expenditure on education by the number of all children of school age. In 1926, it was estimated that the vouchers would be worth £20 to the institutions that received and cashed them. It was stated that the Bourne plan would give to the poor man the same right to choose educational institutions his children were to attend as the rich and middle classes had always held. Whether the plan would have worked out in just this way may be debatable, but one can certainly agree with A. C. F. Beales, an advocate of education vouchers, when he says," . . . one of the profoundest of poverty's degradations . . . is unavailability of choice."[38] It was also stated in the Bourne plan that teachers would become more agreeable and efficient, once they felt market forces of competition. Primarily, however, the plan was advanced to relieve the financial plight of Catholic families who wished to

248

continue to send their children to parochial schools and who were finding the cost of keeping up to the standard being set in the public sector becoming more and more onerous.

There is one clear difference between the Friedman and Bourne voucher plans. The former would have the value of vouchers (or warrants) determined by local standards of expenditure and the latter by national. There is another possible difference. One can interpret Cardinal Bourne's statements to mean that the warrants were to meet the full cost of attending *any* school within commuting distance of a child's home. (He plainly did not suggest that the warrants entitled a person to enroll a child in a residential school, like Eton and Harrow.) If this is the proper interpretation, then the Bourne plan, on the one hand, would have equalized expenditures in the state and non-religious schools, leaving the church free to "add on" to warrant payments in its own schools, and, on the other, would have taken a giant step to give poor families choice in education. Later writers have assumed, however, that the Bourne plan, like Friedman's, would have allowed schools to charge what the market would bear, with parents being required to supplement voucher payments if they wished to enroll their children in expensive schools. This leaves education received substantially a function of parental income, of course.

Economic Efficiency. On the face of it, Friedman vouchers I and II should provide greater educational choice to middle class families than they now possess. (We assume that upper class families already have a good bit; the lower class poses a problem to which we will turn later.) A number of new private educational institutions should open their doors, and surely some of these institutions would seek to establish a certain measure of distinctiveness, in order to increase the potential demand for their services by households of a particular bent. For example, some schools might stress the outdoor life, others might emphasize painting, sculpture and music, and yet others might specialize in mathematics and science.

However, choice would develop not in a planned way but in response, simply, to market forces. Two institutional constraints might impede large-scale establishment of diversified institutions. On the one hand, state governments might be reluctant to relax controls with respect to curriculum, teacher certification, and textbooks. For example, House Bill 3843, considered in the 1970 Session of Massachusetts Legislature, provided that vouchers could be spent only in schools that were accredited by the state and that taught all subjects required in public schools of the Commonwealth. Senate Bill 1082, Chapter 2, 1970, in Michigan required that teachers in aided private schools must hold public school teaching certificates. Ohio Revised Code 3317.06(H) and Regulations states that ". . . services, instructional materials, or programs provided for pupils attending non-public schools shall not exceed in cost or quality such services . . . as are provided for pupils in the public schools of the district." In short, it is not enough simply to adopt a voucher plan and let it go at that. If the objective is to procure choice, and if this choice is to develop in the private sector primarily, then it is necessary to protect new institutions against excessive public controls. One may wonder, accordingly, if it would not be better to try to provide choice within the public sector as a conscious act of planning.

Second, diversity in educational offerings could develop under a voucher plan only if teachers were willing to see it develop. Teachers are unionized. The power of the union against a single school would be many times greater than it is against a public school system. New schools especially cannot withstand strikes, since parents would not willingly tolerate interruptions of their children's schooling. It is difficult to say how teachers' organizations would respond to the development of diversity in education.

Against these (possible) institutional obstacles, one may set the question of how effective would be market pressures in producing diversity. Do middle class parents really want different kinds of education (or educational institutions) or simply the right to try to use their *economic power* more effectively in choosing different qualities of college-preparatory programs? Probably the latter, which is to say that true diversity could not develop as long as (1) parents make educational choices for their children and (2) colleges and universities continue to specify admission requirements in terms of specific courses completed, rather than in terms of knowledge acquired (no matter how) and aptitude.

What now is the degree of choice afforded by the voucher plan to working-class parents? Such parents would have little means to supplement the value of vouchers by private payment. Those living in school districts of low assessed valuation would

250

receive vouchers of small dollar value, moreover. Partly, then, the answer depends on whether diversified private institutions could develop in the low cost range or whether poor families would be limited to public institutions (under Friedman II).

Let us take the favorable view and say that, yes, there would be private schools to which poor parents could send their children. The matter then becomes a bit more complicated. One of the advantages claimed for the voucher plan is that it would increase technological efficiency in education: that is, schools would come to provide more learning per dollar spent in them (or collected in fees), because of competitive market pressures. The most effective (and, relatively speaking, easiest), action for a private school to take under competitive pressures is not to fire bad teachers but bad students. This is true because of the powerful effect of external economies in production of school services. Even in the public sector this is the case, even where, that is, dismissal is closely controlled. How much greater it would be in the private. Not only would disruptive, slow-learning children be got out of the way — no longer to distract the other students or to lower their norms of attainment — but the threat of dismissal would be a major incentive on the remaining students to work hard.

Would dismissal power fall on children or different classes differentially? It would seem likely, for working class children frequently appear slow and disruptive until they come to feel at home in a given school environment. Accordingly, the working class might be expected to take the brunt. Further, working class parents would be less able, probably, to make effective grievance than middle class against a school management for arbitrary treatment or against a teacher (he being backed up, of course, by his union, with its ever present threat of strike.) [39]

It would be unfortunate if the poor had their choices constrained to a local public school, probably one which had been drained of a large share of its teachers and students who were academically superior, at the same time that the middle and upper classes were being given new powers to guide the destinies of their children. This introduction of the poor into the mainstream of American education is what much recent federal legislation has sought to accomplish, though not yet with astounding success. One would not want to make a bad situation worse, and the only way out might be to have the public authorities supervise dismissal power in all institutions, public and

251

private alike. In that case, one may again raise the question of whether it would not be preferable to provide choice within the public sector in a planned manner.

Technological Efficiency. Much of the possibility of raising the level of technological efficiency would depend on whether newly established schools could have a more highly differentiated salary structure, so that teaching could become attractive to very talented people. More money, it should be expected, would be available for the schools (1) because interested parents could add on the value of the vouchers as private supplement to publicly determined expenditures and (2) because all parents, not just public school parents, would have reason to support tax override elections for education (thus to increase the value of the vouchers themselves). The question remains, however, whether teachers would be agreeable to a more highly differentiated salary structure.

And, of course, money is only a necessary, not a sufficient, condition to attract talented people into teaching. The tasks of teaching must themselves be seen to be intellectually intriguing and exciting. The greater freedom to experiment in voucher schools would produce that atmosphere to a greater degree than it exists at present. But can competitive pressure reinforce the remaking of the teacher role? Once a parent has enrolled his child in a school, he cannot easily withdraw him — in the meantime, friendships have been made, routines established, etc. For competitive pressure to work, then, much depends on the quality of knowldge possessed by the household when it makes its choice of school. The technology-efficiency-increasing power of a voucher plan would be raised greatly, it would seem, if parents had the benefit of a "truth in education" act, under which all schools would be required to show not only what resources (number of teachers and their characteristics, library, laboratory, and sport facilities available, etc.) they intended to lay before the student but also what success they had had with students in the past, as revealed by "follow-up" reports from their graduates: which institution of further education they entered, how well they had done there, or what jobs they had gone on to, and so on. Naturally, under such a system, schools would be keen to regulate the quality of their admissions carefully, and unless Friedman's plans were modified in some way technological efficiency would be bought at a price of intensified

252

social stratification in education.

Two comments must immediately be made. First, the Friedman plan should not be introduced in such a manner that a larger number of private, white segregated institutions can be established. It might be desirable to require racial quotas, under which enrollment in any given school is required to conform approximately to the racial composition of the geographic area. Another approach (incorporated in the family-power-equalizing scheme) is to require open admissions. The second comment has to do with the "truth in education" feature. It is not certain that self-reporting by educational institutions can be relied upon to inform parents. On the other hand, state accreditation bodies have not shown themselves over the years to be very imaginative; further, they have grown accustomed to measuring school quality almost exclusively in terms of input variables (number of teachers, proportion of teachers holding certificates, etc.). It might be well to establish an independent, well-financed body to conduct "consumer research" in education and to see it report its findings both locally and regionally.

The last point regarding technological efficiency has to do with economies of scale. If the local district structure is to be retained (which it would not be in the family-power-equalizing plan), then we can expect most students to attend schools within existing district boundaries. Most suburban districts are not large enough to support a plethora of private institutions, especially at the secondary level, laid along side the existing public schools, without sacrificing considerable economies of scale. The Friedman plans, then, would offer a trade-off between some possible gains in effiiciency through technology and some losses through the scale factor.

Social Efficiency. Enough has been said already to indicate that the Friedman voucher plans, both of them, get low marks on this criterion. Unless the plans were modified (possibly in the ways to be discussed below), it seems almost certain that rich and middle class parents would exercise the right to add on to the monetary value of the vouchers in buying private education. Clearly, they have much more power to do this than the poor, especially the poor who happen to have large families. It is very likely, then, that quality of education obtained would come to bear an even closer positive relation to household income than it does now.

Modifications of Friedman Vouchers: Pauly and Otherwise

An interesting addition to the discussion has been made by Mark V. Pauly.[40] He has proposed that the value of vouchers paid to households be made to vary inversely with household income. ". . . a scheme in which the community agrees to pay some fraction of the cost of *each unit* of education purchased by the parents could lead to optimality . . . The optimal structure of these payments is not, however, one in which the community pays the same fraction of the per unit cost at all income levels, but rather it is one in which the fraction paid by the community varies inversely with income."[41] Such a modification could reduce the effect of Friedman vouchers in affecting social efficiency adversely.

Another modification would be to restrict Friedman vouchers to secondary schools and above, while at the same time introducing the "truth in education" feature noted above. There are several arguments in support of this modification: (1) It seems likely that parents are more keen to make choices about education *after* the primary level is passed. Some evidence is given by the fact that many rich and upper middle class families in New England use the local public primary schools, even in the central cities, though they choose private schools for their high school youth. The same pattern prevails in the United Kingdom. (2) The "truth in education" feature is desirable to obtain technological efficiency *and* to allow parents to exercise their access to economic efficiency intelligently. But we do not want to reduce the effectiveness of the educational system in discovering and nurturing talent among the children of the working classes. Introduction of the voucher plan at the secondary level would allow a beneficiary-oriented sharing of costs of that level of education between the non-parent taxpayer and households with school-age children. If the Pauly modification were introduced, the sharing could provide rough equity. Sharing of costs would release public funds from secondary level to strengthen a publicly administered primary system, a chief purpose of which is to discover talent and salvage it while it is still capable of being salvaged — among all the classes. If a real effort were made to eliminate the effects of home background on primary school success, then selectivity, parental choice, and institutional competition at the secondary level might be appropriate stimuli toward higher educational performance, won at no great cost of

254

equity. The use of contract schemes, to be discussed below, would be one device to raise the efficiency of primary schools in getting a closer fit between true abilities of students and actual performance.

Family Power Equalizing

This is a somewhat more complicated proposal than those we have so far considered. Developed by Professor John E. Coons, School of Law, Berkeley, and his colleagues, the plan is not necessarily in final form, but the main outlines of it can be seen.[42] The plan intends to give parents options in the education of their children such that households can select a school at one of four expenditure levels. Tentatively, these expnditure levels are $500, $800, $1,100 and $1,400 per student in primary grades and $800, $1,100, $1,400, and $1,700 in secondary school years. The household, it is held, would have one or more schools available to it at each expenditure level administered by public authorities. It is also expected that most households could choose among a set of privately administered schools, the set including schools operating at each of the different expenditure levels. (School districts, however, would disappear and so would local school district taxes.) Parental choice could be exercised, then, as between different expenditure levels and as between public and private institutions.

Both public and private schools would be subsidized by the state governments from general revenue sources.[43] However, parents, even very poor parents who chose the lowest expenditure type of school, would make a direct financial contribution toward the education of their children. The contribution is in the form of a weighted progressive income tax. For example, suppose a parent has a taxable income of $5,000. If he decides to send his children to the lowest expenditure-category school ($500 a student a year in elementary and $800 a student in secondary), his school tax might be equal to, say, 2.0 percent of his taxable income. If he chooses the highest expenditure category ($1,400 elementary and $1,700 secondary), his tax might be at a rate of 5.5 percent of taxable income. Note that both the amount of school tax paid and the rate are variable as the parent picks a different expenditure level for his children's education.

Call this first parent Mr. Jones. Now, let us consider Mr.

Smith, and suppose that Mr. Smith has a taxable income of $15,000 a year. If Mr. Smith chooses the lowest expenditure schools for his children, he may pay school tax at the rate of 3.0 percent, while if he picks the highest expenditure education he may pay tax at the rate of 8.0 percent. Suppose that Jones picks the 2.0 percent rate (and the kind of schools that such a rate "buys") and that Smith picks 8.0 percent. The extra $1,100 that Smith is paying (Smith pays $1,200 as compared with Jones $100) reflects three things: (a) that Smith picked a more expensive school, (b) that payment is related to income, Smith's being the larger, and (c) that the rate of school tax is progressive.

This is one way to define a price, and, given that we are dealing with a subsidized activity characterized both by external economies in production and by external economies in consumption, it is a rational way. In classical public finance theory, it is shown that the quality of public sector goods can hardly be expected to satisfy anyone. Most people will want either more or less of the given goods or services. The voting mechanism at best is intended to determine a single level of output for a certain service provided by a certain government which is tolerably inoffensive to the majority. Coons makes this point: why not cater to differences of taste within the public sector, at least for services like education where, first, external economies in consumption dictate that we cannot leave matters about minimum levels entirely in parents' hands and, second, where parents, willy nilly, are going to intervene on matters affecting their progeny? The trick is to arrange that they intervene not dysfunctionally with respect to the external economies of production and this means in the future they come to accept more mixing of the social classes in schools and in school programs.

Conventional wisdom answers that household choice is already provided by the system of local government (which governments provide those services, after all, in which differences in tastes are most urgently felt by households), because the household can always move to that community which meets but does not exceed its required standard of service.[44] This solution is inconvenient for all families and infeasible for some—especially the poor. Coons breaks the nexus between consumption of such things as school services and place of residence. His definition of price, moreover, avoids the irrationality of having the price paid for education a function primarily of the amount of assessed real property per student in the hands of the school district. If a private power plant is placed within district X, why should its residents have the price of their children's education reduced, say, three quarters—the connection between economic location of electrical generating capacity and priority for distribution of educational resources (or local tax relief) is not easy to discover.[45] Coons has carried thinking about allocation of public sector goods and services a considerable step forward.

It was said earlier that payments for school services would be made under a "weighted" progressive income tax. We have considered the progressive feature; what, then, about the "weightedness?" This refers simply to the fact that if a family has more than one child in school and if these children attend schools of different expenditure levels, the tax rate charged to the family will be the average of the rates fixed for schools in the categories attended by their children. Actually, it would seem unlikely that most families would practice such invidious discrimination as to send some of their children to expensive schools and some to cheap, unless, *mirabile dictu*, it turned out that high status education, namely, college preparatory, happened to be generally cheaper than low status kinds—vocational, artistic, scientific, and the like.

It is instructive to consider the differences between family-power-equalizing and Friedman vouchers. There are, importantly, two. First, family-power-equalizing, like Pauly's variant of Friedman vouchers, provides a public subsidy that is functionally—and inversely—related to family income. In truth, the distinction between FPE (to use a common abbreviation) and Friedman vouchers is even more interesting than this, in that the amount of subsidy paid a household depends not only on its income (however the progressive tax structure may be laid out) but also on its choice of quality of education. That is, the actual and relative amount of subsidy may be different for different expenditure categories of school chosen, and these latter differences may not be related to household income or size in any obvious or simple way. Indeed, these latter kinds of subsidy valuations are to be empirically determined to assure that some rich and poor families choose expensive schools and that some rich and poor families chose cheap schools—in other words, to provide intermingling of classes within the schools.

The second distinction is this: Coons would allow no private

257

supplements to education expenditures, whereas Friedman sees such private supplements as a vital and necessary part of his plan. Under the Coons arrangements, *schools* would receive the stated amount known to parent and school alike—$500 to $1,400 per student in primary schools, depending on expenditure classification chosen by the school—neither more nor less for each student enrolled. The state, of course, would make up the difference between the stated fee and the yield of the income-determined school tax rate on a given household's income—or receive the excess yield when the household was very rich—but it would pay only the amount of the total fee per student to the school. The household itself would pay nothing directly to the institution. This leaves schools indifferent with respect to fees as between choosing a student from a rich household or a poor one. The provision promotes racial and class integration. But the Coons "no-add-on" feature means that rich families cannot meld public subsidies for education with their own large financial resources to commandeer an unusually large amount of educational resources for exclusive service of their children—not with respect to full-time, formal educational institutions, at least.

It is also instructive to examine the roots of the FPE plan. Coons and his co-authors, William Cline and Stephen Sugarman, developed a lengthy case to indict most existing state school finance plans as unconstitutional. The complex argument emphasizes several factors: that all children are both poor and disenfranchised, thereby deserving special judicial attention under the equal protection guarantee of the Fourteenth Amendment; that education should be an interest judicially favored; and that existing structures for its provision are irrational in the sense that the states have burdened local school districts with the uniform duty to provide education, while leaving those districts grossly unequalized in economic power to carry out that uniform purpose. The results of present arrangements are that poor districts pay taxes at high rates to obtain low-grade school services and rich districts pay taxes at low rates to receive superior services. It is, practically speaking, impossible for poor districts to run good schools. Now, assuming that in most cases poor districts (in terms of local taxable capacity per student) are populated by poor households and rich districts by rich, the pattern of discrimination becomes clear: poor districts cannot buy good educational services on behalf of their inhabitants nor

258

can the residents of those districts provide themselves with such services by private means.

As a guiding principle, Coons, et al., developed the following proposition: "the quality of public education may not be a function of wealth other than the wealth of the state as a whole."[47] The proposition would be satisfied, of course, if the state established equal per student expenditures in all of its public elementary schools, public secondary schools, etc. But Coons, et al., see this as violating another important (though non-constitutional) principle, that of "subsidiarity." "Subsidiarity" is the value we invoke when we prefer local control, decentralization, and district choice. The important thing, then, is to retain the possibility of district choice, but to free that choice of the influence of local taxable wealth. This could be done by a "district-power-equalizing" (abbreviated as DPE) plan, under which school districts choose a quality of school program, measured as expenditure of $x_1, x_2, x_3, \ldots$ dollars per student per year, with each different quality being associated with a specific local tax rate. The schedule of school expenditures vs. tax rates would be positive and would be uniform for all districts. Call district A rich and district B poor. If rich district A decided to spend $900 per student in its elementary/secondary schools and if the associated tax rate was $2.50 on $100 of assessed valuation, then poor district B could get the same $900 for a $2.50 rate. If both wanted a more expensive program, say $1,100 per student, then the tax rate might go to $3.00 but the rate would be the same in the two districts. For the scheme to work with absolute precision, very rich districts not only would not receive a state subsidy but would make a net contribution to the state school fund for redistribution to poorer districts. The magnitude of necessary redistribution of this kind could be minimized either by redrawing the boundaries of the richest and poorest districts or by withdrawing industrial and commercial property from the local base.

While DPE would be a vast improvement over existing state finance plans, it has its shortcomings. Poor families living in poor districts are still left poor. We cannot hold that the fragmentary evidence of some poor districts' being willing to have high tax rates is sufficient to make us certain that poor families in general would see themselves able to buy high-grade schooling for their children. Big cities have high non-school costs in the public sector; these could be said to eat away the local taxable resources for education. It is difficult to accommodate this problem of "municipal overburden" in a DPE formula.[48] DPE was subjected to the criticism that the authors were unduly sensitive to wealth-induced differences in provision and callous toward place-induced (geographic) discrimination. "One difficulty is that children whose families have identical (let us say rather low) incomes and identical (let us say rather avid) tastes for education, and who differ only in where they live, may under a district-power-equalizing system receive substantially unequal treatment depending upon the levels of sacrifice for education which are *collectively* (i.e., politically) preferred by the voters in their respective districts of residence. Here is a systematic, state-sponsored discrimination among the possibly favored class of children, affecting their almost certainly favored interest in education."[49] The illustration can be extended to consider the case of a district which voted minimum (possibly zero) expenditures for schools. The richer parents would turn to private schools, whereas most of the poor could not. Place discrimination, even under DPE, would be turned into wealth discrimination, violating the main proposition, i.e., wealth is not to affect the quality of education.

FPE stands up better, though admittedly not perfectly, to these kinds of problems than does DPE, so what was first put down as a kind of afterthought in Coons', et al., *magnum opus* on DPE has become (rightly, one thinks) their main policy prescription. It is as if Coons and his associates had first seen the existing state financial arrangements as the tail wagging improperly the dog of the American educational system and had set out to give the dog a new tail. Now, they have decided we need a new dog. The question remains, will it bark better than the old one?

Before we make a response (tentative, of course) to that question, let us consider the nature of the family-power-equalizing plan more carefully (recognizing that the proposal may yet be modified in its details). Several principles undergird the plan, and some, such as the desirability of offering householders choice of educational program, the undesirability of allowing rich householders choice of educational program, the undesirability of allowing rich households to "add on" their private resources to the value of public vouchers, etc., have already been mentioned. Others are worth noting. (1) All households, even the poorest, are required to make a private contribution toward the education of their children, and the idea behind this is that people are likely to value more what they directly pay for than what they do not. (2) Direct costs of education (as distinct, say, from indirect costs like income foregone of students, which in the nature of the case are likely to be borne mainly by the student and his household) are to be shifted under family-power-equalizing to some degree from non-parents to parents, though in a progressive way. This would probably be most noticeable in the case of upper middle class families: non-parents would be relieved of *local* school taxes while parents would face the choice of paying $1,000-$2,000 a year (the actual figure would depend on the household's adjusted gross income and on the rate structure for parental contributions finally voted) to government for entrance into a public (or private-aided school) or of meeting the whole bill of their children's education in a private unaided school. On the other hand, family size would not affect the contribution as long as public or private-aided schools were used. (3) Parental judgment is to play a somewhat larger role in selecting programs for students. The authors of family-power-equalizing appear to hold the view that parents have knowledge of their children's interests and capabilities that the public school system, as presently organized, does not easily and frequently recognize. They profess to believe that poor families, including those in which the adults have had only the smallest amount of schooling, will recognize the great bargain offered them when they choose an expensive, rather than a cheap, program for those of their children that can profit from it.[50] But they buttress these assumptions with the requirement that schools furnish a great deal more information to their clients—and prospective clients—than now they do. As a minimum, schools would be required to provide prospective clients with information on expenditures per student, religious affiliation, curriculum specialties, maximum enrollment fixed by statute, and average score of students on achievement tests. (Such tests would be conducted each year in all public and private-aided schools and the results by school and by grade within a school made a matter of public record.) Information might also be provided on physical facilities, size and characteristics of faculty, and special methods of instruction employed, if any.

Certain more detailed features of the plan deserve attention.[51] The Superintendent of Public Instruction would be charged to see that a variety of public schools to compete with the private at all permitted levels of spending was available throughout the state. The superintendent would enforce minimum standards of facilities and staff in the public schools of the state. Private schools would be charged to receive no income other than credits from the tuition account, except with respect to certain closely defined categories of revenue (e.g., grants directly to the institution from the federal government). Where private schools receive services at less than fair market value, the excess of such market value over wages actually paid would be reported, and that sum would be deducted from the tuition credit of the schools. No parent would be taxed an amount greater than twice the expenditure level of the school(s) he chose for his child (children), or the weighted average thereof. What this latter point means is that small rich families would subsidize everybody, to a degree, but the dollar magnitude of the subsidy would be small, relative to the nation's education bill. Schools would be allowed to make contracts with each other for services. This means that a teacher might teach in more than one school at a time, and a student might work in more than one school. Schools could also issue contracts to private, non-school parties for services.

Admissions is a special matter, and, as we shall see later, a special problem. Family-power-equalizing would arrange things in the following ways. Parents would be provided a list of schools in their area or to which transport would be available. The list would indicate the kinds of information about schools mentioned above. The list would include both public and private-aided schools. Parents would make known their first preference for each of their children, as well as alternative choices. Each school would have to *accept any child* for whom it had a place, though it might counsel a parent against entering his child in the given institution. If a school had more applications than it could accommodate, it would determine the names of accepted candidates by lot, having first given preference to students who were in the school the previous year and their siblings. The intent of these provisions is to let parental judgments about a child's capacity, motivation, and interest prevail over the professional's, in the final analysis, and to reduce racial, economic, religious, and social segregation of students. Up to this time, the family-power-equalizing plan appears to be silent in

262

matters of student dismissal: grounds for dismissal, appeal machinery, possibilities for readmittance, etc.

Economic Efficiency. How well would FPE serve the objective of getting a closer fit between educational outputs most highly desired by parents and the actual outputs of schools? In part, the answer would depend on one's subjective view of educational processes and institutions. No doubt, there exist educators who feel that substantial variety can be provided within a single institution — this notion is fundamental to the strong support given in America to the "comprehensive school." If this view is correct, then variety as represented by differences in expenditure level, which is to say differences in generalized quality, is all the additional variety one can ask for, and FPE *might* do the trick. Even under this favorable view, however, one must ask: would any parent choose any but the highest expenditure level school for his children?[52] Let us consider the problem as it might apply first to poor households and, second, to rich.

Any household, poor or rich, rationally would weigh only the marginal cost of moving up from a low expenditure to a high expenditure school. The way to assure that all parents of whatever income level do not choose the most expensive schools is to see that these marginal differences are significant for members of the given income class. If, for example, the dollar choices (household contribution) between the four categories of schools (spending, as noted $500, $800, $1,100 or $1,400 at elementary grades) were $50, $150, $250, $350, respectively, for a $3,000 a year family, the $300 difference between the cheapest and most expensive school would probably discourage most low-income households from picking the most expensive. Only a few of the most dedicated would squeeze their budgets and sacrifice so much for education. But are we then meeting the objective of the proposition that underlies FPE, namely, that differences in wealth shall not influence choice of educational opportunities? We are but only in the relative sense and only if, say, rich households feel similar constraint about choosing the most expensive as compared with the cheapest schools.

So let us see what range of prices one is able to specify for rich households. The household costs of attending a minimum-expense school must be at least slightly greater in absolute terms than the costs for the same type of school laid on a middle income household—otherwise, the prices would not be progressive.[53] This condition puts a kind of *floor* under the price scale offered rich families. The *ceiling* of prices for the rich is functionally related to the costs of attending unaided private schools. Taking account of the present level of fees, etc., if a rich family was told it would have to pay $5,000 to government to enroll its child (children) in a public or private-aided school, it might well respond by opting out of the public system altogether. Only a very large rich family would have much financial reason to feel differently. It is not good enough to say that the rich use public schools where public schools are good—which now means that the rich use suburban schools — because presently the rich buy a style of life and an associated package of local public services through the purchase of housing. FPE breaks education out of this package by requiring that public school attendance (or private-aided school attendance) entail a substantial fee, which fee can be foregone if the parent chooses a wholly private school. The latter choice thus becomes marginally more attractive, and, since the rich live in segregated areas, wholly private schools could spring up conveniently near their neighborhoods.

To keep the rich in the system, then, requires that the top price not be very high. Given that the price to rich families of the lowest cost school is itself inflexibly determined, as noted, the range between prices for cheapest educational services and most expensive is unlikely to be greater, say, than $2,000. This is not enough to dissuade a rich family from choosing the most expensive kind of schooling, especially if it has several children of school-going age.

Accordingly, the range of prices laid before the poor cannot be very wide either, relative to their incomes; otherwise, household income, as distinct from such factors as parental tastes and interests and children's aptitudes, would be seen to play a disproportionately greater role in influencing educational choices as we moved down the income scale, contrary to the guiding principle of FPE. And suppose that wholly private schools were banned, so that the lid on the very top of parental contributions, in effect, was taken off. It would still be a major feat of social engineering to discover that set of prices which minimized (or brought down to a tolerable level) the influence of household income on educational choices over all income classes.

Moreover, there are those, the author included, who feel that within-school variety of programs is no substitute for between-school differences. In other words, what we may want to have is greater specialization by type of institution rather than just by quality of institution. Take the example of instruction in the arts. A teacher of painting in a comprehensive high school, unless it is such an extremely large high school that four or five full-time members are found in the fine arts department, is bound to feel lonely in the professional sense and is likely to regard himself as no more than an ornament to the "regular" programs. Further, only the most common of the arts will be treated in a comprehensive school: drama, painting, band, orchestra, possibly printing, but not ballet, sculpture, chamber music, organ, Oriental music, African music, calligraphy, poetry writing, playwriting, mime, etc., except as these forms of creative expression are touched on in a fleeting and non-professional way. Yet, creative talent blooms early in youth, and its flowering, more than in the case of verbal skills, would be no respecter of classes. A high school of creative arts would offer economy of scale in laying before youth the range of aesthetic expressions; the staff would reinforce and stimulate each other, provided all had both motivation *and* talent, and the administration could reasonably set standards of professional knowledge—as well as of teaching skills and of maintenance of discipline—to regulate advancement of staff. The same case for specialization by type of high school could be made in such fields as mathematics/pure science, mathematics/applied science (technology), social science, commerce, construction trades, machine trades, and languages (including computer languages). It could well be that one of the roots of student unrest is vacuity of courses in the last years of high school and in the first year or two of college. The underlying reason for the malaise may be that in America we delay too long that necessary measure of specialization to serve a student's aptitude and stimulate his interests.

It might appear that FPE would be conducive to the development of such a necessary degree of specialization, but the difficulty is open admissions. Once a student is entered in a school, he is not easily changed therefrom, so an initial improper sorting will have lasting effects. Since external economies of production are important in education, the actual standard of work done in what might appear to be specialized schools would become general. This is more or less admitted by Professor

265

Coons when, speaking of the processes through which open admission would work itself out, he writes, "The overall consequences would probably be more stably integrative for densely populated areas than any of the administrative proposals with which the author has been associated or is familiar."[54] Though the quotation refers to integration of races and classes, the feeling one gets is that it might refer also to aptitudes and interests. It may well be true that specialization of program—and all the benefits which might flow from such specialization—requires admissions standards, differentiated of course, by the particular emphasis of a given school. This would probably yield quantitatively less race and class integration than FPE with open admissions, but there could well be more class and racial tolerance. After all, it doesn't accomplish much to have blacks and whites in the same school if most of the whites are in the college preparatory program and most of the blacks are put in the shop. Under specialization, whites and blacks having similar strong interests would have a chance to work side by side.

Yet a better solution might be to rely on school advertising and guidance to improve initial student (parental) choice and then to allow a one-year tryout for any student (or his household, if final choice is not the student's) who is sufficiently determined and confident to seek to enroll himself against school authorities' statements that he is probably not qualified to work in the given institution. This would reduce reliance on one-shot tests to screen applicants, which is generally a risky business anyway.

In any case, we are left in FPE primarily with choice in terms of expenditure (= quality) but not much in terms of type of program. This at least is likely to be a greater degree of real choice than decentralization (alone) would give, and it is provided in a much fairer way than under Friedman vouchers. However, what we are doing is relying to a greater degree than at present on parental choice and less on the judgments of professional educators, school boards, state legislatures, the Congress, etc., to make choices about the kind and quality of school services that should be laid before a given student. We all now recognize that different students "require" different amounts of educational resources, with programs for the deprived, the handicapped, and the vocationally minded being relatively expensive. Better knowledge of education production functions should someday guide us to make more sensible and sophisti-

266

cated expenditure differentials. Can parental judgment do as well in allocating students to programs as the professionals and public authorities? No one knows, and no one can know until we have some experimental program of FPE type.

Technological Efficiency. To try to assess FPE in terms of technological efficiency is an exercise in raising questions that only experience of structural reform could possibly answer. The substantial range in expenditures per student (low-cost schools vs. high cost schools), together with the autonomy of the administration of the individual schools, might break the present bland uniformity that still characterizes teacher pay arrangements in the United States. One would hope to bring top rates up to the point where a talented person would not mind "being a teacher all my life." On the other hand, teachers' unions might be in a stronger position to bargain with single schools than with school districts. This might result in an undue diversion of school budgets into the teachers' salary item and prevent the introduction of more capital goods into instructional processes.

What about the effects of reporting of test scores and interschool competition? Basically, the results might be to improve the quality of work in the more academically oriented schools, while leaving schools that serve the non-academic (i.e., those students who do not plan to go to four year college) unaffected. Parental choice under a system of graded fees would probably act in a way to segregate serious academic students from the non-serious. This would be even more likely if the schools were required to report the proportion of their expenditures laid on instruction vs. the proportion put on extra curricular activities, etc. A well-to-do family might then choose, for the less intellectual of their progeny, an expensive school, but one that emphasized social life, sports, and so on, to avoid invidious comparisons within the family about the quality of schooling bought for different children. The more academic schools might use their new autonomy to build links with nearby colleges and universities, with provision for the sharing of teaching services between the institutions. This might help to remove the status disparity, under which work in college/university is regarded generally as honorific while work in schools is held to be plebian. But whether these things will actually come to pass is unknown.

Presently, there is beginning to be some sharing of services among school districts. For example, a successful new program launched under, say, Title III of the Elementary and Secondary Education Act, might be spread to neighboring districts through contractual arrangements. The sponsoring district gains a certain amount of prestige when this happens. The forces of competition might encourage the development of local monopolistic practices and protectionism, rather than the sharing of exceptional services (possibly underutilized in the single school) from one institution to another.

A concern might be felt about rewards in the new competitive system: who gets them and how quickly? First, about the schools and the teachers. Do schools that do well, as measured by test results and waiting lists, have the chance to upgrade themselves into some higher category(=expenditure class)? Apparently not, because this would be equivalent to breaking a contract with the parents of students already enrolled.[55] Accordingly, the most successful of teachers would probably bid their way up to the top of the vertical hierarchy of schools (by expenditure status). This is not exactly conducive to building institutional strength in a given school. However, the availability of many schools in high density areas like central cities might draw superior teachers to downtown neighborhoods where promotion opportunities would be good. Further, the great range of choice of schools might draw intellectually avid parents back to the cities. The cities could finally profit, as they long should have been doing, from economies of scale in the social sector.

It is difficult here to do more than speculate, but one final point is worth noting. To make dramatic changes in educational production functions such that substantially greater outcomes are obtained may call for access to resources far beyond the reach of the single school. FPE is no substitute for action at the state level—to see that talented people enter teaching, that they are well trained, that services of specialists are available to schools, possibly under state-financed programs ("aid-in-kind"), that educational research is well financed (so that the struggle to find out useful things about learning processes may continue), etc.

Social Efficiency. FPE seems by far the fairest of the structural changes we have considered so far—from the point of view of parents, at least. If parents want more expensive education for their children, they must find some extra money to pay for it.

268

But because education is important and is, say, in a class of favored interests, it is heavily subsidized by the state. To recognize social benefits of education, all taxpayers contribute toward its support at the state and federal levels, though nonparents might no longer pay at the local. Further, because not only is education favored, but so also is the class of children, fees are steeply progressive with respect to income. So far so good. By the criterion of cutting sharply the nexus between quality of education and wealth, FPE represents a great advance. Things are not necessarily so rosy when we look at the matter from the point of view of the student himself. An intellectually avid student may have parents who do not care. This argues for allowing a degree of student-initiated mobility among schools, supported by merit scholarships. This could be an important matter, since the expenditure differences per student are much greater in FPE than our public education system is now seeking to provide—within, that is, any one state.

However, it is worth noting that rewards for good work in school are themselves skewed in their distribution to the social classes. Take first an upper-middle class boy. If he obtains high marks, he obtains his choice of entering several well-regarded universities or four-year colleges. If he gets poor marks, he may be disbarred from accompanying his friends in that adventure. This reward/penalty for equality of school work has been a powerful incentive for middle class youth to work hard. Take, now, a poor black who is getting C's and D's. To move up to A's and B's may be difficult. Anyway, the young man may not see much point to trying to enter a four-year college or university populated largely by whites. However, assume the student could move up to B's and C's, and complete the high school program. There is little reward, unfortunately, in making the improvement. He would obtain the same job, if any, in either case. Differentiation of the reward system by class lies outside the narrow concern of FPE, strictly speaking, but it would be possible to arrange things, as we shall see later, such that rewards are widely available. If such changes were made, FPE itself would work better.

Contracts

In this case the seminal statement is James S. Coleman's article "Toward Open Schools," in the journal *Public Interest*.[56]

The basic idea is that schools are changed from being self-contained cost centers for instruction to "open" institutions. Parents could choose whether to have their children taught various subjects (1) by public school teachers in their "home base" school, (2) by private contractors operating in the public school, or (3) by private contractors stationed outside the given public school. Contractors would be paid on the basis of results obtained in student achievement, as measured by standardized tests. Schools could be required to provide released time and access to private contractors.[57] For example, ". . . the teaching of elementary-level reading and arithmetic would be opened up to entrepreneurs outside the school, under contract with the school system to teach only reading or only arithmetic, and paid on the basis of performance by the child on standardized tests. The methods used by the contractors may only be surmised; the successful ones would presumably involve massive restructuring of the verbal or mathematical environment . . . The payment-by-results would quickly eliminate unsuccessful contractors, and the contractors would provide testing grounds for innovation that could subsequently be used by the school."[58]

More diversified contractual offerings could be provided at high school level. Controls could be established to assure that contracting was not a means to establish a greater degree of social and racial segregation. Community groups could be encouraged to bid for contracts under which one of the purposes might be to promote integration in extra-curricular affairs, etc.

The idea is catching on. In Texarkana in 1969 Dorsett Educational Systems, a private company, entered into a contract with the Liberty-Eylan School District of the following nature: "If the company (Dorsett) can raise the reading and mathematics level of the students who need the most help . . . by one full grade level in 80 hours, it would receive $1 per hour per student. If it succeeds in 60 hours or less, it can make as much as $110 a student. If the job takes 105 hours or more, payment is reduced to $60 per student. If a student makes no progress, the entire payment for the student is forfeited."[59]

Coleman explained the advantages of the contract system in the following terms. The plan " . . . allows the parent what he has never had within the public school system: a freedom of choice as consumer, as well as the opportunity to help establish special purpose programs, clinics and centers to beat the school at its own game. It allows educational innovators to prove them-

270

selves, insofar as they can attract and hold students. The contract centers provide the school with a source of innovation as well as a source of competition to measure its own efforts, neither of which it has had in the past. The interschool and interscholastic academic events widen horizons of both teachers and children, and provide a means of diffusing both the techniques and content of education. . . ."[60]

Economic Efficiency. The first thing to note is that Coleman contracting definitely conceives of the public school system as remaining in existence and of providing "home base" schools for students. Indeed, successful innovations may be copied and taken over by the public schools from the private entrepreneurs. It is thus hard to see how private contractors can undertake large-scale physical investments. Political uses aside, the Pioneer Palaces of U.S.S.R. offer students an opportunity to explore their interests in scientific, technical, and aesthetic fields that is probably unparalled in the world. As long as contractors are dependent on local governments to renew contracts and provide them access to students through released time, it is unlikely that they will build many well-equipped permanent contract centers. Similarly, it is unlikely in view of all the uncertainties that contractors can gain a great degree of continuity of staff, especially if they seek, as they should, highly talented people. Accordingly, though the contract system would undoubtedly offer a better fit between educational products that are most highly valued by households and services actually received, it would do so under the constraint of a low threshold of capital investment and under the further constraint of contractors' having little means of building on experience acquired through long service of their staff members.

Technological Efficiency. More than the other structural changes we have considered, the contract plan should allow an exploration of new approaches to instructional processes, subject to the proviso, as already noted, that the exploration not require heavy investment in physical capital nor continuity of experience in the contractor's staff. It should also be noted that contractors cannot be expected to provide large sums of money for basic research in educational methods, unless, of course, some assurance can be given that contractual arrangements can be maintained over the long period. At presently envisaged, contracting would allow testing only of approaches that are already known about under the existing state of research of learning processes, student motivation, etc.

Social Efficiency. It would appear that the Coleman contract plan would place the responsibility for arranging contract services on the present local school authorities. This would leave the relation between educational opportunities and wealth as they are at present, at least with respect to levels of money expenditure. However, it might well be true that districts could spend whatever funds they have more effectively through partial reliance on contractual services than if all expenditures are made in the public school system. It might also be true that this kind of advantage would be gained to a greater extent in poor districts than in rich. If both of these points were borne out, the relation (inverse) between educational opportunities and wealth would be moderated.

A Possibly Useful Combination: Family-Power-Equalizing and and the Contract System

It is possible to make combinations of the proposals for structural change that we have been describing. One such would be (1) to adopt family-power-equalizing grants as the general arrangement and (2) to allow families to elect to take a share of their entitlement in vouchers to be redeemed in the purchase of services from state-approved educational contractors. A sliding scale of contract entitlement might be employed, both to protect the child in terms of his receiving a minimum education program and to offer flexibility in choice of services to intellectually avid parents. For example, suppose under FPE a household chose the minimum tax rate and received an entitlement to enter their child in the lowest cost school ($500 per student per year at elementary level, $800 at secondary). That household might be entitled to receive no more than 20 percent of its entitlement in contract vouchers.[61] Now take the case of a family that opted for the highest tax rate and gained entry to schools with $1,400 at elementary and $1,700 at secondary levels (if all the value were used to obtain admittance in a single school). Such a family might be able to claim 50 percent of its entitlement for contract services. No family, of course, would receive actual cash. However, the higher the tax rate chosen, the more expensive school, *and* the more flexibility in purchase of educational services a household would obtain.

As compared with an unmodified FPE program, the flexible family-plan-equalizing scheme (call it FFPE) would appear to offer the following advantages: (1) the amount of choice in education would be substantially increased; hence, the level of economic efficiency would be raised; (2) it would be less likely that families uniformly would choose the most expensive schools (the problem we dealt with at some length above, in terms of the difficulties associated with developing a tax structure to ration educational services independently of household wealth), since many families, one might suppose, would elect to use a cheaper "home base" school in order to have entitlements to design special programs for their children under what could be called a "building block" approach; (3) households could obtain the advantages of specialized secondary institutions without having to breach the education establishment's commitment to the comprehensive high school.

As compared with the simple contract approach, FFPE would be likely to provide these gains: (1) The contractors would be freed from dependence on local school districts for renewal of contracts and for the provision of released time. They would deal directly with parents, having first obtained state approval for the relevance and quality of their offerings. It would, of course, be incumbent on them to provide their services at times that did not conflict with regular school programs or to make an individual arrangement with a school for the release of a given student. In any case, however, the market would be opened in a regular and continuing way, and contractors would gradually come to make appropriate investment in physical plant, training of staff, and applied research in education to exploit more thoroughly the opportunities for obtaining advances in technological efficiency. The continuity of the program and the freedom from arbitrary bureaucratic decisions of local government would make it feasible for contractors to put substantial investments into the quality of their services. Once such investment is made feasible, competition should dictate that it is actually carried out. (2) The provisions that the amount of state subsidy to a household (a) is inverse to household income and (b) is wholly free of extraneous matters, such as the value of local assessed valuation per student, introduces greater equity than was originally provided in the contract plan.

It might be objected that the combination plan loses an essential equity provision of FPE, namely, that parents do not

273

"add on"[62] to the value of their entitlements in purchasing educational services. Under FFPE, it is true that it would be possible to supplement costs for contracted services by private household contribution. To require no "add on" under our suggested modification would not be administratively feasible. The difference between the original proposal for family-power-equalizing and the modified plan is not so great on this score as one might first think: after all, no one could bar a household from supplementing its FPE schooling by wholly private contributions for contractual services. The lack of government commitment toward contractual services would simply mean that they would be of lower quality and, moreover, less well distributed among the social classes.

THE SPECIAL PROBLEM OF
VOCATIONAL AND TECHNICAL EDUCATION

Vocational and technical education is commonly regarded as expensive. It does not have high status in our country. Unless special attention is given to its provision, it is likely that the supply and quality of this kind of schooling will suffer under the structural changes we have described. Yet, the availability of this kind of schooling in good quality is exactly what is needed to provide incentives for all but the most ambitious of poor youth to do well in their early years of general education. (The problem of a class-differentiated incentive structure for students was noted above.)

In his original statement on voucher plans, Friedman suggested that government provide loans to students for their specialized training, with repayment related to the estimated extra income they would earn for having received the instruction.[63] Unfortunately, this laissez-faire approach to the institutional structure under which training is provided may fail to attack the problem of quality of training in sufficient measure. Let us consider the problem in more detail.

What are the difficulties in the present arrangements for supply of skill training in public, formal institutions?

1. Public institutions, especially those offering instruction above secondary level, are subject to extreme political pressures. It is a popular thing for a local authority to establish, say, a new junior college with a vocational wing in a district that has none. Yet, proliferation of institutions and of programs within

274

institutions can quickly lead to a low rate of utilization of specific courses.

2. Drop out rates in such public institutions are notoriously high. Are these high drop out rates related to the control, i.e., public sector control, of training institutions? It is possible to think so: (1) Because there is no legal linkage between the training institutions and employers, the student cannot be assured of a job even if he completes the training program successfully; hence, when the student becomes temporarily frustrated in his academic program, he may view the cost to himself of dropping out as rather low. (2) Since employers, i.e., those persons who have the most intimate knowledge of what is required of new entrants to the work force, do not select students for admission to the training institutions or for assignment to specific programs within the institutions, and since the previous education of students, by which they establish their eligibility to enter the training institutions, has been general in nature, it seems rather a matter of chance whether a given student really has the motivation and aptitude to learn the trade he is studying; hence, an improper fit between the characteristics of a student and the learnings expected of him may force some students out. (3) Students who find their work in training institutions administered by public authorities either too easy or too demanding cannot easily shift to another level of study; hence, certain ones of them would be likely to become bored and drop-out prone for lack of interest, while others would be forced out by academic failure. The tendency of public institutions toward rigidity of program is not a necessary feature of their existence, but is possibly related to the fact that public institutions in the education and training fields are seldom scrutinized closely with respect to their own productivity and cost-effectiveness. (4) The jobs for which the students are trained are often monopolized by trade unions, membership in which may not be open *de facto* to new graduates.

3. Training institutions are expensive to operate in the nature of the case. As compared with general instruction, training institutions require more capital facilities (e.g., laboratories and shops); they also require a greater quantity of consumable materials of instruction. Teachers in training institutions, those who are competent anyway, have good opportunities to work in production rather than in teaching, and they must be paid high salaries, as compared with arts teachers, to retain their services.

275

Thus, it is possible, speaking realistically, to run high-grade training institutions only when those institutions can be made to operate efficiently. This means that courses must be filled with the maximum number of students who can be taught effectively in a given subject and that the drop-out rate must be held to a low point. Yet, as we have indicated above, it is just these kinds of efficiencies that public institutions find it difficult to provide.

The most common alternative to training conducted by public institutions is training provided by the employer in the work place. Now, as we have said above, a certain amount of on-the-job training is characteristic of every human economic activity. The question, however, is whether the employer should bear the major share of the responsibility for the development of work skills in the trades and in the technical fields. Apprenticeship is the form in which this employer responsibility has been most clearly delineated.

On the face of it, training by employers would seem to offer certain advantages. The training would almost certainly be relevant to the future work assignment of the trainee, because there would be no educational vested interests to dictate otherwise, and because employers would have no incentive to provide irrelevant training. The courses would probably be flexible, in the sense that their length would be determined by the time needed for a given group of trainees to learn a particular set of skills. The program would be flexible, in the sense that courses would be started up or dropped in close relation to the current skill requirements of the employer. These kinds of flexibility are possible to attain because the employer can shift his senior staff from production work to part-time training of new workers and back to full-time production with great ease. Under a system of on-the-job training, the trainee should be less drop-out prone in three respects: first, he will feel a closer nexus between success in learning new skills and immediate advancement in the firm than he would feel if he was a full-time student in a public training institution, where desire for success in learning is clouded by uncertainty about how and where he can finally get a job; second, because training is more individualized (which is possible, in turn, because the trainee spends part of his time in production), the pace of learning can be accelerated or slowed down in terms of the trainee's own progress, so that he is unlikely ever to become too bored or too discouraged with his instruction; third, he usually is paid.

However, there would appear to be certain disadvantages in shifting the main burden of training onto the shoulders of employers:

1. If standards of labor productivity are low to begin with, bright, young, eager trainees may regress to those prevailing low standards because they do not have any proper models of performance, if not of skill standards, to look up to.

2. Only in the largest firms—and sometimes not even in them—the exceptionally good craftsman or technician cannot find more than a handful of trainees to work with at any given point in time. He may have, perhaps, three apprentices when he could easily be teaching the more bookish parts of the craft to a group of twenty. On-the-job training does not commonly allow economies of scale in the use of the time of instructors. This is a critical shortcoming, given the scarcity of highly skilled persons in operational fields in this country.

So there are disadvantages both in relying mainly on publicly administered training institutions and in relying mainly on on-the-job training. Some countries have tried to solve this problem by combining the two systems: to have, for example, apprentices receiving instruction in the practical parts of their craft in the work place and simultaneously receiving instruction in the more analytical aspects of their trade in publicly administered training institutions (on a part-time basis). Actually, this solution may preserve the worst features of both plans. The public institutions may still be staffed by not-so-good instructors, on account of the low pay and status that working in such institutions implies. The trainee may tend to regress still to the low standards of productivity he sees about him in the work place. The problem of attaining efficient utilization of training skills, the producers' goods of the human resources industry, would still remain.

Fortunately, there is a "third way" to skill and technical training, namely, to have most of the training performed in institutions which are separate from the work place but to place those institutions under the financial and administrative control of consortia of employers. This plan was adopted in France in 1930, has worked well in Latin America (e.g., the Servicio Nacional de Aprendizaje—SENA of Colombia), and was

277

taken up in England in 1964.[64] What are some of the possible advantages of the "third way?"

1. The system would provide flexibility in the education and training system where it is most needed. Contrast, for example, the planning of programs for medical with that of programs for skilled and technical workers (e.g., machinists, foundrymen, draftsmen, loom fixers, electricians, computer programmers, etc.). In the former case decisions are essentially judgmental: how many doctors per 10,000 of population shall the country have at fixed dates in the future? Once this decision is made, planning of programs for the training of doctors is relatively straightforward. In the latter case, one is dealing with many different types of skills, many of which are substitutable one for the other, or with respect to capital. Demand for specific skills is subject to short-term shifts, accordingly, in production functions. It is also subject to short-term shifts in output markets. Plainly, one should seek a flexible system of training for craftsmen and technical workers. Employer-administered training institutions can provide such flexibility, because employers can second their own craftsmen and technicians into teaching service on short-term assignments, if need be on a part-time basis.

2. At the same time, the training institutions would allow economies of scale to be achieved in the utilization of time of the trainers. The number of persons a given trainer was instructing could be determined more closely by considerations of pedagogical efficiency and less by accidental considerations of how many apprentices, say, a given plant in a given firm happened to have at the moment.

3. If the training institutions were financed by a payroll tax, then the institutions would have an elastic source of revenue and one under which the volume of funds flowing to training activities would be functionally related to the degree to which management was substituting labor for capital and higher grades of labor for lower. The stop-and-go characteristics of training when it is strictly a responsibility of individual employers would be ended (after all, private training programs are generally the first casualty of a downturn in profits in a firm).

4. The training institutions would have the financial resources and the access to data to deal with a number of important topics of applied research, such as the following: what are the strategic learnings from general education necessary to

278

learn specific work skills; how quickly can operational skills be taught to workers of different backgrounds and what are the cost-effectiveness relations involved in acceleration of training, selection of applicants for training, and the provision of remedial education; is a quantitative or analytical set of mind important in developing a high-productivity employee and, if so, how is this way of thinking best developed?

5. Other, somewhat more specific, advantages are the following: (1) Insofar as the training institutions required a permanent faculty, they should find themselves blessed with the financial resources and the prestige to attract competent teachers. (2) Students would benefit from having the intellectual discipline of the classroom but at the same time they would have been placed in a new, work-oriented setting, different from the public educational institutions in which many of them had previously suffered failure and lost commitment to learning. (3) The structure of the training system could easily recognize regional differences in skill requirements and in calibre of students. (4) Individual training institutions could incorporate different levels of instruction (remedial, standard, advanced) and different forms (full-time, sandwich, evening). (5) The program could accommodate high school students, high school leavers, and high school graduates, thus offering an incentive structure consonant with formal educational aspirations of different youth.

Nothing in the structural changes we have considered earlier would be compatible with this type of revision of work-related training.

It is plainly true that we can no longer see our existing educational structure as the only alternative. The various measures of change we have considered appear to have strengths, as nearly we can judge them *in vacuo*, but they may also have weaknesses. What is important is to have experimentation by our state governments with the different structural arrangements *and* with combinations of the various proposals. To ignore the discontent with the present system of education and to ignore the possibilities of fruitful change could be disastrous. However, it is hard to see which kind of system will work well in what various kinds of situations until the experiments are carried out.[65]

New degrees of flexibility could serve to make education more of a life-long process for a larger number of people. It may well be that in America we have exhausted the patience of the young

279

with protracted years of continuing education without having exhausted the possibilities of education for human welfare and happiness. "Discontinuous" education might relieve the impatience, with years of schooling being interspersed (penalty free) with outdoor work, travel, community development, etc. The basic requirement is that education and training be available at times when people want it, under attractive conditions, and at costs that are equitable. It is not to be expected, nonetheless, that absolute reduction in expenditures can be achieved as a direct outcome of the adoption of the kinds of structural changes that have been discussed in this paper. More satisfaction in the public sector, yes, and possibly more social benefits—these would be the likely yields, not dollar savings in the short-run.

This idea of the general availability of educational services is the major American contribution to world educational thought; it stands in stark contrast to the efforts of most countries to regulate educational provision by the government's estimate of requirements for specific types of trained manpower. The structural changes we have discussed here all shift the locus of decision-making about consumption of educational services more directly into the household. For this reason they are in the American tradition.

FOOTNOTES

* The author is grateful for the assistance of Professor John E. Coons, School of Law, University of California, Berkeley, and Professors David Cohen and Martin T. Katzman, Harvard University. Professors R. L. Johns and John E. Coons highly read an earlier draft and provided helpful comments. Dorothy Benson and Ramona Fellom assisted him in editing and preparing the manuscript. The author alone is responsible for the opinions expressed herein.

1. In a developing nation like Pakistan, the pressures for structural changes arise from different kinds of problems: imbalance between numbers of students taking arts as against science courses, shortages of skilled craftsmen and technicians alongside unemployment of college graduates, brain drain, etc. Mostly, these matters are related to labor markets and reflect, in part, the fact that in Pakistan, as in most countries other than the United States, there is a fairly rigid relation between the type of education one receives and the status of occupation one enters—or seeks to enter.

2. Charles S. Benson and Peter B. Lund, *Neighborhood Distribution of Local Public Services* (Berkeley: Institute of Governmental Studies, University of California, 1969), pp. 98-100.

3. James S. Coleman, et al., Equality of Educational Opportunity (Washington: Government Printing Office, 1966); Charles S. Benson, et al., *State and Local Fiscal Relationships in Public Education in California* (Sacramento: State Senate, 1965).

4. "Inexorably," that is, in the absence of more exprexe departures in instructional practices (computer-assisted instructions, classes of size and under, etc.) than our state-local school systems are likely to intro-

280

duce and in the absence of radical revisions in incentives placed before students to work hard in school.

5. See Statement by Frederick O'R. Hayes, Director of the Budget, City of New York on "National Priorities," United States Congress, Joint Committee on the Economic Report (February 24, 1970).

6. The cities in America have absorbed what is probably the largest migration of families from off the farms that the world has ever seen. Earlier, the cities had absorbed a great tide of the poor and spiritually dispossessed of Europe. The second migration, unlike the first, could not be accommodated without it being a contributing factor to a pervasive and lasting deterioration of quality of urban life. With hindsight, one can say that the federal government should have seen to it that the education of the rural poor over the course of the last several decades was of sufficient quality that the agricultural revolution—and the migrations it produced—would not cause such havoc as we see it did.

7. The author is indebted to Professor Martin T. Katzman for discussion on these points.

8. Not only do the rich withdraw their children from the public schools, but so do many middle-class Catholic families. The double "creaming off" has the effect of removing significant numbers of children from the public school environment who have academic ambitions and who are willing to accept academic discipline.

9. The failure rate in schools appears to be a function of city size. For some evidence, note the following estimates of school failure in New York State in 1968-69: New York City, 37 percent; other large cities, 27 percent; medium sized cities, 20 percent; small cities, 17 percent; villages and large central school districts (rural), 13 percent (State Education Department, University of the State of New York, *Education Statistics New York State* [Albany: The Department, 1970], p. 10.) Reasons for the relation are not clear, though it is reasonable to infer that city populations include disproportionate numbers of households who are sufferers from educational deprivation as a part of the southern legacy. See Irving Gershenberg, "The Negro and the Development of White Public Education in the South: Alabama, 1880-30," *The Journal of Negro Education* (Winter, 1970), pp. 50-59. On the other hand, it is possible to view the problem as one of class, not of race. See Alan B. Wilson, "Residential Segregation of Social Classes and Aspirations of High School Boys," *American Sociological Review* (December, 1959), pp. 836-45.

10. We refer here to "consumers" as households in which there are children of school-going age. In a broader sense, every household is a consumer of educational services, because the education industry is characterized by external economies of consumption, i.e., the industry provides "social benefits." In the present context, however, we are using the term "consumer" in its narrower meaning of a household obtaining schooling for its own children.

11. For a major decentralization proposal, we refer to Mayor's Advisory Panel on Decentralization of the New York City Schools, McGeorge Bundy, Chairman, *Reconnection for Learning: A Community School System for New York City* (New York: The Panel, 1967). The voucher proposal was first presented in recent times by Milton Friedman of the Department of Economics, University of Chicago. See his article, "The Role of Government in Education," in Robert A. Solo, ed., *Economics and the Public Interest* (New Brunswick: Rutgers University Press, 1955), pp. 123-42, reprinted in Charles S. Benson, *Perspectives on the Economics of Public Education* (Boston: Houghton Mifflin Company, 1963), pp. 132-42. Family-power-equalizing is developed in John E. Coons, William H. Clune, III, and Stephen D. Sugarman, *Private Wealth and Public Education* (Cambridge: Harvard University Press, 1970). The idea of obtaining educational services through contractual arrangements is presented in James S. Coleman, "Toward Open Schools," *The Public Interest* Fall, 1967 pp. 20-27.

12. Frederick O'R. Hayes. referring to material quoted from Otto Eck-

281

stein in "The Outlook for the Public Finances of State and Local Governments to 1975," in Office of the Mayor, City of New York, *Commission on Inflation and Economic Welfare of the City of New York* (New York: The Office, 1969).

13. And hence, the education industry finds it difficult to show any large amount of productivity gains. See Victor R. Fuchs, *The Service Economy* (New York: National Bureau of Economic Research, 1968), p. 76.

14. Charles S. Benson, *The Economics of Public Education*, (Boston: Houghton Mifflin Company, 1968), pp. 294-305.

15. Joseph M. Cronin, "School Finance in the Seventies: The Prospect for Reform," *Phi Delta Kappan* (November, 1969), p. 117. At the same time, we must recognize that education in the United States is handsomely supported as compared with levels of expenditures in other countries. For example, in the mid-sixties, the United States educational system (all levels) was consuming resources equal in value to four times the Gross National Product of Pakistan, and Pakistan is one of the largest countries in the world in terms of population. In other words, 130 million Pakistanis would have to work for four years to feed the United States' educational system for one year (at the level of school and university expenditures in the mid-sixties).

16. *New York Times*, March 4, 1970, p. 1.

17. Coons, et al. pp. 256-68. See also John E. Coons, William H. Clune, III, and Stephen D. Sugarman, "Educational Opportunity: A Workable Constitutional Test for State Financial Structures." *California Law Review* (April, 1969), pp. 321-22.

18. The general taxpayer, however, would still be required to pay his customary share of state and federal contributions for education, including partial subsidy of tuition for children in above-average schools.

19. Friedman.

20. Arthur E. Wise, "The Constitutional Challenge to Inequities in School Finance, *Phi Delta Kappan* (November, 1969), pp. 145-48; James W. Guthrie, George B. Kleindorfer, Henry M. Levin, and Robert T. Stout, *Schools and Inequality* (Washington, D. C.: The Urban Coalition, 1969), pp. 2-3.

21. This phenomenon can readily be observed in New England. Even in California, it can be seen to exist. See Charles S. Benson, *et al.*, *State and Local Fiscal Relationships in Public Education in California,* Chapter IV, Tables 2 and 4, pp. 45, 48.

22. State Committee on Public Education, *Citizens for the 21st Century* (Sacramento: State Board of Education 1969), p. 63.

23. See Guthrie, et al., Ch. 3, 4, and 5.

24. Coons, et al., p. 388.

25. Frank I. Michelman, "The Supreme Court, 1968 Term Foreword: On Protecting the Poor Through the Fourteenth Amendment," *Harvard Law Review* (November, 1969), pp. 56-59.

26. Mayor's Advisory Panel on Decentralization of the New York City Schools, See also Henry M. Levin, ed., *Community Control of Schools* (Washington, D.C.: The Brookings Institution, 1970).

27. Coons, et al., Private Wealth and Public Education, pp. 268-69.

28. Mayor's Advisory Panel on Decentralization of the New York City Schools, p. 4.

29. *Ibid.*

30. *Ibid.*, p. 10.

31. *Ibid.*

32. It is necessary, of course, to develop financial relationships between the Central Board of Education and the Community School Districts and between both and the state government. These were discussed in Part IV of the Bundy Report. Several alternative patterns were suggested, but no final recommendation was made.

33. *Ibid.*, p. 73. However, the general tenor of the Bundy Report appears to be negative toward open enrollments.

34. Friedman.

35. Ibid., p. 135.

36. *Ibid.*, p. 137.

37. A.C.F. Beales, "Historical Aspects of the Debate on Education," in Institute of Economic Affairs, *Education: A Framework for Choice* (London:, The Institute, 1967), p. 8. More recently, a voucher plan in England has been proposed by Professor Alan Peacock and Jack Wiseman. *Education for Democrats* (London, Institute of Economics, 1964).

38. A.C.F. Beales, p. 20.

39. Grievance procedures are coming to be of increasing importance in education. They need not be confined to resolution of problems between administrators and staff; they could also be used to resolve issues between school staffs and parents.

40. M. V. Pauly, "Mixed Public and Private Financing of Education: Efficiency and Feasibility," *American Economic Review* (March, 1967), pp. 120-30.

41. *Ibid.*, p. 129.

42. John E. Coons, "Recreating the Family's Role in Education," *Inequality in Education* (Harvard Center for Law and Education, Numbers 3 and 4, 1970), pp. 1-5.

43. Each institution would receive from government a given amount of fee per student. The amount of fee would vary by category of institution but not by category of student. Poor families would pay much less in school charges than the amounts of the fees paid to the institutions; rich might pay more; but overall the government would pay out more to the schools than it collected in charges—hence, the public subsidy.

44. It is barely conceivable that the community which met the family's taste with respect to one local public service would also meet its tastes with respect to the remainder of local public services. Apparently, the idea is that the family would choose its residence on the basis of which community met its standards on what were seen by it to be the most important services. Obviously, this is not an ideal solution, especially when there are strong differences in taste *within* a given household.

45. To some extent, the addition to the local community's taxable potential would be offset by a reduction in its receipts of state aid for education, but state aid programs are by no means so finely tuned that the locality would be left indifferent between having or not having the power plant, if the choice is seen strictly in terms of local government finance.

46. They still could make use of unaided private schools, however.

47. Coons, et al., "Educational Opportunity: A Workable Constitutional Test for State Financial Structures," p. 311.

48. In the volume, *Private Wealth and Public Education*, pp. 282-83, Coons et al. suggest that district power equalizing might be applied to all local public services. This would be a comprehensive approach to the problem of municipal overburden.

49. Michelman, p. 51.

50. There remains a question whether the ability to judge true worth, as distinct from the more superficial aspects of style, is randomly distributed in the population.

51. John E. Coons, "The Draft Statute with Comments" (Berkeley: School of Law, University of Califarnia, 1969), mimeo., pp. 1-38.

52. It is a part of the Coons' plan that sufficient places in schools at each expenditure level would be available in all localities.

53. One way around the difficulty, though possibly not a good way, is to make the lowest-priced schools free to all income classes.

54. Coons, "Recreating the Family's Role in Education," p. 16.

55. However, the tuition rates *could* be raised over a period of time, adjusting them year-by-year, starting with the earliest year of enrollment.

56. Coleman.

57. The basic ideas are not new. "Payment-by-results" was the standard of remuneration for state school teachers in mid-nineteenth century England. It is traditional in India and Pakistan that interested (and well-

heeled) parents pay the teacher (who is ostensibly fully employed in a state or private school) an extra fee to come to their homes and give private tuition to their children in off hours. See Nirad C. Chaudhuri, *The Autobiography of an Unknown Indian* (Berkeley: University of California Press, 1968). pp. 150-51. Similarly, in the early nineteen-sixties, the then U.S. Ambassador to India, John Kenneth Galbraith, proposed that teachers in Calcutta be paid ". . . a subsidy in the form of salary to every teacher that sets up in business at any possible place and passes a given number of pupils through carefully conducted examinations each year." *Ambassador's Journal* (Boston: Houghton Mifflin Company, 1969), p. 306.

58. Coleman, p. 25.

59. "Private Firm Wins Performance Contract: If Students Don't Learn, District Doesn't Pay," *Phi Delta Kappan* (November, 1969), p. 135.

60. Coleman, p. 27.

61. The idea is that offering a higher percentage in contract fees at this low level of purchase of educational service might produce too many cases of students failing to receive a minimum amount of schooling in basic subjects. The provision suggested here, it should be noted, destroys Coons' idea that there should be only four levels of prices for school services (or some such small number). Allowing parents to take part of their entitlement in contracts would mean that schools would have to produce a much more diversified price structure.

62. In reading an earlier draft, Professor Coons suggested that it is possible to preserve the features of FPE while providing contract vouchers to a greater degree than indicated here. One approach would be to keep the four school expenditure levels (only) and let families choose a higher tax rate than specified for a given school, taking the excess tuition in contract vouchers. Another would be to provide contract vouchers to families that were willing to pay a small additional (supplementary) tax.

63. Friedman, pp. 139-42. A similar but much more thoroughly developed proposal was made by William Vickery, "A Proposal for Student Loans," in Selma Mushkin, ed., *Economics of Higher Education*, (Washington, Government Printing Office, 1962), p. 270 ff.

64. For a discussion of the corresponding program in Brazil (SENAI), see Nathaniel H. Leff, *The Brazilian Capital Goods Industry, 1929-1964* (Cambridge: Harvard University Press, 1968), pp. 74-81.

65. Indeed, it was recently announced that the Office of Economic Opportunity is sponsoring a pilot program in education vouchers in selected school districts in the fall of 1971. *International Herald Tribune* (June 5, 1970), p. 3.

CHAPTER 9

Alternative State Finance Plans

In this chapter object measures will be used in evaluating alternative finance models applied to a prototype state. These alternative models will be compared by objective methods to determine: (1) the extent to which financial equalization of educational opportunity is provided and (2) the extent to which the taxes used to finance the programs are regressive or progressive.

School finance models have two major dimensions as follows: The *allocation* dimension and the *revenue* dimension. The allocation dimension includes the target populations to be served; the programs, services and facilities provided for the target populations; the computation of unit costs for the programs to be financed; determination of whether local ability and/or effort will be considered in the allocation of state funds; requirements and restraints placed on the use of state funds; and similar matters.

The revenue dimension includes the percent of revenues to be provided from each of the following sources: federal, state and local; the types of taxes to levy at each level of government; the progressivity or regressivity of different types of taxes; the amount of revenue to allocate for school support and similar mat-

285

ters. In this chapter we will deal only with the state and local revenue and allocation dimensions.

The principal finance models in common use in the United States and variations in those models are examined in this chapter. The financial impact of each model is compared with all other models examined on a comparable basis. In order to do this, it was found desirable to construct a prototype state with conditions somewhat representative of the nation, with real data for the districts in that state. The development of data for the prototype state is discussed next.

THE PROTOTYPE STATE

A prototype state was constructed for the purpose of testing alternative models of state support. This prototype state was created by starting from a state which represented a wide range of conditions among the districts of that state and adding a few districts selected from another state which would further diversify the variations among the districts of the prototype state. All of the districts of the prototype state are real school districts and the data are actual data. The prototype state includes data from 32 local school districts. Extensive demographic and educational data were gathered for each district. Pupil population data and the assessed valuation for each district are summarized in Table 9-4. Districts composing the prototype state represent a wide variety of conditions so that an assessment can be made of the impact of each school finance model on a particular type of district. The goal was to represent the full range of districts found throughout the nation; however, it is not claimed that the prototype state is a true sample of the nation. For example, all districts included in the sample have 1,800 or more pupils and all districts operate both elementary and high schools. The prototype state actually is a model of a state with a fairly efficient school district organization. If all 50 states had as efficient a district organization as the prototype state, the total number of school districts in the United States would be reduced from some 17,000 to approximately 2,000-2,500.

It is impossible to develop a school finance plan which is equitable to the children and also equitable to the taxpayers in a state with inefficient small school districts gerrymandered so as to sequester wealth and to disequalize educational opportunity.

286

Therefore, the alternative models presented in this chapter are tested in a state which has a relatively efficient district organization in order that the impact of the *finance model* and not the *district organization* might be evaluated.

The prototype state includes the following types of districts:

1. Large core city districts.
2. Suburban districts.
3. Medium size city districts.
4. Small city districts.
5. Rural districts.
6. Districts with high and low equalized valuation per pupil.
7. Districts with high and low personal income per pupil.
8. Districts with a high and low percentage of the culturally disadvantaged.

DEVELOPMENT OF ALTERNATIVE FINANCE MODELS

There are an infinite number of alternative models of state school financing. No two of the fifty states are using exactly the same model in all respects. Furthermore, some change in each state's school finance plan is made in practically every general session of the legislature of that state. Although there are an infinite number of variations in plans of school financing, it is possible to make certain useful broad classifications of alternative models and to compare the impact of these models assuming that each model is applied to the same total revenue from state and local sources. In this chapter we are dealing only with alternative models of state and local financing which can be controlled by the states. Hopefully, federal funds made available to the states can be integrated with state funds in such a manner as to supplement those funds and, therefore, have the same impact within a state as state funds.

There are, of course, infinite possible variations in the amount or relative adequacy of funds provided for the public schools of a state. In order to test the impact of the alternative models examined in this chapter, the total amount of revenue from all sources combined is held constant for all models but the sources of the revenue and the methods of allocation are varied.

As pointed out above, school finance models have two major dimensions—the allocation dimension and the revenue dimension.

The Allocation Dimension

Following are the principal types of state school finance models classified according to the *allocation dimension*:

1. *Flat Grant Models.* Under this type of model, state grants are allocated to local school districts without taking into consideration variations among the districts in local taxpaying ability. There are two major variations of this model as follows:

> a. A uniform amount per pupil, per teacher or some other unit of need is allotted without taking into consideration necessary variations in unit costs of different educational programs and services.
>
> b. Variable amounts per unit of need are allocated to local school districts which reflect necessary variations in unit costs.

2. *Equalization Models.* Under this type of model state funds are allocated to local school districts in inverse proportion to local taxpaying ability. In other words, more state funds per pupil, per teacher, or other unit of need are allocated to the districts of less wealth than to those of greater wealth. As in the flat grant models, there are two main variations in the equalization models as follows:

> a. In computing the cost of the foundation program equalized, a uniform amount is allowed per pupil, per teacher or other unit of need without giving consideration to necessary variations in unit costs of different educational programs and services.
>
> b. Variable amounts per unit of need which take into consideration necessary variations in unit costs are used in computing the cost of the foundation programs.

The Revenue Dimension

Ignoring federal funds, following are the principal types of state school finance models classified according to the *revenue dimension:*

1. *Complete State Support Model.*
2. *Joint State-Local Support Model.*
3. *Complete Local Support Model.*

If federal revenue is included the following additional revenue models can be added:

1. *Federal-state support model.*
2. *Federal-state-local model.*
3. *Federal-local model.*
4. *Complete federal support model.*

The impact of some of these federal related models is examined briefly in Chapter 11 of this volume.

The revenue dimension includes another variable which substantially affects the equity of state school finance models. That variable is the degree of progressivity (or regressivity) of the taxes used to support the public schools. The degree of the progressivity of a state's tax structure depends upon the type of taxes a state levies. The state has a wide range of choices in the type of taxes it levies. Taxes may be progressive, proportional or regressive. Approximately 98% of local school tax revenue is derived from property taxes. Boards of education in most states do not have much choice in the type of tax to levy. They must depend almost entirely on property taxes which are the most regressive major tax levied. Therefore, the progressivity of the tax structure used to support the public schools depends upon two factors:

1. The proportion of school revenue provided by the state and,
2. The relative progressivity of the state's revenues.

The alternative school finance models tested in this chapter include all of the dimensions described in this section.

Major Policy Decisions

The legislature of every state must make the following major policy decisions with respect to financing the public schools:

1. What educational programs and services will be funded in the states' school finance plan and for whom will these programs be provided?
2. Will state funds be apportioned on the flat grant basis which ignores differences in the wealth of local school districts or on the equalization basis which provides more state

funds per unit of educational need to districts of less wealth than to districts of greater wealth?

3. Will necessary variations in unit costs of different educational programs and services be recognized or ignored in allocating state funds on either the flat grant or equalization basis?

4. What proportion of school revenue will be provided by the state and what proportion from local sources?

5. How progressive (or regressive) will be the state's tax structure?

6. To what extent will the state provide for financial equalization of educational opportunity among school districts of the state?

7. What are the financial needs of the public schools and how nearly can those needs be met taking into consideration needs for other governmental services and the financial ability of the state?

A number of alternative models and variations in those models are examined in this chapter in order to assist decision making authorities in determining the consequences of decisions they make with respect to decision areas 1 to 6 listed above. Prior to testing these models, it is necessary to describe alternative methods of treating the data from the prototype state. Those methods are presented in the following section.

UNIT COST DIFFERENTIALS USED FOR PROTOTYPE STATE

In Chapter 7 of this volume, variations in cost per pupil for different educational programs are presented. Educational programs designed to meet the many different needs of pupils vary widely in per pupil cost. For example, senior high schools cost more per pupil than elementary schools. Exceptional education programs, vocational programs and programs for compensatory education all cost more per pupil than programs provided for pupils not enrolled in these special high cost programs. Two methods are commonly used to adjust for these extra costs—the weighted pupil technique and the adjusted instruction unit, (sometimes called the adjusted classroom unit or teacher unit).

The Weighted Pupil Technique. The weighted pupil technique is based on the assumption that the pupil-teacher ratio is less and operating costs are higher for certain special programs and under certain conditions than for typical elementary school programs. The method usually used is to start the weighting of pupils by assigning the weight of 1 to the cost per pupil of regular pupils enrolled in elementary schools. If it is found that the cost of educating exceptional pupils (handicapped pupils) is approximately twice the per pupil cost of educating regular pupils because the per pupil-teacher ratio is only one-half of the per pupil-teacher ratio for regular elementary pupils and operating and capital outlay costs are also about twice the amount per pupil needed for regular elementary pupils, then the equivalent full time pupils enrolled in exceptional education classes are given a weight of two. Appropriate weights are also assigned to pupils enrolled in the other high cost programs. It costs more per pupil to provide educational opportunities for pupils enrolled in small isolated schools which because of distance or geographical barriers cannot be consolidated with other schools. The pupils enrolled in small, isolated schools can also be appropriately weighted.

Table 9-1 sets forth the scale used for weighting the pupils in average daily membership in the prototype state. The weights for educational programs are average weights computed from the data presented in the special studies reported in Volume 3 of the National Educational Finance Project. The weights for pupils attending necessary isolated schools were developed by the central staff from current practice. It should not be assumed that the weights presented in Table 9-1 are valid for all time. Those weights are based on current practice in school systems reputed to have good programs in the program areas that are weighted. What is current practice today may become outdated tomorrow. Therefore, the weights presented in Table 9-1 should be considered as weights derived from current practice to illustrate the methods used in weighting pupils. Furthermore, the special satellite studies made by the National Educational Finance Project revealed that the cost differentials for special educational programs varied widely among different school systems. Therefore, much additional research is needed before fully reliable cost differentials can be assigned to these special programs. However, the evidence is conclusive that vocational education, exceptional education, and compensatory education all cost more per pupil than regular educational programs. To defer

291

TABLE 9-1

SCALES USED FOR WEIGHTING PUPILS IN THE PROTOTYPE STATE

Programs	Prototype State Target Population[a] (ADM)	Weighting For Cost Differential[c]	Weighted Pupils
Col. 1	Col. 2	Col. 3	Col. 4
Early Childhood			
3 year olds	30,946	1.40	43,324
4 year olds	50,813	1.40	71,138
Kindergarten (5 year olds)	56,231	1.30	73,100
Sub Total	137,990		187,562
Non-Isolated Basic Elementary and Secondary			
Grades 1–6	301,777	1.00	301,777
Grades 7–9	182,961	1.20	219,553
Grades 10–12	124,693	1.40	174,570
Sub Total	609,431		695,900
Isolated Basic Elementary and Secondary[b]			
Elementary Size			
150–200	6,332	1.10	6,965
100–149	3,155	1.20	3,786
less than 100	3,789	1.30	4,926
Junior High			
150–200	2,266	1.30	2,946
100–149	1,177	1.40	1,648
less than 100	1,299	1.50	1,948
Senior High			
150–200	849	1.50	1,273
100–149	381	1.60	609
less than 100	126	1.70	214
Sub Total	19,374		24,315
Special (Exceptional)			
Mentally Handicapped	16,089	1.90	30,569
Physically Handicapped	2,668	3.25	8,671
Emotionally Handicapped	19,696	2.80	55,149
Special Learning Disorder	5,335	2.40	12,804
Speech Handicapped	31,152	1.20	37,382
Sub Total	74,940		144,575
Compensatory Education			
Basic: Income under $4,000	131,165	2.00	262,330
Vocational—Technical	46,502	1.80	83,704
Total All Categories (Preschool—Grade 12)	1,019,402		1,398,386

[a]Full time equivalent membership.
[b]Elementary schools must be 10 miles or more by road from another elementary school in order to be weighted for isolation; junior high schools 15 or more miles from another junior high school and senior high schools, 20 miles or more from another senior high school.
[c]These weights vary slightly from the weights reported in Chapter 7 because a few additional districts were added to the sample from which the averages were computed.

making allowance in state support programs for the extra costs of these special programs until exact information is available on these cost differentials would be self-defeating.

It will be noted from Table 9-1 that there are 1,019,402 pupils in average daily membership in the prototype state but there are 1,398,386 weighted pupils in average daily membership. As will be shown later in this chapter the ratio of weighted pupils in A.D.M. to pupils in A.D.M. varies widely among the districts of the state. Therefore, the use of weighted pupils instead of unweighted pupils in apportioning state school funds substantially improves the equity of a state's school finance plan.

The Adjusted Instruction Unit Technique. This technique is actually a function of the weighted pupil technique. Let us assume that it is desired to express the state guaranteed program in terms of instruction units and that those units include all instruction personnel such as classroom teachers, principals, supervisors, guidance counselors, librarians, etc. Let us also assume that the decision has been made to allot one instruction unit for each 25 pupils in average daily membership in elementary schools for regular elementary pupils (non-high cost pupils). The pupil instruction unit ratios for all types of educational programs can be determined by dividing 25 by the same cost differential weights used to compute weighted pupils. The method of computing adjusted instruction units is set forth in Table 9-2. The number of adjusted instruction units for each program category is shown in column 5 of Table 9-2.

The relationship between weighted pupils and adjusted instruction units can readily be shown by dividing the number of weighted pupils shown in column 4 of Table 9-1 by 25. The quotient is the same number of adjusted instruction units as shown in column 5 of Table 9-2. Therefore, the weighted pupil is exactly 1/25 of the adjusted instruction unit assuming the same weights are used in calculating both units and assuming that an A.D.M. per instruction unit of 25 to 1 is desired for elementary schools. The pupil instruction unit ratio could, of course, be higher or lower and the mathematical relationship between the two units will be determined by the pupil instruction unit ratio selected.

Some states start with higher pupil-teacher ratios and compute adjusted classroom teacher units first and then increase those units by some fraction in order to provide for other in-

TABLE 9-2

SCALE USED FOR COMPUTING ADJUSTED
CLASSROOM UNITS IN THE PROTOTYPE STATE

Programs	Prototype State Target Population (ADM)	Weighting For Cost Differential	Number of Pupils in ADM per Adjusted Instruction Unit[a]	Adjusted Instruction Units[b]
Col. 1	Col. 2	Col. 3	Col. 4	Col. 5
Early Childhood				
3 year olds	30,946	1.40	17.86	1,733
4 year olds	50,813	1.40	17.86	2,845
Kindergarten (5 year olds)	56,231	1.30	19.23	2,924
Sub Total	137,990			
Non-Isolated Basic				
Elementary and Secondary				
Grades 1–6	301,777	1.00	25.00	12,071
Grades 7–9	182,961	1.20	20.83	8,784
Grades 10–12	124,693	1.40	17.86	6,982
Sub Total	609,431			
Isolated Basic				
Elementary and Secondary				
Elementary Size				
150–200	6,332	1.10	22.73	279
100–149	3,155	1.20	20.83	151
less than 100	3,789	1.30	19.23	197
Junior High				
150–200	2,266	1.30	19.23	118
100–149	1,177	1.40	17.86	66
less than 100	1,299	1.50	16.67	78

TABLE 9-2 (Cont.)

Programs	Prototype State Target Population (ADM)	Weighting For Cost Differential	Number of Pupils in ADM per Adjusted Instruction Unit[a]	Adjusted Instruction Units[b]
Col. 1	Col. 2	Col. 3	Col. 4	Col. 5
Senior High				
150–200	849	1.50	16.67	51
100–149	381	1.60	15.62	24
less than 100	126	1.70	14.71	9
Sub Total	19,374			
Special (and/or Exceptional)				
Mentally Handicapped	16,089	1.90	13.16	1,223
Physically Handicapped	2,668	3.25	7.69	347
Emotionally Handicapped	19,696	2.80	8.93	2,206
Special Learning Disorder	5,335	2.40	10.42	512
Speech Handicapped	31,152	1.20	20.83	1,496
Sub Total	74,940			
Compensatory Education				
Basis: Income under $4,000	131,165	2.00	12.50	10,493
Vocational—Technical	46,502	1.80	13.89	3,348
Total All Categories (Preschool—Grade 12)	1,019,402			55,937

[a]Computed by dividing 25 by Column 3.
[b]Computed by dividing Column 2 by Column 4.

structional personnel needed, such as principals, supervisors, guidance counselors, librarians, etc. For example, adjusted classroom teacher units could be computed by starting with 27 pupils in A.D.M. of regular pupils enrolled in elementary schools and weighting for other educational programs as shown in Table 9-2. Then total adjusted instruction units can be computed by multiplying the classroom teacher units by some fraction such as 1/8 and adding the product to adjusted classroom units. Under such a formula adjusted instruction units could be 112.5 percent of adjusted classroom teacher units.

It should not be assumed from the discussion of computation of adjusted instruction units presented in this chapter, that the pupil-teacher ratios presented are the ratios recommended by the National Educational Finance Project. The ratios presented are for the purpose of illustrating the method of calculating weighted pupils and adjusted instruction units. Subsequent research may show that higher or lower pupil teacher ratios are desirable. The pupil-teacher or pupil instruction unit ratio provided for in the state program is one of the major decisions affecting the cost of the educational program made by a legislature in its program for financing the public schools.

Conversion of Weighted Pupils or Adjusted Instruction Units into Costs. Weighted pupils can be converted into costs by multiplying the number of weighted pupils by a uniform allotment per weighted pupil since necessary cost differentials have already been provided for. The cost of the state guaranteed program including all current expenses except the cost of such support services as school transportation, free textbooks and school food service can be computed by multiplying weighted pupils by a uniform amount per weighted pupil. The cost of the guaranteed program can be computed from adjusted instruction units by multiplying the units by a uniform amount also. Let us assume that the legislature has decided to provide $500 per weighted pupil in A.D.M. in order to finance all current expenses other than provisions for school transportation, free textbook and school food service. The cost of the guaranteed program for each district can then be determined by multiplying the weighted pupils for that district by $500. If the cost of the program is computed from adjusted instruction units shown in Table 9-2, the units are multiplied by $12,500. The total cost of the program for each district would be identical regardless of which method is used. Since these methods are equivalent mathematically, the legislature should select the method which it believes will be most acceptable in that state. The weighted pupil technique may be easier to manipulate mathematically but the adjusted instruction unit may be easier for the lay public to understand than the weighted pupil. The weighted pupil is used in this chapter to compare alternative state school finance models although the adjusted instruction unit could have been used just as effectively.

The cost of the state guaranteed program for capital outlay can also be computed fairly equitably in terms of weighted pupils or adjusted classroom units.

Attention is directed to the fact that the use of adjusted instruction units or weighted pupils to adjust for high cost programs in allocating state funds in effect establishes a type of educational program budget because a district cannot obtain adjusted instruction units or weighted pupils for high cost programs unless it actually provides those services. The use of adjusted instruction units or weighted pupils in state apportionment makes it possible for districts that have unusual needs for high cost programs to provide those programs. It also assures the state that target populations who need these programs will have them available. The use of program budgeting in the state plan of apportionment has all the advantages of categorical aids for special educational programs without the disadvantages of the fragmented uncoordinated budgeting resulting from a wide use of categorical grants. The adjusted instruction unit has some advantages over the weighted pupil unit in developing a program budget because the adjusted instruction unit reveals the number of instructional personnel provided for in state finance plans for each educational program area. Since capital outlay needs and other operating costs are closely associated with instruction units, the state legislature is enabled by this method to make a state total estimate of the funds allocated to each educational program area in its finance plan.

Differential Costs of Pupil Transportation. It has long been recognized that the cost per pupil transported varies widely among school districts due largely to variations in the density of transported pupils. States allocating state funds for transportation usually allot more funds per pupil for districts with a low pupil density of transported pupils than to districts with a high

TABLE 9-3

TABLE FOR COMPUTING COST DIFFERENTIALS FOR SCHOOL TRANSPORTATION

Number of Pupils Transported Per Route Mile (One Way)	Allotment Per Pupil Transported Per Year
Below .5	$90.00
.5 – .74	77.00
.75– .99	65.00
1.00–1.24	55.00
1.25–1.49	49.00
1.50–1.74	43.00
1.75–1.99	40.00
2.00–2.24	37.00
2.25–2.99	34.00
3.00–3.49	32.00
3.50–3.99	31.00
4.00 and above	30.00

density. Table 9-3 presents an example of such a scale. It will be noted that the allotment per pupil transported is three times as much in the district with the lowest density of transported pupils as in the districts with highest density. It should not be assumed that this is an ideal scale of cost differentials for pupil transportation. Costs vary from state to state and from year to year. This scale was used for the purpose of illustrating how necessary cost differentials may be computed for transportation and it was used in computing the allotment for transportation in the alternative finance models analyzed in this chapter.

Computing the Cost of Other Programs and Services. As pointed out above, capital outlay costs can be computed fairly equitably in terms of weighted pupils or adjusted classroom units. Alternative plans for financing the capital outlay needs of the public schools are discussed in some detail in Chapter 7 of Volume 3 of the National Educational Finance Project entitled *Planning to Finance Education.*

Costs of the school food service program to include in the state school finance plan should be based on the number of children served, the type of lunch served, the number of needed free and reduced price lunches served and perhaps other factors. Various models for financing the school food service program are discussed in Chapter 8 of Volume 3 of the National Educational Finance Project.

Computations for capital outlay needs and school food service needs are not included in the alternative finance models examined in this chapter, not because these functions are not important but in order to simplify the computations and analyses presented.

Some states provide for school food service, capital outlay, textbooks and certain other items through state categorical grants. This may be desirable for certain budget items but categorical grants should be held to a minimum in order to increase the efficiency of administration. Even if categorical grants are provided, these grants should be included in the same state appropriation package as general aid in order that the legislature may be facilitated in determining relative priorities it assigns to different educational program and service areas provided for in the state's finance plan.

Other Factors that Might be Considered in Determining Necessary Cost Differentials. There are some other factors that might affect unit costs for an equivalent quality of educational services. One of the most commonly mentioned factors is variations in the cost of living among the districts of a state. The National Educational Finance Project did not have the resources to make an in-depth study of necessary variations among the districts of a state in the cost of living for an equivalent standard of living. Usually a board of education spends 75 to 80 percent of its operating budget for salaries and wages. Variation among the districts in rents would affect the living costs of personnel employed by boards of education. Undoubtedly, rents are higher in some urban areas of high density than in some rural areas. However, the cost of obtaining medical services and other amenities of life is higher in remote rural areas than in urban areas because of the extra travel required. Since the National Educational Finance Project did not have data available on which it could make estimates of necessary variations in unit costs of education due to variations in the cost of living, no weighting for this item was provided for in the prototype state.

The quality of teachers provided in a school district or in an individual school within a district undoubtedly affects the quality of education provided more than any other single factor. In order to have substantial equality of educational opportunity the pupils of different districts and different schools within a district should have equal access to the best quality of teachers. Placement bureaus of teacher education institutions find that many of their graduates will not accept positions in remote rural areas with no cultural advantages or in urban ghettos when they have the choice of accepting positions in middle class suburban or urban areas. There is some reason to believe that in order to give the pupils in remote rural areas and in ghetto urban areas equal access to the quality of teachers available in other areas that extra supplements should be made to the salaries of teachers employed in such areas. The National Educational Finance Project did not have the resources to make studies of the cost differentials necessary to accomplish these purposes. Therefore, no weighting for these items was provided for in the prototype state.

It might seem that the National Educational Finance Project is overemphasizing the importance of cost differentials. However, it seems safe to predict that in the future the federal and state governments will inevitably be compelled to provide a much higher percent of school revenues than at the present time if educational needs are to be met. As we move to more central funding of school costs, it is essential that central governments provide for necessary variations among school districts in unit costs or they will disequalize the educational opportunities they are attempting to equalize.

METHODS OF TESTING ALTERNATIVE MODELS

Eighteen alternative models of state school finance programs are analyzed in this chapter. These models encompass all of the major decisions that must be made by a legislature except the adequacy of the program provided. Table 10-4 presents certain information for each of the 32 districts in the prototype state. The districts are listed in order of equalized valuation per weighted pupil in average daily membership. The Table also contains the unweighted and weighted total average daily membership for each district plus the total equalized assessed valuation. This procedure is followed in each of the subsequent tables presented in this chapter. Tables 9-5 to 9-22 present detailed analyses of the application of each model to the districts of the prototype state. Table 9-23 presents a summary of the evaluation of each of the eighteen models by three objective methods. Figures 9-1 to 9-19 present a graphical picture of each model.

Methods of Evaluation of Models

The three objective methods used to evaluate each model are as follows:

1. Average deviation from full equalization.
2. Score on the National Educational Finance Project scale for measuring the extent of financial equalization of the state's finance program.
3. Score on the National Educational Finance Project scale for measuring tax progressivity.

The average deviation from full equalization is computed by assuming that the same total revenue from state and local revenues is available in all eighteen models, but methods of allocation and sources of revenue differ. A computation is made on the basis of weighted pupils and necessary transportation costs showing the total amount of funds each district would have, if each district had the same amount of money available per weighted pupil and its necessary transportation costs. In other words, this computation shows the revenue that each district would have available if complete financial equalization were provided throughout the state. Then, the deviation of each district from complete equalization is computed. This computation shows the financial impact of each model on each district of a state and is reported in Tables 9-5 to 9 -22.

The National Educational Finance Project scale for measuring the extent of financial equalization of educational opportunity has been used in analyzing each model. The score on the NEFP scale is very highly correlated negatively with the measure "average deviation from full equalization." The minimum score on this scale is 1 and the maximum score is 8.4. The advantage of the NEFP scale is that it can be used quickly to evaluate a proposed change in a state's finance model without computing the impact of the change on all districts of a state.

The Tax Progressivity scale has also been applied to the prototype state. The assumption is that the prototype state had a state tax structure equivalent to the progressivity of the tax structure of the

301

average state. Any state could, of course, increase or decrease the progressivity of its state tax structure by increasing or decreasing the proportion of its tax revenue derived from relatively progressive taxes.

Assumption Made for All Models

In order to compare these eighteen models on the same basis it was necessary to make the following assumptions:

1. That the same total revenue was available for all models but the proportion from state and local sources varied.
2. That all districts levied the legal limit of taxes permitted by the state. This might seem unrealistic but it does represent a comparable measure of the local tax revenue potential of each district.

List of Models Tested

Following is a list of the eighteen models tested and a brief description of each:

1. *Flat grant models* with the same total revenue and the same proportion from state and local sources with different methods of apportionment.

MODEL I-A Flat grant of $500 per pupil in A.D.M., unweighted pupils, no aid for transportation, local tax rate 12 mills.

MODEL I-B Same total state funds as Model I-A but state funds are distributed on the basis of weighted pupils, and need for transportation and same local funds as Model I-A.

2. *Equalization models* with the same total state funds and same total local funds as MODEL I-A.

MODEL II-A Strayer-Haig equalization formula, unweighted pupils, transportation allotment, 5 mills required local effort, 7 mills local leeway.

The Strayer Haig equalization formula (or an adaptation of that formula) is the most commonly used model for appor-

302

tioning state school funds. Under this formula the cost of the foundation program which the legislature desires to guarantee for each district is computed and from that cost is deducted the amount of funds which each district can raise locally through a minimum required local tax effort and the difference is allocated to the district from state funds. Although this model seems simple, there are numerous variations in the elements of the model which have a profound impact on the finances of local school districts. The impact of some of these variations is revealed in the tables presented below.

MODEL II-B Same as Model I-A except pupils are weighted.

MODEL II-C Same as Model II-B except required local effort is 10 mills and local leeway 2 mills.

MODEL II-D Complete equalization, same as Model II-A except required local effort is 12 mills and there is no local leeway.

3. *Percentage Equalizing Formula.*

MODEL III The state's share of the cost of the foundation program of a district under this formula is computed by multiplying the cost of the foundation program of any district by 100 percent minus a predetermined percentage figure which, in turn, is multiplied by the quotient of the equalized value of property of the district divided by the state average equalized value of property per weighted pupil. Let A equal the cost of the foundation program; D, the equalized value of property per pupil in the district; S, the state average equalized value of property per pupil; and E, the predetermined constant factor. Then the state aid for district under this formula equals the cost of the foundation program (A) multiplied by $1 - [\frac{D}{S} \times E]$. Despite its seeming complexity, this formula gives exactly the same result as the Strayer-Haig formula when applied to measures of need based on weighted pupils or adjusted instruction units for any given level of foundation program.[2] This is demonstrated in Tables 9-8 and 9-11.

303

4. *Flat Grant* models with the same total revenue as in Model I-A but increasing the proportion of revenues from state sources and decreasing local revenue.

MODEL IV-A Apportionment method the same as Model I-B, but limit local revenue to 7 mills and increase state appropriation the equivalent of 5 mills.

MODEL IV-B Same as IV-A but limit local revenues to 4 mills and increase state appropriation the equivalent of 8 mills.

MODEL IV-C Complete equalization apportionment method same as IV-A except no local millage and state appropriation increased the equivalent of 12 mills.

5. *Equalization models* with the same total revenue as Model I-A but increasing the proportion of revenue from state sources and decreasing local revenue.

MODEL V-A Apportionment according to method of II-B, 7 mill limit on local taxes, 4 mill required effort, 3 mill leeway and state appropriation increased the equivalent of 5 mills.

MODEL V-B Same as V-A except 4 mill limit on local taxes, 2 mill required effort, 2 mill local leeway and increased state funds the equivalent of 8 mills.

MODEL V-C Complete equalization—same as V-A except no local taxes and state appropriation increased the equivalent of 12 mills.

6. *Flat grant* models with the same total revenue as I-A but increasing the proportion of revenue from local sources and decreasing state revenue.

MODEL VI-A Apportionment method the same as I-B, 50% of revenue from state sources and 50% local revenue, local tax rate 16.3 mills.

MODEL VI-B Same as VI-A except state revenue 25%, local revenue 75% and local tax rate 24.452 mills.

7. *Equalization models* with the same total revenue as I-A but increasing the revenue from local sources and decreasing state revenue.

MODEL VII-A 50% of revenue from state sources, 50% from local sources, apportionment according to method II-B, except total local millage of 16.3 mills, 11 mills required effort and local leeway of 5.3 mills.

MODEL VII-B Same as VII-A except state revenue 25%, local revenue 75%, local millage 24.452, required local effort of 10 mills and local leeway of 14.452 miles.

8. *Complete local support model.*

MODEL VIII Same total revenue as Model I-A, all local revenue, local tax rate of 32.6024 mills.

ANALYSIS OF IMPACT OF ALTERNATIVE MODELS TESTED

Some variations among the 32 districts of significance to school financing are presented in Table 9-4. The districts range from 1,811 pupils in average daily membership to 208,014. The range in weighted pupils in average daily membership is from 2,404 to 324,828. The 32 districts in Table 9-4 are listed in order of equalized valuation per weighted pupil from highest to lowest. It will be noted that the district of greatest wealth has approximately six times the equalized valuation per weighted pupil as the district of least wealth.

Variations in the relationship of weighted pupils to pupils in average daily membership are of great significance to school financing. For example, in District 3, a large wealthy, urban district, weighted pupils are 130 percent of pupils in A.D.M. In District 25, a large, urban district of less than average wealth, weighted pupils are 156 percent of pupils in A.D.M. Thus, District 25 not only has a higher percentage of high cost pupils than the state average but it has considerably less wealth per pupil than the state average. All large urban districts do not have the same conditions. Some are much wealthier than others and some have a much higher percent of disadvantaged high cost pupils than other cities similar in size. To ignore these variations in a state school finance plan is to fail to equalize educational opportunity.

The same type of variations exist among small districts. For example, in District 4, a relatively small, wealthy district, weighted pupils are 130 percent of A.D.M. but in District 29, a relatively small district, far below the state average in wealth, weighted pupils are 149 percent of pupils in A.D.M.

The extent to which the alternative finance models tested equalize the financial support of the public schools and provide progressivity in the tax structure for school support is presented in the remainder of this section.

Flat Grant Models with the Same Total Revenue and the Same Proportion from State and Local Sources

Two models are examined under this classification. In Model I-A, the state allotment is computed simply by multiplying $500 times the A.D.M. of each district and each district has the potential of local revenue equal to 12 mills times its equalized valuation. Table 10-5 shows that under this model state funds would total $509,700,000 and local funds $296,874,000 making a total revenue of $806,574,000. All of the alternative models from Model I-A through Model VIII are computed on the basis of approximately $806,574,000 of total revenue available for the support of the public schools but the models vary in the proportions from state and local sources and in methods of apportionment. The $500 per pupil in A.D.M. was arbitrarily selected. It is not suggested that this is the amount of state revenue that a state should provide. The $500 per pupil in A.D.M. was selected purely for purposes of illustration and a basis of comparison.

Model I-A is one of the most primitive methods of apportioning state school funds. It does not recognize variations in local tax paying ability, necessary variations in pupil costs or variations in transportation needs. Table 9-23 shows an average deviation of 15.42 percent from full equalization for Model I-A and a score of 4.3 on the NEFP scale. The average deviation from the full equalization scale is negatively correlated with the score on the NEFP scale. The scores on the NEFP scale range from 1 for no equalization to 8.4 for complete equalization. The scores on the average deviation from full equalization range from 0 for complete equalization to 30.98 for no equalization for the models tested.

The failure of Model I-A to financially equalize educational opportunity is more fully revealed in Table 9-5. This table shows that District 1, the district of greatest wealth per pupil would have revenue equal to 161 percent of the revenue required

306

for complete equalization in the state and that District 31, the district next to the lowest in wealth would have only 70 percent of the revenue required under complete equalization. This is highly significant because under Model I-A the state provides 63 percent of total school revenue but the state appropriation is distributed so crudely in relation to educational need that educational opportunity is far from equalized in the prototype state. Table 9-5 shows that the districts of below average wealth in general do not receive enough state aid under Model I-A to provide educational opportunities comparable to the districts of above average wealth. Despite the inequity of this model, a considerable amount of state school revenue in the nation is still being distributed on some type of a flat per pupil basis in A.D.A., A.D.M. or census basis.

Model I-B is an improvement over Model I-A. Under Model I-B, the same state revenue, $509,700,000 is apportioned to the 32 districts but it is apportioned on a weighted pupil basis after providing for the necessary costs of transportation. The computations for this model are shown in Table 9-6. It is noted that the district of greatest wealth, District 1, will have 154 percent of the revenue available required for complete equalization and District 32, the district of least wealth, 78 percent. Table 9-23 shows an average deviation of 11.40 percent from full equalization and an NEFP score of 5.1. This is some improvement over Model I-A but educational opportunities are still far from equalized under Model I-B.

A profile of the revenue available per weighted pupil from state and local sources under Model I-A is presented for 16 randomly selected districts of the prototype state, ranging from the most wealthy to the least wealthy. Revenue available for transportation was excluded in order to place all districts on a comparable basis. Only 16 districts, the odd numbered districts, are included in the graph in order to simplify the presentation. Comparing Figure 9-1 with Figure 9-2, it is noted that the length of the bars for the 16 districts is more nearly uniform under Model 10-B than Model 10-A. The impact of each finance model on each of the 16 districts is graphically presented for all models examined. The equalization qualities of all models can be compared from these figures because the more nearly uniform the length of the bars for a model, the greater its equalizing qualities.

Equalization Models with the Same Total State Funds and Total Local Funds as Model I-A

Four models are examined under this classification. Under Model II-A, the cost of the foundation program is computed on the basis of A.D.M. (unweighted pupils) and the necessary costs of transportation. Each district is required to contribute the yield of a 5 mill levy on its equalized valuation to the costs of its foundation program and the balance is provided by the state. Each district has 7 mills local leeway. Table 9-23 would indicate that Model II-A would not be any improvement over Model I-B because both models have almost the same average deviation from full equalization scores and NEFP scale scores. However, Table 9-7 shows that Model II-A is a considerable improvement in equalization over Model I-B because the range in percent of complete equalization is much less. Under Model II-A the scores range from 138 percent of full equalization in District 1 to 81 percent in District 31, the district next to the bottom in per pupil wealth. Table 9-6 shows that the range for Model I-B is from 154 percent to 78 percent.

Model II-B is a marked improvement over Model II-A because the pupils are weighted in Model II-B. Other provisions of Model II-B are exactly the same as under Model II-A. Table 9-23 shows that Model II-B has an average deviation from full equalization score of 6.65 and an NEFP score of 6.3. Table 9-8 shows that the district of greatest wealth has 131 percent of the revenue required for complete equalization and the district of least wealth 87 percent.

Model II-C is exactly the same as Model II-B except that the required local effort in support of the foundation program is 10 mills and the local leeway is two mills. Table 9-23 and Figures 9-4 and 9-5 show that Model II-C much more nearly equalizes educational opportunity than Model II-B. The average percent deviation from full equalization is only 1.90 and the score on the NEFP scale is 7.6. Table 9-9 shows that under Model II-C, that the district of greatest wealth has only 109 percent of the revenue required for full equalization and the district of least wealth, 96 percent. A comparison of Models II-B and II-C shows that the greater the *local tax leeway*, the greater the financial *disequalization* from a given amount of state and local revenue. The local tax leeway under Model II-B is 7 mills and under Model

II-C, 2 mills. Furthermore, a comparison of these two models also shows that the *greater the proportion* of the legal limit of local taxes that districts are required to contribute to the cost of the foundation program, the *greater the financial equalization of educational opportunity.*

Model II-D shows what would happen if all districts were required to contribute the full amount of the yield of the legal local tax limit (in this case 12 mills) to the cost of the foundation program. This would provide for complete equalization because its effect would be to convert the local tax levy of 12 mills to a state levy of a like amount for schools. Table 9-23 shows that the average deviation from complete equalization would be 0 under Model II-D and the NEFP score would be 8.4. Table 10-10 shows the amount of revenue each district would have available under full financial equalization assuming total revenue of approximately $806,574,000 from state and local sources is available.

The Percentage Equalizing Formula

Model III is the percentage equalizing formula (sometimes called the state aid ratio formula) described earlier in this chapter. The computations for this formula are shown in Table 10-11. It is noted, that except for deviations due to rounding of totals, the computations for Model III are the same as for Model II-B because they are based on the same unit costs and the same percent of state funds contributed to the cost of the foundation program and a required minimum level foundation program. The percentage equalizing formula is only a mathematical manipulation of the Strayer-Haig formula. Table 9-11 shows that excluding transportation, the state contributes 51.193 percent of the cost of the foundation program to District 1. This same percentage can be computed from Table 9-8 for Model II-B as follows: Deduct $28,140, the amount allocated for transportation from $4,073,537, the total state funds allocated to District 1 and divide the remainder by $7,902,210, the total cost of its foundation program, excluding transportation and the quotient is 51.193 percent.

A state may wish to establish a variable level foundation program for its districts depending upon the local tax effort the district makes. The percentage equalizing formula can be con-

309

verted into a state aid ratio formula as follows: Divide the state percentage for a district by its local percentage and the quotient is the ratio of state aid dollars to local dollars. Using District 1 as an example: 51.193 the state percentage divided by 48.807, the local percentage equals 1.0488. This quotient multiplied by $3,857,000, the yield of a 5 mill levy in District 1, equals $4,045,-000, which is equivalent to the state contribution for the W.A.D.M. allotment computed by the percentage equalizing formula shown in Table 9-11.

The original Strayer-Haig formula has the advantage over the percentage equalizing formula in that under the Strayer-Haig formula, the allowable costs of transportation can be included as a part of the foundation program but under the percentage equalizing formula, the costs of transportation must be provided for under a special categorical appropriation if the penalization of districts with a heavy burden of transportation is avoided. For example, if each district had to provide the same percent of the cost of transportation as the percent required for the remainder of its foundation program, District 2, under the percentage equalizing formula, would be required to use no local funds for this purpose because it has no transportation needs. District 10 has allowable transportation costs totalling $2,275,-000. Under the percentage equalizing formula, it would have to provide 23 percent of this cost from local funds. This would amount to $523,000 or 12 percent of its local revenue whereas District 2 would not have to use any of its local revenue for this purpose.

There is another important difference between the percentage equalizing adaptation of the Strayer-Haig formula and the original Strayer-Haig formula. The percentage equalizing formula can be used to allocate state funds for any level of state support ranging from 0 to no limit. Under the percentage equalizing formula, a district would receive no state funds if it levied no local taxes because under this formula, state funds equal the state aid ratio for that district multiplied by the yield of its local levy. Under the original Strayer-Haig formula, state aid equals the difference between the cost of a district's foundation program and the yield of a required minimum local tax effort. Under the Strayer-Haig formula, the district that levied 0 local taxes would still receive the state's portion of its foundation program. Therefore, the penalty for lack of local tax effort is greater under the percentage equalizing formula. Actually, no state using the percentage equalizing formula could permit a local district to levy 0 taxes because if it did, the public school system would be abolished in a district levying 0 taxes. Therefore, any state using the equalization model, regardless of the formula must set some type of minimum required effort. It would seem better policy for a state to mandate the minimum required minimum local effort regardless of whether the percentage equalizing formula or the Strayer-Haig formula is used. To leave the required minimum effort optional under either formula prevents the state from assuring any foundation program of education for all children in a state.

The percentage equalizing formula has been used as an incentive to increase local tax effort by matching local funds raised by the local school district in addition to the required minimum effort on the same percentage basis as is used in allocating funds for the required minimum foundation programs. This in effect establishes a _variable level_ foundation program varying for each district in proportion to the local effort it is willing to make, but all districts, regardless of variations in per pupil wealth could have the same level of foundation program, if they made the same effort. Exactly the same incentive could be provided under the Strayer-Haig formula if the state would establish a variable level foundation program depending upon variations in local effort instead of setting a uniform fixed level for the foundation program. A financial incentive for increased local tax effort to support schools has some advantages but it also has some disadvantages as is pointed out later in this chapter.

Flat Grant Models with the Same Total Revenue as Model I-A But Increasing the Proportion from State Sources and Decreasing Local Sources

Under Model IV-A, state funds are apportioned under the same method as I-B but total state revenue is increased the equivalent of the yield of a 5 mill levy on the equalized valuation and local taxes are reduced from 12 mills to 7 mills. Table 9-23 shows the flat grant Model IV-A is a considerable improvement over flat grant Model I-B because average deviation from full equalization is reduced from 11.40 to 6.65 and the NEFP score

311

is increased from 5.1 to 6.4. When Table 9-6 is compared with Table 9-12, it is observed that the range in deviation is 154 percent to 78 percent for Model I-B and 131 percent to 87 percent for Model IV-A.

Flat grant Model IV-B greatly advances financial equalization because under this model, the state appropriation is increased the equivalent of 8 mills and local property taxes are reduced from 12 mills to 4 mills. Table 9-23 shows that Model IV-B has an average deviation of only 3.8 percent from full equalization and an NEFP score of 7.2. Table 9-13 shows that the deviations from full equalization of the districts of greatest wealth from full equalization as compared with the districts of least wealth are also greatly reduced. It is noted when comparing Models I-B, IV-A and IV-B, that the higher the percent of total revenue provided from state sources, that the greater the possibility of financial equalization by a flat grant model.

Under Model IV-C, state funds are increased the equivalent of 12 mills and local taxes for schools abolished. This, of course, provides for complete equalization. It is equivalent to the Hawaii plan for school financing.

Equalization Models with the Same Total Revenue as Model I-A But Increasing the Proportion of Revenue from State Sources and Decreasing Local Revenue

Under Model V-A, apportionment is made according to the Model II-B except that state revenue is increased the equivalent of 5 mills, local revenue is reduced to 7 mills, 4 mills of which is used for required local effort to support the foundation programs, leaving a local leeway of 3 mills. Table 9-23 shows that Model V-A provides considerably more financial equalization than Model II-B. Average deviation from full equalization is reduced from 6.65 percent to 2.85 percent and the NEFP score is increased from 6.3 to 7.2.

Model V-B further advances financial equalization. Under this model, the state appropriation is increased the equivalent of 8 mills, local taxes are reduced from 12 mills to 4 mills, 2 mills of which is required for the support of the foundation program and 2 mills is left for local leeway. The average deviation from full equalization of Model V-B is only 1.90 percent and the NEFP score is 7.5. Table 9-16 shows that under Model V-B, the dis-

312

trict of greatest wealth has total revenue available equal to 109 percent of full equalization and the revenue available to the district of least wealth equals 96 percent of full equalization.

A comparison of Models II-B, V-A and V-B also shows that the greater the percent of school funds provided from state sources, the greater the possibility of equalizing financial resources under equalization formulas.

A comparison of all flat grant models with all equalization models reveals that with a given amount of state money, it is possible to more nearly financially equalize financial resources with an equalization model than with a flat grant model.

A comparison of Model IV-B with Model V-B shows that as we approach full state funding, differences between flat grant models and equalizing models begin to disappear provided that necessary variations in unit costs are incorporated in both types of models. Approximately 88 percent of total revenue is provided by the state in Models IV-B and V-B.

Model V-C is identical with Model IV-C showing that the terminal point of both flat grant and equalization models is complete equalization as we approach full state funding.

Flat Grant Models with the Same Total Revenue as Model I-A but Increasing the Proportion of Revenue from Local Sources and Decreasing State Revenue

Under Model VI-A, state funds are apportioned according to the method of I-B but 50% of total revenue is provided from state sources and 50% from local sources. This requires an increase of the local levy from 12 mills to 16.3 mills. Table VI-A shows that this policy decreases equalization. Comparing Model VI-A with I-B, the average deviation from full equalization is increased from 11.40 percent to 15.48 percent and the NEFP score is reduced from 5.1 to 4.1. Comparing Table 9-5 with 9-18, the range in percent of full equalization is increased from 78 to 154 for Model I-B to 70 to 173 for Model VI-A.

Model VI-B is the same as Model VI-A except that local taxes provide 75 percent of total revenue, state sources 25 percent and it is necessary to increase the local tax levy to 24.452 mills. This model further disequalizes financial equalization. As compared with Model VI-A, the average deviation from full equalization is increased from 15.48 percent to 23.23 percent and the NEFP

313

score is reduced from 4.1 to 2.4. Furthermore, Table 9-19 shows that the district of greatest wealth would have revenue available equal to 209 percent of full equalization whereas the district of least wealth would have only 56 percent of the revenue required for full equalization.

Equalization Models with the Same Total Revenue as I-A but Increasing the Revenue from Local Sources and Decreasing State Revenue

Under Model VII-A, 50 percent of the revenue is provided from state sources, 50 percent from local sources, the local levy is 16.3 mills, 11 of which is required in support of the foundation program leaving a local leeway of 5.3 mills. The requirement of 11 mills of local effort was selected so that the district of greatest wealth would receive no state funds. Under this model, average deviation from full equalization is increased from 1.90 percent in Model V-B to 5.03 percent and the NEFP score is reduced from 7.5 to 7.2. Although all of the state's revenue is used for equalization purposes under Model VII-A, it is noted that the possibility of financial equalization under an equalization model is not as great when the state provides 50 percent of state revenue as when it provides a higher percent of school revenue.

Model VII-B shows more clearly the effect on financial equalization of educational opportunity when the percent of local revenue is increased and state revenue decreased. Under this model, 75 percent of revenue is obtained from local sources, 25 percent from state sources, the local tax rate increased to 24.452 mills, 10 mills of which is required in support of the foundation program leaving a local leeway of 14.452 mills. The required local effort of 10 mills was selected because the districts of greatest wealth would receive no state revenue under this requirement. Despite the fact that all of the state revenue is used for equalization, when the state provides only 25 percent of total revenue, the average deviation from full equalization is increased from 5.03 in Model VII-A to 14.25 in Model VII-B and the NEFP score is decreased from 7.2 to 5.1. A comparison of Table 9-6 with Table 9-21 and data presented in Table 9-23 for Models 1-B and VII-B will show that a flat grant model when the state provides 63 percent of the revenue will equalize educational opportunity better than an equalization model when the state provides

314

only 25 percent of the revenue. However, a comparison of Model VI-B with Model VII-B shows that if a state provides only 25 percent of school revenue from state sources, an equalization model will provide much more financial equalization than a flat grant model.

Complete Local Support Model

Under this model, the same total revenue is provided as under Model I-A but all of it is provided from a local levy in each district of 32.6024. This model provides for no financial equalization whatsoever. The average deviation from full equalization is 30.98 percent and the NEFP score is 1, the lowest possible score on that scale. Table 9-22 shows that the wealthiest district would have 248 percent of the revenue required for full equalization and the district of least wealth only 39 percent. It can be computed from data in Tables 9-4 and 9-10 that if there were no limits on the mills of local taxes District 1 could obtain the equalized foundation program shown in Table 9-10 with a levy of only 13 mills whereas it would require a levy of 83 mills in District 32, the district of least wealth. This condition shown in the prototype state is typical of the conditions found in most states.

Comparison of Progressivity of Tax Structure Under Alternative Models

Table 9-23 shows the tax progressivity score for each model. The data indicate that the tax progressivity score is 18.10 for all models from Model I-A through Model III. This is due to the fact that the proportion from state and local sources is the same for each of these models. In making the computations of the progressivity scores for the prototype state the assumption was made that the state's tax progressivity score was the same as for the average state, and the local score was the same as the local score of the average state. NEFP research has found that the state tax progressivity score for the average state in 1969 was 20.49 and the local tax score was 14.00. However, if the assumption had been made that the state tax progressivity score of the prototype state had been as high as Oregon, 26.7%, the progressivity score for all of these models would have been higher. NEFP research on tax progressivity indicate the following:

1. The higher the percent of state revenue derived from relatively progressive taxes, the higher the progressivity score of a state's tax structure.
2. The higher the percent of state revenue in relation to local tax revenue, the higher the progressivity score of the state's school finance plan.
3. The higher the percent of school revenue provided from federal sources in relation to state and local sources, the higher the progressivity score of a state's school finance plan. The progressivity score for federal revenue for 1969 was 39.90 (see Table 9-4).

   For example, the tax progressivity score would be 25.65 under a revenue model with 30 percent of the school revenue provided by the federal government, 60 percent by the state and 10 percent by local school districts.

Table 9-23 shows that the progressivity scores for flat grant Models IV-A through IV-C increase as the percent of state revenue increases. The same trend is observed in equalization Models V-A through V-C. However, when the percent of state funds is reduced, the tax progressivity score decreases as shown in flat grant Models V-A and VI-B and equalization Models VII-A and VII-B. Model VIII, the complete local support model, has a tax progressivity score of 14.00, the lowest possible score.

SOME OTHER ALTERNATIVES

There are numerous other possible variations in school finance models. Some of those possible variations are discussed below.

Other Variations in Models Examined

Following is a list of some of the possible variations:

1. Various program elements, such as pre-school programs and special programs might be added or subtracted.
2. Cost differentials could be varied.
3. Special supporting services and facilities such as school food service, transportation, summer programs and capital outlay could be added or subtracted.

TABLE 9-4

AVERAGE DAILY MEMBERSHIP, WEIGHTED AVERAGE DAILY MEMBERSHIP AND
EQUALIZED VALUATION OF THE PROTOTYPE STATE

District	Average Daily Membership	Weighted Average Daily Membership	Equalized Assessed Valuation (in thousands)	EAV Per Pupil in WADM (in Dollars)
1	14,230	17,934	771,363	43,011
2	10,481	13,644	560,413	41,074
3	32,532	42,274	1,286,623	30,435
4	123,318	160,101	4,624,308	28,884
5	5,197	7,682	181,070	23,571
6	10,179	13,223	293,313	22,182
7	15,220	19,712	429,791	21,804
8	1,811	2,404	51,978	21,621
9	7,058	10,792	226,790	21,015
10	137,329	177,038	3,586,843	20,260
11	3,231	4,070	78,197	19,213
12	4,730	6,164	118,360	19,202
13	4,065	6,014	107,516	17,878
14	165,324	209,378	3,715,068	17,743
15	4,761	7,238	122,025	16,859
16	16,649	22,202	348,643	15,703
17	73,945	97,005	1,512,960	15,597
18	21,240	30,139	458,200	15,203
19	30,017	39,044	555,443	14,226
20	14,861	20,902	292,053	13,972
21	25,011	35,508	495,610	13,958
22	18,968	27,516	341,873	12,425
23	6,124	9,173	110,308	12,025
24	7,245	11,612	129,830	11,181
25	208,014	324,828	3,580,364	11,022
26	13,918	19,042	209,837	11,020
27	13,577	19,353	200,515	10,361
28	2,503	3,131	32,243	10,298
29	11,284	16,838	141,236	8,388
30	5,531	8,139	60,105	7,385
31	6,064	9,116	66,219	7,264
32	4,985	7,171	50,616	7,058
Totals	1,019,401	1,398,386	24,739,630	———

4. Other modifying factors such as training and experience of teachers could be included or excluded.
5. Sources of state revenue could be varied.
6. Sources of local revenue could be varied.
7. Measures of local ability in equalization models could include factors other than equalized valuation.

The National Educational Finance Project has developed a computerized model which can incorporate all of these variations. The details of this model are too extensive to be included in this volume but are available in a technical monograph published by the Project.

TABLE 9-5 — MODEL I-A

FLAT GRANT OF $500 PER PUPIL IN ADM NO ALLOCATION FOR TRANSPORTATION LOCAL TAX RATE OF 12 MILLS

District	State Approp of $500 Per Pupil *ADM In Thousands of Dollars	Local Rev Yield of 12 Mill Levy on EAV In Thousands of Dollars	Total Revenue In Thousands of Dollars	Total Rev Per Pupil In ADM In Dollars	Ratio of Dist Revenue to Complete Equal Revenue in %	Deviation From 100% Equalized
1	7,115	9,256	16,371	1,150	161.27	61.27
2	5,241	6,725	11,965	1,142	155.36	55.36
3	16,266	15,439	31,705	975	132.15	32.15
4	61,659	55,492	117,151	950	126.79	26.79
5	2,599	2,173	4,771	918	106.20	6.20
6	5,090	3,520	8,609	846	112.07	12.07
7	7,610	5,157	12,767	839	108.58	8.58
8	906	624	1,529	844	107.52	7.52
9	3,529	2,721	6,250	886	97.11	-2.89
10	68,664	43,042	111,707	813	109.29	9.29
11	1,616	938	2,554	790	107.00	7.00
12	2,365	1,420	3,785	800	105.61	5.61
13	2,033	1,290	3,323	817	93.98	-6.02
14	82,662	44,581	127,243	770	105.67	5.67
15	2,381	1,464	3,845	808	88.00	-12.00
16	8,325	4,184	12,508	751	95.01	-4.99
17	36,972	18,156	55,128	746	97.74	-2.26
18	10,620	5,498	16,118	759	92.47	-7.53
19	15,009	6,665	21,674	722	94.57	-5.43
20	7,431	3,505	10,935	736	88.75	-11.25
21	12,506	5,947	18,453	738	89.15	-10.85
22	9,484	4,102	13,586	716	85.31	-14.69
23	3,062	1,324	4,386	716	79.45	-20.55
24	3,623	1,558	5,180	715	75.71	-24.29
25	104,007	42,964	146,971	707	80.06	-19.94
26	6,959	2,518	9,477	681	84.58	-15.42
27	6,789	2,406	9,195	677	79.21	-20.79
28	1,252	387	1,638	655	85.81	-14.19
29	5,642	1,695	7,337	650	73.43	-26.58
30	2,766	721	3,487	630	72.07	-27.93
31	3,032	795	3,827	631	70.00	-30.00
32	2,493	607	3,100	622	73.63	-26.37
Totals	509,701	296,876	806,573	—	—	—
Average Weighted Deviation —						15.42

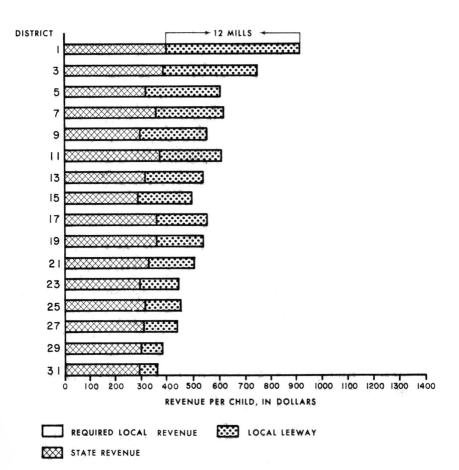

FIGURE 9-1. MODEL I-A REVENUE PER WEIGHTED
PUPIL (EXCLUDING TRANSPORTATION)

DISTRICT

12 MILLS

REVENUE PER CHILD, IN DOLLARS

☐ REQUIRED LOCAL REVENUE   ▨ LOCAL LEEWAY

▧ STATE REVENUE

319

TABLE 9-6 — MODEL I-B

FLAT GRANT OF $352.1696 PER PUPIL IN WADM ALLOCATION FOR TRANSPORTATION LOCAL TAX RATE OF 12 MILLS

District	Amount Alloc for trans in Dollars	State Appropriation $352.1696 Amt Allocated Per WADM In Thousands of Dollars	Total State Alloc In Thousands of Dollars	Local Revenue Yield of 12 Mill Levy In Thousands of Dollars	Total Revenue In Thousands of Dollars	Total Revenue Per WADM In Dollars	Ratio of Dist Revenue to Complete Equal Revenue in %	Deviation from 100% Equalized
1	28,140	6,316	6,344	9,256	15,600	870	153.68	53.68
2	0	4,805	4,805	6,725	11,530	845	149.71	49.71
3	129,600	14,888	15,017	15,439	30,457	720	126.95	26.95
4	2,025,199	56,383	58,408	55,492	113,900	711	123.27	23.27
5	156,585	2,705	2,862	2,173	5,035	655	112.06	12.06
6	217,838	4,657	4,876	3,520	8,394	635	109.28	9.28
7	631,659	6,942	7,574	5,157	12,731	646	108.27	8.27
8	65,285	847	912	624	1,536	639	107.97	7.97
9	344,760	3,801	4,145	2,721	6,867	636	106.69	6.69
10	2,275,609	62,347	64,623	43,042	107,665	608	105.34	5.34
11	89,440	1,433	1,523	938	2,461	605	103.11	3.11
12	104,762	2,171	2,276	1,420	3,696	600	103.12	3.12
13	140,800	2,118	2,259	1,290	3,549	590	100.38	.38
14	2,227,033	73,737	75,964	44,581	120,544	576	100.11	.11
15	283,465	2,550	2,832	1,464	4,297	594	98.35	− 1.66
16	632,443	7,819	8,451	4,184	12,635	569	95.98	− 4.02
17	1,649,358	34,162	35,812	18,156	53,967	556	95.68	− 4.32
18	418,744	10,614	11,033	5,498	16,531	548	94.84	− 5.16
19	879,995	13,750	14,630	6,665	21,295	545	92.92	− 7.08
20	522,555	7,361	7,884	3,505	11,388	545	92.43	− 7.57
21	654,440	12,505	13,159	5,947	19,107	538	92.31	− 7.69
22	394,525	9,690	10,085	4,102	14,187	516	89.08	−10.92
23	342,355	3,230	3,573	1,324	4,897	534	88.70	−11.30
24	287,980	4,089	4,377	1,558	5,935	511	86.74	−13.26
25	230,496	114,395	114,625	42,964	157,589	485	85.84	−14.16
26	456,729	6,706	7,163	2,518	9,681	508	86.39	−13.61
27	683,995	6,816	7,500	2,406	9,906	512	85.33	−14.67
28	141,904	1,103	1,245	387	1,631	521	85.45	−14.55
29	488,345	5,930	6,418	1,695	8,113	482	81.19	−18.81
30	243,705	2,866	3,110	721	3,831	471	79.19	−20.81
31	321,100	3,210	3,531	795	4,326	475	79.13	−20.87
32	162,030	2,525	2,687	607	3,295	459	78.27	−21.73
Totals	17,230,840	492,468	509,698	296,875	806,573	—	—	11.40

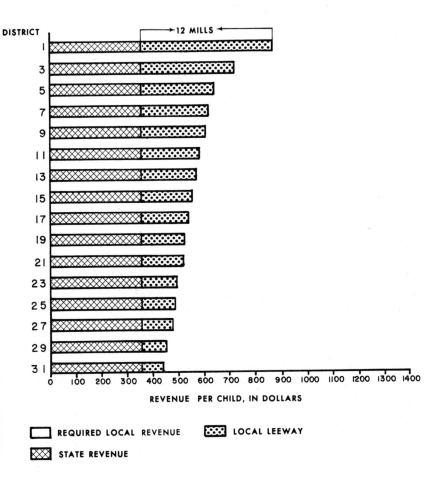

FIGURE 9-2. MODEL I-B REVENUE PER WEIGHTED
PUPIL (EXCLUDING TRANSPORTATION)

REVENUE PER CHILD, IN DOLLARS

☐ REQUIRED LOCAL REVENUE   ▨ LOCAL LEEWAY
▨ STATE REVENUE

TABLE 9-7 — MODEL II-A

MINIMUM FOUNDATION PROGRAM ALLOCATION FOR TRANSPORTATION
ALLOCATION OF $604.4404 PER ADM 5 MILL LEVY CHARGEBACK
7 MILL LEVY LOCAL TAX LEEWAY

District	Amt Alloc For Trans in Dollars	$604.4404 Amt Alloc Per ADM in Thousands of Dollars	State Appropriations Total Found Program in Thousands of Dollars	5 Mills Equal Val in Thousands of Dollars	Total State Appropriation in Thousands of Dollars	Additional Local Rev 7 Mills Equal Val in Thousands of Dollars	Total Revenue in Thousands of Dollars	Total Revenue Per Pupil in ADM in Dollars	Ratio of Dist Revenue to Complete Equal Revenue in %	Deviation from 100% Equalized
1	28,140	8,601	8,629	3,857	4,773	5,400	14,029	986	138.20	38.20
2	0	6,335	6,335	2,802	3,533	3,923	10,259	979	133.19	33.19
3	129,600	19,664	19,793	6,433	13,360	9,006	28,800	885	120.04	20.04
4	2,025,199	74,538	76,564	23,122	53,442	32,370	108,934	883	117.90	17.90
5	156,585	3,141	3,298	905	2,393	1,267	4,565	878	101.61	1.61
6	217,838	6,153	6,370	1,467	4,904	2,053	8,424	828	109.66	9.66
7	631,659	9,200	9,831	2,149	7,682	3,009	12,840	844	109.20	9.20
8	65,285	1,095	1,160	260	900	364	1,524	841	107.14	7.14
9	344,760	4,266	4,611	1,134	3,477	1,588	6,198	878	96.30	−3.70
10	2,275,609	83,007	85,283	17,934	67,349	25,108	110,391	804	108.01	8.01
11	89,440	1,953	2,042	391	1,651	547	2,590	802	108.50	8.50
12	104,762	2,859	2,964	592	2,371	829	3,792	802	105.81	5.81
13	140,800	2,457	2,598	538	2,060	753	3,350	824	94.77	−5.23
14	2,227,033	99,928	102,156	18,575	83,580	26,006	128,161	775	106.43	6.43
15	283,465	2,878	3,161	610	2,551	854	4,015	843	91.90	−8.10
16	632,443	10,063	10,698	1,743	8,953	2,441	13,136	789	99.78	−.22
17	1,649,358	44,695	46,345	7,565	38,780	10,591	56,935	770	100.94	.94
18	418,744	12,838	13,257	2,291	10,966	3,207	16,464	775	94.45	−5.55
19	879,995	18,143	19,023	2,777	16,246	3,888	22,912	763	99.97	−.03
20	522,555	8,983	9,505	1,460	8,045	2,044	11,550	777	93.74	−6.26
21	654,440	15,118	15,772	2,478	13,294	3,469	19,241	769	92.96	−7.04
22	394,525	11,465	11,860	1,709	10,150	2,393	14,253	751	89.49	−10.51
23	342,355	3,702	4,044	552	3,492	772	4,816	786	87.24	−12.76
24	287,980	4,379	4,667	649	4,018	909	5,576	770	81.49	−18.51
25	230,496	125,732	125,963	17,902	108,061	25,063	151,025	726	82.26	−17.74
26	456,729	8,413	8,869	1,049	7,820	1,469	10,338	743	92.26	−7.74
27	683,995	8,206	8,890	1,003	7,888	1,404	10,294	758	88.68	−11.32
28	141,904	1,513	1,655	161	1,494	226	1,881	751	98.49	−1.51
29	488,345	6,821	7,309	706	6,603	989	8,298	735	83.03	−16.97
30	243,705	3,343	3,589	301	3,286	421	4,008	725	82.84	−17.16
31	321,100	3,665	3,986	331	3,655	464	4,450	734	81.40	−18.60
32	162,030	3,013	3,175	253	2,922	354	3,529	708	83.84	−16.16
Totals	17,230,840	616,166	633,396	123,698	509,698	173,178	806,573	—	—	—
Average Weighted Deviation	—	—	—	—	—	—	—	—	—	11.63

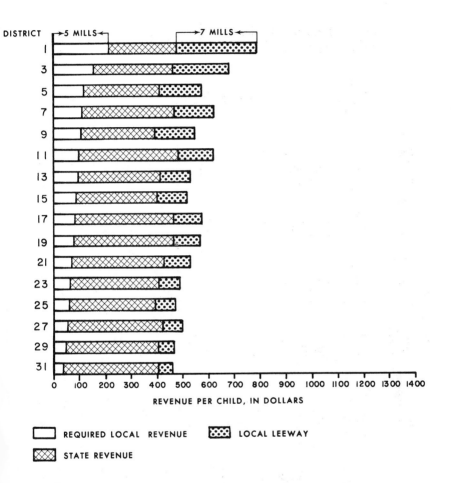

FIGURE 9-3. MODEL II-A REVENUE PER WEIGHTED PUPIL (EXCLUDING TRANSPORTATION)

REQUIRED LOCAL REVENUE   LOCAL LEEWAY
STATE REVENUE

TABLE 9-8 — MODEL II-B

MINIMUM FOUNDATION PROGRAM ALLOCATION FOR TRANSPORTATION
ALLOCATION OF $440.6274 PER WADM 5 MILL LEVY CHARGEBACK
7 MILL LEVY LOCAL TAX LEEWAY

District	Amt. Alloc for Trans in Dollars	$440.6274 Amt Alloc Per WADM in Thousands of Dollars	State Appropriations Total Found Program in Thousands of Dollars	5 Mills X Equal Val in Thousands of Dollars	Total State Appropriation in Thousands of Dollars	Local Rev Revenue 7 Mills X Equal Val in Thousands of Dollars	Total Revenue in Thousands of Dollars	Total Revenue Per Pupil in WADM in Dollars	Ratio of Dist Revenue to Complete Equal Revenue in %	Deviation from 100% Equalization
1	28,140	7,902	7,930	3,857	4,074	5,400	13,330	743	131.31	31.31
2	0	6,012	6,012	2,802	3,210	3,923	9,935	728	129.00	29.99
3	129,600	18,627	18,757	6,433	12,324	9,006	27,763	657	115.72	15.72
4	2,025,199	70,545	72,570	23,122	49,449	32,370	104,940	655	113.58	13.58
5	156,585	3,385	3,541	905	2,636	1,267	4,809	626	107.04	7.04
6	217,838	5,826	6,044	1,467	4,578	2,053	8,097	612	105.41	5.41
7	631,659	8,686	9,317	2,149	7,168	3,009	12,326	625	104.83	4.83
8	65,285	1,059	1,125	260	865	364	1,488	619	104.65	4.65
9	344,760	4,755	5,100	1,134	3,966	1,588	6,688	620	103.90	3.90
10	2,275,609	78,008	80,283	17,934	62,349	25,108	105,391	595	103.11	3.11
11	89,440	1,793	1,883	391	1,492	547	2,430	597	101.82	1.82
12	104,762	2,716	2,821	592	2,229	829	3,649	592	101.82	1.82
13	140,800	2,650	2,791	538	2,253	753	3,543	589	100.22	.22
14	2,227,033	92,258	94,485	18,575	75,909	26,006	120,490	575	100.06	.06
15	283,465	3,189	3,473	610	2,863	854	4,327	598	99.03	− .97
16	632,443	9,783	10,415	1,743	8,672	2,441	12,856	579	97.65	− 2.35
17	1,649,358	42,743	44,392	7,565	36,828	10,591	54,983	567	97.48	− 2.52
18	418,744	13,280	13,699	2,291	11,408	3,207	16,906	561	96.99	− 3.01
19	879,995	17,204	18,084	2,777	15,307	3,888	21,972	563	95.87	− 4.13
20	522,555	9,210	9,733	1,460	8,272	2,044	11,777	563	95.58	− 4.42
21	654,440	15,646	16,300	2,478	13,822	3,469	19,770	557	95.52	− 4.48
22	394,525	12,124	12,519	1,709	10,810	2,393	14,912	542	93.63	− 6.37
23	342,355	4,042	4,384	552	3,833	772	5,156	562	93.41	− 6.59
24	287,980	5,117	5,405	649	4,755	909	6,313	544	92.27	− 7.73
25	230,496	143,128	143,359	17,902	125,457	25,063	168,421	518	91.74	− 8.26
26	456,729	8,390	8,847	1,049	7,798	1,469	10,316	542	92.06	− 7.94
27	683,995	8,527	9,211	1,003	8,209	1,404	10,615	548	91.44	− 8.56
28	141,904	1,380	1,521	161	1,360	226	1,747	558	91.51	− 8.49
29	488,345	7,419	7,908	706	7,201	989	8,896	528	89.03	− 10.97
30	243,705	3,586	3,830	301	3,529	421	4,251	522	87.86	− 12.14
31	321,100	4,017	4,338	331	4,007	464	4,801	527	87.83	− 12.17
32	162,030	3,160	3,322	253	3,069	354	3,676	513	87.32	− 12.68
Totals	17,230,840	616,166	633,396	123,698	509,697	173,178	806,573	—	—	—
Average Weighted Deviation										6.65

324

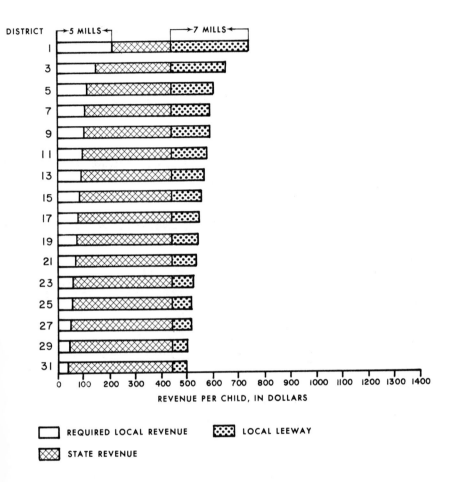

FIGURE 9-4. MODEL II-B REVENUE PER WEIGHTED
PUPIL (EXCLUDING TRANSPORTATION)

TABLE 9-9 — MODEL II-C

MINIMUM FOUNDATION PROGRAM ALLOCATION FOR TRANSPORTATION
ALLOCATION OF $529.0856 PER WADM 10 MILL LEVY CHARGEBACK
2 MILL LEVY LOCAL TAX LEEWAY

District	Amt Alloc for Trans in Dollars	State Appropriations $529.0856 Amt Alloc Per WADM in Thousands of Dollars	Total Found Program in Thousands of Dollars	10 Mills X Equal Val in Thousands of Dollars	Total State Appropriation in Thousands of Dollars	Local Rev Revenue 2 Mills Equal Val in Thousands of Dollars	Total Revenue in Thousands of Dollars	Total Revenue Per Pupil in WADM in Dollars	Ratio of Dist Revenue to Complete Equal Revenue in %	Deviation from 100% Equalization
1	28,140	9,489	9,517	7,714	1,803	1,543	11,059	617	108.95	8.95
2	0	7,219	7,219	5,604	1,615	1,121	8,340	611	108.28	8.28
3	129,600	22,367	22,496	12,866	9,630	2,573	25,069	593	104.49	4.49
4	2,025,199	84,707	86,732	46,243	40,489	9,249	95,981	600	103.88	3.88
5	156,585	4,064	4,221	1,811	2,410	362	4,583	597	102.01	2.01
6	217,838	6,996	7,214	2,933	4,281	587	7,801	590	101.55	1.55
7	631,659	10,429	11,061	4,298	6,763	860	11,921	605	101.38	1.38
8	65,285	1,272	1,337	520	817	104	1,441	599	101.33	1.33
9	344,760	5,710	6,055	2,268	3,787	454	6,508	603	101.11	1.11
10	2,275,609	93,668	95,944	35,868	60,075	7,174	103,118	582	100.89	.89
11	89,440	2,153	2,243	782	1,461	156	2,399	589	100.52	.52
12	104,762	3,261	3,366	1,184	2,182	237	3,603	584	100.52	.52
13	140,800	3,182	3,323	1,075	2,248	215	3,538	588	100.06	.06
14	2,227,033	110,779	113,006	37,151	75,855	7,430	120,436	575	100.02	.02
15	283,465	3,830	4,113	1,220	2,893	244	4,357	602	99.72	−.28
16	632,443	11,747	12,379	3,486	8,893	697	13,076	589	99.33	−.67
17	1,649,358	51,324	52,973	15,130	37,844	3,026	55,999	577	99.28	−.72
18	418,744	15,946	16,365	4,582	11,783	916	17,281	573	99.14	−.86
19	879,995	20,658	21,538	5,554	15,983	1,111	22,648	580	98.82	−1.18
20	522,555	11,059	11,582	2,921	8,661	584	12,166	582	98.74	−1.26
21	654,440	18,787	19,441	4,956	14,485	991	20,432	575	98.72	−1.28
22	394,525	14,558	14,953	3,419	11,534	684	15,637	568	98.18	−1.82
23	342,355	4,853	5,196	1,103	4,093	221	5,416	590	98.12	−1.88
24	287,980	6,144	6,432	1,298	5,133	260	6,691	576	97.79	−2.21
25	230,496	171,862	172,092	35,804	136,289	7,161	179,253	552	97.64	−2.36
26	456,729	10,075	10,532	2,098	8,433	420	10,951	575	97.73	−2.27
27	683,995	10,239	10,923	2,005	8,918	401	11,324	585	97.56	−2.44
28	141,904	1,657	1,798	322	1,476	64	1,863	595	97.58	−2.42
29	488,345	8,909	9,397	1,412	7,985	282	9,680	575	96.86	−3.14
30	243,705	4,306	4,550	601	3,949	120	4,670	574	96.53	−3.47
31	321,100	4,823	5,144	662	4,482	132	5,277	579	96.52	−3.48
32	162,030	3,794	3,956	506	3,450	101	4,057	566	96.38	−3.62
Totals	17,230,840	739,864	757,095	247,397	509,698	49,479	806,573			
Average Weighted Deviation —										1.90

326

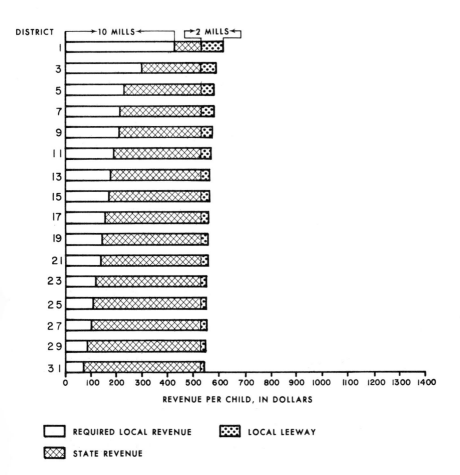

FIGURE 9-5. MODEL II-C REVENUE PER WEIGHTED PUPIL (EXCLUDING TRANSPORTATION)

TABLE 9-10 — MODEL II-D

COMPLETE EQUALIZATION MODEL MINIMUM FOUNDATION PROGRAM
ALLOCATION FOR TRANSPORTATION ALLOCATION OF $564.4685 PER WADM
12 MILL LEVY CHARGEBACK 0 MILL LEVY LOCAL TAX LEEWAY

District	Amt Alloc For Trans in Dollars	$564.4685 Amt Alloc Per WADM in Thousands of Dollars	Total Found Program in Thousands of Dollars	State Appropriations 12 Mill X Equal Val in Thousands of Dollars	Total State Appropriation in Thousands of Dollars	Total Revenue in Thousands of Dollars	Total Revenue Per WADM in Dollars	Ratio of Dist Revenue to Complete Equal Revenue in %	Deviation from 100% Equalized
1	28,140	10,123	10,151	9,256	895	10,151	566	100	0
2	0	7,702	7,702	6,725	977	7,702	564	100	0
3	129,600	23,862	23,992	15,439	8,552	23,992	568	100	0
4	2,025,199	90,372	92,397	55,492	36,905	92,397	577	100	0
5	156,585	4,336	4,493	2,173	2,320	4,493	585	100	0
6	217,838	7,464	7,682	3,520	4,162	7,682	581	100	0
7	631,659	11,127	11,758	5,157	6,601	11,758	597	100	0
8	65,285	1,357	1,422	624	799	1,422	592	100	0
9	344,760	6,092	6,437	2,721	3,715	6,437	596	100	0
10	2,275,609	99,932	102,208	43,042	59,166	102,208	577	100	0
11	89,440	2,297	2,387	938	1,448	2,387	586	100	0
12	104,762	3,479	3,584	1,420	2,164	3,584	581	100	0
13	140,800	3,395	3,536	1,290	2,245	3,536	588	100	0
14	2,227,033	118,187	120,414	44,581	75,833	120,414	575	100	0
15	283,465	4,086	4,369	1,464	2,905	4,369	604	100	0
16	632,443	12,532	13,165	4,184	8,981	13,165	593	100	0
17	1,649,358	54,756	56,406	18,156	38,250	56,406	581	100	0
18	418,744	17,013	17,431	5,498	11,933	17,431	578	100	0
19	879,995	22,039	22,919	6,665	16,254	22,919	587	100	0
20	522,555	11,799	12,321	3,505	8,816	12,321	589	100	0
21	654,440	20,043	20,698	5,947	14,750	20,698	583	100	0
22	394,525	15,532	15,926	4,102	11,824	15,926	579	100	0
23	342,355	5,178	5,520	1,324	4,197	5,520	602	100	0
24	287,980	6,555	6,843	1,558	5,285	6,843	589	100	0
25	230,496	183,355	183,586	42,964	140,621	183,586	565	100	0
26	456,729	10,749	11,205	2,518	8,687	11,205	588	100	0
27	683,995	10,924	11,608	2,406	9,202	11,608	600	100	0
28	141,904	1,767	1,909	387	1,522	1,909	610	100	0
29	488,345	9,505	9,993	1,695	8,298	9,993	593	100	0
30	243,705	4,594	4,838	721	4,117	4,838	594	100	0
31	321,100	5,146	5,467	795	4,672	5,467	600	100	0
32	162,030	4,048	4,210	607	3,602	4,210	587	100	0
Totals	17,230,840	789,343	806,573	296,876	509,698	806,573	—	—	—
Average Weighted Deviation	—	—	—	—	—	—	—	—	0

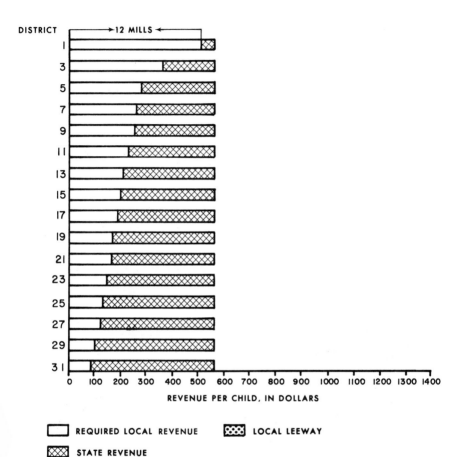

FIGURE 9-6. MODEL II-D REVENUE PER WEIGHTED
PUPIL (EXCLUDING TRANSPORTATION)

DISTRICT

REVENUE PER CHILD, IN DOLLARS

☐ REQUIRED LOCAL REVENUE ▦ LOCAL LEEWAY

▨ STATE REVENUE

TABLE 9-11 — MODEL III

PERCENTAGE EQUALIZING GRANT—STATE REV = $A \times [1 - (D/S \times E)]$
PERCENTAGE BASED UPON LOCAL CONTRIBUTION ON 5 MILL OF EQUAL VALUE OF PROPERTY ALLOCATION FOR TRANSPORTATION WEIGHTED PUPILS

District	Amt Alloc For Trans in Dollars	440.6274 Amt Alloc Per WADM in Thousands of Dollars	% of Program Costs Contrib By State	State Contribution in Thousands of Dollars	Total State Appropriations in Thousands of Dollars	Local Rev 7 Mills X Equal Val in Thousands of Dollars	Total Revenue in Thousands of Dollars	Total Revenue Per Pupil in WADM in Dollars	Ratio of Dist Revenue to Complete Equal Revenue in %	Deviation from 100% Equalized
1	28,140	7,902	51.1931	4,045	4,074	5,400	13,330	743	131.31	31.31
2	0	6,012	53.3914	3,210	3,210	3,923	9,935	728	129.00	29.00
3	129,600	18,627	65.4635	12,194	12,324	9,006	27,763	657	115.72	15.72
4	2,025,199	70,545	67.2242	47,423	49,448	32,370	104,940	655	113.58	13.58
5	156,585	3,385	73.2532	2,480	2,636	1,267	4,809	626	107.04	7.04
6	217,838	5,826	74.8290	4,360	4,578	2,053	8,097	612	105.41	5.41
7	631,659	8,686	75.2585	6,537	7,168	3,009	12,326	625	104.83	4.83
8	65,285	1,059	75.4652	799	865	364	1,488	619	104.65	4.65
9	344,760	4,755	76.1537	3,621	3,966	1,588	6,688	620	103.90	3.90
10	2,275,609	78,008	77.0096	60,074	62,349	25,108	105,391	593	103.11	3.11
11	89,440	1,793	78.1981	1,402	1,492	547	2,430	597	101.82	1.82
12	104,762	2,716	78.2107	2,124	2,229	829	3,649	592	101.82	1.82
13	140,800	2,650	79.7132	2,112	2,253	753	3,543	589	100.22	0.22
14	2,227,033	92,258	79.8657	73,682	75,909	26,006	120,490	575	100.06	0.06
15	283,465	3,189	80.8693	2,579	2,863	854	4,327	598	99.03	- 0.96
16	632,443	9,783	82.1808	8,040	8,672	2,441	12,856	579	97.65	- 2.35
17	1,649,358	42,743	82.3016	35,178	36,828	10,591	54,983	567	97.47	- 2.52
18	418,744	13,280	82.7485	10,989	11,408	3,207	16,906	561	96.98	- 3.01
19	879,995	17,204	83.8570	14,427	15,307	3,888	21,972	563	95.86	- 4.13
20	522,555	9,210	84.1147	7,750	8,272	2,044	11,777	563	95.58	- 4.42
21	654,440	15,646	84.1615	13,168	13,822	3,469	19,770	557	95.51	- 4.48
22	394,525	12,124	85.9013	10,415	10,809	2,393	14,912	542	93.63	- 6.37
23	342,355	4,042	86.3543	3,490	3,833	772	5,156	562	93.41	- 6.59
24	287,980	5,117	87.3127	4,467	4,755	909	6,313	544	92.27	- 7.73
25	230,496	143,128	87.4924	125,226	125,457	25,063	168,421	518	91.74	- 8.26
26	456,729	8,390	87.4954	7,341	7,798	1,469	10,316	542	92.06	- 7.94
27	683,995	8,527	88.2430	7,525	8,209	1,404	10,615	548	91.44	- 8.56
28	141,904	1,380	88.3144	1,218	1,360	226	1,747	558	91.51	- 8.49
29	488,345	7,419	90.4818	6,713	7,201	989	8,896	528	89.03	-10.97
30	243,705	3,586	91.6201	3,286	3,529	421	4,251	522	87.86	-12.14
31	321,100	4,017	91.7571	3,686	4,007	464	4,801	527	87.83	-12.17
32	162,030	3,160	91.9905	2,907	3,069	354	3,676	513	87.32	-12.68
Totals	17,230,840	616,166		492,467	509,697	173,178	806,573			
Average Weighted Deviation										6.65

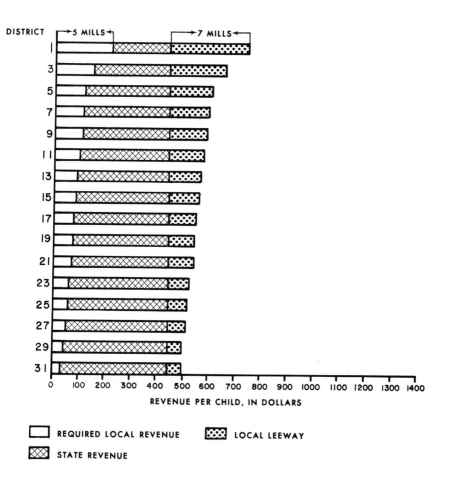

FIGURE 9-7. MODEL III REVENUE PER WEIGHTED
PUPIL (EXCLUDING TRANSPORTATION)

DISTRICT

REVENUE PER CHILD, IN DOLLARS

☐ REQUIRED LOCAL REVENUE   ▨ LOCAL LEEWAY
▧ STATE REVENUE

TABLE 9-12 — MODEL IV-A

FLAT GRANT OF $440.6274 PER PUPIL IN WADM ALLOCATION FOR TRANSPORTATION EQUIVALENT OF 5 MILLS ON EAV PROVIDED TO STATE FOR DISTRIBUTION. LOCAL TAX RATE OF 7 MILLS

District	Amount Alloc For Trans in Dollars	State Appropriation $440.6274 Amt Allocated Per WADM in Thousands of Dollars	Total State Alloc in Thousands of Dollars	Local Revenue Yield of 7 Mill Levy in Thousands of Dollars	Total Revenue in Thousands of Dollars	Total Revenue Per WADM in Dollars	Ratio of Dist Revenue to Complete Equal Revenue in %	Deviation From 100% Equalized
1	28,140	7,902	7,930	5,400	13,330	743	131.31	31.31
2	0	6,012	6,012	3,923	9,935	728	129.00	29.00
3	129,600	18,627	18,757	9,006	27,763	657	115.72	15.72
4	2,025,199	70,545	72,570	32,370	104,940	655	113.58	13.58
5	156,585	3,385	3,541	1,267	4,809	626	107.04	7.04
6	217,838	5,826	6,044	2,053	8,097	612	105.41	5.41
7	631,659	8,686	9,317	3,009	12,326	625	104.83	4.83
8	65,285	1,059	1,125	364	1,488	619	104.65	4.65
9	344,760	4,755	5,100	1,588	6,688	620	103.90	3.90
10	2,275,609	78,008	80,283	25,108	105,391	595	103.11	3.11
11	89,440	1,793	1,883	547	2,430	597	101.82	1.82
12	104,762	2,716	2,821	829	3,649	592	101.82	1.82
13	140,800	2,650	2,791	753	3,543	589	100.22	.22
14	2,227,033	92,258	94,485	26,005	120,490	575	100.06	.06
15	283,465	3,189	3,473	854	4,327	598	99.03	-.97
16	632,443	9,783	10,415	2,440	12,856	579	97.65	-2.35
17	1,649,358	42,743	44,392	10,591	54,983	567	97.48	-2.52
18	418,744	13,280	13,699	3,207	16,906	561	96.99	-3.01
19	879,995	17,204	18,084	3,888	21,972	563	95.87	-4.13
20	522,555	9,210	9,733	2,044	11,777	563	95.58	-4.41
21	654,440	15,646	16,300	3,469	19,770	557	95.52	-4.48
22	394,525	12,124	12,519	2,393	14,912	542	93.63	-6.37
23	342,355	4,042	4,384	772	5,156	562	93.41	-6.59
24	287,980	5,117	5,405	909	6,313	544	92.27	-7.73
25	230,496	143,128	143,359	25,063	168,421	518	91.74	-8.26
26	456,729	8,390	8,847	1,469	10,316	542	92.06	-7.94
27	683,995	8,527	9,211	1,404	10,615	548	91.44	-8.56
28	141,904	1,380	1,522	226	1,747	558	91.51	-8.49
29	488,345	7,419	7,908	989	8,896	528	89.02	-10.97
30	243,705	3,586	3,830	421	4,251	522	87.86	-12.14
31	321,100	4,017	4,338	464	4,801	527	87.83	-12.17
32	162,030	3,160	3,322	354	3,676	513	87.32	-12.68
Totals	17,230,840	616,166	633,396	173,178	806,573	—	—	—
Average Weighted Deviation	—	—	—	—	—	—	—	6.65

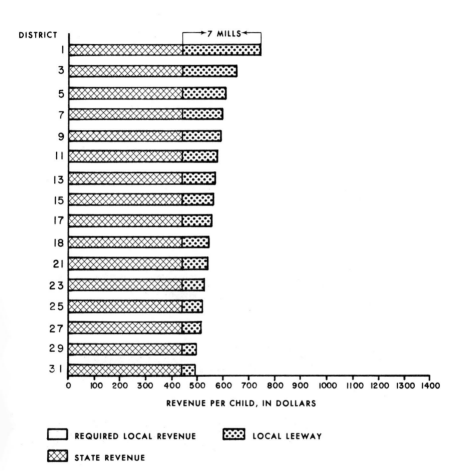

FIGURE 9-8. MODEL Ⅳ-A REVENUE PER WEIGHTED
PUPIL (EXCLUDING TRANSPORTATION)

REVENUE PER CHILD, IN DOLLARS

☐ REQUIRED LOCAL REVENUE   ▨ LOCAL LEEWAY

▨ STATE REVENUE

TABLE 9-13 — MODEL IV-B

FLAT GRANT OF $493.7023 PER PUPIL IN WADM ALLOCATION FOR TRANSPORTATION EQUIVALENT OF 8 MILLS ON EAV PROVIDED TO STATE FOR DISTRIBUTION. LOCAL TAX RATE OF 4 MILLS

District	Amount Alloc for Trans in Dollars	State Appropriation $493.7023 Amt Allocated Per WADM in Thousands of Dollars	Total Alloc State Alloc in Thousands of Dollars	Local Revenue Yield of 4 Mill Levy in Thousands of Dollars	Total Revenue in Thousands of Dollars	Total Revenue Per WADM Complete Equal Revenue in % in Dollars	Ratio of Dist Revenue to Complete Equal Revenue in %	Deviation from 100% Equalized
1	28,140	8,854	8,882	3,085	11,968	667	117.89	17.89
2	0	6,736	6,736	2,242	8,978	658	116.57	16.57
3	129,600	20,871	21,000	5,146	26,147	619	108.98	8.98
4	2,025,199	79,042	81,067	18,497	99,565	622	107.76	7.76
5	156,585	3,793	3,949	724	4,673	608	104.02	4.02
6	217,838	6,528	6,746	1,173	7,919	599	103.09	3.09
7	631,659	9,732	10,364	1,719	12,083	613	102.76	2.76
8	65,285	1,187	1,252	208	1,460	607	102.66	2.66
9	344,760	5,328	5,673	907	6,580	610	102.23	2.23
10	2,275,609	87,404	89,680	14,347	104,027	588	101.78	1.78
11	89,440	2,009	2,099	313	2,412	593	101.04	1.04
12	104,762	3,043	3,148	473	3,621	588	101.04	1.04
13	140,800	2,969	3,110	430	3,540	589	100.13	.13
14	2,227,033	103,370	105,597	14,860	120,458	575	100.04	.04
15	283,465	3,573	3,857	488	4,345	600	99.45	-.55
16	632,443	10,961	11,594	1,395	12,988	585	98.66	-1.34
17	1,649,358	47,892	49,541	6,052	55,593	573	98.56	-1.44
18	418,744	14,880	15,298	1,833	17,131	568	98.28	-1.72
19	879,995	19,276	20,156	2,222	22,378	573	97.64	-2.36
20	522,555	10,319	10,842	1,168	12,010	575	97.48	-2.52
21	654,440	17,530	18,184	1,982	20,167	568	97.44	-2.56
22	394,525	13,585	13,979	1,367	15,347	558	96.36	-3.64
23	342,355	4,529	4,871	441	5,312	579	96.23	-3.77
24	287,980	5,733	6,021	519	6,540	563	95.58	-4.42
25	230,496	160,368	160,599	14,321	174,920	539	95.28	-4.72
26	456,729	9,401	9,858	839	10,697	562	95.46	-4.54
27	683,995	9,555	10,239	802	11,041	570	95.11	-4.89
28	141,904	1,546	1,688	129	1,817	580	95.15	-4.85
29	488,345	8,313	8,801	565	9,366	556	93.73	-6.27
30	243,705	4,018	4,262	240	4,502	553	93.06	-6.94
31	321,100	4,501	4,822	265	5,087	558	93.04	-6.96
32	162,030	3,540	3,702	202	3,905	545	92.76	-7.24
Totals	17,230,840	690,385	707,615	98,959	806,573			
Average Weighted Deviation —								3.80

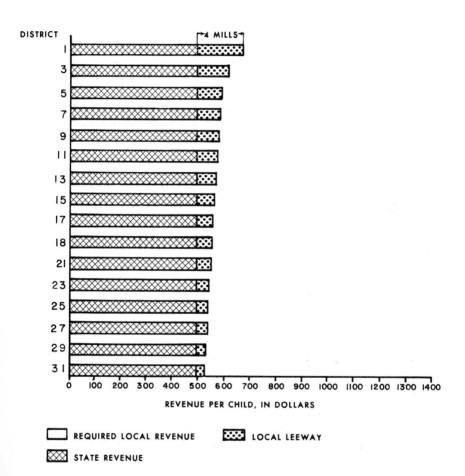

FIGURE 9-9. MODEL IV-B REVENUE PER WEIGHTED
PUPIL (EXCLUDING TRANSPORTATION)

REVENUE PER CHILD, IN DOLLARS

☐ REQUIRED LOCAL REVENUE ▨ LOCAL LEEWAY
▨ STATE REVENUE

335

TABLE 9-14 — MODEL IV-C

FLAT GRANT OF $564.4685 PER PUPIL IN WADM ALLOCATION FOR
TRANSPORTATION EQUIVALENT OF 12 MILLS ON EAV PROVIDED TO THE
STATE FOR DISTRIBUTION. LOCAL TAX RATE OF 0 MILLS

District	Amount Alloc for Trans in Dollars	State Appropriation $564.4685 Amt Allocated Per WADM in Thousands of Dollars	Total State Alloc in Thousands of Dollars	Local Revenue Yield of 0 Mill Levy in Dollars	Total Revenue in Thousands of Dollars	Total Revenue Per WADM in Dollars	Ratio of Dist Revenue to Complete Equal Revenue in %	Deviation from 100% Equalized
1	28,140	10,123	10,151	0	10,151	566	100	0
2	0	7,702	7,702	0	7,702	564	100	0
3	129,600	23,862	23,992	0	23,992	568	100	0
4	2,025,199	90,372	92,397	0	92,397	577	100	0
5	156,585	4,336	4,493	0	4,493	585	100	0
6	217,838	7,464	7,682	0	7,682	581	100	0
7	631,659	11,127	11,758	0	11,758	597	100	0
8	65,285	1,357	1,422	0	1,422	592	100	0
9	344,760	6,092	6,437	0	6,437	596	100	0
10	2,275,609	99,932	102,208	0	102,208	577	100	0
11	89,440	2,297	2,387	0	2,387	586	100	0
12	104,762	3,479	3,584	0	3,584	581	100	0
13	140,800	3,395	3,536	0	3,536	588	100	0
14	2,227,033	118,187	120,414	0	120,414	574	100	0
15	283,465	4,086	4,369	0	4,369	604	100	0
16	632,443	12,532	13,165	0	13,165	593	100	0
17	1,649,358	54,756	56,406	0	56,406	582	100	0
18	418,744	17,013	17,431	0	17,431	578	100	0
19	879,995	22,039	22,919	0	22,919	589	100	0
20	522,555	11,799	12,321	0	12,321	587	100	0
21	654,440	20,043	20,698	0	20,698	583	100	0
22	394,525	15,532	15,926	0	15,926	579	100	0
23	342,355	5,178	5,520	0	5,520	602	100	0
24	287,980	6,555	6,843	0	6,843	589	100	0
25	230,496	183,355	183,586	0	183,586	565	100	0
26	456,729	10,749	11,205	0	11,205	588	100	0
27	683,995	10,924	11,608	0	11,608	600	100	0
28	141,904	1,767	1,909	0	1,909	610	100	0
29	488,345	9,505	9,993	0	9,993	593	100	0
30	243,705	4,594	4,838	0	4,838	594	100	0
31	321,100	5,146	5,467	0	5,467	600	100	0
32	162,030	4,048	4,210	0	4,210	587	100	0
Totals	17,230,840	789,343	806,573	0	806,573	—	—	0
Average Weighted Deviation	—	—	—	—	—	—	—	0

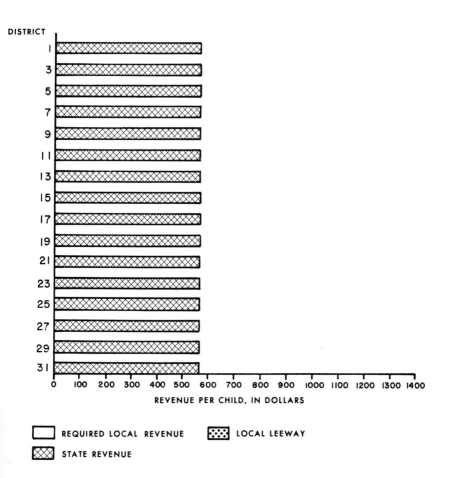

FIGURE 9-10.   MODEL IV-C REVENUE PER WEIGHTED
PUPIL (EXCLUDING TRANSPORTATION)

DISTRICT

REVENUE PER CHILD, IN DOLLARS

☐ REQUIRED LOCAL REVENUE   ▨ LOCAL LEEWAY
▨ STATE REVENUE

337

TABLE 9-15 — MODEL V-A

MINIMUM FOUNDATION PROGRAM ALLOCATION FOR TRANSPORTATION
ALLOCATION OF $511.3937 PER WADM EQUIVALENT OF 5 MILLS PROVIDED
TO THE STATE FOR DISTRIBUTION IN THE MINIMUM FOUNDATION
PROGRAM 4 MILL LEVY CHARGEBACK 3 MILL LEVY LOCAL TAX LEEWAY

District	Amt Alloc for Trans in Dollars	$511.3937 Amt Alloc Per WADM in Thousands of Dollars	State Appropriation Total Found Program in Thousands of Dollars	4 Mills X Equal Val in Thousands of Dollars	Total State Appropriation in Thousands of Dollars	Local Revenue 3 Mills X Equal Val in Thousands of Dollars	Total Revenue in Thousands of Dollars	Total Revenue Per Pupil in WADM in Dollars	Ratio of Dist Revenue to Complete Equal Revenue in %	Deviation From 100% Equalized
1	28,140	9,171	9,199	3,085	6,114	2,314	11,514	642	113.42	13.42
2	0	6,977	6,977	2,242	4,736	1,681	8,659	635	112.43	12.43
3	129,600	21,619	21,748	5,146	16,602	3,860	25,608	606	106.74	6.74
4	2,025,199	81,875	83,900	18,497	65,403	13,873	97,773	611	105.82	5.82
5	156,585	3,929	4,085	724	3,361	543	4,628	602	103.02	3.02
6	217,838	6,762	6,980	1,173	5,807	880	7,860	594	102.32	2.32
7	631,659	10,081	10,712	1,719	8,993	1,289	12,002	609	102.07	2.07
8	65,285	1,229	1,295	208	1,087	156	1,450	603	101.99	1.99
9	344,760	5,519	5,864	907	4,957	680	6,544	606	101.67	1.67
10	2,275,609	90,536	92,812	14,347	78,464	10,761	103,572	585	101.33	1.33
11	89,440	2,081	2,171	313	1,858	235	2,405	591	100.78	.78
12	104,762	3,152	3,257	473	2,784	355	3,612	586	100.78	.78
13	140,800	3,076	3,216	430	2,786	323	3,539	588	100.09	.09
14	2,227,033	107,075	109,302	14,860	94,441	11,145	120,447	575	100.03	.03
15	283,465	3,701	3,985	488	3,497	366	4,351	601	99.95	-.41
16	632,443	11,354	11,986	1,395	10,592	1,046	13,032	587	98.99	-1.01
17	1,649,358	49,608	51,257	6,052	45,205	4,539	55,796	575	98.92	-1.08
18	418,744	15,413	15,832	1,833	13,999	1,375	17,206	571	98.71	-1.29
19	879,995	19,967	20,847	2,222	18,625	1,666	22,513	577	98.23	-1.77
20	522,555	10,689	11,212	1,168	10,043	876	12,088	578	98.11	-1.89
21	654,440	18,159	18,813	1,982	16,831	1,487	20,300	572	98.08	-1.92
22	394,525	14,072	14,466	1,367	13,099	1,026	15,492	563	97.27	-2.73
23	342,355	4,691	5,033	441	4,592	331	5,364	585	97.18	-2.82
24	287,980	5,938	6,226	519	5,707	389	6,616	570	96.69	-3.31
25	230,496	166,115	166,346	14,321	152,024	10,741	177,087	545	96.46	-3.54
26	456,729	9,738	10,195	839	9,355	630	10,824	568	96.60	-3.40
27	683,995	9,897	10,581	802	9,779	602	11,183	578	96.33	-3.67
28	141,904	1,601	1,743	129	1,614	97	1,840	588	96.36	-3.64
29	488,345	8,611	9,099	565	8,534	424	9,523	566	95.30	-4.70
30	243,705	4,162	4,406	240	4,166	180	4,586	563	94.80	-5.20
31	321,100	4,662	4,983	265	4,718	199	5,182	568	94.78	-5.22
32	162,030	3,667	3,829	202	3,627	152	3,981	555	94.57	-5.43
Totals	17,230,840	715,124	732,355	98,959	633,396	74,219	806,573	—	—	—
Average Weighted Deviation	—	—	—	—	—	—	—	—	—	2.85

338

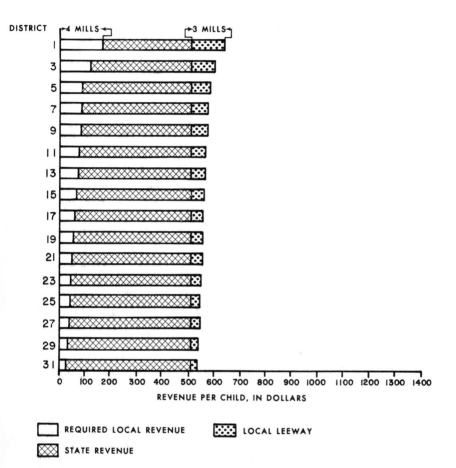

FIGURE 9-11. MODEL $\underline{V}$-A REVENUE PER WEIGHTED
PUPIL (EXCLUDING TRANSPORTATION)

TABLE 9-16 — MODEL V-B

MINIMUM FOUNDATION PROGRAM ALLOCATION FOR TRANSPORTATION
ALLOCATION OF $529.0854 PER WADM EQUIVALENT OF 8 MILLS PROVIDED
TO THE STATE FOR DISTRIBUTION IN THE MINIMUM FOUND PROGRAM
2 MILL LEVY CHARGEBACK 2 MILL LEVY LOCAL TAX LEEWAY

District	Amt Alloc for Trans in Dollars	$529.0854 Amt Alloc Per WADM in Thousands of Dollars	State Appropriation Total Found Program in Thousands of Dollars	2 Mills × Equal Val in Thousands of Dollars	Total State Appropriation in Thousands of Dollars	Local Revenue 2 Mills × Equal Val in Thousands of Dollars	Total Revenue in Thousands of Dollars	Total Revenue Per Pupil in WADM in Dollars	Ratio of Dist Revenue to Complete Equal Revenue in %	Deviation from 100% Equalized
1	28,140	9,489	9,517	1,543	7,974	1,543	11,059	617	108.95	8.95
2	0	7,219	7,219	1,121	6,098	1,121	8,340	611	108.28	8.28
3	129,600	22,367	22,496	2,573	19,923	2,573	25,069	593	104.49	4.49
4	2,025,199	84,707	86,732	9,249	77,484	9,249	95,981	600	103.88	3.88
5	156,585	4,064	4,221	362	3,859	362	4,583	597	102.01	2.01
6	217,838	6,996	7,214	587	6,627	587	7,801	590	101.55	1.55
7	631,659	10,429	11,061	860	10,201	860	11,921	605	101.38	1.38
8	65,285	1,272	1,337	104	1,233	104	1,441	599	101.33	1.33
9	344,760	5,710	6,055	454	5,601	454	6,508	603	101.11	1.11
10	2,275,609	93,668	95,944	7,174	88,770	7,174	103,117	582	100.89	.89
11	89,440	2,153	2,243	156	2,086	156	2,399	589	100.52	.52
12	104,762	3,261	3,366	237	3,129	237	3,603	584	100.52	.52
13	140,800	3,182	3,323	215	3,108	215	3,538	588	100.06	.06
14	2,227,033	110,779	113,006	7,430	105,577	7,430	120,436	575	100.02	.02
15	283,465	3,830	4,113	244	3,869	244	4,357	602	99.72	-.28
16	632,443	11,747	12,379	697	11,682	697	13,076	589	99.33	-.67
17	1,649,358	51,324	52,973	3,026	49,947	3,026	55,999	577	99.28	-.72
18	418,744	15,946	16,365	916	15,448	916	17,281	573	99.14	-.86
19	879,995	20,658	21,538	1,111	20,427	1,111	22,648	580	98.82	-1.18
20	522,555	11,059	11,581	584	10,997	584	12,166	582	98.74	-1.26
21	654,440	18,787	19,441	991	18,450	991	20,432	575	98.72	-1.28
22	394,525	14,558	14,953	684	14,269	684	15,637	568	98.18	-1.82
23	342,355	4,853	5,196	221	4,975	221	5,416	590	98.12	-1.88
24	287,980	6,144	6,432	260	6,172	260	6,691	576	97.79	-2.21
25	230,496	171,862	172,092	7,161	164,932	7,161	179,253	552	97.64	-2.36
26	456,729	10,075	10,532	420	10,112	420	10,951	575	97.73	-2.27
27	683,995	10,239	10,923	401	10,522	401	11,324	585	97.56	-2.44
28	141,904	1,657	1,798	64	1,734	64	1,863	595	97.58	-2.42
29	488,345	8,909	9,397	282	9,115	282	9,680	575	96.86	-3.14
30	243,705	4,306	4,550	120	4,430	120	4,670	574	96.53	-3.47
31	321,100	4,823	5,144	132	5,012	132	5,277	579	96.52	-3.48
32	162,030	3,794	3,956	101	3,855	101	4,057	566	96.38	-3.62
Totals	17,230,840	739,864	757,095	49,480	707,615	49,479	806,573	—	—	—
Average Weighted Deviation	—								—	1.90

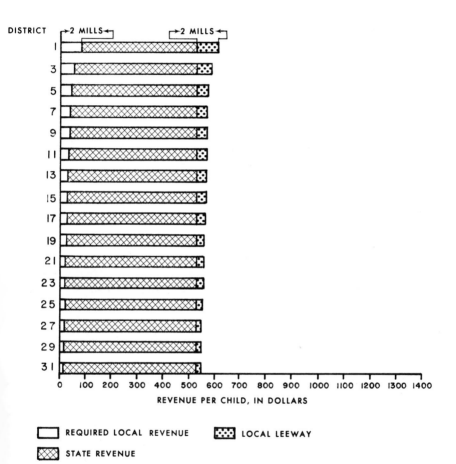

FIGURE 9-12. MODEL $\overline{V}$-B REVENUE PER WEIGHTED
PUPIL (EXCLUDING TRANSPORTATION)

TABLE 9-17 — MODEL V-C

MINIMUM FOUNDATION PROGRAM ALLOCATION FOR TRANSPORTATION
ALLOCATION OF $564.4685 PER WADM EQUIVALENT OF 12 MILLS PROVIDED
TO THE STATE FOR DISTRIBUTION IN THE MINIMUM FOUND PROGRAM
0 MILL LEVY CHARGEBACK 0 MILL LEVY LOCAL TAX LEEWAY

District	Amt Alloc for Trans in Dollars	$564.4685 Amt Alloc Per WADM in Thousands of Dollars	Total Found Program in Thousands of Dollars	State Appropriations 0 Mills Equal Val in Dollars	Total State Appropriation in Thousands of Dollars	Local Revenue 0 Mills Equal Val in Dollars	Total Revenue in Thousands of Dollars	Total Revenue Per Pupil in WADM in Dollars	Ratio of Dist Revenue to Complete Equal Revenue in %	Deviation From 100% Equalized
1	28,140	10,123	10,151	0	10,151	0	10,151	566	100	0
2	0	7,702	7,702	0	7,702	0	7,702	564	100	0
3	129,600	23,862	23,992	0	23,992	0	23,992	568	100	0
4	2,025,199	90,372	92,397	0	92,397	0	92,397	577	100	0
5	156,585	4,336	4,493	0	4,493	0	4,493	585	100	0
6	217,838	7,464	7,682	0	7,682	0	7,682	581	100	0
7	631,659	11,127	11,758	0	11,758	0	11,758	597	100	0
8	65,285	1,357	1,422	0	1,422	0	1,422	592	100	0
9	344,760	6,092	6,437	0	6,437	0	6,437	596	100	0
10	2,275,609	99,932	102,208	0	102,208	0	102,208	577	100	0
11	89,440	2,297	2,387	0	2,387	0	2,387	586	100	0
12	104,762	3,479	3,584	0	3,584	0	3,584	581	100	0
13	140,800	3,395	3,536	0	3,536	0	3,536	588	100	0
14	2,227,033	118,187	120,414	0	120,414	0	120,414	575	100	0
15	283,465	4,086	4,369	0	4,369	0	4,369	604	100	0
16	632,443	12,532	13,165	0	13,165	0	13,165	593	100	0
17	1,649,358	54,756	56,406	0	56,406	0	56,406	581	100	0
18	418,744	17,013	17,431	0	17,431	0	17,431	578	100	0
19	879,995	22,039	22,919	0	22,919	0	22,919	587	100	0
20	522,555	11,799	12,321	0	12,321	0	12,321	589	100	0
21	654,440	20,043	20,698	0	20,698	0	20,698	583	100	0
22	394,525	15,532	15,926	0	15,926	0	15,926	579	100	0
23	342,355	5,178	5,520	0	5,520	0	5,520	602	100	0
24	287,980	6,555	6,843	0	6,843	0	6,843	589	100	0
25	230,496	183,355	183,586	0	183,586	0	183,586	565	100	0
26	456,729	10,749	11,205	0	11,205	0	11,205	588	100	0
27	683,995	10,924	11,608	0	11,608	0	11,608	600	100	0
28	141,904	1,767	1,909	0	1,909	0	1,909	610	100	0
29	488,345	9,505	9,993	0	9,993	0	9,993	593	100	0
30	243,705	4,594	4,838	0	4,838	0	4,838	594	100	0
31	321,100	5,146	5,467	0	5,467	0	5,467	600	100	0
32	162,030	4,049	4,210	0	4,210	0	4,210	587	100	0
Totals	17,230,840	789,343	806,573	0	806,573	0	806,573	—	—	—
Average Weighted Deviation —									—	0

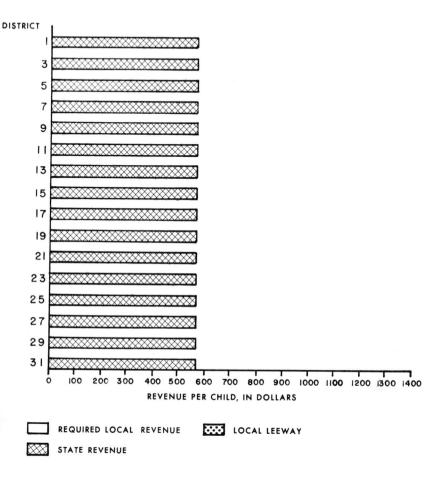

FIGURE 9-13. MODEL $\underline{V}$-C REVENUE PER WEIGHTED PUPIL (EXCLUDING TRANSPORTATION)

343

TABLE 9-18 — MODEL VI-A

FLAT GRANT OF $276.0942 PER PUPIL IN WADM 50% OF REVENUE FROM STATE FUNDS 50% OF REVENUE FROM LOCAL FUNDS ALLOCATION FOR TRANSPORTATION LOCAL TAX RATE OF 16.3 MILLS

District	Amount Alloc for Trans in Dollars	State Appropriations 276.0942 Amt Allocated Per WADM in Thousands of Dollars	Total State Alloc in Thousands of Dollars	Local Revenue Yield of 16.3 Mill Levy in Thousands of Dollars	Total Revenue in Thousands of Dollars	Total Revenue Per WADM in Dollars	Ratio of Dist Revenue To Complete Equal Revenue in %	Deviation from 100% Equalized
1	28,140	4,951	4,980	12,573	17,553	979	173	72.91
2	0	3,767	3,767	9,135	12,902	946	168	67.52
3	129,600	11,672	11,801	20,972	32,773	775	137	36.60
4	2,025,199	44,203	46,228	75,376	121,604	760	132	31.61
5	156,585	2,121	2,278	2,951	5,229	681	116	16.38
6	217,888	3,651	3,869	4,781	8,650	654	113	12.60
7	631,659	5,442	6,074	7,006	13,080	664	111	11.24
8	65,285	664	729	847	1,576	656	111	10.83
9	344,760	2,980	3,324	3,697	7,021	651	109	9.08
10	2,275,609	48,880	51,155	58,466	109,620	619	107	7.25
11	89,440	1,124	1,213	1,275	2,488	611	104	4.23
12	104,762	1,702	1,807	1,929	3,736	606	104	4.23
13	140,800	1,660	1,801	1,753	3,554	591	101	.516
14	2,227,033	57,808	60,035	60,556	120,591	576	100	.147
15	283,465	1,998	2,282	1,989	4,271	590	98	- 2.25
16	632,443	6,130	6,762	5,683	12,445	561	95	- 5.47
17	1,649,358	26,783	28,432	24,661	53,093	547	94	- 5.87
18	418,744	8,321	8,740	7,469	16,209	538	93	- 7.01
19	879,995	10,780	11,660	9,054	20,714	531	90	- 9.62
20	522,555	5,774	6,293	4,760	11,054	529	90	-10.28
21	654,440	9,804	10,458	8,078	18,536	522	90	-10.44
22	394,525	7,597	7,992	5,573	13,564	493	85	-14.83
23	342,355	2,533	2,875	1,798	4,673	509	85	-15.35
24	287,980	3,206	3,494	2,116	5,610	483	82	-18.01
25	230,496	89,683	89,914	58,360	148,274	456	81	-19.23
26	456,729	5,257	5,714	3,420	9,134	480	82	-18.48
27	683,995	5,343	6,027	3,268	9,296	480	80	-19.92
28	141,904	864	1,006	526	1,532	489	80	-19.76
29	488,345	4,649	5,137	2,302	7,439	442	74	-25.55
30	243,705	2,247	2,491	980	3,471	427	72	-28.26
31	321,100	2,517	2,838	1,079	3,917	430	72	-28.34
32	162,030	1,980	2,142	825	2,967	414	70	-29.52
Totals	17,230,840	386,085	403,315	403,255	806,572	—	—	—
Average Weighted Deviation	—	—	—	—	—	—	—	15.48

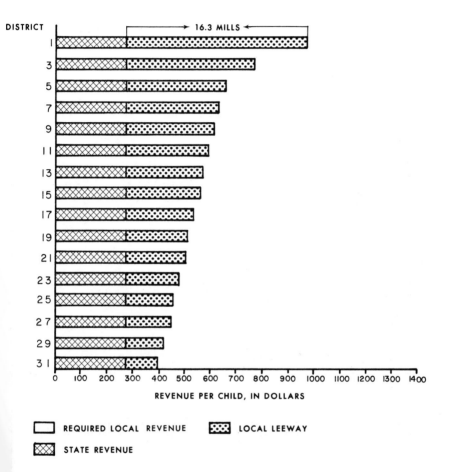

FIGURE 9-14. MODEL VI-A REVENUE PER WEIGHTED
PUPIL (EXCLUDING TRANSPORTATION)

DISTRICT

16.3 MILLS

REVENUE PER CHILD, IN DOLLARS

REQUIRED LOCAL REVENUE   LOCAL LEEWAY

STATE REVENUE

345

TABLE 9-19 — MODEL VI-B

FLAT GRANT OF $131.8751 PER PUPIL IN WADM 25% OF REVENUE FROM
STATE FUNDS 75% OF REVENUE FROM LOCAL FUNDS ALLOCATION FOR
TRANSPORTATION LOCAL TAX RATE OF 24.452 MILLS

District	Amount Alloc for Trans in Dollars	State Appropriations $131.8751 Amt Allocated Per WADM In Thousands of Dollars	Total State Alloc In Thousands of Dollars	Local Rev Yield of 24.452 Mill Levy In Thousands of Dollars	Total Revenue In Thousands of Dollars	Total Revenue Per WADM in Dollars	Ratio of Dist Revenue to Complete Equal Revenue in %	Deviation From 100% Equalized
1	28,140	2,365	2,393	18,861	21,255	1,185	209.38	109.38
2	0	1,799	1,799	13,703	15,503	1,136	201.29	101.29
3	129,600	5,575	5,704	31,461	37,165	879	154.91	54.91
4	2,025,199	21,113	23,139	113,074	136,212	851	147.42	47.42
5	156,585	1,013	1,170	4,428	5,597	729	124.58	24.58
6	217,838	1,744	1,962	7,172	9,134	691	118.90	18.90
7	631,659	2,600	3,231	10,509	13,740	697	116.86	16.81
8	65,285	317	382	1,271	1,653	688	116.24	16.24
9	344,760	1,423	1,768	5,545	7,313	678	113.62	13.62
10	2,275,609	23,347	25,623	87,706	113,328	640	110.88	10.88
11	89,440	537	626	1,912	2,538	624	106.34	6.34
12	104,762	813	918	2,894	3,812	618	106.35	6.35
13	140,800	793	934	2,629	3,563	592	100.77	.77
14	2,227,033	27,612	29,839	90,841	120,680	576	100.22	.22
15	283,465	955	1,238	2,984	4,222	583	96.63	− 3.37
16	632,443	2,928	3,560	8,525	12,085	544	91.80	− 8.20
17	1,649,358	12,793	14,442	36,995	51,437	530	91.19	− 8.81
18	418,744	3,975	4,393	11,204	15,597	518	89.48	−10.52
19	879,995	5,149	6,029	13,582	19,611	502	85.56	−14.44
20	522,555	2,756	5,337	7,141	10,420	499	84.57	−15.43
21	654,440	4,683	4,023	12,119	17,456	492	84.33	−15.66
22	394,525	3,629	1,552	8,359	12,383	450	77.75	−22.25
23	342,355	1,210	1,210	2,697	4,249	463	76.98	−23.02
24	287,980	1,531	1,819	3,175	4,994	430	72.98	−27.02
25	230,496	42,837	43,067	87,547	130,614	402	72.28	−28.85
26	456,729	2,511	2,968	5,131	8,099	425	71.15	−27.72
27	683,995	2,552	3,236	4,903	8,139	421	70.12	−29.88
28	141,904	413	555	788	1,343	429	70.35	−29.65
29	488,345	2,221	2,709	3,454	6,162	366	61.67	−38.33
30	243,705	1,073	1,317	1,470	2,787	342	57.60	−42.40
31	321,100	1,202	1,523	1,619	3,142	345	57.48	−42.52
32	162,030	946	1,108	1,238	2,345	327	55.71	−44.29
Totals	17,230,840	184,412	201,643	604,933	806,573	—	—	—
Average Weighted Deviation	—	—	—	—	—	—	—	23.23

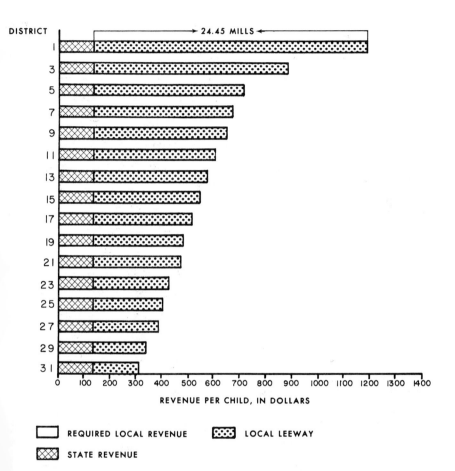

FIGURE 9-15. MODEL $\overline{VI}$-B REVENUE PER WEIGHTED
PUPIL (EXCLUDING TRANSPORTATION)

DISTRICT

24.45 MILLS

REVENUE PER CHILD, IN DOLLARS

☐ REQUIRED LOCAL REVENUE   ▨ LOCAL LEEWAY
▨ STATE REVENUE

TABLE 9-20 — MODEL VII-A

MINIMUM FOUNDATION PROGRAM ALLOCATION FOR TRANSPORTATION
ALLOCATION OF $470.7028 PER WADM 11 MILL LEVY CHARGEBACK
5.3 MILL LEVY LOCAL TAX LEEWAY 50% REVENUE FROM STATE FUNDS
50% REVENUE FROM LOCAL FUNDS

District	Amt Alloc For Trans in Dollars	470.7028 Amt. Alloc Per WADM in Thousands of Dollars	State Appropriations Total Found Program in Thousands of Dollars	11 Mill X Equal Val in Thousands of Dollars	Total State Appropriation in Thousands of Dollars	Local Revenue 5.3 Mills X Equal Val in Thousands of Dollars	Total Revenue in Thousands of Dollars	Total Revenue Per Pupil in WADM in Dollars	Ratio of Dist Revenue To Complete Equal Revenue in %	Deviation From 100% Equalized
1	28,140	8,442	8,470	8,485	-15	4,088	12,558	700	123.71	23.71
2	0	6,422	6,422	6,165	258	2,970	9,392	688	121.95	21.95
3	129,600	19,898	20,028	14,153	5,875	6,819	26,847	635	111.90	11.90
4	2,025,199	73,360	77,385	50,867	26,518	24,509	101,894	616	110.28	10.28
5	156,585	3,616	3,773	1,992	1,781	960	4,732	616	105.33	5.33
6	217,838	6,224	6,442	3,226	3,216	1,555	7,996	605	104.10	4.10
7	631,659	9,278	9,910	4,728	5,182	2,278	12,188	618	103.65	3.65
8	65,285	1,132	1,197	572	625	275	1,472	612	103.52	3.52
9	344,760	5,080	5,425	2,495	2,930	1,202	6,627	614	102.95	2.95
10	2,275,609	83,332	85,608	39,455	46,153	19,010	104,618	591	102.36	2.36
11	89,440	1,916	2,005	860	1,145	414	2,420	595	101.37	1.37
12	104,762	2,901	3,006	1,302	1,704	627	3,633	589	101.38	1.38
13	140,800	2,831	2,972	1,183	1,789	570	3,541	589	100.17	.17
14	2,227,003	98,555	100,782	40,866	59,916	19,690	120,472	575	100.05	.05
15	283,465	3,407	3,690	1,342	2,348	647	4,337	599	99.27	-.73
16	632,443	10,450	11,083	3,835	7,248	1,848	12,931	582	98.22	-1.78
17	1,649,358	45,660	47,310	16,643	30,667	8,019	55,329	570	98.09	-1.91
18	418,744	14,187	14,605	5,040	9,565	2,428	17,034	565	97.72	-2.28
19	879,995	18,378	19,258	6,110	13,148	2,944	22,202	569	96.87	-3.13
20	522,555	9,839	10,361	3,213	7,149	1,548	11,909	570	96.66	-3.34
21	654,440	16,713	17,368	5,452	11,916	2,627	19,995	563	96.60	-3.40
22	394,525	12,951	13,346	3,761	9,586	1,812	15,158	551	95.18	-4.82
23	342,355	4,318	4,660	1,213	3,447	585	5,245	572	95.01	-4.99
24	287,980	5,466	5,754	1,428	4,326	688	6,442	555	94.14	-5.86
25	230,496	152,897	153,128	39,384	113,744	18,976	172,104	530	93.75	-6.25
26	456,729	8,963	9,420	2,308	7,112	1,112	10,532	553	93.99	-6.01
27	683,995	9,110	9,794	2,206	7,588	1,063	10,856	561	93.52	-6.48
28	141,904	1,474	1,616	355	1,261	171	1,787	571	93.57	-6.43
29	488,345	7,926	8,414	1,554	6,860	749	9,163	544	91.69	-8.31
30	243,705	3,831	4,075	661	3,414	319	4,393	540	90.81	-9.19
31	321,100	4,291	4,612	728	3,884	351	4,963	544	90.78	-9.22
32	162,030	3,375	3,537	557	2,981	268	3,806	531	90.40	-9.60
Totals	17,230,840	658,223	675,453	272,136	403,316	131,120	806,573	—	—	—
Average Weighted Deviation	—	—	—	—	—	—	—	—	—	5.03

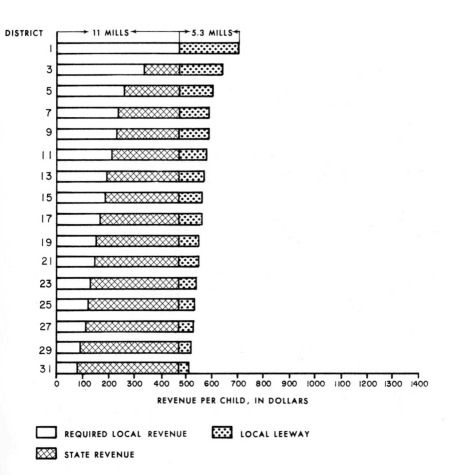

FIGURE 9-16. MODEL VII-A REVENUE PER WEIGHTED PUPIL (EXCLUDING TRANSPORTATION)

TABLE 9-21 — MODEL VII-B

MINIMUM FOUNDATION PROGRAM ALLOCATION FOR TRANSPORTATION ALLOCATION OF $306.2128 PER WADM 10 MILL LEVY CHARGEBACK 14.452 MILL LEVY LOCAL TAX LEEWAY 25% OF REVENUE FROM STATE SOURCES AND 75% OF RESERVE FROM LOCAL SOURCES

District	Amt Alloc for Trans in Dollars	$306.2128 Amt WADM Per WADM in Thousands of Dollars	Total Found Program in Thousands of Dollars	State Appropriations 10 Mills X Equal Val in Thousands of Dollars	Total State Appropriation in Thousands of Dollars	Local Revenue 14.452 Mills X Equal Val in Thousands of Dollars	Total Revenue in Thousands of Dollars	Total Revenue Per Pupil in WADM in Dollars	Ratio of Dist Revenue to Complete Equal Revenue in %	Deviation From 100% Equalized
1	28,140	5,492	5,520	7,714	0	11,148	18,861	1,052	185.80	85.80
2	0	4,178	4,178	5,604	0	8,099	13,703	1,004	177.93	77.93
3	129,600	12,945	13,074	12,866	208	18,594	31,669	749	132.00	32.00
4	2,025,199	49,025	51,050	46,243	4,807	66,831	117,881	736	127.58	27.58
5	156,585	2,352	2,509	1,811	698	2,617	5,126	667	114.09	14.09
6	217,838	4,049	4,267	2,933	1,334	4239	8,506	643	110.73	10.73
7	631,659	6,036	6,668	4,298	2,370	6,211	12,879	653	109.53	9.53
8	65,285	736	801	520	282	751	1,553	646	109.16	9.16
9	344,760	3,305	3,649	2,268	1,382	3,278	6,927	642	107.62	7.62
10	2,275,609	54,211	56,487	35,868	20,618	51,837	108,324	612	105.98	5.98
11	89,440	1,246	1,336	782	554	1,130	2,466	606	103.31	3.31
12	104,762	1,887	1,992	1,184	809	1,711	3,703	601	103.31	3.31
13	140,800	1,842	1,982	1,075	907	1,554	3,537	588	100.02	.029
14	2,227,033	64,114	66,341	37,151	29,191	53,690	120,031	573	99.68	-.32
15	283,465	2,216	2,500	1,220	1,280	1,764	4,263	589	97.58	-2.42
16	632,443	6,799	7,431	3,486	3,945	5,039	12,470	562	94.72	-5.28
17	1,649,358	29,704	31,354	15,130	16,224	21,865	53,219	549	94.35	-5.65
18	418,744	9,229	9,648	4,582	5,066	6,622	16,270	540	93.34	-6.66
19	879,995	11,956	12,836	5,554	7,281	8,027	20,863	534	91.03	-8.97
20	522,555	6,400	6,923	2,921	4,002	4,221	11,144	533	90.44	-9.56
21	654,440	10,873	11,527	4,956	6,571	7,163	18,690	526	90.30	-9.70
22	394,525	8,426	8,820	3,419	5,402	4,941	13,761	500	86.40	-13.60
23	342,355	2,809	3,151	1,103	2,048	1,594	4,745	517	85.96	-14.04
24	287,980	3,556	3,844	1,298	2,545	1,876	5,720	493	83.59	-16.41
25	230,496	99,467	99,697	35,804	63,893	51,743	151,440	466	82.49	-17.51
26	456,729	5,831	6,288	2,098	4,189	3,033	9,320	489	83.18	-16.82
27	683,995	5,926	6,610	2,005	4,605	2,898	9,508	491	81.91	-18.09
28	141,904	959	1,101	322	778	466	1,567	500	82.05	-17.95
29	488,345	5,156	5,644	1,412	4,232	2,041	7,685	456	76.91	-23.09
30	243,705	2,492	2,736	601	2,135	869	3,605	443	74.51	-25.49
31	321,100	2,791	3,113	662	2,450	957	4,070	446	74.44	-25.56
32	162,030	2,196	2,358	506	1,852	732	3,089	431	73.38	-26.62
Totals	17,230,840	428,202	445,433	247,397	201,658	357,537	806,590			
Average Weighted Deviation										14.29

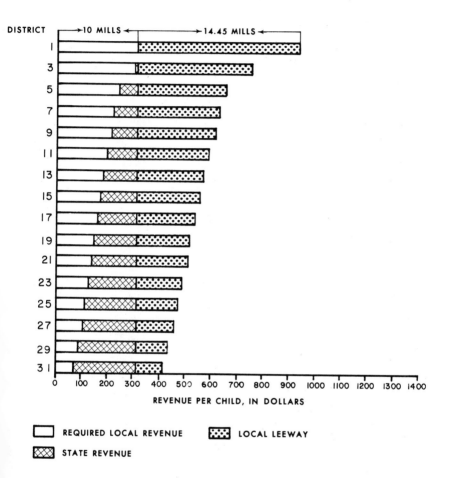

FIGURE 9-17. MODEL VII-B REVENUE PER WEIGHTED
PUPIL (EXCLUDING TRANSPORTATION)

351

TABLE 9-22 — MODEL VIII

TOTAL LOCAL FUNDING OF REVENUE TOTALING $806,571,200 32.6024 LOCAL MILL LEVY AUTHORIZED FOR ALL DISTRICTS

District	Local Rev 32.6024 Mills × Equal Val in Thousands of Dollars	Revenue Per Pupil in WADM in Dollars	Ratio of Dist Revenue to Comp Equal Revenue in %	Deviation From 100% Equalized
1	25,148	1,402	247.73	147.73
2	18,271	1,339	237.23	137.23
3	41,947	992	174.84	74.84
4	150,764	942	163.17	63.17
5	5,903	768	131.40	31.40
6	9,563	723	124.49	24.49
7	14,012	711	119.17	19.17
8	1,695	705	119.15	19.15
9	7,394	685	114.87	14.88
10	116,940	661	114.41	14.41
11	2,549	626	106.81	6.81
12	3,859	626	107.66	7.66
13	3,505	583	99.15	− .85
14	121,120	578	100.59	.59
15	3,978	550	91.06	− 8.94
16	11,367	512	86.34	−13.66
17	49,326	508	87.45	−12.55
18	14,938	496	85.70	−14.30
19	18,109	464	79.01	−20.99
20	9,522	456	77.28	−22.72
21	16,158	455	78.07	−21.93
22	11,146	405	69.98	−30.02
23	3,596	392	65.14	−34.85
24	4,233	365	61.86	−38.14
25	116,728	359	63.58	−36.42
26	6,841	359	61.06	−38.95
27	6,537	338	56.32	−43.68
28	1,051	336	55.06	−44.94
29	4,605	273	46.08	−53.92
30	1,960	241	40.50	−59.50
31	2,159	237	39.50	−60.51
32	1,650	230	39.20	−60.60
Totals	806,571	———	———	———

Average Weighted Deviation — — — — — — — — — 30.98

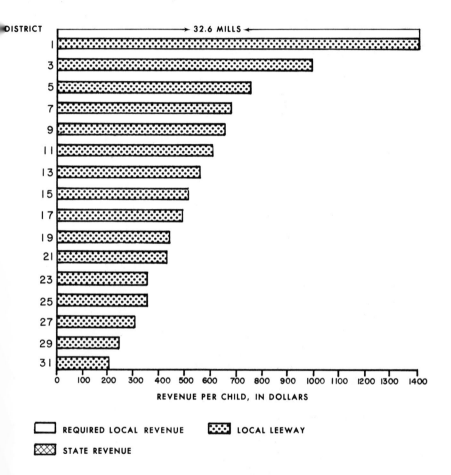

FIGURE 9-18. MODEL VIII REVENUE PER WEIGHTED
PUPIL (EXCLUDING TRANSPORTATION)

REVENUE PER CHILD, IN DOLLARS

REQUIRED LOCAL REVENUE   LOCAL LEEWAY

STATE REVENUE

353

TABLE 9-23

RATING OF MODELS

Models	Average Deviation From Full Equalization	Score On NEFP Scale	Tax Progressivity Score
1. *Flat grant models* with the same total revenue and the same proportion from state and local sources with different methods of apportionment			
MODEL I-A — Flat grant of $500 per pupil in ADM, unweighted pupils, no aid for transportation, local tax rate 12 mills[a]	15.42	4.3	18.10
MODEL I-B — Same total state funds as Model I-A but state funds are distributed on the basis of weighted pupils, and need for transportation and same local funds as Model I-A.	11.40	5.1	18.10
2. *Equalization models* with the same total state funds and same total local funds as Model I-A			
MODEL II-A — Strayer-Haig equalization formula, unweighted pupils, transportation allotment, 5 mills required local effort, 7 mills local leeway	11.63	5.2	18.10
MODEL II-B — Same as Model I-A except pupils are weighted	6.65	6.3	18.10
MODEL II-C — Same as Model II-B except required local effort is 10 mills and local leeway 2 mills	1.90	7.6	18.10
MODEL II-D — Complete equalization, same as Model II-A except required local effort is 12 mills and there is no local leeway	0.	8.4	18.10

TABLE 9-23 — RATING OF MODELS (Cont.)

Models		Average Deviation From Full Equalization	Score On NEFP Scale	Tax Progressivity Score
3. *Percentage equalizing formula*				
MODEL III	Compared with Model II-B	6.65	6.3	18.10
4. *Flat Grant* models with the same total revenue as in Model I-A but increasing the proportion of revenues from state sources and decreasing local revenue				
MODEL IV-A	Apportionment method the same as Model I-B, but limit local revenue to 7 mills and increase state appropriation the equivalent of 5 mills	6.65	6.4	19.03
MODEL IV-B	Same as IV-A but limit local revenues to 4 mills and increase state appropriation the equivalent of 8 mills	3.80	7.2	19.69
MODEL IV-C	Complete equalization, apportionment method same as IV-A except no local millage and state appropriation increased the equivalent of 15 mills	0.	8.4	20.49
5. *Equalization models* with the same total revenue as Model I-A but increasing the proportion of revenue from state sources and decreasing local revenue				
MODEL V-A	Apportionment according to method of II-B, 7 mill limit on local taxes, 4 mill required effort, 3 mill leeway increase state appropriation the equivalent of 5 mills	2.85	7.1	19.03

TABLE 9-23 — RATING OF MODELS (Cont.)

Models		Average Deviation From Full Equalization	Score On NEFP Scale	Tax Progressivity Score
MODEL V-B	Same as V-A except 4 mill limit on local taxes, 2 mill required effort, 2 mill local leeway and increase state funds the equivalent of 8 mills	1.90	7.5	19.69
MODEL V-C	Complete equalization, same as V-A except no local taxes and state appropriation increased the equivlent of 12 mills	0.	8.4	20.49

6. *Flat grant* models with the same total revenue as I-A but increasing the proportion of revenue from local sources and decreasing state revenue

MODEL VI-A	Apportionment method the same as I-B, 50% of revenue from state resources and 50% local revenue, local levy 16.3 mills	15.48	4.1	17.25
MODEL VI-B	Same as VI-A except state revenue 25%, local revenue 75% and local tax rate 24.452 mills	23.23	2.4	15.62

7. *Equalization models* with the same total revenue as I-A but increasing the revenue from local sources and decreasing state revenue

MODEL VII-A	50% of revenue from state sources, 50% from local sources, apportionment according to method II-B, except total local millage of 16.3 mills, 11 mills required effort and local leeway of 5.3 mills	5.03	7.2	17.25

TABLE 9-23 — RATING OF MODELS (Cont.)

Models	Average Deviation From Full Equalization	Score On NEFP Scale	Tax Progressivity Score
MODEL VII-B Same as VII-A except state revenue 25%, local revenue 75%, local millage 24.452, required local effort of 10 mills and local leeway of 14.452 mills	14.29	5.1	15.62
8. *Complete local support* model			
MODEL VIII Same total revenue as Model I-A, all local revenue, local tax rate of 32.6024 mills	30.98	1.0	14.00

ᵃIn all of these models, the assumption is made that all districts levy the legal maximum tax rate because that rate represents the local revenue potential.

The Incentive Grant Model

As pointed out above, an incentive grant can be added to the percentage equalizing or state aid ratio model and the Strayer-Haig model. It is difficult to examine the impact of the incentive grant model by all of the same methods used to examine the other models presented above. However, it is possible to compare an incentive grant model with an equalization model with a fixed level foundation program by graphical methods if assumptions are made with respect to variations among districts in local tax effort.

The incentive grant model is compared with Equalization Model II-C below. Table 9-24 shows the revenue per weighted pupil in average daily membership (excluding transportation) from: (a) the required local levy, (b) the state and (c) from local leeway taxes for Model II-C. The data are shown only for one-half of the districts in the prototype state, randomly selected in order of wealth in order to simplify the chart developed from this table. Data for transportation are also excluded in order to simplify the two models, the assumption being made that the allowable costs of transportation would be funded by the state in both models.

TABLE 9-24

REVENUE PER WEIGHTED PUPIL IN ADM FROM REQUIRED LOCAL EFFORT,
FROM THE STATE AND FROM LOCAL LEEWAY LEVY UNDER MODEL II-C,
TABLE 9-9 (EXCLUDING REVENUE FOR TRANSPORTATION) FOR
SAMPLE DISTRICTS FROM THE PROTOTYPE STATE

District	Revenue Per Weighted Pupil From Required Local Effort[a]	Revenue Per Weighted Pupil From The State[b]	Revenue Per Pupil From Local Leeway Taxes[c]	Total Revenue Per Pupil[d]
Col. 1	Col. 2	Col. 3	Col. 4	Col. 5
1	430.	99.	86.	615.
3	304.	225.	61.	590.
5	236.	293.	47.	576.
7	218.	311.	44.	573.
9	210.	319.	42.	571.
11	192.	337.	38.	567.
13	179.	350.	36.	565.
15	169.	360.	34.	563.
17	156.	373.	31.	560.
19	142.	388.	28.	558.
21	140.	390.	28.	558.
23	120.	409.	24.	553.
25	110.	419.	22.	551.
27	104.	425.	21.	550.
29	84.	445.	17.	546.
31	73.	456.	15.	544.

[a]Column 5 of Table 9-9 ÷ Column 3 of Table 9-4.

[b]Column 6 of Table 9-9 — Column 2 of Table 9-9 ÷ Column 3 of Table 9-4.

[c]Column 7 of Table 9-9 ÷ Column 3 of Table 9-4.

[d]The sum of Columns 2 + 3 + 4 of Table 9-24.

Table 9-25 shows the computation of the funds available to the same selected sixteen districts under an incentive grant formula with the following assumptions:

1. The same weighted pupils are used in the incentive grant model as in Model II-C.

2. A mandated minimum levy of 10 mills is required for the incentive grant model and districts have the option of levying up to 17 mills.

3. The same percentage of state funds for the district of average wealth is provided for in the incentive grant formula as in Model II-C for the same mandated local effort.

4. The sixteen districts levy the tax rates indicated.

Table 9-26 shows the revenue per weighted pupil in average daily membership for the sixteen districts from: (1) local taxes and (2) the state for the incentive grant model.

358

Table 9-25

THE PERCENTAGE EQUALIZING OR STATE AID RATIO MODEL FOR SELECTED
DISTRICTS FROM THE PROTOTYPE STATE WITH THE PERCENT OF STATE AID
PROVIDED FOR THE DISTRICT OF AVERAGE WEALTH EQUIVALENT TO THAT
PROVIDED IN MODEL II-C (EXCLUDING REVENUE FOR TRANSPORTATION)

District	Number of Mills of Local Taxes Levied	Local Tax Revenue[a]	State Aid Ratio[b]	State Appropriation[c]	Total Revenue[d]
Col. 1	Col. 2	Col. 3	Col. 4	Col. 5	Col. 6
1	12	9,256,347.	.2301–1	2,129,885.	11,386,232.
3	17	21,872,591.	.7383–1	16,148,534.	38,021,125.
5	15	2,716,048.	1.2446–1	3,380,393.	6,096,441.
7	14	6,017,066.	1.4226–1	8,583,946.	14,601,012.
9	16	3,628,637.	1.5177–1	5,507,182.	9,135,819.
11	16	1,251,148.	1.7537–1	2,194,138.	3,445,286.
13	13	1,397,720.	1.9594–1	2,738,693.	4,136,413.
15	14	1,708,349.	2.1383–1	3,652,963.	5,361,312.
17	17	25,720,337.	2.3922–1	61,528,190.	87,248,527.
19	12	6,665,308.	2.7191–1	18,123,639.	24,788,947.
21	15	7,434,142.	2.7906–1	20,745,717.	28,179,859.
23	13	1,434,003.	3.3997–1	4,875,180.	6,309,183.
25	17	60,866,171.	3.8001–1	231,297,536.	292,163,707.
27	14	2,807,209.	4.1065–1	11,527,804.	14,335,013.
29	15	2,118,538.	5.3077–1	11,244,564.	13,363,102.
31	12	794,627.	6.2836–1	4,993,118.	5,787,745.

[a]Column 2 of Table 9-26 × Column 4 of Table 9-4.
[b]Column 6 of Table 9-9 — Column 2 of Table 9-9 ÷ Column 5 of
Table 9-9. Use decimals to 4 places.
[c]Column 3 of Table 9-25 × Column 4 of Table 9-25.
[d]The sum of Columns 3 and 5 of Table 9-25.

Figure 10-5 shows the data for Model II-C and Figure 10-19
for the incentive grant model. The following conclusions can be
drawn from a comparison of these two charts:

1. The financial equalization of educational opportunity is
   disequalized by the incentive grant model as compared
   with Model II-C because under the incentive grant model,
   the level of the program guaranteed by the state in a district depends upon its local tax effort rather than variations in educational need as compared with other districts.
2. Both local tax revenue and state appropriations are increased under the incentive grant model.

The incentive grant model was developed some years ago primarily to stimulate innovation and the improvement of the quality of education. It had been observed in some states that there
was a tendency for the public to become satisfied with a fixed

359

TABLE 9-26

REVENUE PER WEIGHTED PUPIL UNDER THE INCENTIVE GRANT MODEL FROM
LOCAL SOURCES AND FROM THE STATE FOR SELECTED DISTRICTS FROM
THE PROTOTYPE STATE (EXCLUDING REVENUE FOR TRANSPORTATION)

District	Revenue Per Weighted Pupil From Local Taxes[a]	Revenue Per Weighted Pupil From the State[b]	Total Revenue Per Weighted Pupil[c]
Col. 1	Col. 2	Col. 3	Col. 4
1	516.	119.	635.
3	517.	382.	899.
5	354.	440.	794.
7	305.	436.	741.
9	336.	510.	846.
11	307.	539.	846.
13	232.	455.	687.
15	236.	505.	741.
17	265.	634.	899.
19	171.	464.	635.
21	210.	584.	794.
23	156.	531.	687.
25	187.	712.	899.
27	145.	596.	741.
29	126.	668.	794.
31	87.	548.	635.

[a]Column 3 of Table 9-25 ÷ Column 3 of Table 9-4.
[b]Column 5 of Table 9-26 ÷ Column 3 of Table 9-6.
[c]Total of Column 3 and 3 of Table 9-26.

level foundation program and it was difficult to change the level
of the program. It was theorized that if the state rewarded increases in local effort by state grants that this would stimulate
an increased level of school financing. This policy, of course, establishes various foundation program levels within a state depending upon the level of local effort. The incentive grant idea
was generally supported by most of the experts on school finance
including some of the researchers for the National Educational
Finance Project. However, experience with this model and evidence presented in Figures 9-5 and 9-19 raise some serious
questions concerning the desirability of the incentive grant
model. Following are some of the objections to this model:

1. It tends to disequalize educational opportunity within a
   state.
2. It stimulates an increase in local property taxes for school
   support despite the fact that too high a proportion of the
   school budget is already obtained from property taxes in
   most states.

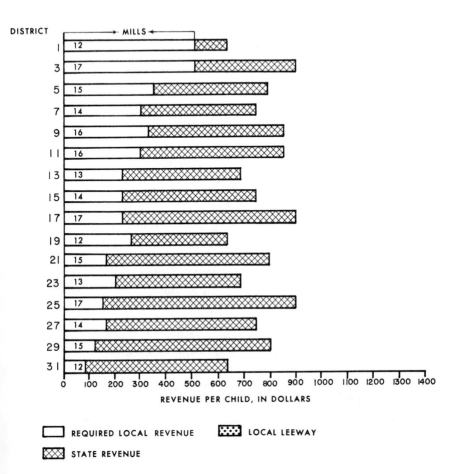

FIGURE 9-19. INCENTIVE GRANT MODEL REVENUE
PER WEIGHTED PUPIL (EXCLUDING TRANSPORTATION)

3. Although under the incentive grant computed by the state aid ratio method, all districts regardless of wealth, could have the same foundation program level for an equivalent level of effort, there is no assurance that the districts which at present have the lowest quality of education will make the extra local effort needed. As a matter of fact, the districts which already have a high level of education of the electorate are the districts that place the highest value on education and those districts are the districts that are most likely to make a high local effort. The schools in such districts usually are not in as great a need of improvement as in the districts with a low educational level of the electorate.

4. If no limit is placed on the local taxes for schools which will be matched on the state aid ratio, necessary noneducational functions of local government may be underfinanced in relation to education. This is especially true if the state does not reward local governments for financing local governmental functions. To base the allocation of state funds on the basis of "the more you spend locally, the more you get from the state" seems irrational because it may cause a misallocation of the priorities needed for various governmental functions.

Although the incentive grant model has some desirable purposes, it certainly has some undesirable side effects. It seems that better methods of stimulating innovation and change in the educational program could be developed than the incentive model. For example, the state could provide in its foundation program allotments to school systems for research and development and program improvement which would constitute a more desirable type of incentive. Although adequate financing is necessary for educational improvement, factors other than money such as state and local leadership, long range planning, evaluation of alternative means for achieving desired educational goals, improved district organization, improved internal organization of districts, and other means can be used to improve the quality of education. It is beyond the scope of this volume to discuss these other means. Suffice it to say that it would seem a better policy for improvement of the educational program to utilize factors aimed directly at improvement of the educational program rather than a factor aimed directly at increasing local property taxes for schools. It is true that local property taxes for schools are negligible in some states. In such states it would seem to be better policy for the state to directly mandate the needed increase in local property taxes for schools than to use the carrot approach.

Negotiated Budgets

It has been suggested that the variation among the districts of a state in educational needs and unit costs are so great that no state formula of apportionment could be developed that would adequately reflect those variations and therefore that each district should negotiate its budget of state funds with a state agency. This is hardly a model. Even if this plan were instituted, the state agency would have to use allocation guidelines similar to a formula in negotiating the budget for a school district or the agency would be subjected to intolerable political pressures. In any event the negotiated budget would give entirely too much power to a state agency. The research conducted by the National Educational Finance Project shows that it is possible to develop reasonably equitable formulas for the allocation of state funds. Therefore, there is no need to risk the many dangers of negotiating budgets.

State Aid for Non-Public Schools[3]

The National Educational Finance Project did no research on finance models providing state aid for non-public schools for the following reasons:

1. The Project staff considered state aid to non-public schools a political problem rather than a financial problem. If all private schools in the United States were abolished and absorbed in the public schools, it is estimated that school costs would be increased nationally only approximately 10 percent. This is a relatively small increase compared with an increase of 152 percent in public school expenditures between 1960 and 1970. It is true the increase would not be uniform throughout the United States. However, the greatest concentrations of pupils in private schools are generally found in the states of greatest wealth. Those states should be able to finance those extra

363

costs. It is true that districts within a state vary greatly in the percent of pupils enrolled in non-public schools in the states that have a high percent of pupils enrolled in non-public schools. If there is a wholesale closing of non-public schools in those districts (as has been feared by some) those districts would have critical housing problems. In such states, the state legislature should provide special capital outlay assistance to the districts having a critical housing shortage due to the closing of non-public schools. This special capital outlay aid could be used either to construct new facilities or to purchase suitable facilities from non-public school authorities who no longer need the facilities if they desire to sell them. It would also be sound policy to provide special federal aid on a temporary basis for this purpose. It is not being suggested that there should be wholesale closing of non-public schools, but if it does occur in any school district, financial provisions should be made for an orderly transfer of non-public school pupils to public schools without unduly burdening that district. When the students become public school students, the districts having an influx of non-public school pupils will receive additional state funds for operating purposes on a continuing basis.

2. The United States Supreme Court in June, 1971 ruled that it was unconstitutional to provide tax funds for the direct support of parochial schools. Approximately 90 percent of all of the pupils enrolled in non-public schools are enrolled in parochial schools. Any finance model which provided general aid for parochial schools would be unconstitutional. Therefore, it would be futile to develop such a model.

Municipal Overburden

It has been suggested by some that the financial ability of large urban districts as measured by the equalized value of property be reduced appropriately in the state's apportionment formula because of the extra local tax burdens those cities are required to bear. There is no doubt that large core cities have these extra costs as compared with many suburban and rural areas. However, the costs of those cities for public safety, welfare, sewage disposal, control of air and water pollution, trans-

364

portation and other services are so great that they cannot be substantially met by manipulations of the school apportionment formula. The cities should be provided direct financial aid in accordance with these needs for municipal services and their relative financial ability. Both the federal and state governments should contribute financial aid to the cities for this purpose.

Core cities as a rule have a higher percent of high cost pupils than surrounding suburban districts. It has already been recommended in this chapter, that pupils should be weighted appropriately in order to provide for the extra costs of culturally disadvantaged pupils.

These provisions, if implemented, would solve the problem of municipal overburden without inserting special provisions in the school apportionment formula for that purpose.

Measures of Local Effort

The measures of local effort in proportion to ability in the equalization models examined in this chapter are based upon millage levies on the equalized value of property because 98 percent of all local school tax revenue is derived from property taxes. It is true that some school boards have the authority to levy a limited amount of local property taxes. The local taxpaying ability of school districts in reality is not their theoretical taxpaying ability, but rather a measure of their accessibility to local tax revenue. If a district only has the authority to levy property taxes then its local taxpaying ability (or effort to support schools) should be measured only in terms of the equalized value of the taxable property in that district. However, if a district has the power to levy local nonproperty taxes, such as payroll taxes, sales taxes, utility taxes, etc., then the yield of such local nonproperty taxes can justly be incorporated in the measure of the taxpaying ability of that district. Since local nonproperty taxes for schools are unimportant in most states, no measures of local taxpaying ability were examined which incorporated ability to pay nonproperty taxes. As pointed out in Chapter 6 of Volume 4 of the National Educational Finance Project entitled *Status and Impact of Educational Finance Programs*, supporting schools by local nonproperty taxes disequalizes school financial support more than local property taxes. The state can levy and collect practically all important types of nonproperty taxes more efficiently than local governments. Since the use of local non-property taxes for school support increases inequalities in school support and promotes inefficiency in tax administration, it does not seem wise policy to encourage this practice.

SUMMARY OF CONCLUSIONS DERIVED FROM THE MODELS TESTED

Following are some conclusions that can be derived from the analyses of the alternative finance models presented in this chapter:

1. State funds distributed by any model tested provide for some financial equalization but some finance models provide more equalization than others. Even the flat grant model provides for some equalization despite the fact that under this model each district, regardless of wealth or necessary variations in unit costs, receives the same amount of state money per pupil or other unit. This is due to the fact that the less wealthy districts receive more state aid per pupil than the revenue per pupil they contribute to the state treasury.

2. The flat grant model by which state funds are apportioned on the basis of a flat amount per pupil unit or other unit which does not take into consideration necessary variations in unit costs or variations in wealth per unit of need of local districts provides the least financial equalization for a given amount of state aid of any of the state-local support models tested.

3. The flat grant model under which necessary cost variations per unit of need are provided for but variations in the per pupil wealth of local districts are ignored provides for more equalization than the flat grant model described in 2 above. But it does not equalize financial resources as well as the equalization models providing for cost differentials and variations in wealth.

4. Equalization models under which necessary unit cost differentials are provided for in computing the cost of the educational program equalized and which take into consideration differences in the wealth of local school districts in computing state funds needed by a district are the most

366

efficient models examined for equalizing financial resources in states which use a state-local revenue model for financing schools.

5. In equalization models the greater the local effort required in proportion to the legal limit of local taxes for schools, the greater the equalization.

6. In equalization models the greater the local tax leeway above the required local tax effort required for the support of the foundation program, the less the equalization.

7. Complete equalization is attained only under full state funding or under an equalization model which requires school districts to contribute the full legal limit of local taxes to the cost of the foundation program.

8. The higher the percent of school revenues provided by the state, the greater the equalization of financial resources under both flat grant and equalization models but there is always more equalization under an equalization model than a flat grant model for any given amount of state funds apportioned.

9. As full state funding is approached (100 percent of school revenue provided by the state) the difference between the equalizing potential of flat grant models and equalization models begins to disappear, assuming that cost differentials are provided for under each model. For example, with 90 percent or more state funding of schools, the differences between flat grant models and equalization models in equalizing financial resources would not be significant but the equalization models would always be slightly superior until full state funding is reached.

10. As the percent of local revenue is increased, the possibility of equalizing financial resources decreases.

11. A complete local support model provides for no equalization whatsoever. In the prototype state under this model, the least wealthy district would have only 1/6 of the resources per pupil available in the most wealthy district.

12. The higher the percent of state funds provided, in relation to local revenue, the greater the progressivity of the tax structure for school support.

13. The higher the percent of federal funds provided in relation to state and local revenues the greater the progres-

sivity of the tax structure for school support. This is due to the fact that federal taxes are on the average more progressive than state taxes and state taxes more progressive than local taxes.

14. Many states can increase the progressivity of state taxes by increasing the proportion of state revenue obtained from relatively progressive taxes.

Which school finance model is the best model? That depends entirely on the values and goals of those making decisions on school fiscal policies. Following are some options:

1. If one believes that educational opportunities should be substantially equalized financially among the districts of a state, but that districts should be left with some local tax leeway for enrichment of the foundation program, an equalization model is the best model. However, the higher the priority one gives to equalization, the more he will prefer the equalization model that provides the most equalization.

2. If one believes that educational opportunities should be completely equalized financially, among the districts of a state, the complete state support model is the preferred model. If the decision of the Supreme Court of California in August, 1971 is upheld by the United States Supreme Court, complete state and federal support of the public schools or complete equalization of local ability by a Strayer-Haig model will be the only legal alternatives. The California Supreme Court ruled that the use of local property taxes to finance schools violated the 14th Amendment to the federal constitution.

3. If one believes that all children regardless of variations in ability, talent, health, physical condition, cultural background, or other conditions which cause variations in educational needs, have a right to the kind of education that meets their individual needs, he will select school finance models which incorporate the programs needed and which provide for necessary cost differentials per unit of need.

4. If one believes that educational opportunity should be substantially equalized among the states he will support a revenue model which provides a substantial percent of

368

school revenue in general federal aid apportioned in such a manner as to tend to equalize educational opportunities among the states.

5. If one believes that the taxes for the support of the public schools should be relatively progressive rather than regressive, he will prefer revenue models which provide a high percent of school revenue from federal and state sources.

6. If one believes that publicly financed education should tend to remove the barriers between caste and class and provide social mobility, he will oppose any plan of school financing which promotes the segregation of pupils by wealth, race, religion or social class.

7. If one believes that all essential functions of state and local government should be equitably financed in relation to each other, he will oppose any finance model for any function of government, including education, under which either federal or state funds are allocated to local governments on the basis of "the more you spend locally, the more you get from the central government" rather than on the basis of need.

8. If one believes that the educational output per dollar of investment in education should be maximized, he will support finance models that will promote efficient district organization and efficient organizations of school centers within districts.

9. If one believes in a federal system of government, he will support finance models which will not require a decision governing public education to be made at the federal level when it can be made efficiently at the state level, and will not require a decision to be made at the state level when it can be made efficiently at the local level, regardless of the percent of revenue provided by each level of government.

10. If one believes that education is essential to the successful operation of a democratic form of government in a free enterprise society and if he believes that education is essential to the economic growth of the nation and to the fulfillment of the legitimate aspirations of all persons in our society, he will support revenue models sufficiently financed to meet educational needs adequately.

FOOTNOTES

1. It should not be assumed that the National Educational Finance Project is recommending that 1,800 pupils is the most desirable minimum size of school district. Actually, maximum economy of scale cannot be reached until the minimum size of school district is made much larger. The minimum size of 1,800 was selected because it should be reasonably attainable in all states and because inefficiencies of scale increase rapidly as districts fall below 1,800 in size.

2. Adapted from Edgar L. Morphet and David L. Jesser, eds. *Emerging Designs for Education*, Denver, Col.: Designing Education for the Future, 1968. P. 227. (Republished by Citation Press, Scholastic Magazine, New York, N. Y.)

3. The so-called "voucher plan" was not considered because its constitutionality is in doubt at this writing. Furthermore, if the law prohibited the redeeming of the vouchers by parochial schools and also by private schools which enrolled a lower percent of blacks than the percent of blacks enrolled in public schools of the district in which the private school was located, there would probably be few advocates of the voucher plan.

CHAPTER 10

Historical Development of Federal
Aid Programs

One of the most persistent problems in American education has been determining the role of the federal government in education. What role, for example, should the federal government play in funding, organizing, and improving education? From the beginning of our country the role of the federal government has never been clear, for education began as a local responsibility and concern and was, therefore, embodied as a state responsibility. Only recently have we begun to explore the potential role of the federal government in influencing American education. It is hoped that this chapter will be able to highlight some of the questions and issues in this area of social and public policy.

Today, we find many writers who are concerned essentially with the economics of education, pointing up the importance of education not only as a cost, but also as an investment. We no longer justify education on individual and cultural grounds alone, but have become aware of education as a basis for economic, political, social, and in fact, international development.

One of the fastest growing aspects of our economy is the Knowledge Industry. Writers have estimated that half of the total income of the United States in 1985 will be derived from the Knowledge Industry. Machlup defines knowledge in "The

371

Production and Distribution of Knowledge in the United States"[1] as "anything somebody knows." Thus, education is clearly included, as is research development, printing and publishing, the theater, films, television, telephone, and the telegraph. Machlup defines education, furthermore, as "the business of retailing old knowledge and inculcating the habit of acquiring further knowledge." He points out that the education enterprise has quadrupled since 1930 and accounts for approximately 45% of the so-called Knowledge Industry. He corroborates the increased importance of education, citing the fact that the average member of the work force in 1960 had spent nearly twice as many days in school as a similar worker in 1910.

We can conclude that education is not only big business, but is intimately involved in our economic system and in our total society. Matters concerning education, therefore, literally concern the whole nation. In this chapter we will focus on determining (1) the background of the federal government's present involvement in education and (2) the arguments pro and con regarding the government's involvement in education.

BACKGROUND

It is generally conceded that public education began in this country with the enactment of the Massachusetts Bay Laws of 1642 and 1647. These acts were an attempt to educate people sufficiently to enable them to read the Bible. These laws exemplify an early use of education to serve societal aims, for it was the concern of seventeenth century society that the Old Deluder, Satan, be kept from corrupting the minds and the hearts of the good New England men.

Ordinances of 1785 and 1787

One of the first examples of the government's direct involvement in education in pre-federal days is the Ordinance of 1785. The Survey Ordinance of 1785 reserved section 16 in every township to be used for the endowment of schools within the township. These ordinances also serve as one of the few examples of *general* types of federal aid to education as opposed to the *categorical* type.

One of the few statements of government policy pertaining

372

to education is stated in the Northwest Ordinance of 1787, "Religion, morality, and knowledge being necessary to good government and the happiness of mankind, schools and the means of education shall forever be encouraged." There remains some doubt whether the primary purpose of this ordinance was to aid education, for a prime objective was also obviously that of settling the great land that was available at the time. Daniel Webster, however, in discussing the Northwest Ordinance of 1787, clearly states, "It set forth and declared it to be a high and binding duty of government to support schools and the means of education."

The Morrill Act

In 1862, President Lincoln signed the Morrill Act. This act, seen by some authorities as one of the first attempts by the federal government to establish policy in regard to education, provided 30,000 acres per Congressman for the support of an institution of higher education. Part of the concern of Congress in passing this act was to provide for a college which would improve knowledge in agriculture and the mechanical arts. Presently, the colleges and universities established under this act now include 68 institutions with an enrollment of approximately 20% of all undergraduates.

Office of Education

President Andrew Johnson, in 1867, provided for a department of education with Henry Barnard as its first commissioner. At one time the Department of Education was in the Interior Department. In 1930, however, it was placed under the administration of the Federal Security Agency, and in 1953, it became part of the Department of Health, Education, and Welfare where it resides at the present time. In the early days, the U.S. Office of Education acted chiefly as a collection agency, collecting statistics and information about education and publishing such statistics. In recent years, however, the United States Office of Education has taken on additional duties relating to the administration of increased federal funds for education and also increased is emphasis on leadership and encouragement of innovation and research in education.

Another way of looking at the change taking place in the United States Office of Education is to compare the size of the

Office for the fiscal year of 1956 and that of 1970. In 1956 the Office had 555 employees and a budget of $166.3 million, while fourteen years later, in 1970, it had 2,900 full time employees, plus 500 part-time employees, and its budget was $3.6 billion.[2]

Smith-Hughes Act

The Smith-Hughes Act had as its major purpose the fostering of vocational education and home economics for high school students. Historically, the Smith-Hughes Act is one of the first examples of federal participation in education below the college and university level. Passed in 1917, the act provided for the salaries of teachers and supervisors of agricultural activities and salaries of teachers of certain trades, home economics, and industrial subjects. It also provided aid for teacher trainees in these subject areas and supplied additional monies for the administration of the bill.

Lanham Act and Impact Laws

The Lanham Act, passed in 1941, was aimed at equalizing the tax load through federal payments that were, in effect, "in lieu of taxes." During the Second World War many towns and school districts were overwhelmed by influxes of people employed by defense industries and military establishments. The act made monies available to school districts for buildings and school services, depending upon the number of individuals employed on federal properties.

Although this act was little noted at the time, it has proved to be one of the most politically popular of the federal measures to aid education. During the Korean War the so-called Impact Laws, Public Laws 815 and 874, were enacted. These laws were essentially the same type of law as the Lanham Act of 1941, for the idea was that the federal government had a responsibility to help school districts to care for increased population due to federal activity. It should also be clarified that, since the federal government pays no local taxes, these monies were meant to redress the balance.

The Impact Laws, passed originally in 1950, are still in effect and are very popular with the school administrators, as well as with Congress. The executive branch of the government has made several attempts to reduce the Impact Laws, but even such

374

a staunch opponent of federal aid to education as Senator Barry Goldwater has supported the Impact Laws. Public Law 874, part of this Impact group, is especially significant for it represents the first time that the federal government granted funds to school districts for general operating costs; that is, the grants made can be used for any aspect of the education program. Public Law 815 provides monies essentially for school construction.

National Defense Education Act

The National Defense Education Act, known by the acronym, NDEA, was passed in 1958, a direct response on the part of Congress to Soviet space successes. This reaction resulted in a major re-evaluation of our school system. NDEA, aimed at stimulating and strengthening education in science, foreign languages, and mathematics, consisted of ten titles. Below is a listing of these titles which should provide some conception of the scope of the act.

I. General Provisions—Purpose and Definition.
II. Loans To Students in Higher Education.
III. Financial Assistance For Strengthening Science, Mathematics, and Modern Foreign Language Instruction.
IV. National Defense Fellowships.
V. Guidance, Counseling, and Testing; Identification and Encouragement of Able Students; Counseling and Guidance Training.
VI. Language Development Centers for Research and Studies; Language Institutes.
VII. Research and Experimentation In More Effective Utilization of Television, Radio, Motion Pictures, and Related Media For Educational Purposes.
VIII. Area Vocational Education Programs.
IX. Science Information Service.
X. Improvement of Statistical Services of State Educational Agencies.

Several examples will suffice to note the tremendous impact of NDEA on education. Since its passage, state departments of education have approved more than 200,000 projects for local schools covering the purchase of equipment in science, mathematics, and foreign language.[3] The number of language labs, for example, has increased from 46 in 1938 to nearly 6,000 in 1963.[4] The major criticisms of the original NDEA was that it tended to unbalance the school curriculum with its emphasis on mathematics, science, and the foreign languages. The second criticism pertains to the fact that it aided both private and public institutions. In general, however, the kindest compliment of all is to have an act not only continued, but to have it expanded. In 1963, the act was expanded and amended to include guidance, counseling, and testing programs, and in 1964 it was further expanded to cover almost all areas of the school curriculum.

Higher Education Facilities Act

Sometimes called the Morse-Green Bill after the former Senator and Representative from Oregon, the Higher Education Facilities Act of 1963 states its purpose thus: "To assist the nation's institutions of higher education, to construct needed classrooms, laboratories, and libraries in order to accommodate mounting student enrollments and to meet the demands for skilled technicians and for advanced graduate education."

This Higher Education Act might be called a "bricks and mortar" act, for the major provisions are ones that involve expenditures to schools to encourage construction. The following are the major areas covered by the Higher Education Facilities Act:

(1) Funds to all four year colleges, junior colleges, and technical institutions to build libraries and classrooms for instruction in science, language, and mathematics,

(2) Loans extending over a period of fifty years, carrying an interest of 3 5/8% for all types of classroom construction,

(3) Approximately 50 million dollars to communities for constructing junior and community colleges, and

(4) Finally, funds to establish graduate centers throughout the country.

In making its allocations, priority is given to institutions that are expanding. Matching funds in this bill were required on a two-to-one basis, thus generating a great deal of money for school construction.

One of the issues posed by the passage of this act was its inclusion of church-supported and private schools. However, generally the concern has not been so great for the aiding of private colleges as has been the concern for aiding private and parochial schools at the elementary and secondary levels.

Civil Rights Act

While not directly pertaining to education, the Civil Rights Act passed in 1964 had as one of its major purposes the desegregation of public schools. Several titles, therefore, of the Civil Rights Act directly involve education. For example, Title IV allows the Attorney General to initiate action against school boards that deny equal rights to children. Further, it states, "No person in the United States shall, on the grounds of race, color, or national origin, be excluded from participation in or denied the benefits of, or be subject to discrimination in any program or activity receiving federal financial assistance." The emphasis in the Civil Rights Act, in spite of the strong language of the above portion, remains on voluntary compliance.

Title IX requires the U.S. Office of Education to determine whether, in effect, equality of educational opportunity is being denied any individual. The law further provides a great deal of help to individuals carrying out programs of desegregation. In fact, one of the portions of Title IX provides financial assistance for colleges and universities to conduct institutes that would provide aid to school people facing desegregation problems. Like the Economic Opportunity Act, the Civil Rights Act is not directly an education bill; yet certainly its strong thrust is towards helping educators provide for educational opportunity.

Economic Opportunity Act

This bill, sometimes called the War on Poverty Bill, was passed in 1964 as part of the whole program known as the Johnson Administration's *Great Society*. While not strictly an aid to education or a public schools bill, this bill did carry educational implications.

Title I of the Economic Opportunity Act established the Job Corps to provide training for 40,000 men and women in residential centers throughout the country. These youngsters were of high school age and in all probability were the ones who had dropped out of school. The program essentially was one intended to provide basic literacy skills for youngsters, as well as training in job-related skills. One interesting innovation is that several of the job centers were operated by private industry. For instance, the job center in Northern California was operated by Litton Associates, a diversified electronics company.

Title II covers urban and rural community action programs. Under this proposal the federal government funded up to 90% of the cost of projects in areas such as job training, vocational rehabilitation, health, and welfare. A part of this program provided training courses for basic education and work experience demostration.

A type of domestic peace corps program provided in the Economic Opportunity Act was a program called Volunteers in Service to America (VISTA). These volunteers serve throughout the country helping students and work not only in schools, but on Indian reservations, with migratory workers, and in mental hospitals.

One of the most popular features of this act has been the Head Start Program. This is, of course, directly related to education, particularly the pre-school aspect of education, and has proved to be a very popular method of up-grading the deficient backgrounds of poor youngsters. The only problem so far has been that the children in the programs tend to lose their gain when they enter into the regular school program. The Head Start Program provides for teacher aides, physical exams, and many desirable classroom instructional aids that make for better teaching.

Elementary and Secondary Education Act

Sometimes designated as the centerpiece of the Great Society, the Elementary and Secondary Education Act (ESEA), passed in 1965, is indeed a landmark piece of legislation. Broad in its concept and hope, it directly involves over 90% of the nation's school districts. The purpose of this act can be stated broadly as follows: (1) to strengthen the elementary and secondary education of the educationally disadvantaged child, (2) to provide school libraries, resources, textbooks, and other instructional materials, (3) to fund supplemental education centers, (4) to broaden cooperative research, and finally (5) to strengthen state departments of education.

The purpose of Title I is to provide (through extension of

378

Impact Law 874) assistance to school districts for the education of children of low income families. To qualify for aid, school districts must have students whose family income was less than $2,000 per year. This was raised to $3,000 in 1966. Roughly 90% of the school districts in the country, it is estimated, will be eligible for aid under this criterion. Payments are made on the basis of the average per pupil expenditure in any state. The cost of this program for the first year for this one title was 1.06 billion dollars.

Basically the philosophy behind Title I assumes a very close relationship between lack of educational opportunity and poverty. It has been pointed out, for example, that the ten states with the lowest per capita personal income have draft rejection rates based on mental tests well above the average for all fifty states. Further information tells us that dropout rates are high where income rates are low.

The local school district under the Elementary and Secondary Education Act can use the funds allocated to it for almost any purpose as long as the benefit accrues to the disadvantaged student. State departments have set up bureaus, departments, and offices whose function it is to see that local plans are functional in terms of providing the best possible education for the disadvantaged youngster with the money allocated. The bill also provides, furthermore, that funds can be shared with private and parochial schools if the person benefitting is the disadvantaged child.

Under this act the President is to provide for a National Advisory Council on the education of disadvantaged children. The council reviews the various state and local plans to determine how well the purpose of this act is being carried out by the school districts. Some of the programs that are operated by school districts under Title I of the Elementary and Secondary Education Act include:

Teacher aides.
Classes for talented youngsters.
Pre-school education programs.
Enrichment programs after school, on Saturday mornings, and during the summer.
Special programs for non-English-speaking youngsters.
Provisions for books, clothing, and meals.
School health and psychological services.

Increased guidance services.

In-service education for teachers.

Additional teaching personnel to provide for smaller classes.

Providing new curriculum material for the disadvantaged.

Remedial reading centers.

Remedial language centers.

Day camp programs.

On-the-job training for high school students.

Work experience programs.

Title II of the Elementary and Secondary Education Act provides money for school library resources, textbooks, and other instructional materials. Research has pointed out the relevance of the school library to academic programs in the school. Where there are central libraries, children not only read more, but also have significantly greater achievement records. In spite of this knowledge, however, almost half of the public and non-public elementary schools have no central library. In general, the high schools are better off, but it is estimated that nearly 1/3 of all elementary and secondary school youngsters attend a school without a central library.

The provisions provided under Title II originally amounted to $100 million, which is allotted to the states for the purchase of books, periodicals, documents, magnetic tapes, records, and other printed and published materials. The basis for allotment is the number of students enrolled in both public and non-public elementary and secondary schools within the state. Since materials are to be provided to both public and non-public institutions, the arrangement is usually made that local districts hold Title II materials that are then provided to private schools on a loan basis. Finally, funds are not to be used to substitute for local or state funding, but are to be used rather for improvement of instruction. Each state, of course, will set up its own program in accord with its constitutional and legal requirements. Thus, administration of the program will vary greatly from state to state.

Title III provides for supplemental education centers and services. The difference between the good school and the poor school is frequently that the good school is able to provide special services in math, science, and foreign language, the arts, and music, as well as technical services. Research reveals that approximately 75% of our elementary schools do not have the serv-

380

ices of a guidance counselor, 70% of our secondary schools do not have language laboratories, and in some forty states there are a few high schools that do not have science laboratories.

Under the provisions for Title III, supplemental education centers are set up for three basic purposes: (1) to provide educational services that the community is not able to provide it-self, (2) to up-grade the existing services provided by local educational authorities, and (3) to develop exemplary model programs for the community. The aim of this title is to provide for a great many services to school districts that no one district could provide. Services might include adult education, remedial instruction, special programs for gifted children, provisions for health, as well as language centers, and so forth.

Title IV provides for educational research and training. Many writers have noted the small percentage of the school budget that is devoted to research and development. It is estimated that before the passage of this act in 1965, approximately 1/5 of 1% of the education budget was spent on research and development. (It might be noted, in comparison, that many private industries allocate as much as 10% of their annual expenditures to research and development activities.) The Cooperative Research Act in 1954 provided a stimulus to research in education. Title IV of ESEA amended the Cooperative Research Act and authorized $100 million over the succeeding five years to provide for national and regional research facilities. The major purpose of this program was to develop and test educational ideas, and at the same time disseminate these ideas to the schools that they serve. It is also the purpose of Title IV to involve other groups in research, for instance, artists, historians, and mathematicians, as well as private research organizations.

Title V strengthens state departments of education. It is felt that in order for education to improve, the state departments must play a more significant role. Title V authorized $25 million annually for the improvement and expansion of state department programs. These funds are utilized to improve the effectiveness of the present state departments.

National Foundation of the Arts and the Humanities

In 1965 the President established the National Foundation of the Arts and the Humanities. This foundation, similar in some ways to the National Science Foundation, is an independent agency with two branches. One is a National Endowment for the Arts, while the other is a National Endowment for the Humanities. Each endowment is provided with a council consisting of private citizens who give the endowment advice and guidance.

The National Foundation of the Arts and the Humanities Act allows the chairman of the National Endowment of the Arts to provide a program of grants and aid to groups, or in appropriate cases, to individuals engaged in or concerned with the arts. Thus, persons could be involved in projects of cultural and artistic significance—production of artistic efforts, projects that would encourage and assist artists, workshops to develop the appreciation and enjoyment of the arts by the citizenry, and other projects that might include research, surveys, or general planning in the arts.

The chairman of the National Endowment for the Humanities has similar authorization to promote progress and scholarship in the humanities and to support research that strengthens the research potential in the United States in the humanities. This might be done through grants, loans, or other types of assistance in the form of fellowships to institutions or individuals, to encourage the interchange of information, to foster greater understanding in this area, and to support the publication of scholarly works in the humanities.

This act represents one of the few attempts on the part of the government to aid the arts. It is obviously an attempt to redress the balance somewhat between the two cultures identified by C. P. Snow, science and humanities.

International Education Act

President Johnson recommended to Congress a broad, long-range plan of educational development in the field of international education. In his original message to Congress the President made twenty recommendations—some of which were contained in the International Education Act of 1966 (PL89-698). The most important part of this program is under Title I, which consists of two grant programs. The first authorizes the establishment of centers for advanced international study at the graduate level. Providing national and international centers for research and training, these centers might concentrate on specific geographic areas or they might focus on particular fields or issues.

The second part of Title I creates undergraduate programs of a wide variety. These grants are aimed at helping colleges and universities in planning programs that will improve their undergraduate instruction. Programs created might include training of faculty members in foreign countries, expanding foreign language offerings, visiting programs that encourage foreign teachers to visit institutions, teaching and research, and curriculum development. Congress authorized $40 million for the fiscal year 1968 and $90 million for 1969. This act, very broadly conceived, did not, however, gain the required funding.

Educational Professions Development Act

President Johnson, in 1967, signed into law the Education Professions Development Act with the stated purpose "To coordinate, broaden, and strengthen programs for the training and improvement of the qualifications of educational personnel in order to provide a better foundation for meeting critical needs for such personnel." In order to carry out this mandate, the Act is divided into the following major parts:

Part A has three major operations:

1. A fifteen member National Advisory Council is to be created.

2. The Commissioner of Education is to assess the needs of education at all levels and in all subject areas.

3. The staff of the Bureau of Education Professions Development is to encourage better qualified people to enter the education professions.

Part B has two major parts:

1. Calls for expansion of the Teacher Corps.

2. A new state grant program to attract teachers and teacher aides.

Part C continues graduate programs originally under the Higher Education Act.

Part D expands and extends the NDEA institute programs formerly under Title V-B and XI of the NDEA.

Part E provides grants for inservice and pre-service training for members of institutions of higher education.

383

Part F provides for the training program for vocational educators.

The Education Professions Development Act is an attempt to consolidate all training programs involving educational personnel under one act.

Vocational Education Amendments of 1968

The major purpose of these amendments was to redirect, reorganize, and expand the nation's vocational education effort. One of the major thrusts of this act is to give special attention to the training of individuals who have in the past been ignored. Twenty-five percent of all new funds, and a substantial part of existing funds, must go for education of the disadvantaged. Another example is the requirement that ten percent of all permanent funds must go for the education of handicapped children.

The federal government has been involved in vocational education since the Smith-Hughes Act of 1917, which emphasized primarily the areas of vocational agriculture and home economics. The George-Barden Act of 1946 was an attempt to bring up to date the manpower skills in our nation. More flexibility came into existence with the Vocational Education Act of 1963. The Vocational Education Amendment of 1968 provided even greater flexibility in programs for state and local school districts, something that has not always existed in previous vocational legislation. Further, the 1968 Amendment doubled the authorization for vocational education. Authorizations for the first four years are:

1969	$542,100,000
1970	$857,650,000
1971	$870,150,000
1972	$910,150,000

One must keep in mind that these are authorizations, not appropriations. That is another question requiring its own legislative enactment. However, as one looks at the Vocational Education Amendments of 1968, one must concede that it represents a massive attempt to bring vocational education up to date.

384

Higher Education Amendments of 1968

Like the Education Professions Development Act, the Higher Education Amendments Act of 1968 brings together most, if not all, of the legislation involving higher education into one Act.

The Higher Education Amendment of 1968 extends and improves four education acts, the National Defense Education Act, the Higher Education Facilities Act, the International Education Act, and the Higher Education Act of 1965.

Six new programs were launched with the Higher Education Amendments of 1968:

1. *Networks for Knowledge.* The basic idea is to strengthen smaller colleges by having them cooperate and coordinate their efforts with stronger colleges and universities. This will be done by pooling resources, staff, and information.

2. *Education for Public Service.* The purpose is to provide training for individuals working in the area of public service on the federal, state, or local levels. This authorization will allow colleges and universities to provide appropriate education for those students wishing to enter the public service.

3. *Cooperative Education.* This provision enables colleges and universities to initiate or enlarge their programs of Cooperative Education.

4. *Improvement of Graduate Programs.* This portion of the bill provides for the improvement of graduate programs.

5. *Special Services for Disadvantaged Students.* This is a program to help economically deprived students enter college. It pulls together many of the programs such as Upward Bound, which is transferred from the Office of Economic Opportunity to the Office of Education, and puts them under the rubric of the Higher Education Amendments Act.

6. *Law School Clinical Experience Program.* This section authorized the expenditure of funds to provide for clinical experience in the training of law students.

Summary of Federal Legislation Affecting Education—1777 to 1968

Following is a chronological summary of the principal federal legislation affecting education from 1777 to 1968:

777 Initiation of direct administration of education programs

—the instruction of military personnel, including schooling in mathematics.

1785 Commencement of aid to territories for education by endowment of schools with public lands.

1787 Commencement of endowment of public institutions of higher education with public lands—Northwest Ordinance: "Schools and the means of education shall forever be encouraged."

1802 Establishment of the first federal institution of higher education—Military Academy at West Point.

1804 District of Columbia—federal provision for education begins.

1862 The First Morrill Act—initiated federal policy of aid to states for agricultural and industrial education through land grants for colleges.

1867 Federal Department of Education established by Congress; later the Office of Education.

1874 Introduction of the principle of federal-state matching of funds for education.

1887 Hatch Act—encouraged scientific investigation in agriculture.

1890 The Second Morrill Act—introduction of federal grants of money for college instruction in specified areas of learning.

1914 Smith-Lever Act—matching of funds for agricultural and home economics instruction.

1917 The Smith-Hughes Act—began policy of promoting vocational education below college level through assistance with teachers' salaries.

1918 Rehabilitation training for disabled veterans.

1919 Federal surplus property available to educational institutions.

1920 The National Defense Act of 1920—direct relationship between the federal government and educational institutions.

1920 Smith-Bankhead Act—federal-state cooperation in vocational rehabilitation; education for people disabled in industry.

1933 Federal Emergency Relief Administration—supported educational programs.

1933 Civilian Conservation Corps—provided vocational education.

1935 National Youth Administration—employment for college students.

1935 Bankhead-Jones Act—increased support for land-grant colleges.

1936 Promotion of Inter-American Cultural Relations Convention—international educational exchanges.

1936 George-Deen Act—extended the Smith-Hughs Act.

1937	National Cancer Institute Act—provided fellowship grants.
1941	Lanham Act—provided educational assistance for schools in communities affected by the federal government's activities.
1943	Vocational Rehabilitation Act—aid for disabled veterans.
1944	The Servicemen's Readjustment Act—G.I. Bill, educational aid for veterans.
1944	Surplus Property Act—government surplus given to educational institutions.
1946	National School Lunch—gave funds and food to public and non-public schools; school milk program added in 1954.
1946	George-Barden Act—extended Smith-Hughs Act by increasing appropriation.
1948	Smith-Mundt Act—program of international educational exchanges.
1949	Federal Property and Administrative Services Act—surplus property disposal for educational, health, and civil defense purposes.
1950	The National Science Foundation Act—promoted progress in science through scholarships and fellowships in fields of science.
1950	The Housing Act—low interest rates for loans to institutions of higher learning for building of housing facilities.
1950	Federal Impact Laws (P.L. 815 and P.L. 874)—extended the Lanham Act of 1941; provided assistance to communities affected by activities of the federal government for construction and operation of schools.
1952	National Science Foundation—fellowship program.
1954	Cooperative Research Act—authorized the Office of Education to conduct cooperative research with colleges, universities, and state educational agencies.
1956	Library Services Act—grants for improvement of library facilities.
1958	United States and Union of Soviet Socialist Republics agree to exchange study groups in educational and cultural fields.
1958	The National Defense Education Act—provided for graduate fellowships in science, mathematics, foreign languages, counseling and guidance, educational technology.
1958	Fogarty-McGovern Act—federal grants to train teachers of mentally retarded children.
1961	Area Redevelopment Act—training of persons in redevelopment areas.
1961	Peace Corps Act—supplied teachers and technicians to underdeveloped nations.
1961	Juvenile Delinquency and Youth Offenses Control—study of problem.

1962   Manpower Development and Training Act—up-to-date training for the unemployable.

1963   Health Professions Educational Assistance Act—construction of facilities and student loans.

1963   Mental Retardation Facilities and Community Mental Health Centers Construction Act—training of teachers and demonstration projects.

1963   Higher Education Facilities Act of 1963—grants to all colleges, public and private, for improvement of facilities.

1963   Amendments to the Manpower Development and Training Act—expansion of provisions of law, 1962.

1963   Vocational Education Act of 1963—construction of vocational schools with expanded offerings; extended Impact Laws (1950) and NDEA (1958).

1964   The Civil Rights Act of 1964—desegregation of the schools enforced and assisted.

1964   Juvenile Delinquency and Youth Offenses Control Act Amendment—new programs and special studies.

1964   Economic Opportunity Act of 1964—war on poverty through retraining and remedial education and other opportunities.

1964   Amendments to National Defense Education Act—extended and expanded to include areas of English, reading, history, and geography.

1965   Elementary and Secondary Education Act—federal grants to states for allocation to school districts with low income families.

1965   National Foundation for the Arts and Humanities—foundation to support humanities and the arts through grants.

1965   Higher Education Act of 1965—aid to colleges, students, and teachers.

1966   International Education Act—to provide a strengthening of American educational resources for international studies and research.

1967   Education Professions Development Act—to coordinate, broaden and strengthen programs for the training and the improvement of educational personnel.

1968   Vocational Educational Amendments of 1968—redirect, reorganize and expand vocational education.

1968   Higher Education Amendments of 1968—extended and improved four major education acts and authorized six new programs.

1968   Handicapped Children's Assistance Act—federal effort to help handicapped children at pre-school level.

ARGUMENTS FOR AND AGAINST FEDERAL AID

Some of the historical arguments will be presented in this section. The arguments presented are those generally considered

388

the most cogent and powerful. It is important to review these arguments, not only for their historical importance, but also for their present impact.

Arguments in Opposition to Federal Aid to Education

In this section an analysis will be made of the major arguments presented by those individuals and groups who are opposed to any increase in the federal government's involvement in education.

Equalizing Educational Opportunity. Opponents to federal aid believe that it is impossible to equalize educational opportunity, that the task is far too difficult for any government to carry out. Even if it were possible to equalize educational opportunity, they maintain, they are not sure that it would be for the betterment of education. Equalizing educational opportunity is seen as dragging down the educational standard to a mediocrity that would eliminate the outstanding schools. This attempt, which sounds at first blush as one that would improve schools, would actually be detrimental to our system.

Schools should differ from each other because states, communities, and neighborhoods differ, and in our great pluralistic society, this is seen as a strength of our educational system. It is not possible to equalize education without equalizing our system economically, politically, and socially. It is not possible to equalize education without bringing all of society to a level of conformity that has never existed before and should never exist in a free and open community.

Lack of need. The point is made by the opponents to federal aid that there exists at the present time no need for massive federal aid to education. The need, rather, is to tighten up the present curriculum, to eliminate the frills, and to use existing facilities more efficiently. Thus, through more effective utilization of our facilities we will receive more education for the same amount of money.

The point is also made that there is fiscal ability on the part of states to support good educational programs. The states have the potential for doing the job if they have the will. In fact, state governments are in a better position to finance education than is the federal government. If we want proof of this, all we have to do is look at the classrooms that have been built by the states, and look at the way teachers' salaries have improved. These illustrations should answer the question of whether the states have been doing the job or not. The American Farm Bureau, an active opponent of federal aid, states: "There is massive evidence to demonstrate that we are making real progress at the state and local levels in meeting the educational needs of our nation."[5]

Federal control. One of the strongest arguments used against federal aid to education has been that control will necessarily and inevitably follow any program of federal aid. This is seen as a disaster, for in truth, the last stronghold of states' rights is that of the school. Aid to education is seen as yet another wedge in the overpowering drive of the federal government to seize control of all endeavors and use this wedge to diminish and abolish individual rights.

In aid to education, the purpose is to improve schools. Whenever there is change, there is the possibility of federal control. Why would the federal government spend its money without demanding an educational accounting as well as a fiscal accounting? The National Defense Education Act, while supporting certain areas of the curriculum, particularly in mathematics, science, and foreign language, has in effect unbalanced the curriculum in other areas. This affects not only elementary and secondary levels, but also the college. Increased availability of funds has undoubtedly drawn more able students, effective faculty, and improved equipment toward the sciences. This is cited as an example of what happens when the federal government enters the field of education.

Unconstitutionality. As it has been pointed out, education is not mentioned in the Constitution. The 10th Amendment to the Constitution has had the effect of making education essentially a state responsibility, which might conceivably *prohibit* the federal government's involvement at all. Article X states, "The powers not delegated to the United States by the Constitution, nor prohibited by it to the states, are reserved to the states respectively, or to the people."

Senator Goldwater pointed out in a speech to Congress in 1961, that "No constitutional amendment to extend federal powers or responsibilities into education has ever been considered. If proposed, it would be overwhelmingly rejected."[6]

Cost. The opponents to federal aid to education are vehement in their position that the government, which is already funding war efforts past, present, and future, is in no position to fund our most expensive domestic cost, that of education. They point out that the federal income tax is already as high as it can possibly be and that the property tax, which represents only 13% of the national tax bill, if used more effectively and efficiently, could provide the necessary monies for education.

It is clear, too, that all sources of tax money are the same, that is, they all come from the individual citizen. There really are no tax monies available, therefore, to the federal government that are not also available to the states.

Individual Initiative. Any federal assistance will lessen the sense of local pride and responsibility the people feel for their schools. The federal government will come between the schools and the local community, which is one of the most detrimental things that could ever happen to education. In most areas of our lives we see tremendous increases in centralization, but the schools historically have been close to the people and the people have been close to the schools. This is the best way to insure freedom and equality of education for our children.

Most writers who are opponents to the involvement of the federal government make this point. They feel that the federal government's involvement will weaken the schools because the people will be less willing to make decisions about their schools. They feel that the schools, once out of the hands of the individuals, will get into the hands of the bureaucrats. The purpose of any aid to education should be to help people to help themselves. No aid should involve the taking away of this right through federal interference. It is felt that through federal involvement the responsibility for the local school will disappear.

Historical precedent. It has been pointed out that most education bills have been passed not to aid education or to improve education, but in effect, to aid the federal government. Some recent research has pointed out that the ordinances of 1785 and 1787, often times cited as the beginning of the federal government's involvement in education, were really passed to encourage the settlement of large parcels of land and to develop our country, rather than to aid education. It has been pointed out also that railroads were given much more land than was education.

In more recent times it has been pointed out that our international role, our concern with the space race, and military preparedness, led to the passage of the National Defense Education Act. Even the wording of this bill, it could be pointed out, with national defense coming before education, would indicate the primacy of the concern. The Impact Laws 815 and 874 are, in effect, payment in lieu of taxes and are not meant to aid education. It can be pointed out also that the Morrill Act was really meant to aid agriculture and that the School Lunch Act originally was set up to get rid of surplus food products. In spite of many enactments pertaining to education, the federal government has been basically involved in other issues—settling land, utilizing surplus food products, improving agriculture, and most recently, the space race.

Individual Freedom. One of the most frequent arguments used is that expanding the role of the federal government in education will be another way of losing our political and intellectual freedom. Individuals subscribing to this point of view hold that the family is the basic unit in American society. Although the family has delegated to local government some duties that it was unable to carry out, it has never seen fit to give to the federal government the power over the education of its children.

Some people have recently, with the passage of the Elementary and Secondary Education Act in 1965, become concerned also with this question. Many of them feel that the government has been too vehement in dictating how certain monies should be spent and in setting up regulations, checks, and requirements that must be fulfilled by local school districts before they can obtain the money to which they are entitled.

On the college and university level it can be pointed out that the concern for federal research monies has to some extent upset the delicate balance that previously existed between research and teaching and that this has made the situation of the college student even more intolerable than it was before. The student and the professor are thus directly influenced by bureaucratic decisions in Washington. The college professor's skill is to some extent judged by his facility in obtaining research grants rather than in his skill as a college teacher. Students, too, are influenced in their choice of a profession or in their field of further study by the availability or non-availability of government funds.

392

Arguments in Favor of Federal Aid to Education

A variety of arguments have been presented by individuals and groups that favor a greater role for the federal government in education. In this section are outlined nine of the major arguments made by these individuals and groups.

Local control. Local control represents the first and strongest argument for both the proponents and the opponents of federal aid. Historically our schools have developed as local institutions and there has consistently been great concern on the part of individuals connected with education that education remain a local concern.

This concern is shared, moreover, by the U.S. Office of Education and the great majority of those in both houses of the Congress. There are few individuals, it is argued, who believe that local control of education will be lost if federal aid is received. Since no one really likes or desires federal control of education, there appears to be little reason to fear that this will be an outcome of any federal legislation to aid educational efforts. Experience with federal grants to districts has demonstrated, furthermore, that it is possible to draw up legislation and to administer this legislation without inhibiting local control.

Equalization of Educational Opportunity. Individuals who favor federal aid to education take the position that we must equalize educational opportunity throughout our country, for at the present time, there are sections of our country where youngsters are not receiving an equal opportunity in the field of education. It is stated, furthermore, that it is impossible for some states, due to the large number of children and the lack of wealth, to provide this education. It is only through the efforts of the federal government, therefore, that all youngsters may receive a fair distribution. In the year 1968-69, for example, New York state spent approximately $1,159 per child on education while the state of Mississippi spent only $466 per child.[7]

Failure to provide superior education is not due to the lack of willingness on the part of states, it is pointed out, but rather a lack of fiscal ability. The personal income per child index shows that in 1968 Mississippi had approximately $7,195 behind each child of school age, whereas the state of New York had approximately $17,233. This discrepancy is even further complicated by the fact that the number of school-age children per hundred adults, 21-64 years of age, was 63 in Mississippi, while at the same time, the number of school-age children was only 46 per 100 adults in New York.[8]

National Concern. Another argument favoring greater federal involvement in education is that our nation's welfare is directly affected by what happens in education. This attitude is illustrated most effectively by the national response to Sputnik in 1957, which resulted almost immediately in passage of the National Defense Education Act in 1958, with its concern for subjects vital to national welfare; e.g., mathematics, science, and foreign language. A host of subsequent bills illustrate the national concern for the disadvantaged, for the War on Poverty which led to the Elementary and Secondary Education Act in 1965, which focused on compensatory education for economically deprived students.

Stemming from this position is the argument that our nation as a whole is directly affected by whatever happens in any sector of society. Deficiencies in any sector, for example, education, present a problem for all of society. The many failures in the draft test is only one instance of an educational deficiency that affects national welfare and has caused concern regarding the efficacy of education. For this reason, education is seen as more than a local responsibility and a state function. It is recognized as a national concern.

Need. The need for an improved educational system is one of the strongest arguments made by the proponents of increased federal aid. Not only is need stated in terms of housing the existing group of students and improving teachers' salaries, but stress is also placed on the need to provide a generally improved educational system for all youngsters. Since 1957, and Sputnik, our educational system has seen a greater and greater concern for excellence as we develop curricular innovation, new materials, and better trained teachers to improve our educational system across the board.

It is felt that the only way to insure this improvement in education and the only way to assure that it is carried out in all fifty states is for the federal government to be an innovative agent. The federal government has become involved, therefore, in improving teacher education, supervision, curriculum, and materials of instruction. Proponents of federal involvement in education are not looking for mere improvement of minimum

394

standards in some locales, but are aiming at raising the level of the total educational program.

The Tax Base. According to persons advocating federal participation in education, only the federal government has a tax base sufficiently broad to pay for a broad program of education. It is pointed out, for example, that the federal government collects approximately 2/3 of the taxes in this country, yet it pays only a little over 6% of the cost of education.

It is noted, furthermore, that money for education comes primarily from the local property tax, a very inflexible, regressive type of tax. Property is no longer considered the index of wealth that it was when this country was chiefly rural. A truer index, it is maintained, is that of income, which is tapped effectively and efficiently by the national government. Approximately 90% of taxes on personal and corporate income are paid to the national government.

Mobility of the People. Closely related to the national concern for education is the fact that we are one of the most mobile people ever to exist on this earth. It is estimated that each year 40 million people change their addresses and approximately 1 million youngsters cross state lines. Each month, for example, California receives enough new people to create a town of 30,000. We have both mass migration from the south to the north, as well as movement from smaller communities to the megalopolis.[9]

Thus, it can be seen that the individual child, who through no fault of his own, receives a poor education, is hampered. In moving to another state, he also penalizes that state for something with which it had nothing to do. From these observations it can be quickly reasoned that, since mobility is a fact in our society, place of residence should not be allowed to have the deleterious effect that it might on a person's future. It is the rare individual who is born, reared, educated, works, lives, and retires in the same community. Furthermore, most of the people do not spend their entire lives even in one state. Our national mobility, therefore, indicates the need for a strong minimum education program in every state.

Acceptance. From all information available, it appears that the majority of people in our society are in favor of federal aid to education. In 1960 Gallup found that approximately 65% of the American voters favored federal aid to school construction. The Lou Harris Poll in 1963 found that 70% of the voters favored federal aid to education.[10] As might be expected, a high percentage of teachers favored federal aid. *Phi Delta Kappan* reported that 85% of its membership list favored federal aid to education. The Los Angeles Teachers' Association found that 80% of its teachers were in favor.[11]

Efficiency of the Federal Government. Earlier the point was made that the federal government not only collects a high percentage of the taxes in this country, but that it also collects them very efficiently, by and large, more efficiently than do state and local agencies. The federal government is efficient not only in collection of funds, moreover, but in the dispersing of these same funds. The "freight bill" that is sometimes attributed to monies going to the federal government and returning to the local district, furthermore, has not proved to be large. For instance, one of the Hoover commissions found that administrative overhead for the school lunch program was only 1.7% of the total cost and for such school legislation as Public Law 874 and Public Law 815, the overhead was under .9%, very economical rates for administrative costs.[12]

History. Historically, there is nothing new or unusual about federal involvement in education. In 1785, Congress began passing federal laws involving education and has since that time passed approximately 200 laws. Edith Green, Representative from Oregon, stated that the issue of federal involvement in education was decided over 100 years ago and that presently we have at least 42 federal agencies providing aid to education in the amount of over two billion dollars a year.[13] We have had federal aid and help for education since 1785, and it appears that we are no closer to federal control of our schools now than we were in the 18th century.

The Constitution. Many writers have pointed out that the constitution of the United States does not mention education in its main body or in any of the amendments. Opponents to federal aid to education point out that this omission indicates a clear lack of interest in education on the part of the federal government. This omission has not in any way, however, hindered the government's involvement when involvement was deemed desirable or necessary.

The General Welfare Clause of the Constitution, Article I Section 8, is used by many people as a justification for the federal government's involvement in education. The clause reads, "The

Congress shall have power: To lay and collect taxes, duties, imposts, and excises, to pay the debts and provide for the common defense and general welfare of the United States. . . ." Education was certainly in the minds of the founding fathers, for Washington's farewell address states, "Promote then as an object of prime importance institutions for the general diffusion of knowledge."

FOOTNOTES

1. *Phi Delta Kappan*, Volume XLV, No. 3 (December, 1964) : p. 207.
2. Edith Green, "Education: Our Largest Enterprise," *College Management*, (March, 1970) : pp. 4-5.
3. Sidney W. Tiedt, *The Role of the Federal Government in Education.* Fair Lawn, New Jersey: Oxford University Press, 1966, p. 30.
4. *Op. cit.*, p. 30.
5. United States Senate Committee on Labor and Public Welfare, *Proposed Federal Aid for Education: A Collection of Pro and Con Excerpts and a Bibliography.* Washington, D. C.: U. S. Government Printing Office, 1961.
6. Barry Goldwater, "Historic and Current Federal Role in Education," *Congressional Record*: Speech, September 23, 1961.
7. Research Discussion-National Education Association, *Estimates of School Statistics, 1969-70.* Washington, D. C.: The Association.
8. Research Discussion-National Education Association, *Rankings of the States*, Washington, D. C.: The Association, 1970.
9. National Education Association, *Research Bulletin*, Washington, D. C.: The Association, 36:4, pp. 99-100.
10. *Christian Science Monitor.* Lou Harris Poll (September 13, 1963).
11. Tiedt, *Ibid.*, p. 37.
12. United States Department of Health, Education and Welfare, Office of Education, *Digest of Educational Statistics.* Washington, D. C.: U. S. Government Printing Office, 1964.
13. United States House of Representatives Committee on Education and Labor, *The Federal Government and Education.* Washington, D. C.: U. S. Government Printing Office, 1963.

SELECTED BIBLIOGRAPHY

Allen, Hollis P. *The Federal Government and Education.* New York: McGraw-Hill, 1950.
American Association of School Administrators. *The Federal Government and Public Schools.* Washington, D. C.: The Association, 1965.
American Council on Education. *Source Book on Federal-State Relations in Education.* Washington, D. C.: The Council, 1945.
Bendiner, Robert. *Obstacle Course on Capital Hill.* New York: McGraw-Hill, 1964.
Benson, Charles S. *The Economics of Public Education.* Boston: Houghton Mifflin, 1961.
Buehler, Ezra C. *Federal Aid for Education.* New York: Noble, 1934.

Burke, Arvid J. *Financing Public Schools in the United States.* Rev. ed. New York: Harper & Row, 1957.

Conant, James B. *Shaping Educational Policy.* New York: McGraw-Hill, 1964.

Educational Policies Commission. *Educational Responsibilities of the Federal Government.* Washington, D. C.: National Education Association, 1964.

Edwards, Newton. *The Courts and the Public Schools.* 2nd ed. Chicago: University of Chicago Press, 1955.

Harris, Seymour E. *How Shall We Pay for Education?* New York: Harper, 1948.

Johns, Roe L. and Edgar L. Morphet, *The Economics and Financing of Education,* Englewood Cliffs, N. J.: Prentice Hall, Inc., 1969.

Kursh, Harry. *The United States Office of Education; a Century of Service.* New York: Chilton, 1965.

Kurth, Edwin L. *Federal Aid to Education.* Gainesville, Florida: The Florida Educational Research and Development Council, 1968.

Labovitz, I. M. *Aid for Federally Affected Schools.* Syracuse, New York: Syracuse University Press, 1963.

La Noue, George R. *Public Funds for Parochial Schools?* New York: National Council of the Churches of Christ in the U.S.A., 1963.

Lee, Gordon C. *The Struggle for Federal Aid.* New York: Teacher's College, Columbia University Bureau of Publications, 1949.

Morphet, Edgar L., Roe L. Johns, and Theodore L. Reller. *Educational Organization and Administration: Concepts, Practices, and Issues.* 2nd ed. Englewood Cliffs, New Jersey: Prentice-Hall, Inc., 1967.

Mort, Paul R. *Federal Support for Public Education.* New York: Teachers College, Columbia University Bureau of Publications, 1936.

Munger, Frank J. and Richard F. Fenno, Jr. *National Politics and Federal Aid to Education.* Syracuse, New York: Syracuse University Press, 1962.

Pierce, Truman M. *Federal, State and Local Government in Education.* New York: The Center for Applied Research in Education, Inc., 1965.

Quattlebaum, Charles A. *Federal Aid to Elementary Education.* Chicago: Public Administration Service, 1948.

Quattlebaum, Charles A. *Federal Educational Policies, Programs and Proposals,* Parts I, II, and III. Washington, D. C.: Government Printing Office, 1960.

Sly, John F. and others. *Financing Education in the Public Schools.* Princeton, New Jersey: Tax Institute Incorporated, 1956.

Spurlock, Clark. *Education and the Supreme Court.* Urbana, Illinois: University of Illinois Press, 1955.

Tiedt, Sidney W. *The Role of the Federal Government in Education.* New York: Oxford University Press, 1955.

United States House of Representatives Committee on Education and Labor. *The Federal Government and Education.* Washington, D. C.: U. S. Government Printing Office, 1961.

Wise, Arthur E. *Rich Schools, Poor Schools.* Chicago: University of Chicago Press, 1968.

398

CHAPTER 11

Federal Responsibilities for Financing Educational Programs

Since the founding of the Republic, the role of the Federal Government in the field of education has been the subject of recurring controversy. While Congress is empowered to "levy and collect taxes . . . for the common defense and general welfare of the United States," education is not one of the powers explicitly delegated to Federal Government. However, in recent years the general welfare clause has been interpreted broadly enough to permit effective participation in the field of education by the Federal Government. This interpretation, unfortunately, did not immediately usher in a period of effective participation in education by the Federal Government. Instead, it ushered in a prolonged controversy between advocates of federal categorical aids for education and advocates of federal general support for public schools.

In 1931, the National Advisory Committee on Education, appointed by President Hoover, issued a report entitled "Federal Relations to Education." In this report, the Committee declared that the American people are justified in using their federal tax system to give financial aid to education in the states, provided they do this in a manner that does not delegate to the Federal Government any control of the social purposes or specific processes of education. The Committee also emphasized that federal funds should be granted to the states to aid education as a whole

399

and not as special grants for the stimulation of particular types of training, and that the Federal Government should render large "intellectual assistance" to the states in matters of education through scientific research.

This report, issued in 1931, suggested criteria which would be relevant today. A few years later, in 1938, a new committee appointed by President Roosevelt gave its views concerning the role of the Federal Government in education. The report of the United States Advisory Committee on Education stated that grants should be made available to the states for "all types of current operating expenses for public elementary and secondary schools"; that the states should be permitted to use part of their federal funds for books, transportation, and scholarships for children attending both public and non-public schools; and that the American people would rightly object to any attempt to use the Federal aid as a means of controlling the content or processes of education in school.

These and subsequent studies emphasized the need for general purpose grants to states to supplement state and local school tax revenues. They sought to minimize federal direction and control of the educational process. Despite these recommendations for general purpose grants for public education, federal participation in education during the past fifteen years has moved rapidly toward categorical grants for narrowly-defined educational purposes.

A recent publication entitled, "Guide to OE-Administered Programs, Fiscal Year 1970," in which the U.S. Office of Education listed 132 programs, reveals how far we have gone down the categorical aid route. Illustrative of the narrowly defined categories are the following programs selected from the list:

1. Aid in the acquisition and installation of equipment for ETV broadcasting;
2. Construct or improve undergraduate academic facilities;
3. Construct vocational education facilities in the Appalachian region;
4. Aid construction of public libraries;
5. Strengthen instruction in ten critically important subjects;
6. Support provision of school library resources, textbooks, and other instructional materials;

400

7. Assist in establishing and maintaining guidance, counseling, and testing programs;
8. Support visits by foreign consultants to improve and develop resources for foreign language and area studies;
9. Train prospective and experienced school administrators;
10. Provide a loan fund to aid Cuban refugee students;
11. Meet educational needs of deprived children;
12. Provide additional educational assistance to Indian children in federally-operated schools;
13. Improve leadership resources of State education agencies;
14. Develop new agency for teacher training in metropolitan areas;
15. Retrain experienced teachers for service in desegregating schools;
16. Enable institutions to assist undergraduates' intensive study of a non-Western language;
17. Increase opportunities throughout the Nation for training in librarianship;
18. Support research on improved instruction in modern foreign languages and materials development and area studies;
19. Development and testing of educational innovations until ready for classroom use;
20. Conduct research in areas of physical education and recreation for handicapped children.

In addition to the 132 programs administered by the U.S. Office of Education, there are programs administered by other agencies. The School Lunch Program is administered by the Department of Agriculture. Programs for the education of native Indian children are administered by the Bureau of Indian Affairs. The National Science Foundation is responsible for most federal programs in science education. This list would be expanded even more if a broader definition of education were used.

The proliferation of categorical aids represents a federal policy which would have been rejected fifteen years ago when interstate equalization of public school resources was the role most commonly recommended for the Federal Government. This role called for general support for public schools, granting greater amounts per pupil to low-wealth states with virtually no federal direction over the expenditure of the granted funds.

This concept of the federal role is based upon an historical distrust of the concentration of power. In America, where diversity and the free marketplace of ideas are the dominant ingredients of our educational system, national controls seemed wholly inappropriate. Moreover, under state and local control, public schools have prospered. Local school boards generally have been highly respected, and local property taxpayers have contributed more than one-half of all school revenue. More innovative educational programs have been developed in the United States under state and local control of education than are generally found in nations that have nationally controlled systems of public education.

During this period, some states made great progress, while others lagged far behind. There were shocking differences in the level of education among the states. During World War II and during the Korean War, the number of young men who were unacceptable for military service because of educational deficiencies was intolerably great in some states.

A careful examination of the facts revealed that most of the states with inadequate schools were also the states in which personal income was far below the national average. In general, the people in those states were making as great an effort to finance their schools as were people in other states. They were devoting a fair share of their income to the support of schools, but the funds available to the schools were inadequate.

These facts indicated that the Federal Government should provide general support for public schools without federal control, granting larger amounts per unit of need to low-wealth states, precisely as state governments had done for local school districts. The assignment of this role to the Federal Government was based upon the assumption that the causes of inadequate schools are basically fiscal and that state and local school leadership exists, or can be found, that will make wise choices in the use of additional funds.

Despite these persuasive arguments for general purpose aid to the states for public schools, categorical grants-in-aid have proliferated beyond all expectation, ushering in a new kind of Federal control. Why? The U.S. Congress, consistently, has been vigilant in its opposition to Federal control of education and to the growth of a federal educational bureaucracy. Yet, during the 1960's, Congress enacted laws which created this complex assortment of categorical aids for education.

This abrupt shift in federal educational policy was accepted by some as an expediency—hopefully temporary in nature—to get needed federal dollars started. Efforts to enact laws granting federal general purpose aid to states for public schools encountered two insurmountable roadblocks—the school segregation issue and the church-school controversy. While it is possible to design federal categorical aids so that parochial schools receive some benefit, the United States Supreme Court has recently ruled that general purpose grants to parochial schools would probably violate the First Amendment to the U.S. Constitution.

To others, however, the new emphasis upon categorical aids for education is not a device for getting around historical roadblocks to general federal support funds. Instead, they are part of the "necessary revolution in American education." This view is expressed clearly in a publication of the U.S. Office of Education entitled, *Education 1967 : A Report to the Profession,* which declared :

> The 88th and 89th Congresses, responding to the desires of the people, enacted laws enabling the Federal Government to take its place in the local-State-National educational partnership . . . Toward this end, the Congress has enacted 24 major pieces of education legislation in the past 3 years. These new laws are channels through which billions of federal tax dollars will go into our elementary schools, high schools, vocational schools, colleges, and universities.
>
> But this money is not simply handed out in the pious hope that it will be put to good use. Each of the education laws . . . is quite specific. Categories and conditions of aid have been established to insure that these funds are spent in an efficient and prudent manner.

The sharp distinction between the basic philosophy of those who favor federal general purpose aid without federal control and those who favor the new, highly controlled, categorical-aid approach is startlingly clear. During the months and years ahead, this issue will be sharply debated as Congress considers expansion of the categorical-aid system or shifts toward "block" grants.

EVALUATION OF FEDERAL CATEGORICAL-AID PROGRAMS[1]

To evaluate this complex assortment of federal educational programs, it is necessary to examine the purpose of each program and ask the question: *Is the purpose of the program worthy and appropriate for the Federal Government?*

In deciding what educational purposes are worthy and appropriate for the Federal Government, first consideration should be given to those educational problems which transcend state lines. Since educational deficiencies cannot be quarantined within state boundaries, educational isolationalism practiced by individual states cannot be sound national policy. The Federal Government clearly has a responsibility to act to strengthen public schools in all states. Only by so doing can a state be protected from the spillover effects of educational neglect in other states. Thus, one worthy and appropriate purpose of federal action is to make general purpose grants to states to supplement state and local funds and to encourage states to expend for public schools amounts needed to maintain an adequate basic school program for all children and youth who choose to attend the public schools.

In addition to this general concern for strengthening the total ongoing public school program in each state, the Federal Government has a special responsibility to assist in the education of disadvantaged children. This responsibility has its origins deep in the history of our country, although immediate concern arises partly from the large number of educationally disadvantaged families that have migrated from one state to another in recent years. Thus, a second worthy and appropriate purpose of federal action is to provide special purpose grants for compensatory or remedial education to assist states in educating disadvantaged children.

The Federal Government has increasingly accepted responsibility for reducing unemployment, and Congress has, in recent years, enacted a number of laws to this end. But unemployment cannot be eliminated without suitable vocational education programs in all states. In order to meet its responsibility for full employment, a worthy and appropriate purpose of federal action is to provide special grants to states for vocational education including vocational programs for adults.

The chief source of local revenues for public schools is the

404

property tax. More than half of all revenues of public schools are derived from this source. The Federal Government is the largest property owner in the United States and its property is tax-exempt. This condition obviously leaves a large gap in the tax base of America's public schools. A worthy and appropriate purpose of federal action is to remedy this gap by making contributions to public schools to compensate for deficiencies in the school tax base resulting from the tax-exempt status of federal property.

In the past, the Federal Government has made contributions for the education of individuals for whom it accepts a special responsibility. The education of native Indian children is a case in point. More recently, contributions have been made for the education of veterans and for Cuban refugees. These obligations have been properly accepted by the Federal Government. It is, therefore, a worthy and appropriate purpose of Federal action to contribute toward the cost of education for veterans and for other individuals for whom the Federal Government has accepted a special responsibility.

For many years, the Federal Government has recognized that "promotion of the general welfare" includes assisting in the elimination of hunger, the improvement of the health of the nation, and in the assurance of an adequate and stabilized supply of food for the nation. These are certainly legitimate national purposes. The appropriation of federal funds for school food service programs, including school lunch, school milk, special assistance for the needy, nutrition education, distribution of surplus commodities, and similar programs are consistent with legitimate national purposes.

The National Educational Finance Project made no special study of federal appropriations for higher education, including junior colleges. However, more than 100 years ago, the Federal Government judged that the promotion of certain types of higher education was consistent with national purposes when the Morrill Act was passed. During recent years, numerous federal acts have provided financial assistance, not only for the higher institution, but also scholarships and loans for college students. If federal financial assistance for elementary and secondary education is consistent with national purposes, it seems that federal financial assistance to higher institutions and to students attending those institutions is also consistent with national purposes.

Common to all states is a need to improve education through research and development programs. If each state were to finance all of its own educational research and development, duplication of effort, excessive costs, or inadequate programs would be inevitable. Therefore, as a service to all schools, it is a worthy and appropriate purpose of federal action to finance research and development programs designed to improve the quality of education in all states.

These are all worthy and appropriate purposes for federal action in the field of education. Most of the current list of federal programs in education meet the test of worthiness of purpose. But this test alone is not enough; in addition, federal programs must be effectively administered. For this reason, it is necessary to ask a second question: *Are the administrative arrangements effective and conducive to sound federal-state-local relationships?*

If the federal-state-local partnership is to function to maximum advantage, the assignment of responsibilities to each partner must utilize the special strengths of each, while compensating for each one's weaknesses. Moreover, each partner must perform his duties without interfering unnecessarily with the essential contribution of the other two partners.

Historically and legally, the state government occupies a central role in the public school partnership. If the total public school program is to function effectively, the state must be in a position to coordinate federal programs with state and local programs, and to provide needed supervision and direction. For this reason, federal programs should not by-pass state governments; instead, federal grants for public schools should be made to state departments of education to be allocated to local schools by them in accordance with state plans. This arrangement not only respects the central role of state governments in the field of education, but also avoids excessive growth of the federal bureaucracy.

Over a period of years, states have developed elaborate plans for granting state funds to local school systems. More recently, as we have previously noted, the Federal Government has launched a number of categorical aid programs. Inevitably, some of the new federal programs duplicate the purpose of some existing state-aid programs. For example, some states have provided aid to local school districts for compensatory or remedial education. With the recent entrance of the Federal Government into this field, it may be in the best interest of education for the state to transfer some of its funds to other equally important purposes. To permit such flexibility in the use of state funds, when the Federal Government and a state grant funds to local school districts for the same or for closely related purposes, the federal grant should not be contingent upon continuation of the state grant. Only by preserving the right of the state to adjust its grant program can the state discharge its obligation to the overall education partnership.

The amounts of federal funds to which individual states or local school districts are entitled should be determined by objective formulas, reducing to a minimum discretionary power of federal officers in the allocation of school funds. Any grant-in-aid program which authorizes federal officers to use broad discretion in allocating school funds among states or local school systems will encourage political favoritism, and the proliferation of expert proposal and justification writers.

In order to promote the efficient use of federal funds and to encourage sound state and local planning, federal contributions should be generally predictable for long-range planning purposes and specifically for year-to-year planning. Effective use of federal grants not only requires planning, but also sufficient lead time to recruit personnel and obtain facilities and equipment. Boards of education should know at budgetmaking time the amount of federal funds they will receive during the ensuing year.

In the interest of effective administration and sound intergovernmental relations, the Federal Government should avoid having several departments grant funds for the same or closely related public school purposes. For example, in the field of vocational education there are several programs administered by different agencies making grants to local school systems. A single federal program, working through a comprehensive state plan for vocational education, would avoid much confusion and would be more effective in achieving the purposes of the Federal Government.

The accounting and auditing safeguards for federal grant funds should utilize the procedures that the states require to safeguard their grants to local school systems. Although the U.S. Office of Education should continue to recommend public school accounting procedures, separate accounting and auditing procedures for federal funds should be superimposed on state requirements only if the latter are inadequate.

Moreover, although the Federal Government might, in the case of categorical grants, specify the purpose for which the funds are to be used, great freedom should be allowed to the local school system in selecting the method by which the purpose is to be achieved. This type of operational freedom is necessary if the local partner is to do his job effectively.

These criteria should be helpful in determining if the administrative arrangements of a federal program are effective and conducive to sound federal-state-local relations. However, if all federal programs in education have worthy and appropriate purposes and sound administrative arrangements, there is still the possibility that gaps exist in the total program. For this reason, it is necessary to ask a third question: *Does the combined effect of all federal programs promote the development of adequate public school programs in all states?* Evaluation of the Federal Government's activities in the field of education cannot be made by looking only at each individual program; in addition, the combined effect of all programs must be considered. It is only in this way that gaps can be detected and that the cumulative effect of various programs can be assessed.

Using this criterion raises serious questions about the effective operation of federal aid programs. There is evidence that the combined effect of numerous categorical aids has produced a deluge of red tape that has hampered public schools; that educational talent is being wasted in writing up applications for small amounts of federal money; that the emphasis upon innovataion, and the search for funds to subsidize it, has resulted in the neglect of programs which have proved valuable in the past. In short, there is a growing conviction that the expanding list of federal categorical aids has produced confusion, instability, and distortion of educational emphasis.

A final criterion to be used in evaluating federal categorical appropriations for education is: *Does the appropriation tend to disequalize the financial resources available for education among the states?* In order to meet this criterion the federal appropriation should either tend to equalize financial resources per pupil (or per unit of need) among the states or at least be neutral in its effect. Any appropriation which provides a greater amount of

408

federal aid per pupil (or per unit of need) to the states of greatest wealth than to the states of least wealth has a disequalizing effect. The National Educational Finance Project made a careful analysis of the ten principal federal categorical aids to elementary and secondary education and found that all of these appropriations either had an equalizing or neutral effect on the financial equalization of educational opportunity except Title 2 of ESEA and that appropriation was a very small percent of the total (see Chapter 8 of Volume 4 of the National Educational Finance Project, entitled *Planning to Finance Education*).

Temporary Versus Continuing Programs

Some federal educational programs are intended to be temporary, but, like temporary buildings, they tend to persist beyond their planned termination dates. When a temporary program is established, a unit is created within the Federal Government to administer it. The employees of the unit tend to feel that their importance and their tenure of employment are related to the continuance of the program. Outside of the government, a lobbying group is formed to represent the program "beneficiaries." Often an association is formed and its employees acquire personal interests in the continuance of the program. Finally, in the local school system which receives federal funds under the temporary program, people are employed to provide the services required to accomplish the purposes of the program. These employees must be prepared to search for new jobs when the program is terminated. Understandably, they seek another job at a time convenient to them, creating staffing problems for the program.

For these reasons, as well as the value of the program itself, temporary programs are often continued beyond their usefulness. Temporary categorical grants are intended to provide a financial stimulant for selected programs or items in the school budget. These grants often provide temporary aid to try out new ideas. The grant programs are expected to terminate and not become part of the continuing school support program. Title II of the Elementary and Secondary Education Act of 1965 and some of the titles of the National Defense Education Act are of this type.

On the other hand, continuing categorical grants are intended to finance, on a continuing basis, selected high cost school programs such as vocational education, compensatory education, and school lunches. These federal grant programs cannot be terminated without curtailing public school programs which contribute to important national goals. The programs supported in this way are usually above average in per student cost and are often related to other concerns of the Federal Government (e.g., vocational education to full employment; compensatory education to the war on poverty).

This distinction between temporary and continuing categorical federal grant programs suggests what the "next steps" should be. First, definite plans should be made to terminate temporary categorical aid programs when they have served their purpose and, second, the continuing categorical grant programs should be consolidated.

If temporary programs are excluded, it should be possible to consolidate continuing categorical aids into a few major "blocks" such as:

1. Vocational education
2. Education of children from low-income families
3. Compensation to schools for federal tax-exempt property
4. Education of handicapped children
5. School food service
6. Educational research and development

With the consolidation of continuing categorical aids into major blocks, it should be possible to simplify application and reporting procedures under approved state plans. Along with these consolidated continuing grants-in-aid, it is necessary to have a few temporary aid programs directed at specific national problems, such as devising better ways for schools to combat drug abuse among young people. Such temporary grants-in-aid, however, should be held to a minimum because they often lead to inefficient planning and unjustifiable efforts to make them permanent.

AID TO FEDERALLY-AFFECTED SCHOOL DISTRICTS

One rationale for federal grants-in-aid for education is that the Federal Government should compensate states and school districts for deficiencies in the school tax base. Under this concept of the federal role, federal payments are based upon inade-

410

quacies of the school tax base. For many years, the Federal Government has compensated local school districts and other local units of government for deficiencies in the property tax base resulting directly from federal ownership of property.

Three distinctly different methods have been used to determine the amounts of payments to be made to school districts, or to other local units of government, to compensate for gaps in the property tax base created by the tax-exempt status of federal property. First, payments-in-lieu-of-taxes based upon the value of the federal property multiplied by a local tax rate are paid by the Federal Government for some types of tax-exempt property. This method of determining the federal payment parallels the methods used to determine the tax obligation of owners of private property, but it is used for only a few types of federal property. Moreover, some federal laws authorizing payments-in-lieu-of-taxes exclude the value of improvements made by the Federal Government in determining the amount to be paid. For example, payments-in-lieu-of-taxes paid by TVA are based upon tax losses incurred by local governments as a result of the acquisition by the Federal Government of property which formerly was taxable. The value of dams and power plants constructed by TVA is not considered in determing the payment. The limitations of this approach are obvious.

If the federal project becomes a basic industry employing thousands of people, large sums of tax funds will be needed by local jurisdictions to build and maintain schools, sewers, and streets. If the federal payments-in-lieu-of-taxes are based upon the value of the unimproved land, the payments will be grossly inadequate to finance the local governmental needs for the expanded population. On the other hand, the exclusion of improvements in determining the amount of the payments is often justified. For example, a costly isolated missile base requiring no public services should not be the basis for a large payment-in-lieu-of-taxes, since the funds would not be needed for schools and local governmental services. In such cases, exclusion of the value of the improvements made by the Federal Government seems reasonable enough.

A second approach to the problem is found in several federal laws relating to public land. For example, 12.5 percent of the revenue derived from grazing fees collected in national grazing districts and 50 percent of the grazing fees collected for other

411

federal lands are paid to states in which the lands are located. Similarly, 37.5 percent of revenues collected by the Bureau of Land Management for rentals and royalties from mineral rights on federal lands are paid to the state in which leased federally-owned mineral lands are located. Under another law enacted in 1908, 25 percent of all revenues derived from the sale of timber and other rights on national forests are paid to states for the benefit of schools and roads in the county in which the forest is located.

This method of determining a federal payment avoids the problem of determining the value of federally-owned property, since payments are based strictly upon the earnings of these properties. However, payments show a marked irregularity from year to year, creating windfalls some years and virtually no revenues in others. For this reason, it is difficult to incorporate these funds into sound budgeting and planning practices by school districts and other local governments. Thus, payments based upon annual earnings are not related to need and are not conducive to efficient use by the recipients.

The third, and perhaps most satisfactory, method of determining payments-in-lieu-of-taxes for school districts is found in Public Laws 815 and 874 enacted in the fall of 1950. These laws stem from an extensive study of school problems in "federally-affected areas" by the House Committee on Education and Labor. These investigations convinced members of the Committee that public schools located near tax-exempt federal installations are unable to maintain satisfactory educational programs unless the federally-owned housing and places of employment in the area contribute a fair share toward the cost of constructing and operating public schools. Taxes levied upon privately-owned residences, many of which were modest in value, could not be expected to make up entirely for the failure of a federally-owned basic industry, such as a tax-exempt navy yard, to pay its fair share of the local tax requirements of the school district.

Based upon these findings, the United States Congress in 1950 enacted Public Laws 815 and 874. The purpose was not only to compensate school districts for gaps in the property tax base resulting from the tax-exempt status of federal property, but also to assure that good public schools would be available near military and other federal installations.

The method of determining federal payments under Section

412

3 of Public Law 874 to local school districts recognizes the tax-exempt status of federally-owned properties and the basic justification for the payments. But under this section of the law, which is the basis for 99 percent of all payments to school districts under Public Law 874, the presence of tax-exempt property alone is not sufficient to justify the federal payment. In addition, there must be children attending public schools who either live on, or whose parents are employed on, the federal tax-exempt property. In this sense, the method of determining the payment is related to the burden on public schools associated with the federal activity.

No "means test" is employed; and the federal payment is regarded as an entitlement of the school district. Thus, the Federal Government assumes the responsibility of paying local school "property taxes" for both the residential and industrial property it owns. The amount it pays is not related directly to the value of the federal property, but rather to the number of public school children associated with it. Since no means test is employed, these federal contributions are often made to "wealthy" school districts, violating a concept that federal payments should only be made to school districts which demonstrate need. This would not be an objectionable feature of this Act if the states utilizing the equalization method of apportioning state funds were permitted to charge back against the districts receiving such funds the same percentage of local funds that is charged back under their apportionment formulas. Unfortunately, recent amendments prohibit this policy.

REVENUE SHARING AND FEDERAL AID TO EDUCATION

Numerous proposals have been advanced for the sharing of federal revenue with the states. Following are some factors that have caused interest in federal revenue sharing:

1. The Federal Government collects approximately two-thirds of all tax revenue.
2. The federal tax structure is more responsive to the economy than state and local tax structures.
3. The federal tax structure is less regressive than state and local tax structures.

413

4. Federal taxes eliminate tax competition among the state and local governments.
5. The great increase in state and local taxes during the past two decades has created major opposition in many places to further increases in state and local taxes.
6. The rapid urbanization of American society accompanied by the development of extra governmental costs in the core cities without compensating increases in taxpaying ability has created serious financial difficulties in many cities.

The impact of federal revenue sharing on the public schools depends largely on the type of the plan and the amount of funds provided.

Let us assume that Congress has decided to share a certain percent of federal revenue with the states and it has the following alternatives under consideration:

1. *Plan A.* All of the federally shared revenue is allocated to the states on a population basis with no federal requirements with respect to its allocation to governmental services. States at present vary widely in the percent of state revenue allocated to the public schools. With no federal requirement with respect to the percent of the shared federal revenue to allocate to the public schools, the states would undoubtedly vary widely in the percent of the shared federal revenue allocated to the public schools. Therefore, no estimate could be made of the financial impact of shared federal revenue in each state under Plan A.
2. *Plan B.* A fixed percent of the shared federal revenue would be allocated to the states on a population basis and a fixed percent to the large cities either on a population basis or on the basis of municipal taxes paid. The percent of shared federal revenue allocated to the states under Plan B would have the same financial impact on the public schools as Plan A. The financial impact on the public schools of the federal revenue shared with the great cities would be still more difficult to analyze. Some cities do not share municipal revenue with the public schools and the cities that do share such revenue vary widely in the percent of municipal revenue allocated to the public schools. In some states the boundaries of the school district are

not coterminous with those of the municipality. This is especially significant in a school district county unit state such as Florida. Therefore, it is impossible to assess the financial impact on the public schools of federal revenue shared with the cities.

3. *Plan C.* Shared federal revenue is allocated to the states on the basis of population with the requirement that a fixed percent be allocated to the public schools. It would be possible to estimate the amount of the shared federal revenue that would be allocated to the public schools under Plan C once the total amount of federal revenue to be shared with each state is determined and the percent to allocate to the public schools is also fixed. For example, let us assume that it has been determined that $18,000,-000,000 of federal revenue will be shared with the states in a given fiscal year and that each state must allocate a minimum of 40 percent of this revenue to the public schools. This equals $7,200,000,000 or slightly more than 20 percent of state and local revenue for the public schools in 1969-70. Assuming that each state allocates exactly 40 percent of the shared revenue, Plan C for shared federal revenue would have roughly the same financial impact on the public schools as Plan II for general federal aid analyzed in Tables 2 and 5. The principal difference would be that under Plan C, federal funds would be allocated on the basis of total population and under Plan II on average daily membership in the public schools. If some states allocated to the public schools more than the required minimum of 40 percent of shared federal revenue, then the public schools would receive more federal revenue under Plan C than Plan II.

Congress, of course, could consider numerous other alternatives for allocating shared federal revenue. The principal issues are:

1. How much federal revenue should be shared?
2. How much control over the allocation of shared federal revenue to competing governmental services should be exercised by the Congress?

As already pointed out above, the public schools should receive at least 22 percent and preferably 30 percent of their total revenue from the federal government in order for the schools to have an adequate tax base and in order for the federal government to accomplish legitimate and appropriate federal purposes. Therefore, any long range revenue sharing plan which would assure the public schools substantially less than the 22 to 30 percent of total revenue would be inadequate.

If the Congress wishes to exercise no control whatsoever over the allocation of shared federal revenue to various state and local governmental functions in the states, then Plan A would be the preferred plan.

If Congress wishes to assure that the cities will receive what Congress deems to be an appropriate portion of shared federal revenue and Congress is not concerned about the amount of the shared federal revenue that will be allocated to the public schools, Plan B would be the preferred plan.

If Congress wishes to assure that the public schools will receive what it deems to be an appropriate percentage of shared federal revenue and it is not concerned about the amount of the shared federal revenue that would be allocated to the cities, Plan C would be the preferred plan.

If Congress wishes to assure that both the public schools and the cities receive what it deems to be appropriate percentages repectively, of federal shared revenue, then a combination of Plans A, B and C would be the preferred plan. Under such a plan, the Congress would determine the percentage of the federal shared revenue to be allocated to the public schools, the percentage to be allocated to the cities and the percentage to be allocated to the states to be appropriated for such governmental services as determined by the respective state legislatures.

Insofar as the public schools are concerned, Plan C or a combination of Plans A, B and C would provide the most favorable financial impact on the public schools, assuming that the amount of federal revenue shared with the states is adequate to substantially accomplish the purposes of federal aid to the schools. It is beyond the scope of this report to analyze all plans that have been proposed for revenue sharing. Almost any plan for federal revenue sharing under which federal revenue is collected nationwide and distributed back to the states by some objective measure of need such as population will have a desirable financial impact on public school financing, provided the amount of revenue shared is substantial. Any such plan has an equalizing effect by redistributing income. Some plans, of course, would provide more financial assistance to the public schools than others. About the only type of revenue sharing plan that would be of no financial assistance to the public schools nationwide is a plan under which the federal government allocated back to each state a uniform percentage of the federal revenue collected in that state. Such a plan would have no equalizing effect whatsoever.

GENERAL PURPOSE GRANTS-IN-AID TO STATES FOR EDUCATION

Proposals for general purpose federal grants-in-aid for public elementary and secondary schools have been presented to the U. S. Congress regularly for more than a third of a century. With equal regularity, the Congress has declined to enact a general support program for public schools. During recent years, however, there has been renewed interest in "block grants" for education as well as proposals to share federal revenues with state governments. These proposals reflect a general concern that federal fiscal dominance has led to a highly centralized control of public services. They are intended to strengthen decentralized control of education and other public services.

Federal grants for vocational education, compensatory education, special education, and research and development are not sufficient to produce needed improvements in elementary and secondary education. In addition to these "block grants," federal action is needed to increase general purpose income available for elementary and secondary schools.

One approach to the problem is to relieve states of other burdens, especially welfare costs, so that they will have sufficient funds to support education. While such federal action would aid states materially, it probably would fall short of assuring an adequate financial base for elementary and secondary schools in all states. Even if this approach is supplemented with a revenue sharing program, adequate educational programs in all states would not be achieved unless part of the shared revenues were earmarked for education.

In considering proposals for general federal aid for education, three approaches or plans and one combination plan are analyzed:

417

1. Plan I - The national foundation program financed from a combination of federal, state and local funds.
2. Plan II - Equal federal grants per student with no requirement of state and local effort to support education.
3. Plan III - Equal federal plan grants per student for equal state and local effort in proportion to ability.
4. Plan IV - A combination of Plan I and Plan II.

Each of these approaches emphasizes different federal purposes.

Following are some of the principal purposes of general federal aid:

1. To equalize educational opportunity among the states.
2. To transfer the administration and control of federal aid from Washington to the states.
3. To relieve the state and local tax burdens of all states.
4. To stimulate or at least preserve state and local effort to finance education.
5. To develop a plan which is politically acceptable in all or most states.

In the following sections of this chapter, these three approaches and one combination approach to general federal aid are presented and analyzed in terms of these purposes. In order to compare these three approaches, tables are presented showing the impact of each approach on all 50 states. In order to make these three approaches comparable, approximately the same amount of federal aid is allocated under each formula and applied to data for 1969-70. The total amount of general federal aid used to demonstrate the impact of each of these formulas was calculated at approximately 20 percent of state and local revenues for the public schools for 1969-70. The figure of 20 percent of state and local revenue was selected for the following reasons: (1) the federal appropriation must be at least 20 percent of state and local revenue for schools in order to effectively accomplish the principal purposes of general federal aid and (2) such a percentage figure or a higher figure could be written into the general federal authorizing act thus providing a long range plan for determining the federal appropriations for general federal aid.

Plan I—The National Foundation Program

In this approach to federal support for public schools, each state would receive a federal contribution based upon its need

Obviously, the need could not be based upon the actual deficit in the public school budget. Such an approach would encourage states to spend more and allocate less state and local tax funds to public schools.

When the foundation program approach is suggested, it is assumed that objective formulas can be developed to determine: (1) the amount of money a state needs annually to provide suitable schooling for all public school students, and (2) the amount of money a state should be expected to provide annually from state and local sources for this purpose. The difference between these two sums for each state determines the amount of federal aid it needs.

Various formulas for determining the amount a state needs to spend for public schools and the amount it should be expected to raise from state and local sources have been suggested. The simplest formula is obtained by assuming that each state (1) needs to spend the same amount per public school student, and (2) should contribute annually for this purpose the same percent of its total personal income payments.

To illustrate the operation of such a formula, let the needed annual expenditure rate be $800 per student and the expected state contribution rate be 4 percent of its total personal income.[2] The amount of federal funds needed in each state under this formula, based on 1969 personal income and 1969-70 A.D.M., is calculated in Table 11-1. Some states would receive no federal payments under this plan, since 4 percent of their personal income exceeds $800 per pupil. The total amount of federal aid required for such a national foundation program is $7,160 millions. The federal contribution under such a foundation program would have been approximately 20 percent of state and local school revenues in 1969-70. The amount of federal funds required would, of course, be less if the $800 per student were reduced, or if the 4 percent state contribution rate were raised to 5 percent. This plan is identical to the Strayer-Haig formula for apportioning state funds described in Chapter 9 of this volume.

Such adjustments in the formula fail to resolve certain other issues—the implied assumption (1) that the average cost per student of suitable education is the same in all states, and (2) that the states of greatest wealth should receive little or no general

419

federal revenue for the public schools despite the fact that such states pay the greatest amount of federal taxes per capita.

Actual expenditure rates per student differ greatly from state to state primarily because salaries paid school employees differ greatly. In the state with the greatest personal income per capita, the average annual salary of public school teachers is approximately twice the average annual salary paid in the state with the lowest income per capita.

One interpretation is that since per capita income measures the prevailing average wage rates for all workers in a state, teachers tend to occupy similar positions within the salary hierarchy in each state. Under this interpretation, differences in teachers' salaries and other school employees reflect general wage rates in each state and can be expected to continue until there has been a change in per capita income and the prevailing wage rates in the state.

This line of reasoning would seem to imply that low income states should provide low quality schools for their children assuming that there is a relationship between the quality of education and the expenditure level. Numerous studies have shown that the low per pupil expenditure states on the average have a considerably higher percent of draftee rejections because of educational deficiencies than the high expenditure states.

A different interpretation stresses per capita income as a measure of fiscal capacity. Under this interpretation, teachers are underpaid in the low per capita income states, not because they are paid in accordance with prevailing wage rates, but because the state has an inadequate school tax base due to poverty. If this analysis is correct, then it is appropriate to ask the federal government to compensate for deficiencies in the school tax base by providing substantial amounts of general aid for low income states. Some would recommend that the federal government provide sufficient funds to assure an acceptable level of education in all states. Such a program would substantially reduce the present wide differentials among the states in teachers' salaries.

If it is assumed that the per pupil cost of education for an *equal quality of education* varies among the states, it should be possible to determine by research what causes those differences and what cost differentials should be provided. Such differentials might be due to difference in cost of living or differences in

420

sparsity or density of population or possibly other factors. The National Educational Finance Project did not have the resources to undertake that research. However, it should be technically possible to solve this problem.

In Chapter 7 of this volume, it is pointed out that the cost per pupil for certain target populations such as vocational students, the handicapped and the culturally disadvantaged is considerably higher than for other students. It has already been recommended in this chapter that the federal categorical aids for these high cost students be continued. If the federal categorical appropriations for these high cost pupils are adequate, there is no need to provide for cost differentials for these target populations in the general federal aid appropriation.

It will be noted that under the national foundation program computed in Table 11-1, high income states, though they are paying the greatest amount of federal taxes per capita, would receive little, if any, federal aid. This form of general purpose aid for elementary and secondary schools was widely supported during the 1930's and 1940's when the per capita income of New York (the state of greatest wealth) was four times as great as in Mississippi, the state of least wealth. Now the ratio between the per capita income in New York and Mississippi has been reduced to 2 to 1. Furthermore, a generation ago, the public school systems and governmental services generally of the wealthy urban states were considered satisfactory and the tax burden for state and local governments in those states was not considered heavy. However, that situation has changed. With the rapid urbanization of American society and the concentration of low income and disadvantaged persons in the core cities, the costs of state and local government, including the public schools, have increased enormously in those states and tax burdens have become onerous. Furthermore, governmental services, including the public schools are not now considered adequate in these states.

For this reason, a federal aid program which fails to increase financial support for schools in the so-called wealthy urban states falls short of national goals at this time.

Summarizing, the national foundation program approach equalizes the financial resources available per pupil better than any other approach. In 1969-70, the state, local and federal categorical revenue available per pupil ranged from a high of $1,325 to a low of $523, a ratio of 2.53 to 1. Table 11-5 shows that Plan

I, the national foundation approach, (assuming that general federal aid would be equal to approximately 20 percent of state and local revenue) would have provided a total of $1,325 per pupil from state, local and federal categorical and federal general aid in the state with the most revenue per pupil and $844 per pupil in the state with the least revenue, a ratio of 1.57 to 1. A comparison of each of the plans analyzed is presented in Table 11-5.

The national foundation approach would also tend to transfer the control of federal aid from Washington to the states. However, the national foundation program approach would not relieve state and local tax burdens in all states, nor would it stimulate state and local effort in all states because under this approach, a number of states would receive little or no federal aid. Furthermore, there is but little reason to believe that this approach would be politically acceptable because of the reasons pointed out above. Therefore, the national foundation program approach would fail to accomplish a number of important federal purposes.

Plan II—Equal Federal Grants per Student with No Requirement of State and Local Effort

The simplest plan for providing federal aid to the states for the general support of elementary and secondary schools is to grant each state an equal amount per student without reference to variations in taxpaying ability or effort. If the amount provided on this basis is substantial, then considerable equalization of public school support among states would be achieved.

Under such a plan, all states would start with unequal amounts of state and local funds per student, and then each state would receive an equal amount per pupil in general federal aid. This approach would reduce the ratio between the funds available per pupil in the state of greatest wealth to the funds available per pupil in the state of least wealth but not as much as under the national foundation program plan. Table 8-5 shows that under the national foundation program plan, the ratio of funds available per pupil in the most wealthy state to the state of least wealth was 1.57 to 1 and under the equal grant amount of general federal aid, the ratio would be 2.18 to 1. Table 11-2 shows the allocation to each state under Plan II.

Moreover, the high income states, through the operation of

422

the progressive federal income tax, would contribute in federal taxes much more than they would receive, while the low income states would receive more than their citizens contribute to the federal government in taxes.

Attention has been directed in the previous section of this chapter that states vary considerably in per capita income and also they probably vary somewhat in the cost of living. Generally speaking the high per capita income states are also the states with the highest living costs. Therefore, a flat grant of an equal amount per pupil probably over allocates in terms of living costs to the states of least wealth but it also over allocates to the states of greatest wealth in terms of taxpaying ability. Therefore, the flat grant formula of an equal amount per pupil tends to be partly self corrective although variations in the cost of living among the states are no doubt considerably less than variations in taxpaying ability.

Summarizing, Plan II provides for some equalization of financial resources among the states but not nearly as much as Plan I, it transfers the administration and control of federal aid from Washington to the states, it relieves state and local tax burdens in all states as well as or better than any other plan, it does not stimulate or preserve state and local effort to finance education and it is perhaps as politically acceptable or more acceptable than any of the plans analyzed.

Perhaps the greatest weakness of this plan is the inherent danger that states might gradually reduce their contribution to public school support, making public schools increasingly a federal responsibility and perhaps even reducing the total revenue available for the support of the public schools in some states.

To avoid this danger, the equal federal grant for equal effort in proportion to ability plan is suggested.

Plan III—Equal Federal Grant Per Pupil for Equal Effort in Proportion to Ability[3]

The federal government could provide an incentive to the states for making a reasonable effort in relation to their ability to support their public schools from state and local funds. It has been argued that the personal income a state has available to support education is the net personal income available after providing for at least the subsistence of all of its citizens and after paying federal personal income taxes (see Chapter 4 of this volume). It has also been argued for example, that a state with a total population of five million, and a school enrollment of one million and total personal income of 12 billion has less taxpaying ability than a state with a total population of 4 million, a school enrollment of one million and a total personal income of $12 billion. This seems reasonable because one of these states has one million more population than the other state for whom at least subsistence must be provided. The measure of ability described in Chapter 4 of this volume and applied to Plan III in this section meets these objections because net income is computed by this method by deducting $750 per capita for subsistence and also deducting federal personal income taxes paid. It could well be argued that this measure of net income could be improved by deducting a more realistic figure, such as $1,200 per capita, for subsistence. It could also be argued that the per capita subsistence cost varies among the states due to variations in the cost of living. This is no doubt true and with adequate research, defensible variations among the states in per capita costs of subsistence could be determined.

Plan III, shown in Table 11-3, simply provides that each state is allotted $158 per pupil in average daily membership by the federal government if it makes a state and local tax effort to support its schools equal to or greater than 6.24 percent of net income which was the average effort made by the states in 1969-70. If a state makes an effort of less than 6.24 percent of its net income, it would receive proportionately less. For example, in 1969-70, Alabama made only 88 percent of the national average effort to support its schools and under Plan III, it would receive only 88 percent of $158 per pupil or $139. It is not suggested under Plan III that the national average effort of the states be computed each year but rather that the Congress would set some figure, for example 6.5 percent of net income as the minimum effort each state would be required to make in order to obtain its full allotment of federal funds. This provision should stimulate the states to preserve a reasonable state and local effort to support schools if the federal government provides from 20 to 30 percent of school revenue. The greater the proportion of federal revenue provided, the greater would be the incentive to continue state or local effort under Plan III.

424

Plan III would provide an even more powerful incentive for the state and local governments to preserve and even increase state and local effort to support education if no limit is placed by the federal government on the percent of personal income allocated to education it would reimburse. If no limit were placed on the reimbursable percentage of income, the states might be encouraged to make a misallocation of resources simply to obtain more federal funds because without a limit, the more state and local funds a state expended on education, the more federal funds it would receive. It is sound public policy for the federal government to require the states to make a reasonable effort in proportion to ability to finance a governmental service which is jointly funded as a condition of receiving federal funds. However, it does not seem to be sound public policy for the federal government to allocate federal funds for any governmental service such as highways, welfare, education, etc. on the basis of "the more you spend, the more federal funds you get." It would seem to be sound public policy to allocate available public funds among competing governmental services on the basis of relative needs and anticipated benefits.

Summarizing, Plan III equalizes financial resources per pupil among the states about as well as Plan II but much less than Plan I, it transfers the administration and control of state aid from Washington to the states as well as any plan, it relieves state and local tax burdens in all states proportionally as much as Plan II and more uniformly than Plan I, it stimulates all states to preserve state and local effort to support education and is more politically acceptable than Plan I. Plan III should be politically as acceptable or even more acceptable than Plan II. It might be argued that neither Plan III nor any of the other plans presented for allocating general federal aid relieve state and local tax burdens because all of these plans assume continued state and local effort which would be supplemented by general federal aid. It is not anticipated that any of these plans would result in a reduction of present state and local effort to support education. However, it is assumed that the need for further increases in state and local taxes, in order to meet increasing school costs, will not be so urgent if the federal government provides an appropriation for general aid, at least equivalent to 20 percent of state and local revenues for the public schools.

425

Plan IV—A Combination of Plan I and Plan II

Under this plan, one-half of the federal appropriation for general aid would be apportioned under Plan I and one-half under Plan II. Table 11-4 shows the allocation that would be received by each state under this plan. Table 11-5 shows that the 1969-70 ratio of revenue per pupil in the state with the greatest revenue per pupil to the state with the least revenue would be reduced from 2.53 to 1 to 1.72 to 1 under Plan IV.

Analyzed in terms of some of the principal purposes of federal aid: Plan IV provides for more equalization of financial resources among the states than Plan II or Plan III but less than Plan I, it transfers the administration and control of federal aid from Washington to the states; it provides some relief of the burden of state and local taxes in all states but not as uniformly as Plans I and II, it provides some stimulus for preserving state and local effort but not as great a stimulus or as uniformly as Plan III; it is probably more politically acceptable than Plan I but probably not as politically acceptable as Plans II and III.

Other Alternative Plans for Allocating General Federal Aid

A large number of alternative plans for apportioning general federal aid could be developed from various combinations of the alternatives analyzed above. For example, Plan V might be the allocation of one-half of the federal appropriation on the basis of Plan I and one-half on Plan III. No table is presented for showing the impact of Plan V on the states. However, Plan V could be evaluated as follows: It would provide for about the same equalization of financial resources as Plan IV, more than Plans II and III but less than Plan I; it would transfer the administration and control of federal aid from Washington to the states as well as any plan analyzed; it would relieve state and local tax burdens of all states as well as Plan IV, better than Plan I but not as much as Plans II and III; it would stimulate the preservation of state and local effort to finance education in all states more than Plans I, II and IV but not as much as Plan III; and it would probably be more politically acceptable than Plan I, equally acceptable as Plan IV, but probably less politically acceptable than Plans II and III.

What is the best plan for apportioning general federal aid

426

TABLE 11-1

PLAN I—FEDERAL CONTRIBUTION TO EACH STATE, BASED ON A NATIONAL
FOUNDATION PROGRAM OF $800 PER PUPIL, WITH A LOCAL CONTRIBUTION
EQUAL TO FOUR PERCENT OF 1969 STATE PERSONAL INCOME
(DOLLARS IN MILLIONS)

State	1969-1970 ADM in Public Elem. & Sec. Schools (in thousands)	ADM × $800	4% of Personal Income	Federal Contribution[c]	Federal Contribution Per Pupil in ADM
U. S. TOTAL	45,100[a]	$36,080	$29,628	$7,160	
Alabama	820	656	365	291	355
Alaska	77	62	50	12	156
Arizona	417	334	228	106	254
Arkansas	436	349	199	150	344
California	4,925	3,940	3,336	604	123
Colorado	534	427	303	124	232
Connecticut	640	512	551	0	0
Delaware	129	103	89	14	109
Florida	1,408	1,126	896	230	163
Georgia	1,098	878	570	308	281
Hawaii	179	143	122	21	117
Idaho	185[b]	148	85	63	341
Illinois	2,232	1,786	1,894	0	0
Indiana	1,274	1,019	755	264	207
Iowa	654	532	395	137	209
Kansas	496	397	324	73	147
Kentucky	692	554	368	186	269
Louisiana	843	674	417	257	305
Maine	239	191	119	72	301
Maryland	884	707	613	94	106
Massachusetts	1,132	906	909	0	0
Michigan	2,141[b]	1,713	1,400	313	146
Minnesota	913	730	538	192	210
Mississippi	559	447	209	238	426
Missouri	976[b]	781	643	138	141
Montana	173	138	87	51	295
Nebraska	329	263	209	54	164
Nevada	122	98	81	17	139
New Hampshire	149	119	100	19	128
New Jersey	1,449	1,159	1,212	0	0
New Mexico	276	221	115	106	384
New York	3,449	2,759	3,255	0	0
North Carolina	1,171	937	601	336	287
North Dakota	147	118	74	44	293
Ohio	2,399	1,919	1,606	313	130
Oklahoma	606	485	313	172	284
Oregon	467	374	290	84	180
Pennsylvania	2,320	1,856	1,727	129	56
Rhode Island	178	142	141	1	6
South Carolina	640	512	281	231	361
South Dakota	165	132	80	52	315
Tennessee	880	704	448	256	291
Texas	2,598	2,078	1,458	620	239
Utah	302	242	125	117	387
Vermont	103	82	57	25	243
Virginia	1,063	850	618	232	218
Washington	823	658	524	134	163
West Virginia	397[b]	318	189	129	325
Wisconsin	926	741	615	126	136
Wyoming	85	68	43	25	294

a—estimated by NEA Research Division.
b—estimated by staff, based on ADA figures for 1969-1970.
c—Total for states which would get funds. No state is credited with a negative amount. Hence, this is more than U. S. total ADM x $800 minus 4% of U. S. personal income, which is only $6,452 million.
SOURCES: *Column 2*: Research Division, National Educational Association, *Estimates of School Statistics, 1970-71* (NEA: Washington, D.C., 1970) Table 3, column 5. *Column 3*: Column 2 multiplied by $800. *Column 4*: Personal Income multiplied by 4 percent. Personal Income for 1969 obtained from U. S. Department of Commerce, Office of Business Statistics: *Survey of Current Business*, (Washington, D.C.: U. S. Government Printing Office) Volume 50, No. 8, August 1970, p. 34. *Column 5*: Column 3 minus column 4.

assuming that approximately the same amount of federal revenue is received by the states from each plan? Obviously the *best* plan can be determined only in terms of the purposes desired to be served by general federal aid and the relative priority assigned to each purpose. It is the responsibility of the people exercised through their elected officials serving at the federal level to make these determinations. Insofar as the public schools are concerned, they would be greatly benefited by any alternative plan of apportionment analyzed above or any combination thereof provided that the amount of general federal aid appropriated would be equal to or greater than the minimum amount suggested in this

TABLE 11-2

PLAN II—EQUAL GRANT OF $158 PER PUPIL IN ADM WITH NO
REQUIRED STATE AND LOCAL EFFORT

State	Total Contribution $158 Times ADM of Each State (in millions)	State	Total Contribution $158 Times ADM of Each State (in millions)
(1)	(2)	(1)	(2)
U. S. TOTAL	$7,122		
Alabama	130	Montana	27
Alaska	12	Nebraska	52
Arizona	66	Nevada	19
Arkansas	69	New Hampshire	24
California	778	New Jersey	229
Colorado	84	New Mexico	44
Connecticut	101	New York	545
Delaware	20	North Carolina	185
Florida	222	North Dakota	23
Georgia	173	Ohio	379
Hawaii	28	Oklahoma	96
Idaho	29	Oregon	74
Illinois	353	Pennsylvania	367
Indiana	201	Rhode Island	28
Iowa	103	South Carolina	101
Kansas	78	South Dakota	26
Kentucky	109	Tennessee	139
Louisiana	133	Texas	410
Maine	38	Utah	48
Maryland	140	Vermont	16
Massachusetts	179	Virginia	168
Michigan	338	Washington	130
Minnesota	144	West Virginia	63
Mississippi	88	Wisconsin	146
Missouri	154	Wyoming	13

TABLE 11-3

EQUAL GRANT PER PUPIL FOR EQUAL EFFORT IN PROPORTION TO ABILITY

State	State and Local Revenue for the Schools as a Percentage of Net Personal Income[a]	Relative Effort of Each State[b]	Federal Grant Per Pupil[c]	Total Federal Grant[d] (in thousands)
(1)	(2)	(3)	(4)	(5)
U. S. Total	6.24	1.00	158	7,125,800
Alabama	5.50	.88	139	113,980
Alaska	6.21	1.00	158	12,166
Arizona	7.71	1.24	158	65,886
Arkansas	6.15	.99	156	78,016
California	6.48	1.04	158	778,150
Colorado	6.61	1.06	158	84,372
Connecticut	5.64	.90	142	90,880
Delaware	7.19	1.15	158	20,382
Florida	6.33	1.01	158	222,464
Georgia	5.74	.92	145	159,210
Hawaii	6.37	1.02	158	28,282
Idaho	7.13	1.14	158	29,230
Illinois	5.39	.86	136	303,552
Indiana	6.55	1.05	158	201,292
Iowa	7.03	1.13	158	103,332
Kansas	6.67	1.07	158	78,368
Kentucky	5.74	.92	145	100,340
Louisiana	7.45	1.19	158	133,194
Maine	6.45	1.03	158	37,762
Maryland	6.76	1.08	158	139,672
Massachusetts	5.22	.84	133	150,556
Michigan	6.44	1.03	158	338,436
Minnesota	7.36	1.18	158	144,254
Mississippi	7.84	1.26	158	88,322
Missouri	5.52	.88	139	135,664
Montana	8.06	1.29	158	27,334
Nebraska	5.00	.80	126	41,454
Nevada	5.93	.95	150	18,300
New Hampshire	5.37	.86	136	20,264
New Jersey	5.72	.92	145	210,105
New Mexico	8.90	1.43	158	43,608
New York	6.99	1.12	158	544,942
North Carolina	5.89	.94	149	174,479
North Dakota	7.14	1.14	158	23,226
Ohio	5.30	.85	134	321,466
Oklahoma	5.66	.91	144	87,264
Oregon	8.02	1.29	158	73,786
Pennsylvania	6.15	.99	156	361,920
Rhode Island	5.15	.83	131	23,318
South Carolina	6.66	1.07	158	101,120
South Dakota	5.91	.95	150	24,750
Tennessee	5.86	.94	149	131,120
Texas	5.43	.87	137	355,926
Utah	8.40	1.35	158	47,716
Vermont	7.53	1.21	158	16,274
Virginia	6.28	1.01	158	167,954
Washington	6.25	1.00	158	130,034
West Virginia	7.63	1.22	158	62,726
Wisconsin	6.61	1.06	158	146,308
Wyoming	6.54	1.05	158	13,430

[a]See Chapter 4 of this volume for the method of computation.
[b]Column 2 ÷ 6.24.
[c]Column 3 not in excess of 1.00 times $158.
[d]Column 4 times the ADM of each state.

TABLE 11-4

PLAN IV—APPROXIMATELY ONE-HALF OF FEDERAL APPROPRIATION ON BASIS OF FLAT GRANT OF $79 PER PUPIL AND ONE-HALF OF THE NATIONAL FOUNDATION PROGRAM BASIS

	Flat Grant	National Foundation Program of $695				
	ADM of 1969-70 × $79	ADM of 1969-70 × $695	4 Percent of Personal Income 1969	Federal Contribution (Col. 3-4)	Total Federal Contribution ΔCol. 2+5	Federal Contribution Per Pupil in ADM
(1)	(2)	(3)	(4)	(5)	(6)	(7)
U. S. Total	3,565*	31,350*	29,628*	3,489*	7,054*	
Alabama	65	570	365	205	270	329
Alaska	6	54	50	4	10	130
Arizona	33	290	228	62	95	228
Arkansas	34	303	199	104	138	317
California	389	3,423	3,336	87	476	97
Colorado	42	371	303	68	110	206
Connecticut	51	445	551	0	51	79
Delaware	10	90	89	1	11	85
Florida	111	979	896	83	194	138
Georgia	87	763	570	193	280	255
Hawaii	14	124	122	2	16	89
Idaho	15	129	85	44	59	319
Illinois	176	1,551	1,894	0	176	79
Indiana	101	885	755	130	231	181
Iowa	52	455	395	60	112	171
Kansas	39	345	324	21	60	121
Kentucky	55	481	368	113	168	243
Louisiana	67	586	417	169	236	280
Maine	19	166	119	47	66	276
Maryland	70	614	613	1	71	80
Massachusetts	89	787	909	0	89	79
Michigan	169	1,488	1,400	88	257	120
Minnesota	72	635	538	97	169	185
Mississippi	44	389	209	180	224	401
Missouri	77	678	643	35	112	115

* In millions

TABLE 11-4 (Cont.)

	Flat Grant	National Foundation Program of $695				
	ADM of 1969-70 × $79	ADM of 1969-70 × $695	4 Percent of Personal Income 1969	Federal Contribution (Col. 3-4)	Total Federal Contribution ΔCol. 2+5	Federal Contribution Per Pupil in ADM
(1)	(2)	(3)	(4)	(5)	(6)	(7)
Montana	14	120	87	33	47	272
Nebraska	26	229	209	20	46	140
Nevada	10	85	81	4	14	115
New Hampshire	12	104	100	4	16	107
New Jersey	114	1,007	1,212	0	114	79
New Mexico	22	192	115	77	99	359
New York	272	2,397	3,255	0	272	79
North Carolina	93	814	601	213	306	261
North Dakota	12	102	74	28	40	272
Ohio	190	1,667	1,606	61	251	105
Oklahoma	48	421	513	108	156	257
Oregon	37	325	290	35	72	154
Pennsylvania	183	1,612	1,727	0	183	79
Rhode Island	14	124	141	0	14	79
South Carolina	51	445	281	164	215	336
South Dakota	13	115	80	35	48	291
Tennessee	70	612	448	164	234	266
Texas	205	1,806	1,458	348	553	213
Utah	24	210	125	85	109	361
Vermont	8	72	57	15	23	223
Virginia	84	739	618	121	205	193
Washington	65	572	524	48	113	137
West Virginia	31	276	189	87	118	297
Wisconsin	73	644	615	29	102	110
Wyoming	7	59	43	16	23	271

Column 5: Column 3 − Column 4
Column 6: Column 2 + Column 5
Column 7: Column 6 ÷ ADM

431

TABLE 11-5

RELATIVE IMPACT ON EQUALIZATION OF FINANCIAL RESOURCES OF PLANS I, II, III AND IV—TOTAL REVENUE PER PUPIL FROM ALL SOURCES UNDER PLANS I, II, III AND IV COMPARED WITH TOTAL REVENUE FROM ALL SOURCES AVAILABLE PER PUPIL IN 1969–70

(1)	(2) Total Revenue from Federal, State and Local Sources Per Pupil in ADM 1969–70	(3) Total Revenue Per Pupil in ADM 1969–70 Plus Amount Proposed Under Plan I	(4) Total Revenue Per Pupil in ADM 1969–70 Plus Amount Proposed Under Plan II	(5) Total Revenue Per Pupil in ADM 1969–70 Plus Amount Proposed Under Plan III	(6) Total Revenue Per Pupil in ADM 1969–70 Plus Amount Proposed Under Plan IV
U. S. Average	$ 842	$1,001	$1,000	$1,000	$ 998*
Alabama	523	878	681	662	852
Alaska	1,129	1,285	1,287	1,287	1,259
Arizona	864	1,118	1,022	1,022	1,092
Arkansas	570	914	728	726	887
California	773	896	931	931	870
Colorado	810	1,042	968	968	1,016
Connecticut	1,155	1,155	1,313	1,297	1,234
Delaware	1,056	1,165	1,214	1,214	1,141
Florida	804	967	962	962	942
Georgia	589	870	747	734	844
Hawaii	1,066	1,183	1,224	1,224	1,155
Idaho	588	929	746	746	907
Illinois	1,064	1,064	1,222	1,200	1,143
Indiana	688	895	846	846	869
Iowa	844	1,053	1,022	1,002	1,015
Kansas	914	1,061	1,072	1,072	1,035
Kentucky	660	929	818	805	903
Louisiana	703	1,008	861	861	983
Maine	725	1,026	883	883	1,001
Maryland	968	1,074	1,126	1,126	1,048

TABLE 11-5 (Cont.)

(1)	Total Revenue from Federal, State and Local Sources Per Pupil in ADM 1969-70	Total Revenue Per Pupil in ADM 1969-70 Plus Amount Proposed Under Plan I	Total Revenue Per Pupil in ADM 1969-70 Plus Amount Proposed Under Plan II	Total Revenue Per Pupil in ADM 1969-70 Plus Amount Proposed Under Plan III	Total Revenue Per Pupil in ADM 1969-70 Plus Amount Proposed Under Plan IV
	(2)	(3)	(4)	(5)	(6)
Massachusetts	882	882	1,040	1,015	961
Michigan	798	944	956	956	918
Minnesota	903	1,113	1,061	1,061	1,088
Mississippi	561	987	719	719	962
Missouri	771	912	929	910	886
Montana	821	1,116	979	979	1,093
Nebraska	708	872	866	834	848
Nevada	864	1,003	1,022	1,014	979
New Hampshire	761	889	919	897	868
New Jersey	1,079	1,079	1,237	1,224	1,158
New Mexico	749	1,133	907	907	1,108
New York	1,325	1,325	1,483	1,483	1,404
North Carolina	670	957	828	819	931
North Dakota	754	1,047	912	912	1,026
Ohio	758	888	916	892	863
Oklahoma	560	844	718	704	817
Oregon	980	1,160	1,138	1,138	1,134
Pennsylvania	970	1,026	1,128	1,126	1,049
Rhode Island	850	856	1,008	981	929
South Carolina	655	1,016	813	813	991
South Dakota	673	988	831	823	964
Tennessee	607	898	695	756	873
Texas	652	891	810	789	865
Utah	707	1,094	865	865	1,068
Vermont	933	1,176	1,091	1,091	1,156

433

TABLE 11-5 (Cont.)

(1)	Total Revenue from Federal, State and Local Sources Per Pupil in ADM 1969–70 (2)	Total Revenue Per Pupil in ADM 1969–70 Plus Amount Proposed Under Plan I (3)	Total Revenue Per Pupil in ADM 1969–70 Plus Amount Proposed Under Plan II (4)	Total Revenue Per Pupil in ADM 1969–70 Plus Amount Proposed Under Plan III (5)	Total Revenue Per Pupil in ADM 1969–70 Plus Amount Proposed Under Plan IV (6)
Virginia	781	999	939	939	974
Washington	905	1,068	1,063	1,063	1,042
West Virginia	703	1,028	861	861	1,000
Wisconsin	967	1,103	1,125	1,125	1,077
Wyoming	879	1,173	1,037	1,037	1,150
Ratio of State with Greatest Amount of Revenue Per Pupil to State with Least Amount	2.53 to 1	1.57 to 1	2.18 to 1	2.24 to 1	1.72 to 1

Column 2: Computed from *NEA Estimates of School Statistics 1969–70* (Revised).
Column 3: Federal Revenue per pupil proposed under Plan I added to Column 2.
Column 4: Federal Revenue per pupil proposed under Plan II added to Column 2.
Column 5: Federal Revenue per pupil proposed under Plan III added to Column 2.
Column 6: Federal Revenue per pupil proposed under Plan IV added to Column 2.

*The national average for Plans III and IV would have been approximately the same as the national average for Plans I and II if all states had made a state and local effort equal to or greater than 4.7736 percent of personal income.

chapter. The minimum amount of federal aid needed in order to at least make some significant impact on the accomplishment of legitimate federal purposes, including present categorical aids plus the proposed general aid of 20 percent of state and local school revenue, would total approximately 21 percent of total school revenue. Those purposes would be much more adequately accomplished if the federal government would provide 30 percent of total school revenues.

It has been recommended earlier in this chapter that block categorical grants for the education of certain high cost target populations such as vocational students, the handicapped and the culturally disadvantaged be continued. The percent of the total school enrollment of these high cost pupils varies from state to state, especially the percent of the culturally disadvantaged. If the categorical appropriations for these high cost pupils are discontinued, the allocations per pupil for general aid should be varied appropriately in order to reflect these higher costs.

Finally, numerous proposals have been made concerning the controls the federal government should retain over general aid. Those proposals range all the way from no controls whatsoever to detailed controls similar to those now being exercised over some categorical grants. The National Educational Finance Project favors the minimum of federal controls over general federal aid necessary to attain the basic federal purposes in providing general aid.

FOOTNOTES

1. NOTE: This section draws extensively from a paper by Erick Lindman entitled "Criteria for Coordinating Federal Programs" reported in *Proceedings of Tenth Annual Conference on School Finance*, Washington, D. C.: National Education Association, 1967.

2. A better measure of the relative measure of the state to support education is described in Chapter 4 and applied to Plan III in this chapter.

3. This is sometimes called the equalized matching plan.

CHAPTER 12

The Effect of Different Levels of
Expenditure on Educational Output

To the man on the street and to many educators alike, the quality of education in a school district is closely related to that district's expenditures. Historically, "quality education" and additional financial support for the schools have been tied together inextricably by those who wished to improve the schools. Over the past four decades, professional educators and their organizations have exhorted legislators and taxpayers alike that better schools mean more dollars, and clearly the guardians of the public purse strings believed the message. Annual per pupil expenditures for elementary and secondary schools increased seven-fold from $108 in 1930 to $750 in 1968.[1]

Even when these figures are adjusted for the declining purchasing power of the dollar during that period, per pupil expenditures showed an increase of 350 percent. That is, in dollars valued at 1967-68 prices, the average expenditure per student in public elementary and secondary schools rose from about $215 in 1930 to approximately $750 in 1968.

During the decade of the sixties, two important changes in this scenario took place which raised doubts about a simple and straightforward relationship between educational expenditures and quality. Suddenly the public had been made aware that the schools were failing to teach basic skills to large numbers of youngsters from low income backgrounds.[2] Following the usual Pavlovian pattern of response to criticism, educational agencies

436

and organizations asserted that any failures of the schools—if there were failures at all—were due to inadequate finances. They suggested that more educational dollars spent on students from low income backgrounds would remedy the problem. And, indeed, more dollars for so-called disadvantaged students were squeezed from federal, state, and local treasuries. The Elementary and Secondary Education Act of 1965 itself provided over $1 billion a year to support educational and related services for students from low income families. Almost every major city set up its own compensatory education program, and states also provided additional funds for these purposes.

Surprisingly, the evidence gathered from compensatory education programs suggested that additional dollars rarely produced any measurable improvement in educational outcomes for most disadvantaged students. That is, the mere fact that more dollars were spent on particular children in no way assured that those children would be better off educationally. For example, the U.S. Office of Education in evaluating the effect of monies allocated under Title I of the Elementary and Secondary Education Act of 1965 found that on the basis of reading scores, ". . . a child who participated in a Title I project had only a 19% chance of a significant achievement gain, a 13% chance of a significant achievement loss, and a 68% chance of no change at all (relative to the national norms)."[3] Further, the projects included in the investigation were ". . . most likely to be representative of projects in which there was a higher than average investment in resources. Therefore, more significant achievement gains should be found here than in a more representative sample of Title I projects."[4]

Other evaluations of compensatory education showed consistent evidence that additional dollars in the school coffers did not improve ostensibly the quality of education received by disadvantaged children. Of some 1,000 programs reviewed for the U. S. Office of Education, only 21 seemed to have produced significant pupil achievement gains in language or numerical skills.[5]

Moreover, cost-benefit analyses of such programs suggested that spending on conventional compensatory education approaches represented a poor social investment for the reduction of poverty.[6]

The theory that additional educational expenditures automatically led to better schools was also challenged directly by

437

the findings of the Coleman Report.[7] Coleman directed a national survey of schools and their relation to student achievement. On the basis of extensive analysis of pupil, teacher, and other school data, Coleman concluded that per pupil expenditures, books in the library, and a number of other school measures show very little relation to student achievement if the social background of individual students and their classmates are held constant.[8]

While the statistical techniques and data of the report led clearly to an understatement of school effects, the pessimistic finding on school effects dealt a severe blow to the widely held view that higher expenditures would improve educational outcomes.[9] Moreover, the extensive circulation of the Coleman Report and its loose interpretation by many commentators and reviewers gave wide currency to the claim that increases in school expenditures would produce *no* gains in student achievement. Both the compensatory education experience and the Coleman Report raised serious challenges to the theory that money, itself, represented a good general remedy for curing the infirmities of the schools.

HOW DO EXPENDITURES AFFECT EDUCATIONAL OUTCOMES ?

The purpose of this paper is to explore the relationship between educational expenditures and educational effectiveness. In order to trace out this linkage we will first use economic analysis to develop the conceptual ties between expenditures and educational outcomes. Second, we will review empirical studies of resources effectiveness in education. Finally, we will present some policy recommendations for improving the efficiency of educational expenditures.

In order to understand how expenditures are translated into educational outcomes it is necessary to define several concepts from economics as they relate to the production of education. For these purposes the school or school district can be considered to be a firm that is expected to maximize educational output within the limits of a fixed budget.[10] That is, faced with a given budgetary constraint on expenditures, the school district is expected to obtain the largest possible educational outcome. In order to observe the conditions under which this would be accomplished, it is necessary to consider an educational production function.

438

Educational Production Functions

An educational production function can be depicted as a technological relationship showing the maximum amount of educational output that could be produced by each and every set of specified inputs or factors of production.[11] Equation (1) represents a production function for an educational enterprise where A signifies a measure of educational outcomes, B denotes the nature of the student clientele, and $X_1, X_2, \ldots, X_n$ represents a set of inputs or resources used by the schools to produce education. For the moment,

$$(1) \quad A = f\ (B, X_1, X_2, \ldots, X_n),$$

let us assume that A is a composite measure of educational outcomes that we expect from the schools such as increases in learning, changes in attitudes, social consciousness, and so on.[12] Ideally, A should represent the "value-added" to the student body and to the larger society in a given period that is attributable to the school production process over that period. That is, changes in attitudes, performance, cultural appreciation, and so on are the outputs that schools produce. A "value-added" measure tacitly accounts for the fact that some children begin the schooling process with different levels of performance, and the schools should only be held accountable for that part of the change in such measures that is attributable to the schooling influence. Attempts at using the value-added approach have fallen short of success, however, primarily because of measurement problems.[13]

B represents the various characteristics of the students that affect educational outcomes. These include racial and cultural factors as well as ones that reflect the socioeconomic background of the student and his community. The educational outcomes A are affected by student characteristics B for two reasons. First, the objectives that we have for the schools are often based upon the values of the dominant group in society and reflect the cultural attributes of that group. Thus, tests of verbal aptitudes are culture-specific reflecting the vocabulary and syntax of middle class whites rather than lower class whites, blacks, or other minority groups. Second, middle class families tend to emphasize learning in the home to a greater extent than those of lower socioeconomic strata. This advantage is reinforced by the greater ability of middle class families to give their children a wider range of experiences and learning materials, and by the

439

tendency of more highly educated parents to impart substantial vocabularies to their children and to teach their children certain skills which can be transferred to the school experience.[14]

The variables X_1, X_2, . . ., X_n represent the inputs provided by the educational firm for affecting changes in A, educational outcomes. These include all types of personnel, materials, facilities, and buildings that are used to produce education. The Xs may signify not only the quantities of such inputs but also their qualitative characteristics. Thus, X_1 may be a variable denoting the number of teachers, X_2 may represent teacher verbal ability, X_3 may signify teacher experience, and so on.

The assumption is made that an increase in B or in any school input X will increase school output A. Yet, it is also assumed that A will not increase indefinitely at the same rate as increases in B or one of the other school inputs. Rather, the law of diminishing marginal returns should apply, meaning that at some point the addition to A attributable to each additional unit of B or X will begin to diminish. In essence this suggests to the educational decision-maker that the gains in output from increases in an input such as teacher experience, teacher degree level, library size, and so on will be smaller the larger the intensity of those inputs. When a school library has 1,000 volumes, an additional 1,000 volumes may have a substantial impact on the language skills of the students. On the other hand, if the library already contains 10,000 volumes, an additional 1000 volumes may show only a nominal effect.

The production function for education is the means by which school resources are transformed into educational outcomes. Yet we have not established the link between outcomes and school expenditures since the inputs entering the production function are physical and psychological ones rather than dollars. But dollars are used to purchase those physical and psychological inputs. Accordingly, (2) shows the relationship between the dollar budget accorded educational decision makers and the transformation of that budget into school inputs.

$$(2) \quad R = P_1X_1 + P_2X_2 + . . . + P_nX_n$$

R represents the total dollar expenditure or budget allocated to the educational firm; P_1 signifies the price per unit of input X_1; P_2 is the price per unit of input X_2; and so on. The budget equation can be interpreted to mean that the entire dollar allocation R will be devoted to expenditures on the inputs (X_1, X_2,

. . ., X_n) where the expenditure on each input is defined by the amount of each input used multiplied by its price. If X_1 is years of teacher experience and the cost for obtaining teacher experience is $100 per additional year per teacher, the $100 multiplied by the number of years of experience (X_1) will be that part of the total budget R that will be devoted to teacher experience. The sum of all of the inputs multiplied by their prices can not exceed the total budgetary allocation R.

The production function for education (1) and the budget relationship (2) are the two relations that the educational firm operates on to tie educational expenditures to educational outcomes A. In order to obtain the greatest increase in A, for any given budget R, the decision maker must determine that combination of the various inputs X that will maximize output within the expenditure constraint. At that point dollar expenditures will be allocated most effectively. In general, this condition is satisfied by purchasing and utilizing each of the inputs X_1, X_2, . . ., X_n in such a combination that the additional contribution to output from the last dollar expended on each input yields the same effect on output. That is, if an additional dollar spent on X_1, yields a greater contribution to output than one spent on X_2, then more X_1 should be applied to producing education and less X_2 should be used. The law of diminishing marginal returns suggests that an increase in the use of X_1 will be accompanied by a decline in the rate of increase in A due to more X_1, so at some point the marginal or additional impact of X_1 on A relative to that of X_2 on A will be equal for the last dollar spent on each.

Stated in more specific terms we would expect to obtain the largest impact on educational output A by satisfying the conditions described in (3).

(3)
$$\frac{Additional\ output\ from\ X_1}{P_1} = \frac{Additional\ output\ from\ X_2}{P_2} =$$
$$\ldots = \frac{Additional\ output\ from\ X_n}{P_n}$$

The additional output from each input relative to its price should be equal for all inputs. If any particular input yields a higher increment to A relative to its price, then more of that input should be applied so that the law of diminishing returns will equalize the additional output/price ratios.[15] This solution

441

FIGURE 12-1

Flow Diagram of Educational Resource Transformation

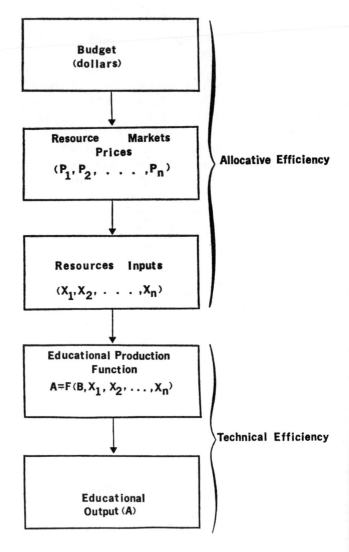

will maximize the effectiveness of the educational budget in producing educational output.

The accompanying flow diagram in Figure 6-1 illustrates the

transformation from dollars to educational outcomes. Dollar budgets are used to purchase school inputs in resource markets. Such markets include those for various types of personnel, equipment, physical space, and so on. These resources inputs are combined by educational managers into the educational production function, thereby producing the educational outcomes represented by A. The first three stages refer to allocative efficiency and the last two refer to technical efficiency. These concepts will be explained below. If all educational firms used dollars in their most efficient ways, then conditions (3) set out above would hold and A would be maximized for any specified level of expenditures, R.

Yet, in order for educational firms or schools to satisfy the criterion of efficiency, we would expect that several factors would be present. Each of these underlies the analogous model of profit maximization for business firms. (1) Substantial management discretion exists over which inputs are purchased and how they are organized to produce education; (2) reliable measures of output for the educational firm are available on a systematic basis; and (3) some system of incentives exists to spur educational managers to maximize output A, for any budget level R.

In fact, none of these factors are present. School principals and superintendents are bound by state education codes, regional accreditation requirements, contracts with educational personnel, and an inbred reverence for existing practices. Under such conditions and traditions, school managers show very little discretionary control over the purchase and utilization of school inputs.

Further, there are few outcomes of the schools that are measured systematically. While some achievement data from paper and pencil testing are available, even these are not adjusted for differences in performance due to student backgrounds and other non-school influences. Thus, they are of little operational value in assessing the schools' effects on achievement. Moreover, such tests measure such a limited range of outcomes, that even if they were useful on their own terms, they would not be appropriate as exclusive foci for school policy. Indicators of student attitudes, feelings, cultural aptitudes, and other skills that might be developed by the schools are not obtained in any regular and systematic way.

Even the accounting systems used by the schools are unable

to link the ingredients of particular programs or the programs themselves to either costs or outcomes. Traditional line-item budgets yield only the information that money was spent on particular items serving functions such as administration, instruction, and so on, and even these so-called functions are misnomered.[16] While the trend is clearly toward accounting systems that do tie resources, costs, programs, and outcomes together for the educational sector, so called planning-programming-budgeting systems (PPBS) are at a very early stage in their application to the schools.[17] In summary, there do not exist school information systems that provide useful data to school managers for educational decision-making.[18]

Finally, incentives for maximizing educational outcomes for a given budget do not seem to be important characteristics of schools as organizations. Financial rewards and promotions for school personnel are handed out in a mindless fashion according to the years of service and accumulation of college credits.[20] Individual schools, teachers, or administrators who are successful in achieving important educational goals are treated similarly to those who are unsuccessful, mediocre, or downright incompetent. In lockstep fashion the schools reward all equally. It is no wonder, then, that schools can fail persistently to teach children to read, or to foster the formation of healthy attitudes, for there are no direct incentives to change the situation. That is, success is not compensated, or formally recognized, and the reward structure is systematically divorced from educational effectiveness.[21] In contrast, commercial enterprises tend to compensate their personnel on the basis of their contributions to the effectiveness of the organization. Commissions for sales personnel, bonuses, promotions, profits, and salary increases all represent rewards for individual or organizational proficiencies.

TECHNICAL AND ALLOCATIVE EFFICIENCY

Given the facts that educational managers lack the discretionary control, the information, and the incentives to maximize educational output for any dollar constraint, it is reasonable to expect massive inefficiencies in the operations of schools. That is, dollar expenditures applied to the schools could probably be used far more effectively than they presently are. Of course, it is important to point out that there are likely to be large differences from school to school, some schools being more

444

efficient than others. Differences in efficiency among schools will depend upon differences in managerial skills as well as differences in the three characteristics outlined above, discretionary control, information, and incentives.

For purposes of analysis it is useful to divide inefficiencies into two types, *technical* and *allocative*. Technical inefficiencies refer to those attributable to using the physical resources of the school in such a way that less educational output is achieved than might be done under some alternative utilization. Allocative inefficiencies refer to those attributable to using the dollar budget of the school in such a way that less output is achieved than could be attained if a different combination of physical resources were purchased even when technical efficiency is satisfied.

More specifically, with any set of physical resources that the schools purchase—the various types of administrators, teachers, other personnel, materials, and facilities — there is some way of organizing them that will maximize the educational output of the school. For example, there is abundant evidence of so-called aptitude-treatment interaction such that some resources are effective for one type of child and relatively ineffective for another type.[22] Some children thrive on structured classroom situations, while others develop more fully in a freer atmosphere. Yet students are not assigned to teachers on the basis of these characteristics. Rather the assignment practices seem to derive from bookkeeping traditions more than from educational rationale.

Most of the technical inefficiencies of the schools reflect the mindlessness of the educational decision-making, and no practice illustrates this better than that relating to class size. The goal of most elementary schools seems to be that of making class size uniform at each grade level if not throughout the enterprise. But the relevance of class size to the learning situation must surely depend on the nature of the students, the subject, the teacher's behavioral style, as well as many other factors. In some situations very small groups are needed in order to individualize instruction, while in other contexts 40-60 students would be more appropriate. These concepts are not recognized by the bland uniformity of current class-size practice.

Often, innovational equipment and curricula are not properly integrated into the school organization, leading to other technical inefficiencies. Typically, the innovations are chosen by

445

administrators rather than the teachers who must implement them; teachers are given inadequate training and lack appropriate commitment; and meaningful evaluation of the innovation does not follow its adoption. Accordingly, the new curriculum or innovational equipment is rarely utilized in a technically efficient way.

Given the resources that schools purchase, greater educational effectiveness could be obtained if they were organized differently, that is, if they were technically efficient. Technical efficiency, then refers to the linkage between the last two blocks in the flow diagram in Figure 12-1, the tie between the educational production function *and* output. Yet, even if the schools were technically efficient (maximizing output for a set of physical inputs) it does not follow that the school is allocatively efficient. Allocative efficiency occurs when the dollar budget is spent in such a way that the resources that are purchased yield the best outcome that can be attained for the given budget. That is, any other combination of resources that could be purchased with that budget would obtain a lower level of output.

Schools are generally allocatively efficient when equation (3), above, holds. That is, more of each resource would be purchased until the additional output from another unit of the resource relative to its price is equal to the additional output from any other resource relative to its price. Both the relative prices and the accretions to output must be considered in obtaining allocative efficiency. Yet, the schools do not have knowledge of either the additional outputs or prices of hiring additional inputs. Thus allocative decisions are made on the basis of conventional wisdoms, and even massive increases in budgets are allocated to such costly resources as more personnel for reducing class size while alternative ways of improving the schools are either not considered or are rejected out-of-hand without considering whether they yield greater increases in output for the additional expenditures.

The quest for allocative efficiency is represented by the linkages among the first three boxes in Figure 12-1 where the budget is applied in the market place to obtain resource inputs. One tool for seeking allocative efficiency is that of cost-effectiveness analysis. Yet, cost-effectiveness analysis has been used very rarely in making educational decisions, in part, because educators are generally unfamiliar with its underlying concepts and complexities. But certainly the limited data base with which

446

educators must work represents a severe limitation to its present application.[23]

Size and Efficiency

Technical and allocative efficiencies are not the only determinants of educational effectiveness for a given level of expenditure. The size, or enrollment, of a school or school district is also a crucial factor. That is, the size or scale of the school enterprise can affect the economic efficiency with which it produces educational services even if the school is allocatively and technically efficient. Translated into costs, the same level of educational output will incur differences in costs depending upon the enrollment of the school or school district.

In general we would expect a U-shaped cost curve as in Figure 12-2.

FIGURE 12-2

Average Cost as a Function of Enrollment

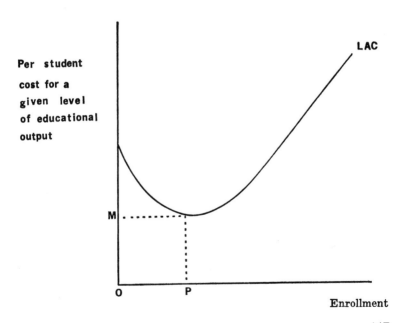

447

The long run average cost curve LAC shows declining costs per student as enrollments increase up to enrollment level P. This phenomenon reflects the fact that minimum teacher and other resources required for any level of educational outcome will not be fully utilized at very low enrollments. That is, these resources represent minimum "fixed capital" requirements that are necessary just to provide an educational offering of a given quality. Thus, at very low levels of enrollment the cost per student is very high. It is this phenomenon which fed the school consolidation movement during the first half of this century.

Beyond enrollment level P, costs rise as the size of schools or school districts increase. The reason for increased costs as a function of enrollment is that the existing organization and technology of schools can not be administered efficiently at very high enrollment levels. The difficulties of governing and administering such large units means that higher resource inputs per student are required to achieve a given outcome.[24] That is, diseconomies of scale set in as enrollments move beyond P.

Thus, a third type of efficiency that will be reflected in the effectiveness of educational dollars is that of size or scale of enterprise. At enrollment level P, the unit cost for a given educational outcome is minimized. As schools diverge from this optimal size they will face increasing costs without increases in the educational output for each student. Accordingly, for an educational firm to maximize educational product for a given budget it must satisfy not only the criteria of technical and allocative efficiency, but also those of scale. That is, it must be the appropriate size to operate at P. In the next section we will review briefly the empirical findings on education efficiency.

EMPIRICAL FINDINGS ON EDUCATIONAL EFFICIENCY

Three types of studies exist which seek to determine the relationships between school inputs and educational outcomes. The first type of study attempts to link total educational expenditures to output measures. The second group includes those that have attempted to estimate the effects of various functional components of expenditure on school outcomes, and the third set of studies represents estimates of the relationships between resources as measured in physical terms and school outputs (educational production functions). Sometimes the latter two

448

approaches have been combined so that resources are measured in dollars for some inputs and in physical qualities and quantities for others.

Expenditure Studies

Expenditure studies seek to examine the gross relations between dollar inputs and educational processes and outcomes. While several of these inquiries have been carried out in recent years, this approach has been pursued, broadly speaking, for at least three decades.[25] Such studies shed little light on the economic efficiency of schools for a variety of reasons.

First expenditures are an aggregate dollar amount that is not decomposed into the actual educational resources that are being used. Thus, we do not know from these studies why expenditures affect outcomes in the samples or which particular composition of expenditures is most productive (the question of allocative efficiency). Second, the measures of expenditure are generally crude ones that are not adjusted for price level differences. Such adjustments are crucial when one is considering national, regional, and statewide samples of schools. Even in metropolitan areas the cost of equivalent teachers, construction, and land is generally higher in the cities than in the suburbs.[26] Moreover, inconsistencies among school districts and states in accounting procedures as well as imprecise survey questions on expenditures have likely led to important measurement errors in several studies.[27]

Early studies tracing the link between expenditure levels and school performance were carried out by specialists in school administration. These so-called cost-quality studies were carried out in order to see how dollar support levels were associated with school quality.[28] In addition to the measurement problems outlined above, these studies suffer from two other severe deficiencies. First, a lack of data on educational outcomes necessitated the use of such indirect measures of school quality as perceived innovation and change or other subjective ratings. Second, these works ignored completely the social class aspects of the school in explaining "school quality." Thus, while the cost-quality studies are provocative when placed in historical perspective, they can not provide an empirical basis for improving our understanding of the effect of educational expenditures on school outcomes.

In contrast, several recent studies have examined the relationships between school expenditures and student achievement scores while attempting to control for differences in socioeconomic backgrounds of students. Thomas Ribich addressed himself specifically to the effects that higher school expenditures might have on the educational attainment of disadvantaged children.[29] Adjustment for student backgrounds, B in equation (1), was attempted by carrying out the analysis only for students from the lowest socioeconomic origins.

Using the Project Talent data, Ribich examined achievement levels of some 6,300 twelfth grade males who were ranked in the bottom 20 percent of a nationally representative sample on a socioeconomic index. He concluded:

> "... it seems clear that low status boys in higher expenditure schools do accumulate more knowledge than their counterparts in low expenditure schools. The effect of increased school expenditures on test performance is shown to be the strongest at the lower end of the expenditure range. A difference of more than a full year of achievement appears between boys in school districts spending less than $200 and districts spending between $200 and $300. The apparent power of increased expenditures to improve performance diminishes progressively with each successive expenditure level.[30]

Much of this increase was due simply to higher costs for a constant level of school services. Thus Ribich observed a tendency for lower-status students to have greater achievement scores the higher the level of school district expenditures, but the relationship was a declining one as expenditures rose.

Kiesling also explored the tie between school district expenditures and student achievement; but his analysis covered the full range of social class backgrounds and several grade levels.[31] More specifically, Kiesling estimated the expenditure-performance relationship for school districts at various grade levels between grades 4 and 11 and by the occupational status of the father. In addition he carried out separate analyses by size and type of school district. Using such explanatory variables as school expenditures, measured IQ of the students, and school district size, Kiesling found a varying association of expenditures on achievement from sample to sample.[32]

What is particularly interesting is his finding that for low socioeconomic status children the relationship between school expenditures and achievement was negative. Kiesling concluded "It seems that high expenditure (per pupil) districts do a poorer job of educating their low background students than low expenditure districts do."[33] This finding supports the possibility that spending money on those school resources that improve the performance of middle-class children may have a deleterious impact on the performance of lower-class students by under-mining the cultural attributes of the latter.[34]

Just as Ribich found that additional expenditures seemed to have a greater impact on pupil achievement at low expenditure levels than at high ones, so did Kiesling. For large urban districts an additional $100 of expenditure per pupil was associated with an additional pupil gain of 2.6 months in standardized test units at the low end of the expenditure range but only 1.4 months at the upper end of the range.[35] In summary, Kiesling found that the apparent effect of additional expenditures on achievement varied according to the initial expenditure level, the type and size of the school district, and the socioeconomic class of the student sample.

Expenditure-Component Studies

The studies examining the relation between total per student expenditures and school outcomes can throw little light on how to improve the technical and allocative efficiency of schools, since they can reveal—at best—only the "state of the art" linkages under the existing inefficient organization of resources. That is, in no way can such inquiries tell us which specific inputs are making a difference and whether that difference could not be achieved by some cheaper input combination. The expenditure component studies disaggregate total expenditures into constituent parts in order to see if expenditures on particular types of inputs have an impact on educational outcomes as well as to explore the relative dollar payoffs. Since these studies do not address themselves to how the resources are used they can not reveal insights into technical efficiency. Rather, they are addressed to yielding information on which group of resources that the school purchases gives the highest educational returns per dollar input, a matter of allocative efficiency. Many of the problems in measuring expenditures that were outlined in the previous section are also reflected in the expenditure-component studies.

A fairly large number of recent studies that make the necessary attempt to account for the influence of student socioeconomic class on school outputs have used an expenditure-component approach.[36] These explorations measure some inputs in physical terms and other ones in dollar values. Perhaps the most interesting aspect of these studies is the rather consistent finding that teacher salary levels show a positive and significant association with student achievement when other measurable influences are held constant.[37]

Presumably, at higher teacher salary levels the quality of teachers recruited by school districts improves. That is, the higher the salary the larger the pool of candidates for teaching positions. At lower teaching salaries many of these candidates would prefer to seek more lucrative teaching employment. Out of this larger applicant pool the schools can obtain a more competent teaching force.[38] Indeed, the empirical evidence on the tie between teacher quality and salaries also supports this interpretation.[39]

Estimates of Educational Production Functions

The most prevalent recent work on educational production relates school resources measured in physical and psychological terms to school outcomes. These studies represent attempts to estimate variants of equation (1) described in the introductory section of this paper, and they can be thought of as the closest approximations to educational production functions that are currently available.

Most of these studies apply multivariate statistical models to large-scale surveys of schools and students.[40] Consistent with the findings of the expenditure-component studies, the characteristics of teachers seem to be the most important determinant of school outputs as reflected in pupil achievement scores.

The landmark study by Coleman and his associates showed that other than possible student influences on each other, the attributes of the teachers appeared to be the most important in school determinant of scholastic achievement.[41] The fact that these effects were probably understated by the statistical model used by Coleman to analyze the data reinforces the apparent prominence of teacher characteristics in influencing educational outcomes.[42] Since schools focus on teacher-student interactions and teacher inputs account for the preponderant share of school budgets, this finding is not surprising. Yet, the particular attributes of teachers which have been shown to be statistically related to student achievement do raise questions about conventional concepts of teacher quality.

Perhaps the most intriguing finding is the observed association between teacher verbal abilities and student achievement. The survey on which the Coleman Report was based included a short vocabulary test that was appended to the teacher questionnaire. Both in the Coleman study and in re-analyses of the Coleman data, the teacher's verbal score was found to be related rather consistently to pupil achievement at the several grade levels and for samples of both black and white students.[43] In a later study that relied upon a different sample and data base, Hanushek also found the teacher's verbal score to relate to pupil performance.[44] Of course it is important to point out that the teacher's verbal score may be a proxy for a large number of possible cognitive and personal traits of the teacher; so that the observed relationship between the teacher's verbal pattern and student achievement may derive from these associated traits rather than the teacher's verbal proficiencies *per se*.

While teacher experience has also been found to be related to student achievement on a fairly consistent basis, the teacher's degree level has rarely shown such an effect.[45] Moreover, variables reflecting the teacher's certification status on the basis of existing state requirements seem to show no apparent association with student achievement. Finally, most studies have found no statistical effect of differences in class size on pupil performance.

While these findings seem reasonable, they should be interpreted within the present context of the research that produced them. The educational models underlying these studies are not yet so refined, nor are the techniques of measurement so perfect, that we can consider the results as final ones. There is a great deal of knowledge that must be accumulated before we can be more nearly certain of our present insights into the production process. Moreover, since it is reasonable to believe that schools are operating inefficiently, even these insights must be viewed as ones derived from schools that are not technically efficient. Rather, the results are based on the "average" state-of-the-art, not the most productive one.

Finally, and most important, no one set of average findings is readily applicable to all student populations under all conditions. A good approach for teaching white children does not seem to be very effective for black ones or Mexican American ones, and the same differentiations must probably be made for other sociocultural types with different learning characteristics.[46] Some other complications are introduced by the multi-dimensional nature of educational outputs.[47] Thus, while educational production function estimates are interesting in an explorative sense, their direct application to public policy must be done with great circumspection.

Allocative Efficiency and Empirical Results

The fruits of educational production function analysis can be used to derive implications for allocative efficiency in two ways. As the reader will recall from equations (1), (2), and (3) above, an allocatively efficient school is one that purchases that combination of inputs which maximized the potential educational impact of its budget. Under such conditions the school is obtaining an equal addition to output from an additional dollar spent on any input. If the production function analysis suggests that no additional output is forthcoming from increasing a particular input (e.g. teacher degree level), then to devote additional resources to that input is inefficient. That is, if a resource shows no relation to output, allocative efficiency would require that none of the resource be purchased regardless of its price. One must be very cautious, however, in applying this principle to the findings of present studies since the lack of an observable relation may be attributable to the crudeness of the measurements and the models underlying the analysis rather than to the lack of a true relation.

Given significant statistical associations between several inputs and educational output, one might like to explore the relative efficiency of allocating more of the budget to each of the several inputs. As in equation (3), one requires both the marginal product or accretion to output for each additional unit of input as well as the prices of each input. On the basis of these data one can estimate the allocative pattern among inputs that will yield the largest increase in output within a limited budget. Few such studies have been carried out for educational

454

production, in part because the "prices" of such inputs as teacher characteristics are difficult to derive.

An early investigation into this area has suggested that obtaining teachers with higher verbal scores is five to ten times as effective per dollar of expenditure in raising student verbal score than a strategy of obtaining teachers with more experience.[48] The implications of this finding are that schools might derive higher student verbal performance by emphasizing the recruitment of more verbally able teachers rather than a more experienced teacher complement. The nascent stage of development of cost-effectiveness applications in education must surely qualify the use of such findings until they are firmly validated by additional inquiry.

Empirical Findings on Size and Efficiency

The theoretical reasons for expecting both very large and very small schooling units to be inefficient were outlined above. What are the empirical findings on this subject? Studies on efficiency and size can be divided into two types: those that explore the relationship for individual schools and those that examine it for school districts. Clearly, adequate studies in this area must consider the nature of the student population as well as educational outcomes in examining the association between size and performance.[49]

Studies of school district size have indicated no evidence of economies of scale for the range of districts under consideration. That is, the larger districts did not appear to be outperforming smaller ones in standardized achievement scores once student inputs and school expenditures were accounted for.[50] Indeed, Kiesling found that under certain conditions the size-performance relation was negative, suggesting that large districts were less efficient than smaller ones.[51] These studies did not concentrate on the very small rural districts where economies of scale in resource use are obvious. Even when such districts were consolidated they often had a student population for all grades that was a fraction of the enrollment of a single, urban elementary school.[52]

Neither have these studies examined the particular implications for educational efficiency of the very large, urban school districts, those with over 100,000 students. The very poor performance of those units has recently become a topic of immense

455

concern as evidenced by the major inquiries carried out for New York City and Los Angeles, the two largest school districts in the country.[53] Apparently, the cumbersome nature of the very large urban districts leads to substantial waste and inefficiencies in their operation.

For example, it was found that reading scores in schools attended by middle-class children in Los Angeles were no better than those of children from much lower socioeconomic backgrounds who were attending schools in the smaller districts surrounding Los Angeles.[54] Furthermore, the relative deficiencies in performance of the Los Angeles students did not appear to be related to differential expenditures among districts.[55]

The studies on high school size, too, indicate no evidence of economies of scale and at least some suggestion of diseconomies of scale. Kiesling examined the relationship between standardized test scores of students and school size while statistically adjusting for differences in school expenditures and student background.[56] In addition, he carried out separate analyses for students at each of four socioeconomic levels. Using achievement tests in different skills as measures of educational outcome, Kiesling found a rather consistent negative relationship between high school size, as measured by average daily attendance and average test scores. That is, over a large range of school sizes—less than 200 to almost 4,000 in average daily attendance—the apparent relation between school size and student performance was negative.

Burkhead and his associates found no significant statistical association between school enrollments and several measures of educational outcome once differences in student backgrounds and school resources were accounted for.[57] The Burkhead analysis was carried out separately for high schools in Chicago, Atlanta, and a set of small communities. The measures of educational outcomes included test scores, relative changes in test scores among high schools between grades, dropout rates, and post-high school educational plans or actual college attendance of graduates. While two studies have suggested that the optimal high school size is in the 1500 to 1700 student range, neither study takes account of differences in student characteristics among its sample.[58] It might be noted that the Project Talent sample of large city high schools showed an average daily attendance level of 2,500.

456

The evidence on the size-performance relationship suggests that high schools and school districts at the high end of the spectrum probably suffer from substantial diseconomies of scale. No study has found that such units yield economies of scale, and several inquiries have obtained the opposite result. In this area as in others there are data gaps. For example, there exist no rigorous studies on elementary school size, and the major sources of scale inefficiencies have not been delineated in adequate detail. Yet, the reduced effectiveness of very large schools has certainly been documented in other types of studies, for example, reduced student participation.[59]

IMPROVING THE EFFECTIVENESS OF EDUCATIONAL DOLLARS

In the preceding sections the conceptual linkages between expenditures and educational outcomes were described. Moreover, empirical studies of the educational production and expenditure relationships were surveyed in order to suggest certain insights into improving the effectiveness of educational dollars. In this final portion we will focus on the implications of this analysis for financing education.

As we stated previously, there are at least three obstacles to obtaining schools that are more productive. These hurdles include (1) the lack of an information system; (2) seemingly limited management discretion over inputs; and (3) the absence of incentives to stimulate the achievement of the school's putative goals. If schools are to improve their performance, all three of these institutional impediments must be overcome.

Information Systems

Given the complex nature of the educational process, the need for information on which to evaluate and make decisions is crucial. Yet, the schools lack such capabilities. This is not to say that the schools lack data, for most of them have reams of computer printout, shelves of reports, and files of records as a testimony to their penchant for numbers. It is the dearth of appropriate data for management decision-making at all levels that is the problem. That is, most of the existing numbers serve no useful function other than to be stored or compiled in reports that themselves have little usefulness.

457

In order for the schools to monitor their on-going operations, to improve their decision-making capabilities, and to raise the proficiencies of their research and evaluation functions it is necessary to develop a school information system that would provide data for both management and research needs. Moreover, this information system must be linked to a school management system that would use these data to make optimal educational decisions at the school district, school, department, classroom, and individual student levels.[60]

What would be some of the requirements of such a system? First, the educational enterprise needs better information about its own operations and performance. In this regard there must be emphasis on evaluation and outcomes of existing programs as well as on the linking of costs to particular programs. Moreover, this process should feed in to a planning, programming, budgeting system that will improve the allocative efficiency of educational expenditures.[61] Second, such a system would devise better ways to communicate the priorities of the various clientele of schools to decision-makers. The schools serve a large number of different constituencies, and the communication of goals from many of these is largely a roundabout process. Students, teachers, administrators, parents, taxpayers, and the various levels of government represent some of the groups with legitimate but often conflicting views on educational matters. The priorities of these groups and their own information needs to judge the schools should be reflected in the information system.[62]

Third, the educational system needs better information about available educational technologies. In order to evaluate alternative processes such data are crucial; yet, often the only source of information is that of the progenitors or promoters of the technologies. A good information system would develop objective descriptions and analyses of alternative approaches with comparable information on costs, required resources, organizational support, and documented outcomes.

Fourth, the educational systems need to develop improved techniques for decision-making in order to utilize properly their information systems. Decision-makers at all levels must learn alternative ways of making decisions as well as data requirements and uses. That is, concomitant with the development of the information system, there needs to be a growing capability to use information feedbacks proficiently.

458

Management Discretion

Even with better information, the productivity of schools will not rise unless those data are used to improve the schooling process. Yet, there is abundant evidence that even the present impoverished data system is not used to any great degree. While testing is a standard feature of the educational system, the results are rarely used in a systematic way to diagnose the educational needs of particular students or groups of students.[63] Moreover, the present use of such information seems to be plagued with errors in a system where few meaningful decisions are made.[64]

For a variety of reasons the schools seem to lack the capacity to deviate from tradition, even when those traditions are failing. Each participant in the process sees himself as a hired hand with little decision-making authority. The school board perceives a very limited role by virtue of the State Education Code, tax-payer pressures, student activity, contractual agreements with teachers and administrators, and other obligations. The superintendent must deal with the same forces and with his school board besides. Moreover, the teachers, administrators, and students see their decision-making options truncated severely by all of the other forces. All of these countervailing perceptions result in a form of institutional constipation where no substantive decisions are made or can be made. Thus, the schools are run on the basis of archaic mandates, written and unwritten, which all of the participants have tacitly accepted.

Under such conditions, what is publicized as change and innovation is only skin deep, yet neither the director not the producer, actors, stagehands, or audience have the real power to alter the direction of the drama. Rather the scenery is changed with the hope that the script will change too. Instead, the traditional litany whines on and on.

A way must be found to free the logjam of decision-making power so that information feedbacks can be used at all levels to improve the functioning of schools. Management discretion in this sense refers to the ability of all of the participants to make meaningful decisions that affect the educational setting at the level in which they are involved. Within this context, management discretion is required at the individual classroom and individual student level as well as those levels more remote from the classroom situation. Only when incentives are granted

459

for improving educational outcomes can we expect the participants to place their judgments on the line.

Incentives and the Educational Enterprise

By far the most important ingredient for improving the productivity of schools is that of an appropriate set of incentives. Both adequate information systems and managerial discretion are themselves functions of the nature of the rewards and sanctions for developing data and for making decisions. If these two activities are essentially unrewarded or even penalized, they will be discouraged by the schools. Indeed, the fact that the educational enterprise focuses its rewards on seniority rather than on either of these two activities or educational outcomes is itself an explanation of the reverence for an educationally insensitive form of traditionalism.

It is only when the rewards of the educational organization are linked more closely to the goals of the schools that substantial improvements in dollar productivity will occur. It would appear that the systematic incentives that are appropriate are ones which would reward primarily educational responsiveness to the needs of the students and families who are served. Two kinds of models have been posited that would pursue these goals: the market approach to schooling and the political or community control approach.[65]

The Educational Marketplace

The market approach is based upon a plan suggested by Professor Milton Friedman of the University of Chicago.[66] Schools are essentially monopolists in that they provide services for a captive audience. Since most children and their parents have little choice but to attend their local schools—no matter how poor the performance of such institutions—the students are locked in to a system which does not have to satisfy their educational needs. The proponents of the market approach believe that by giving students and their families a choice of schools, and by requiring schools to compete for students, substantial increases in educational effectiveness would result. For, if schools had to compete for students in order to survive, they would likely be much more responsive to the particular needs of their potential clientele.

What are the mechanics of such an arrangement? The state

460

would provide tuition vouchers to parents for a specified maximum sum per year for each child. Parents would be free to use these vouchers at any approved institution of their choice. Institutions would be encouraged to enter the marketplace to compete for students, and any school that met minimal requirements in such areas as curriculum and personnel would be eligible to participate. Thus a system of non-public schools would compete with the public ones for students. Applying this model to the residents of the inner-city, this arrangement ". . . would allow that one section of our population that suffers most seriously from segregated schooling—the poor—to move at their own incentive, and if they want to, in schools of their choice outside their neighborhood."[67] The result of this approach is that ". . . Parents could express their views about schools directly, by withdrawing their children from one school and sending them to another to a much greater extent than is now possible."[68] Information on alternative schools would be provided to all potential participants, in order to ensure an effectively functioning educational marketplace. That is, data on school costs, programs, strategies, effectiveness, and student populations might be required of all approved schools in order to keep parents and potential educational sellers informed of available alternatives. Such an arrangement would induce innovation and experimentation in that each school would try to obtain competitive advantages over the others. Only those public schools which would be responsive to the needs of their students could survive such competition, so a healthy infusion of nonpublic schools into the market would also tend to keep the remaining public schools on their toes.[69]

In addition to the basic Friedman plan there are many other ways of using an educational marketplace to fulfill the social goals set out for the schools. In an excellent discussion on the subject, Anthony Downs has suggested that the cities modify existing attendance boundaries so that all students within a given area of the city can attend any of a number of schools within that boundary.[70] That is, several traditional attendance areas would be merged to form a new one. Schools within the merged area would compete for students, and teachers and other resources would be shifted from the less successful schools—those whose enrollments decline—to those attracting new enrollments. Portable classrooms could also be added to the

461

latter schools, if necessary. Thus, principals would have an incentive to maximize the important educational outputs desired by the residents of the merged attendance areas or face a loss of clientele and resources.

In a similar vein James S. Coleman has suggested contracting out such services as reading and arithmetic and paying educational contractors only on the basis of their students' results on standardized tests.[71] There are many ways to create competition within the schools, and virtually all of them would provide market-type incentives for utilizing educational resources far more effectively than they had been applied in the past.

Political Incentives

Yet, for large urban school districts the market schema is not the only means of providing incentives for ensuring that schools will fulfill the needs of their clientele. It is also possible to redirect the efforts of such institutions through revamping the political processes by which decisions are made. At the present time educational strategies are set out at some highly centralized level for all children and all classrooms in the urban schools. Personnel, curriculum, and materials are chosen or approved by central school boards and are imposed on a large variety of educational settings for which they are totally inappropriate. Yet, as we pointed out previously, good educational strategies are ones which are made on the basis of the particular characteristics and needs of the children being served. They cannot be set out at a highly centralized, abstract, and depersonalized level just to satisfy an administrative compulsion for order. The drab uniformity imposed by the urban school boards has been particularly disastrous for the inner-city schools where institutions seem to perform the futile exercise of going through motions that have little educational substance.

Under such conditions it becomes imperative to decentralize decision-making from a central school board to some lower level in order to adapt to the different needs of different segments of the population. Indeed, the market approach is an example of such decentralization, while political decentralization is another form. The latter method would put authority for governing the inner-city schools into the hands of groups of citizens who were representative of the community being served by those schools

462

which are characterized by the greatest failures in fulfilling the educational needs of their students.[72]

How would such a system work? Decentralized school districts would be formed in urban areas based upon proximity and commonality of needs among schools. Each decentralized or community school district would elect a representative school board to govern its constituent schools. The central school board would provide each decentralized school board with a lump-sum budget, and each local board would possess substantial discretion in allocating its budget.[73] Financial accounts and accountability would remain in the hands of the central school authority, but the actual disbursements for each school could be authorized only by the local governing board for that school. On the basis of this decision-making power the local governing boards, in conjunction with administrators and teachers (and perhaps student representatives), would construct their programs and purchase the necessary components to implement them, a course of action which is not permitted under the existing regulations. Political decentralization would then enable schools to reflect more closely the educational needs of their constituents. The inner-city schools would be pressured to break out of the pattern of ineptitude fostered by the mindless universalism of traditional big-city school administration.

Both political and market incentives could be combined to make the schools more effective. Under a system of decentralized schools, students should be given a choice of attending a school in their own community or in any other community. Moreover, the central school board would continue to operate a few schools as alternatives to both individual students and parents—via market choice—and to groups of students and parents—via political action within the community.

Further, the decentralized school districts might find it desirable to purchase some services from private contractors. The community school board would plan its educational requirements and compare these with its capabilities. The school board would then solicit bids from industry, universities, and nonprofit groups for fulfilling objectives in those areas where the local district had the least proficiencies. Educational contractors would compete for the particular services which the community wished to buy, and remuneration might be based on the success of the programs.

A Purview of the Future

What are the prospects for widespread reforms in the structure of education, ones that would improve the functioning of schools and the effectiveness of educational dollars? If one were to use a historical perspective, one could not be very optimistic. After all, almost 200 years ago writers like Adam Smith pointed out what might happen to schools if the clientele possessed no sanctions for keeping schools accountable for results.[74] In a more general context Jeremy Bentham issued a similar analysis.[75]

Yet, ideas that were merely on the drawing board in past decades or were not even yet pipedreams some ten years ago have emerged as operational plans in several settings. The state legislatures of Michigan and New York have mandated forms of political and administrative decentralization for the schools of Detroit and New York respectively. The California Legislature was considering such a plan for Los Angeles in the summer of 1970.

Educational performance contracting is being implemented at several sites by both the U. S. Office of Education and the Office of Economic Opportunity. Under such arrangements contractors are being paid to produce particular results, for example raising reading scores. Provisions of the contract specify greater remuneration for succeeding beyond a prescribed level as well as financial penalities for failure to achieve that level. At this date it even appears that a tryout of an educational voucher plan seems imminent in an experiment to be financed by the Office of Economic Opportunity.[76]

Perhaps the most prophetic sign is the grotesque world that the schools are entering. Expenditures are rising very rapidly with little or no demonstrated increase in educational outcomes. Local taxpayers are revolting and state coffers are stretched, but costs continue to rise while little educational progress is being made. Suddenly we are caught as Alice was in *Through the Looking Glass* when a bedraggled Alice running as fast as she possibly could always found herself back in the same place that she started from. The Queen told Alice that in order to actually get anywhere one must run at least twice as fast as that. Given this hopeless alternative, a widespread movement towards educational reform seems inevitable.

464

FOOTNOTES

1. Kenneth A. Simon and W. Vance Grant, *Digest of Educational Statistics*, 1968 edition, (Washington: U.S. Department of Health, Education and Welfare, 1968), p. 61.
2. For some detail on the educational aspects of these youngsters, see A. Harry Passow et al., *Education of the Disadvantaged* (New York: Holt, Rinehart, and Winston, 1967).
3. Harry Picariello, "Evaluation of Title I" (mimeo, 1969), p. 1. To be published in *Inequality: Studies in Elementary and Secondary Education*, Joseph Froomkin and Dennis J. Dugan, eds., Office of Program Planning and Evaluation. Planning Paper 69-2, U. S. Office of Education.
4. *Ibid.*
5. David G. Hawkridge, Albert B. Chalupsky, and Oscar H. Roberts, "A Study of Selected Exemplary Programs for the Education of Disadvantaged Children," Part I, Final Report, Project No. 089013 for the U. S. Office of Education, Office of Program Planning and Research in Behavioral Sciences, 1968).
6. Thomas I. Ribich, *Education and Poverty* (Washington, The Brookings Institution, 1968).
7. James S. Coleman et al., *Equality of Educational Opportunity*, OE 38001, (Washington: U.S. Office of Health, Education and Welfare, 1966).
8. *Ibid.*
9. For an analysis of the understatement of school effects see, Samuel S. Bowles and Henry M. Levin, "Determinants of Scholastic Achievement—An appraisal of Some Recent Evidence" *The Journal of Human Resources*, III, 1 (Winter, 1968), 3-24.
10. The analysis that follows assumes some knowledge of economic theory. Readers who do not have familiarity with these aspects can obtain background by referring to any textbook that addresses itself to the theory of the firm. A good source is William J. Baumol, *Economic Theory and Operations Analysis*, 2d ed. (Englewood Cliffs, N. J.: Prentice Hall, 1963).
11. For a comprehensive study on educational production functions see Samuel S. Bowles, "Towards an Educational Production Function," Paper Prepared for the Conference on Research in Income and Wealth (Madison, Wisconsin, November 1968), mimeo.
12. While the effectiveness of schools is often measured by student scores on standardized achievement tests, the measure of outcomes suggested by *A* would be far more comprehensive. See for example, Benjamin Bloom, ed., *Taxonomy of Educational Objectives, Handbook I: The Cognitive Domain* (New York: David McKay Co., Inc., 1956); and D. R. Krathwohl, B. S. Bloom, and B. B. Masia, *Taxonomy of Educational Objectives* (New York: David McKay Co., Inc., 1964).
13. For example, see Jesse Burkhead et al., *Input and Output in Large-City High Schools* (Syracuse, N. Y.: Syracuse University Press, 1967). For some technical problems encountered in measuring change scores see L. J. Cronbach and L. Firby, "How We Should Measure Change—Or Should We?" *Psychological Bulletin* (Forthcoming, 1970).
14. For an interesting study that gives insights into these differences see Ellis G. Olim, Robert D. Hess, and Virginia Shipman, "Role of Mothers' Language Styles in Mediating Their Pre-School Children's Cognitive Development," *School Review*, 75, 4 (Winter, 1967), 414-24.
15. In the standard terminology of price theory that combination of inputs is utilized which equalizes the marginal product/price ratios of all of the inputs while just exhausting the budget.
16. For example, such *administrative* expenses as those for principals, clerical, and secretaries in a school building are attributed to the *instructional* budget. See U.S. Department of Health, Education, and Welfare, Office of Education, *Financial Accounting for Local and State School Systems*, State Educational Records and Reports Series: Handbook II OE-22017 (Washington, 1957).
17. See Harry J. Hartley, *Educational Planning-Programming-Budget-*

465

ing: A Systems Approach (Englewood Cliffs, N. J.: Prentice-Hall, Inc., 1968).

18. A proposal for developing such systems is found in Eric Hanushek and Henry M. Levin, "Educational Information Systems for Management and Evaluation—A Proposed Program," Rand Document D-20073, The Rand Corporation (Santa Monica, California, 1969).

19. Indeed, it is not at all clear what the schools are trying to maximize. For a discussion of the school as an organization see Charles E. Bidwell, "The School as a Formal Organization," in *Handbook of Organizations*, James G. March, ed. (Chicago: Rand McNally and Company, 1965), pp. 972-1022.

20. Of course these are not mindless if one accepts the view that the primary goal of the schools is to provide career jobs to persons supporting entrenched political interests. See Peter Schrag, *Village School Downtown* (Boston: Seacon Press, 1967).

21. For a more general analysis of constructing performance incentives in the public sector see Charles L. Schultze, *The Economics and Politics of Public Spending* (Washington: The Brookings Institution, 1968).

22. See for example Lee J. Cronbach and Richard Snow, *Individual Differences in Response to Instruction* (Stanford, California: Stanford University, 19693 mimeo. Obtainable from the ERIC System of the U. S. Offices of Education, ED- 029001. For an economic interpretation see Stephan Michelson, "Equal Protection and School Resources," *Inequality in Education*, 1, 2 _____, 4, 9-16.

23. See Henry M. Levin, "Cost-Effectiveness Analysis of Instructional Technology–The Problems," to be published in a volume by the Commission on Instructional Technology (Washington, D.C.), forthcoming in 1970.

24. A good description of the cumbersome and unwieldy nature of the large-city schools is found in Christopher Jencks, "Is the Public School Obsolete?" *The Public Interest*, 2 (Winter 1966), 18-27.

25. For a review of early studies see William E. Barron, Measurement of Educational Productivity," in *The Theory and Practice of School Finance*, Warren E. Gauerke and Jack R. Childress, eds. (Chicago: Rand McNally Company, 1967), pp. 279-308.

26. Evidence on some of these cost differences is found in Henry M. Levin, "Financing Education for the Urban Disadvantaged," pp. 5-6.

27. A good example of this inadequacy is found in the expenditure information for the massive, nationwide survey of secondary schools, *Project Talent*. The Talent questionnaire made no attempt to be precise about which one of the many school expenditure measures that school districts tally was the one desired by the survey. School districts report several measures of total expenditure, some including capital costs, summer school adult education, and so on, while the best overall measure that reflects elementary and secondary resources is that of the operating budget. Capital costs tend to be lumpy, varying substantially from period to period because the financing period for capital construction is generally considerably shorter than the life of the capital. Thus it is an inaccurate reflection of capital inputs for an annual accounting period. The Coleman Report also used an erroneous expenditure measure. See Samuel S. Bowles and Henry M. Levin, "Determinants of Scholastic Achievement—An Appraisal of Some Recent Evidence," pp. 8-10.

28. See particularly Paul Mort, "Cost Quality Relationships in Education," *Problems and Issues in School Finance*, edited by R. L. Johns and Edgar L. Morphet (New York: National Conference of Professors of Educational Administrational Administration, 1952). Also see William E. Barron.

29. Thomas I. Ribich, *Education and Poverty* (Washington: The Brookings Institution, 1968).

30. Pp. 86-87. It should be pointed out that the dollar comparisons should be interpreted as relative ones since they reflect school expenditures in 1960. Current expenditures per pupil in public elementary and secondary schools increased from $375 in 1959-60 to about $620 in 1967-68.

466

31. Herbert J. Kiesling, "Measuring a Local Government Service: A Study of School Districts in New York State, " *Review of Economics and Statistics*, XLIX, 3 (August, 1967), 356-67.

32. Kiesling's use of IQ scores as an explanatory variable probably biases downward the observed expenditure effect since so-called IQ tests measure school influences as well as other environmental influences and innate abilities. Accordingly, there is reason to believe that some of the variance in achievement scores attributed by Kiesling to student IQ is, in fact, a proxy for the effect of expenditures on IQ. In a later study Kiesling found that by removing IQ from the equation both the magnitude and significance levels of the estimated expenditure effect rose markedly, usually by almost half or more. See Herbert J. Kiesling. "High School Size and Cost Factors," Final Report for the U.S. Office of Education, Bureau of Research, Project No. 6-1590 (processed; U.S. Department of Health, Education, and Welfare, March, 1968), p. 41.

33. P. 359.

34. For a fuller discussion see Stephan Michelson, "The Association of Teacher Resourceness with Children's Characteristics," in *Do Teachers Make a Difference?*, Alexander M. Mood, ed., OE 58042, U.S. Department of Health, Education and Welfare (Washington: U.S. Government Printing Office), pp. 120-68.

35. P. 365.

36. For example, see Jesse Burkhead et al., *Input and Output in Large City High Schools* (Syracuse: Syracuse University Press, 1967); Samuel S. Bowles and Henry M. Levin, "More on Multicollinearity and the Effectiveness of Schools *The Journal of Human Resources*, 3 (Summer, 1968), 393-400; Charles S. Benson et al., *State and Local Fiscal Relationships in Public Education in California*, Report of the Senate Fact Finding Committee on Revenue and Taxation (Sacramento: Senate of the State of California, March 1965); Richard Raymond, "Determinants of the Quality of Primary and Secondary Education in West Virginia," *The Journal of Human Resources*, Vol. 3, 4 (Fall 1968), 450-70; and J. Alan Thomas, "Efficiency in Education: A Study of the Relationship Between Selected Inputs and Mean Test Scores in a Sample of Senior High Schools," (Ph.D. dissertation, Stanford University, School of Education, 1962). For a more extensive set of references see James Guthrie et al., "A Survey of School Effectivness Studies," in *Do Teachers Make a Difference?*, pp. 25-54.

37. See all of the studies cited in the previous footnote.

38. The economic theory of teacher markets as it reflects on this phenomenon is described in Henry M. Levin, "Recruiting Teachers for Large-City Schools" (Unpublished manuscript, The Brookings Institution, 1968), to be published by Charles E. Merrill.

39. *Ibid.*, Ch. 5-7.

40. For example, see James S. Coleman et al. Jesse Burkhead et al.; Eric Hanushek, "The Education of Negroes and Whites (Ph.D. dissertation, Department of Economics, Massachusetts Institute of Technology, 1968); Samuel S. Bowles, "Toward an Educational Production Function."

41. James S. Coleman et al., p. 316.

42. See Bowles and M. Levin, "The Determinants of Scholastic Achievement," and John F. Kain and Eric A. Hanushek, "On the Value of Equality of Educational Opportunity as a Guide to Public Policy," Discussion Paper No. 36, Program on Regional and Urban Economics, Harvard University (Cambridge, 1968).

43. See Eric Hanushek, Stephan Michelson, "The Association of Teacher Resourcefulness with Children's Characteristics," and Bowles M. Levin, "More on Multicollinearity and the Effectiveness of Schools."

44. Eric Hanushek, "The Production of Education, Teacher Quality, and Efficiency," in *Do Teachers Make a Difference?*, pp. 120-68.

45. See all of the studies cited in the preceding section.

46. See Lee J. Cronbach and Richard Snow, "Individual Differences in Response to Instruction"; Stephan Michelson, "The Association of Teacher Resourcefulness with Children's Characteristics"; also see Hanushek's

comparison of effectiveness of a similar set of resources for whites and for Mexican-Americans in "The Production of Education, Teacher Quality, and Efficiency."

47. Henry M. Levin, "A New Model of School Effectiveness," in *Do Teachers Make a Difference?* pp. 55-78.

48. Henry M. Levin, "A Cost-Effectiveness Analysis of Teacher Selection," *The Journal of Human Resources*, 5, 1 (Winter, 1970), 24-33.

49. A number of studies have examined the gross relation between per pupil expenditure and average daily attendance or enrollment levels. The fact that these inquiries have not controlled for differences in student characteristics or educational outcomes invalidates them for consideration of the size-performance question.

50. See Herbert J. Kiesling, "Measuring a Local Government Service," for a study of districts in New York State. For California see M. C. Alkin, C. S. Benson, and R. H. Gustafson, "Economy of Scale in the Production of Selected Educational Outcomes," a paper prepared for the American Education Research Association Meetings, Chicago, (February, 1968), mimeo.

51. *Ibid.*

52. See Leslie L. Chisholm, *School District Reorganization* (Chicago: Midwest Administration Center, 1957), Ch. V.

53. Analysis of the 1.1 million student New York City situation is contained in Mayor's Advisory Panel on Decentralization of the New York City Schools, *Reconnection for Learning: A Community School System for New York City* (1967). For the 650,000 student Los Angeles School District see Arthur D. Little, Inc., *Alternative for Reorganizing Large Urban Unified School Districts*, A Report to the California State Legislature, Joint Committee on Reorganization of Large Urban Unified School Districts, 2 vols. (June, 1970).

54. Henry M. Levin, "A Comparison of the Performance of the Los Angeles City School District with That of Other School Districts" in Memorandum to Assembly Committee on Education, State of California Legislature, from the Joint Committee on Reorganization of Large Urban Unified School Districts, August 10, 1970.

55. *Ibid.*

56. Herbert Kiesling, "High School Size and Cost Factors."

57. Jesse Burkhead et al.

58. John Riew, "Economies of Scale in High School Operation," *Review of Economics and Statistics*, 41 (May, 1959), 232-41; and Elchnan Cohn, "Economies of Scale in Iowa High School Operations," *Journal of Human Resources*, 3, 4 (Fall, 1968), 422-34. The Riew study also lacks measures of educational outcome and bases its findings on "educational offerings."

59. Roger G. Barker and Paul V. Gump, *Big School, Small School* (Stanford: Stanford University Press, 1964).

60. For greater detail see Hanushek and Levin, "Educational Information Systems For Management and Evaluation."

61. See Harry J. Hartley. Also see Selma J. Mushkin and James R. Cleaveland, "Planning, Programming, Budgeting System," in *Interdependence in School Finance: The City; The State; The Nation*, NEA Committee on Educational Finance (Washington: 1968), pp. 59-98.

62. See James S. Coleman and Nancy Karweit, "Multi-Level Information Systems in Education," Rand Document 19287-RC (Santa Monica, California: The Rand Corporation, 1969), processed.

63. Richard M. Jaeger, *Designing School Testing Programs for Institutional Appraisals An Application of Sampling Theory* (Ph.D. dissertation, School of Education, Stanford University, 1970).

64. See James S. Coleman and Nancy Karweit, "Measures of School Performance," R-488-RC (Santa Monica, California: The Rand Corporation, 1970).

65. The following description is substantially similar to a section of my paper, "Financing Education For the Urban Disadvantaged" in *Education*

for the Disadvantaged, Sterling M. McMurrin ed., to be published by the Committee on Economic Development (1970).

66. "The Role of Government in Education," in Robert A. Solo ed., *Economics and the Public Interest* (New Brunswick, New Jersey: Rutgers University Press, 1955), pp. 123-44.

67. Theodore Sizer, "Reform and the Control of Education," 1967, p. 14, (mimeo.) For similar views see Christopher Jencks, "Is the Public School Obsolete?" *The Interest* (Winter, 1966), pp. 18-28.

68. Milton Friedman, p. 129.

69. For a fuller discussion of the benefits and problems associated with the market plan, see Henry M. Levin, "The Failure of the Public Schools and the Free Market Remedy," *The Urban Review,* 2, 7 (June 1968), 32-37 Also available as Brookings Institution Reprint 148.

70. See "Competition and Community Schools," in *Community Control of the Schools,* Henry M. Levin, ed., (Washington: The Brookings Institution, 1969).

71. See James S. Coleman, "Towards Open Schools," *The Public Interest* (Fall, 1967), pp. 20-27.

72. For an extensive discussion of many of the issues see Henry M. Levin, ed., *Community Control of the Schools* (Washington: The Brookings Institution, 1969).

73. For more details see H. Thomas James and Henry M. Levin, "Financing Community Schools," in Levin, *Community Control of the Schools.*

74. Adam Smith, *The Wealth of Nations,* Modern Library Edition (New York: Random House, Inc., 1937), p. 737.

75. Jeremy Bentham, *The Handbook of Political Fallacies,* Harper Torchbooks (New York: Harper and Brothers, 1952), pp. 17-24.

76. See *Education Vouchers,* A Preliminary Report Financing Education by Payments to Parents (Cambridge, Massuchetts: Center for the Study of Public Policy, March, 1970).

469

CHAPTER 13

Constitutional Alternatives
For State School Finance*

Recent court decisions holding state school aid formulas unconstitutional as violative of the equal protection clause of the 14th amendment represent an evolutionary step in the courts' expansion of constitutional protections of individual rights. These decisions represent a major extension of judicial precedent in the area of students' rights. During the past few years the constitutional rights of students have been continually expanded, placing new limitations and restrictions on the police power of the state to regulate and control education. Courts once obliquely maintained that education was a privilege bestowed upon the individual by the goodwill of the state and that it could be altered or even taken away at state discretion. Today, however, this judicial attitude has changed to the concept that the student now possesses a constitutional right to an education. The theory that education is a right has manifested itself in constitutional protections for students in both the substantive and procedural aspects of constitutional law. More notable substantive protections acknowledged

*This chapter was written especially for this book by Kern Alexander and K. Forbis Jordan and was not included in the original National Educational Finance Project volumes.

by the courts include the basic freedoms of the first amendment,[1] fourth amendment rights with regard to unauthorized search and seizure,[2] and the pervasive interpretation of the equal protections clause[3] of the 14th amendment. Guaranteeing the accommodation of these rights are the procedural due process requirements[4] of the 5th and 14th amendments. Court decisions conveying these rights to the student have resulted in a formidable network of constitutional standards within which the public educational system must operate and beyond which the state cannot proceed in denial of individual rights and freedoms.

The equal protection clause of the 14th amendment has been the primary vehicle by which the courts have expanded individual rights. With the desegregation cases as the basic source of precedent, the courts have recently reached the point of invoking equal protection rights as a means of forcing redistribution of state tax sources for education. The cases harbor vast legal implication, not the least of which is their impact on the traditional role of the legislature with regard to governmental finance. Of all of the powers possessed by the legislative branch of government, the discretionary power to tax and distribute resources is the most fundamental and jealously guarded. The court, in treading on this hallowed ground, is boldly entering a "political thicket" at least as formidable as reapportionment and desegregation.

These cases, therefore, represent a giant step in constitutional legal precedent because they involve limitations not only on the police power of the state to regulate and control education but also restrict a state's power to devise and regulate its own system of taxation. Both of these issues have traditionally formed almost entirely separate precedents in constitutional law.

This discussion will give the reader a view of these precedents as they affect both the police power of the state to provide for education and the constitutional limitations on state taxation as they impact on alternative methods for state school financing. The subject may be divided into three generations of constitutional development. The first generation covers a period stretching from 1912 to approximately 1968. Throughout this period the courts handed down several decisions which established constitutional precedent concerning school finance programs. The unique feature of these cases is that they contested the constitutionality of state school finance programs only from the position of taxation. In these situations the taxpayer was the agrieved party and was, in the tradition of most taxpayers, simply instituting the action to save himself a few tax dollars. The second generation cases depart from the taxpayer equity argument and approach the issue of equalization of resources from that of the agrieved student, the student maintaining that his educational opportunity should not be dependent on the fiscal ability of his school district. This issue cannot, of course, be totally removed from the purview of taxation and the power of the state to set up whatever tax system it chooses. The problem lies, though, where it usually rests in constitutional matters, in the extent to which a state can exercise its governmental power and ignore the impact on the rights of the individual. The third generation cases are closely akin to the second; however, they raise the additional problem of how far must the state go in providing equal educational opportunity. Does the state have an affirmative constitutional duty to compensate for variations in educational needs among children? Must the state correct for educational disabilities and disparities which may be the result of social, economic, or individual mental or physical deficiencies?

FIRST GENERATION

State School Finance Programs in the Taxation Context

> Where constitutionality of a statute is questioned, all reasonable doubt will be resolved in favor of the questioned authority and the act will be declared constitutional unless it can be clearly demonstrated that the legislature did not have the power or authority exercised or that its authority was exercised arbitrarily and capriciously, for instance, as to classification or delegation of authority, to the prejudice of the rights of some of the citizens. Particularly, is this true where the act in question is . . . of great public concern involving the performance of an absolute duty imposed on the legislature by the basic law of the state.[5]

This statement describes the traditional and fundamental position of the courts toward the judicial regulation of such important legislative functions as public education and taxation. Nonintervention has been the password for decades when courts have been asked to examine the constitutionality of legislatively prescribed methods of taxation for financing of education.

The courts have steadfastly adhered to the philosophy that an act of the legislature will not be rendered invalid unless the act without a doubt violates certain prescribed constitutional stan-

472

dards. With regard to the constitutionality of state school finance programs, the courts have traditionally only been asked to determine whether such programs create unconstitutional classifications or violate equality and uniformity of taxation requirements. The equal protection clause of the 14th amendment encompasses, but is not limited to, the same protections as the equality and uniformity of taxation provisions of most state constitutions. Even though the federal equal protection clause encompasses much more than mere equality and uniformity of taxation, its broader aspects were not invoked to challenge state school finance programs until recently.

The equal protection clause of the 14th amendment was first described as a limitation on state revenue legislation by the Supreme Court of the United States in 1890.[6] The "test" devised by the Supreme Court to determine constitutionality of state taxation has been restated by Justice Jackson:

> Equal protection does not require identity of treatment. It only requires that classification rest on real and not feigned differences, that the distinction have some relevance to the purpose for which the classification is made, and the different treatment be not so disparate, relative to the difference in classification, as to be wholly arbitrary.[6]

The equal protection clause establishes a minimum standard of uniformity to which state tax legislation must conform in addition to and over and beyond similar limitations imposed by state constitutional requirements.[7]

In practically all cases state constitutions have the equivalent of an "equal protection" provision — that is, some constitutional restriction against "unreasonable classifications." While the United States Supreme Court has the last word regarding "reasonableness" under the federal equal protection clause, state courts have the last word as to the meaning of reasonableness under their respective state constitutions.[8] The primary problem is, of course, the definition of reasonableness with regard to appropriate classification. There are apparently no universally applicable tests by which to determine the reasonableness or unreasonableness of a classification. The cases merely indicate a vague outline of reasonableness and in some instances a given basis may be valid with respect to one tax and invalid with another.[9] Justice Bradley, in dictum in the *Bell's Gap* case,[10] however, did give this explanation.

[The equal protection clause] was not intended to prevent a state from adjusting its system of taxation in all proper and reasonable ways. It may, if it chooses, exempt certain classes of property from any taxation at all, such as churches, libraries, and the property of charitable institutions. . . . We think we are safe in saying, that the Fourteenth Amendment was not intended to compel the state to adopt an iron rule of equal taxation. If that were its proper construction it would not only supersede all those constitutional provisions and laws of some of the states, whose object is to secure equality of taxation, and which are usually accompanied with qualifications deemed material; but it would render nugatory those discriminations which the best interests of society require. . . .[10]

The equal protection clause of the 14th amendment is no stranger to disputes over the distribution of school funds. As early as 1912 the Supreme Court of Maine in *Sawyer* v. *Gilmore* handed down an opinion which examined constitutional equality under both the Maine and United States Constitutions as applied to both taxation and distribution of funds by the state.[11] The plaintiff contended that a statewide 1.5 mill property tax violated both the Maine constitution's equality of taxation[12] provision and the 14th amendment because it was collected statewide from cities, towns, plantations, and unorganized townships but was redistributed back only to cities, towns, and plantations, leaving unorganized townships with no revenues from the fund. The plaintiff in this case, a property owner in an unorganized township, thus complained as both a taxpayer and as the parent of a child. The plaintiff specifically attacked the method of distribution as being unconstitutional because it distributed ". . . one-third according to the number of scholars and two-thirds according to valuation, thus benefiting the cities, and richer towns more than the poorer." The plaintiff did not reveal, however, that when all state and local expenditures were taken into consideration the unorganized townships the year before (1911) had expended $19 per student while the state average was only $2.52. The overall impact of the legislature's action was allegedly to equalize the expenditures among the classes of schools.

The court answered the plaintiff's assertion by saying that the equality of taxation provision of the state constitution required only equality of assessment, not equality of distribution. The court then drew a hard and fast line between judicial and legislative prerogative by saying that:

The method of distributing the proceeds of such a tax rests in the wise discretion and sound judgment of the Legislature. If this discretion is unwisely exercised, the remedy is with the people, and not with the court. . . . We are not to substitute our judgment for that of a coordinate branch of government working within its constitutional limits. . . . In order that taxation may be equal and uniform in the constitutional sense, it is not necessary that the benefits arising therefrom should be enjoyed by all the people in equal degree, nor that each one of the people should participate in each particular benefit.

The court in *Sawyer* dismissed the federal equal protection question rather curtly by pointing out that the object of the 14th amendment was to prohibit discriminatory legislation and did not apply where all persons subject to a law are treated alike in both privileges conferred and liabilities imposed. Further, the court quoting the United States Supreme Court said:

The provision in the Fourteenth Amendment that no state shall deny to any person within its jurisdiction the equal protection of the laws was not intended to prevent a state from adjusting its system of taxation in all proper and reasonable ways.[13]

The logic conveyed in this case reflected a judicial philosophy which was relied upon for over half a century. The courts steadfastly refused to apply state constitutional uniformity and equality of taxing provisions to school fund distribution formulas. In all fairness to the courts, however, seldom if ever was a statute challenged where the legislature was not attempting itself to move toward greater equity in distribution of resources among school districts. Plaintiffs were typically attempting to retard such progress. Indeed, in most cases, state equality of taxation and the federal Constitution were invoked in an attempt to prevent the equalization of resources among school districts.

In a relatively recent case in South Dakota, *Dean* v. *Coddington* (1964), the constitutional equality and uniformity arguments were again raised in an attempt to prevent the initiation of a foundation or equalization program.[14] The plaintiff, a taxpayer, asserted that the state foundation program act was unconstitutional, violating both the equal and uniform provision of the South Dakota constitution and the equal protection clause of the 14th amendment. The plaintiff was a resident of Lakeview School Dis-

475

trict which had no elementary and secondary schools and transferred its children to nearby Scotland School District. Since the Lakeview district had no school, the foundation program law appropriated no funds to it. Further, the Lakeview students attending school in the Scotland district were counted as part of Scotland's enrollment, giving it more state funds. This method of distribution, the plaintiff claimed, effectively lowered the taxes in the Scotland district while leaving them constant in Lakeview.

The plaintiff admitted that the taxes were probably uniformly raised, but contended that uniformity requirement is not satisfied unless the funds derived from the taxes are uniformly distributed. The court, in upholding the constitutionality of the foundation program, commented on equality and uniformity of taxation of both the state and federal constitutions and then laid down guidelines to govern the legislature's apportionment of public funds. First, the court pointed out that the test of the uniformity of taxation provision under the South Dakota constitution was substantially the same as that required by the 14th amendment to the United States Constitution. The rule was stated by the court as:

> It is generally held that the constitutional provisions requiring equality and uniformity relate to the levy of taxes and not to the distribution or application of the revenue derived therefrom; and hence statutes relative to the distribution or application of such money cannot be held invalid on this ground.[15]

In justifying state taxation programs the courts have not always adhered strictly to their philosophy of separation between taxation and distribution of revenues. Indeed, a court is forced into this very dilemma when it seeks to justify a legislative act on the basis of its rationality. In fact, the court in seeking to determine the reasonableness of a classification cannot avoid analyzing the impact of tax revenues on local school districts. Such an analysis forces a court to look at such things as fiscal ability, educational needs, high costs of programs, and other conditions peculiar to particular school districts.

A case illustrating this came out of Ohio in 1923 where plaintiffs attempted to enjoin county officials from the levy of a tax and redistribution of the proceeds of a county equalization fund designed to more nearly equalize resources.[16] The plaintiffs, from a relatively wealthy part of the county, stood to lose about $4,000

476

to other, poorer school districts in the county if the state law were carried out. In distributing the funds within the county, the city and certain village school districts retained the revenue from their full tax levy and received, in addition, a portion of the proceeds raised from school districts outside the city and village districts. Such an apportionment, the plaintiffs claimed, created two classes of school districts, the benefits derived by each being different. This, they maintained, was an unconstitutional classification denying them equal protection of the law under both the Ohio and federal constitutions. In addition, the plaintiff claimed the "uniform taxing" provision of the state constitution was violated.

The court upheld the unconstitutionality of the classification* saying that "... it was easily conceivable that the greatest expense might arise in the poorest districts; that portions of great cities, teeming with life, would be able to contribute relatively little in taxes for the support of schools ... while districts underpopulated with children might represent such taxation value that their school needs would be relatively oversupplied. Could there be a more *reasonable classification* [emphasis added] than that provided for in this act — that school districts should receive aid in varying proportions according to their educational needs."

This vague "educational need" provision was supported as being constitutional in light of a provision of the Ohio constitution[17] which required the general assembly to "secure a thorough and efficient system of common schools throughout the state." This court further substantiated its argument by bringing forth the two primary points of the *Sawyer* case in Maine that (a) inequality of taxation is necessarily fatal, while inequality of distribution is not and (b) the particular method of distribution rests in the wise discretion and sound judgment of the legislature.

This decision pointed out some interesting aspects which were not present in *Sawyer*: first, a clear cut constitutional defense of a legislative classification of types of school districts; second, a state constitutional mandate directing the general assembly to provide a "thorough and efficient system" of common schools was cited as justification for equalization of resources; and third, the court held that varying educational needs of school districts constitute a sound and reasonable constitutional classification.

As state legislatures attempted to provide greater equalization

*For an example of an unconstitutional classification see *Stewart* v. *Davidson*, 218 Ga. 760, 130 S.E. 2d 822 (1963).

of resources among school districts through various taxing and funding techniques, disputes arose over the constitutionality of these methods. Many states had constitutional provisions which required that state school funds be distributed in a particular manner, usually a flat amount per school census or population count. [18] Such constitutional provisions were an impediment to legislatures seeking to equalize resources for poorer school districts. In the earlier cases these constitutional provisions were invoked by taxpayers from the wealthier school districts which sought to prevent state equalization of resources. A case in point is a 1924 Oklahoma case[19] where the legislature enacted a law providing additional money from the state general fund to support school districts which could raise enough resources from a 15 mill levy to operate an eight-month school term. The plaintiff maintained such legislation was unconstitutional because the state constitution mandated that moneys from the state permanent school fund must be allocated on the basis of school population to all common school districts and also complained that state aid provided for only financially weak districts was special legislation constituting an unconstitutional classification. With regard to the first argument, the court held that the equalization moneys were to be paid out of the state general fund and not out of the constitutionally restricted permanent school fund, thereby allowing the legislature flexibility in its method of allocation. The court dismissed the latter argument saying that the state aid to weak school districts applied to all districts alike, extending aid to those which were similarly situated in terms of the lack of resources.

This court also pointed out that the Oklahoma constitution placed the duty on the legislature to "establish and maintain a *system* [emphasis added] of free public schools wherein all children of the state may be educated."[20] Significantly, the court maintained that such wording meant that the legislature was to provide an "effiicient and sufficient system, with competent teachers, necessary general facilities" and adequate length of school terms. The word "system," the court said, indicates a degree of uniformity and equality of opportunity, and by assuming the responsibility to provide for public education the state had the duty to provide "insofar as it is practical, equal rights and privileges to its youth, to obtain such mental and moral training as will make them useful citizens. . . ." This equality of treatment, the court said, was an "imperative governmental duty." In upholding the state's equalization allocation and denying the plaintiffs' argument against equalization, the court concluded:

478

And so we hold that under this constitutional mandate, the state legislature has the power — and, in fact, unless some other way be found to properly maintain in all parts of the state an efficient free public school system, *it owes it as a duty* [emphasis added] to appropriate from available state funds the money necessary to enable each school district to maintain a reasonable school term each year.[19]

This court, while deciding in favor of the legislative provision, went several steps further in support of equalization than did the hands-off courts in either *Sawyer* or *Miller*. Even though no mention was made of the requirements of the 14th amendment, it should be emphasized that the Supreme Court of Oklahoma not only acknowledged the power of the legislature to provide for a "system" of education, but also placed a *duty* on the legislature to furnish a "degree of uniformity and equality" of education and to afford as "far as practical, equal rights and privileges to all its youth" for education. Such words placed this court many strides beyond the earlier cases, but still its position was characterized by words of condition such as "for a degree" and "as far as practical," leaving very wide discretion in the hands of the legislature as to the limits and extent of equality it chose to provide.

Courts have been hesitant to invalidate legislative acts on the basis of unconstitutional classification because the source of taxation is often tightly interwoven with the government's plan for distribution of funds to local districts. The essence of an illegal constitutional classification is to arbitrarily classify local districts or persons with no regard for their actual conditions or needs. The United States Court of Appeals, Ninth Circuit, speaks of this as fitting tax programs to needs:

Traditionally classification has been a device for fitting tax programs to local needs and usages in order to achieve an equitable distribution of the tax burden. It has, because of this, been pointed out that in taxation, even more than in other fields, legislatures possess the greatest freedom in classification. Since the members of a legislature necessarily enjoy a familiarity with local conditions which this court cannot have, the presumption of constitutionality can be overcome only by the most explicit demonstration that a classification is a hostile and oppressive discrimination against particular persons and classes. The burden is on the one attacking the legislative arrangement to negate every conceivable basis which might support it."[21]

This United States Court of Appeals made this statement with reference to a case testing an Alaskan statute which levied property taxes among various types of governmental units for the purpose of supporting municipal and public school functions. The principal claim of inequality arose essentially not from lack of uniformity in the taxation but rather from the fact that the property tax collected in a municipality or school district could be retained by the collecting entity while such property taxes collected outside the designated municipalities and school districts reverted to the territorial treasurer. The court, in answering this charge, said that in the absence of unquestionable systematic geographical discrimination,[22] no requirements of equality and uniformity of the Organic Act of Alaska or the equal protection clause of the 14th amendment limit the power of the legislature in respect to allocation and distribution of public funds.[23]

Even though the court denied that equality and uniformity of taxation requirements of both state and federal constitutions applied to the distribution of funds, the court proceeded nevertheless to lay down "guiding principles" which govern the legislatures' distribution of tax funds. Quoting *Corpus Juris Secundum,* the court said:

> In the absence of constitutional regulation the method of apportioning and distributing a school fund, accruing from taxes or other revenue, rests in the wise discretion of the state legislature, which method, in the absence of abuse of discretion or violation of some constitutional provision, cannot be interferred with by the courts. . . . the fact that the fund is distributed unequally among the different districts or political subdivisions does not render it invalid.[24]

In other words, the needs of the various types of school districts and the resulting impact of methods of taxation is a matter which is to be determined by the legislature.

Observing the First Generation

At the end of the first generation, the courts had made some points which were probably more profound for their implications than for their actual value as precedent. As with most court decisions, they generally raised more questions than they answered. There are, however, some observations which can be made.

480

The first generation cases were generally brought by taxpayers seeking some relief under the state equality and uniformity of taxation provision and in some cases also invoking the equal protection clause of the federal Constitution. In most instances, the taxpayer was seeking tax relief for himself without regard for equalization of educational opportunity. State school financing provisions were usually under attack, not because of the lack of fiscal equalization, but because they tended to provide too much equalization. Generally, the taxpayer was attempting to maintain the preferred position of his school district as an enclave of relatively high wealth.

Since the cases were usually brought by taxpayers, the courts tended to view the situation merely in terms of the precedents which had been established. These governed only the equality and uniformity of taxation provisions of state constitutions and those precedents which had been established with a view of the equal protection clause of the 14th amendment solely in the context of taxation. The courts' adamant position, that the relief was confined to taxation precedents and not to distribution of state resources, restricted the plaintiffs' redress to the narrower taxation category of precedents established under equal protection of the federal Constitution. These courts acknowledged the existence of varying educational needs among local school districts created by special local conditions. According to the courts, such needs can give logical and reasonable rationale for apparently otherwise arbitrary classifications. For example, to allow a city the right to levy a special tax while denying the same taxes used by other districts in a state may on its face appear to be arbitrary if we were unaware of special conditions and needs of cities. However, by the identification of special local conditions and needs, a particular system of finance may be justified.

The courts, although dealing with taxpayer suits, established that the words "system"[25] and "thorough and efficient system"[26] in state constitutions created an affirmative duty on the part of the legislature to afford students an educational program with some degree of equality and uniformity. Unfortunately, the degree of equalization required by the state constitutions was never fully explored by the courts. The courts' use of words of condition such as "insofar as it is practical" indicated that the judicial perception of equalization of educational opportunity would have fallen short of full fiscal equalization among school districts. This short-sightedness on the part of the courts is at least partly responsible for the lack of motivation on the part of state legislature to fully equalize educational opportunity.

SECOND GENERATION

A Child's Education Cannot be a Function of School District Wealth

The several years since *Brown* v. *Board of Education*[27] have been marked with an ever-widening application of the individual's civil rights as guaranteed by the equal protection clause of the 14th amendment. During the years subsequent to *Brown*, the United States Supreme Court established a pattern of equal protection concepts which have substantial bearing on the current philosophy of the scope of individual rights.

The importance of an education has been presumed to be a constitutionally protected right since the Supreme Court in *Brown* said:

> Today, education is perhaps the most important function of state and local government. . . . In these days, it is doubtful that any child may reasonably be expected to succeed in life if he is denied the opportunity of an education. Such an opportunity, where the state has undertaken to provide it, is a right which must be made available to all on equal terms.[3]

This statement by the court has two important aspects: first, it confirmed the Supreme Court's recognition of the state's responsibility to provide education; second, it also pointed out that education was of such importance that it was a constitutionally protected right which must be provided to all on equal terms. This philosophy has been echoed several times since by the court.[28]

Arthur Wise in 1965 advanced the theory that since education was a constitutionally protected right and must be provided to all on equal terms, a state which gives fewer dollars for the child in a poorer school district may be denying the child his constitutional rights.[29] Wise argued that the state had no reasonable constitutional basis on which to justify making a child's education contingent on the wealth of his school district. The United States Supreme Court had laid the groundwork for such a conclusion by previously holding that to classify persons on either the basis

482

of poverty[30] or the basis of their location, homesite, or occupation was unreasonable.[31]

This rationale characterizes the second generation cases, that is, the quality of a child's education cannot be contingent upon the wealth of his school district. A state and local taxing and fund distribution system which is based on the property wealth of the local school district is unconstitutional.

By 1968, several suits had been filed, each seeking to have state school finance programs rendered unconstitutional through the application of this legal logic. A three-judge federal district court in Florida[32] was the first court to hold that a state school finance mechanism was unconstitutional as violative of the equal protection rights of a child. This court, relying largely on precedent by the United States Supreme Court in *Reynolds* v. *Sims*,[33] reasoned that the equal protection clause requires "the uniform treatment of persons standing in the same relation to the governmental action." The court then departed from the traditional line of reasoning of the courts in the first generation cases which had held that so long as the act in question applies uniformly there is no violation of equal protection, reasoning to the contrary that a uniform act of the legislature may indeed violate the equal protection clause if its effect is discriminatory. The court adopted the "rational basis" standard and concluded that a state must show a rational basis for its act or the act will be held unconstitutional.

The dispute here had arisen over a statutory millage cap which the state had placed on all school districts in the state. This millage cap reduced the amount of money which could be derived from local taxes for educational purposes. The plaintiffs contended that the millage limit violated the equal protection rights of children in poorer counties because the millage cap did not allow their county to levy a greater rate to obtain more dollars in order to have equal educational opportunity. The court in holding for the plaintiffs showed that the same ten mills in the richest county in Florida would raise $725 per student and in the poorest county the ten mills would raise only $52 per student. The three-judge court therefore concluded that "the act prevents the poorer counties from providing *from their own taxes* the same support for public education which the wealthy counties are able to provide.[32]"

Ironically, the net effect of the court's decision was to do exactly the opposite of what it apparently intended to do. As anyone who is familiar with school finance realizes, a school district with less than one-tenth the wealth of another district can never obtain equal educational resources by relying on local revenues. The poorest county in this particular instance would be forced to levy over 100 mills to raise the equivalent of a mere 10 mills in the wealthiest county. This, of course, will not be done, and without the millage cap the wealthier districts by merely raising one additional mill can continue to outstrip the less fortunate counties. Removal of the millage cap also sets in motion another phenomenon known as "tax substitution," whereby the wealthier with all their educational needs solved at the local level will not opt for greater amounts of state taxes to equalize resources among counties. The *Hargrave* decision, if allowed to be implemented, would have effectively demolished state-wide equalization in Florida. Here the legislative act was infinitely more equitable to children in poor counties than was the court decision. The court ignored or did not understand the rather sophisticated plan of the legislature which capped off disequalizing local moneys and gradually replaced them with equalizing state revenues.

Fortunately, this decision was vacated and remanded on other grounds by the Supreme Court of the United States. However, *Hargrave* probably stands as a double monument: first, as the first court decision to apply equal protection clause in holding a state school finance program unconstitutional, and second, as an admonishment to the judiciary that a vague understanding of the issues by the courts can produce great inequality of educational opportunity while obstensively invoking the equal protection clause to remedy that very situation.

Only a year elapsed between the lower federal court decision in *Hargrave* and the now famous decision by the California Supreme Court in *Serrano* v. *Priest.*[50] In *Serrano,* the court handed down a well reasoned decision which strongly documents the establishment of the new equal protection precedent. The court here spoke of equalization only in terms of the relative wealth of fiscal ability of the local school districts as measured in terms of property valuation. It did not attempt to define the equal protection argument in terms of educational needs of children or educational programs. In fact, the court was forced to distinguish cases which had sought to relate equal protection to educational needs to avoid adverse precedent previously established by the United States Supreme Court.[34]

484

In order for the court to answer the primary constitutional question, does the California public school financing scheme violate the equal protection clause, it was first necessary to determine whether (1) education is a fundamental interest protected by the constitution, (2) wealth is a "suspect classification," and (3) the state has a "compelling interest" in creating a system of school finance which makes a child's education dependent on the wealth of his local school district. In a short treatise on constitutional law, the court pointed out that the United States Supreme Court had employed two tests for determining the constitutionality of state legislation under the equal protection clause. In the first and more lenient test, the Supreme Court presumed that state legislation is constitutional and merely required the state to show that the distinctions drawn or classifications created by the challenged statute had some "rational relationship to a conceivable legitimate state purpose." On the other hand, if the state legislation touched on a "fundamental interest" of the individual or involved a "suspect classification," then the court would subject the challenged statute to "strict scrutiny" or active and critical analysis. If a fundamental interest or suspect classification is involved, the presumption of constitutionality is not with the state; on the contrary, the burden of establishing the necessity of the classification is with the state.

After reviewing precedents established in desegregation,[35] criminal law,[36] and voting rights[37] cases, the court concluded, "We are convinced that the distinctive and priceless function of education in our society warrants, indeed compels, our treating it as a fundamental interest." With regard to wealth as a "suspect classification" the court relied on inferences made by the United States Supreme Court to the effect that "lines drawn on the basis of wealth or property, like those of race, are traditionally disfavored."[38] This established, to the satisfaction of the court, that wealth was a "suspect classification." The court then critically analyzed the present California finance system and pointed out that although the basic state aid program in California tends to equalize among school districts, the total system, including state and local funds combined, creates great disparities in school revenues and the system as a whole generates school revenue proportional to the wealth of the individual school district.

Finally, after concluding that education was a "fundamental interest" and property wealth was a "suspect classification," the court then applied the "strict scrutiny" standard to determine

485

if the financing system was "necessary to accomplish a compelling state interest." The defendant sought to establish a compelling state interest by alleging that the state school finance program in California "strengthened and encouraged local responsibility for control of public education," essentially maintaining that local control of education was inseparable from local discretion in financing. The court acknowledged that local administrative control of education may be a compelling state interest but denied that the present system of financing was necessary to further that interest. The court said, "No matter how the state decides to finance its system of public education, it can still leave this decision-making power in the hands of local districts."

The defense also asserted that a "compelling interest" of the state is to allow the local school district the authority to choose how much it wishes to spend for education of its children. Countering this argument, the court pointed out that the poor school district did not have such a choice and could not so long as the assessed valuation of property was the major determinant of how much it could spend for schools.

> The poor district cannot freely choose to tax itself into an excellence which its tax rolls cannot provide. Far from being necessary to promote local fiscal choice, the present financing system actually deprives the less wealthy districts of that option.[50]

Striking down these and other arguments by the defense, the court held that the state did not have a "compelling interest" in classifying children according to the wealth of the school district. Said another way, a statutory classification which makes the quality of a child's education dependent on the wealth of the parents and neighbors is unconstitutional.

Closely following *Serrano*, a United States District Court in Minnesota entertained a class action suit[39] wherein plaintiffs alleged denial of equal protection and violation of the Civil Rights Act.[40] Plaintiffs showed that rich districts in Minnesota enjoy both lower tax rates and higher spending. The court, in viewing the facts, arrived at the inescapable conclusion that, "The level of spending for publicly financed education in Minnesota is profoundly affected by the wealth of each school district." Education was considered to be a "fundamental interest" and wealth to be a "suspect classification" as held in *Serrano*.

486

When the state defended its finance system by claiming that local control was a "compelling interest" the court pointed out that the state, by creating erratic disparities in the economic power of the local district, has itself limited local initiative, with poor districts having to spend low with high taxes and rich districts spending high with low taxes. The court further observed that local control and local financing are not inextricably intertwined; local administrative control and local effort can be maintained even though wealth is held neutral. Finally, the court concluded that the plaintiffs stated an appropriate cause of action and that a "system of public school financing which makes spending per pupil a function of the school district's wealth violates the equal protection guarantee of the Fourteenth Amendment." *Van Dusartz* has limited utility as precedent because the court's comments were made merely in support of an order denying the defendant's motion to dismiss the action and the court deferred further action until after the 1972 Minnesota legislative session.

A significant decision by a federal three-judge court in Texas[41] followed both the California and Minnesota cases and reached the same conclusion. Here it was held that plaintiffs had been denied equal protection of the law by the Texas system of financing its public schools. Plaintiffs contended that the educational finance system of the state makes education a function of the local property tax base. In "strict scrutiny" of the Texas system, a survey of 110 school districts in Texas indicated that the school districts with over $100,000 market value of property enjoyed a tax rate per $100 of only thirty-one cents, while the poorest four districts with less than $10,000 in property per pupil had more than double the tax burden of seventy cents per $100 property valuation. The lower rate of the rich districts yielded $585 per pupil while the higher rate in the poorer districts yielded only $60 per pupil. Relying on these data, the court observed that the school finance system of Texas erroneously assumes that the value of property in the various districts will be sufficiently equal to maintain comparable expenditures among districts. This inequality is not corrected to any substantial degree by state funds, because when all state and local funds were combined, the poor district of Edgewood had only $231 per pupil while the rich district of Alamo Heights had $543. Expert testimony substantiated . . . . that the Texas system of school finance "tends to subsidize the rich at the expense of the poor."

To correct this unconstitutional inequality, *Rodriguez* established a standard of "fiscal neutrality." As was the case in both *Serrano* and *Van Dusartz*, the court maintained that fiscal neutrality did not require that all educational expenditures be equal for each child. The standard simply requires that "the quality of public education may not be a function of wealth, other than the wealth of the state as a whole."

In commenting further on educational expenditures, *Rodriguez* made it clear that the "fiscal neutrality" standard does not involve the court in the intricacies of affirmatively requiring expenditures be made in a certain manner. "On the contrary, the state may adopt any financial scheme desired so long as the variations in wealth among the governmentally chosen units do not affect spending for the education of any child."

The *Rodriguez* court made it very clear that it would not become involved in the nebulous concept of educational needs. Such an undertaking would involve the court in "endless research and evaluation for which the judiciary is ill-suited." To the court, judicially manageable standards could only be established along the definable lines of valuation of property wealth.

Observing the Second Generation

Unlike the first generation, these cases were brought on behalf of school children who were alleging denial of equal access to educational fiscal resources. In these cases, the equal protection clause of the 14th amendment was invoked to force greater equalization of resources among school districts. This represented a significant departure from the first generation cases which were characterized by taxpayer actions generally attempting to restrain equalization measures taken by state legislatures. The interests of taxpayers and school children, apparently, seldom had the same equalization objectives.

Second generation decisions established that a child's education cannot be a function of school district wealth. Following United States Supreme Court precedents, these courts, with the exception of *Hargrave*, established that education is a "fundamental interest" of every child. In addition, wealth was held to be a "suspect classification." These legal presumptions required the state to establish a "compelling interest" to justify the classification of school districts on the basis of wealth. Utilizing these constitutional standards, the courts strictly scrutinized the Cali-

488

fornia, Minnesota, and Texas school finance systems and held them unconstitutional. The guideline applied by the courts is one of fiscal neutrality. All of the courts were careful to observe that fiscal neutrality does not require equal expenditures per pupil.

The courts of the second generation scrupulously avoided the question of educational needs. While acknowledging that variations in educational needs probably exist, they, nevertheless, refused to elevate educational needs to a constitutionally protected level. To these courts, the constitutional standard of equality of educational opportunity requires equal fiscal resources as measured in terms of property value, but does not require the incorporation of educational need standards.

THIRD GENERATION

Educational Needs and High Cost Programs

Contemporaneous with and even preceding the second generation cases is another type of case which promises to be the focal point of much litigation in the future. Educators for some time have recognized that all children cannot be educated equally with equal resources. Some children with special learning deficiencies caused by cultural deprivation or mental or physical incapacities must be given special educational services. On reflection, no one can sensibly contend that a non-English speaking child or a child with speech or hearing difficulties does not need special instructional programs. Such programs cost more than regular programs geared to normal children possessing no particular learning disorders or deficiencies. The higher costs of such programs have been documented by the National Educational Finance Project.[42] Today, some state aid programs partially take into account the differences in educational needs of children. Most state finance programs, however, do not adequately measure or compensate such educational needs by providing proportionately greater funds to school districts with high incidences of high cost children. Since education is generally considered by the courts today to be a "fundamental right," can state legislatures constitutionally avoid recognizing special learning problems? Is a child denied his constitutional right of an equal education if he cannot hear the teacher, cannot enunciate his words clearly enough to progress normally in school, or his cultural background has placed him at such a learning deficit that he will be unable ever to catch up or compete? In such cases, equal expenditures or regular programs for all children may provide equal learning opportunity for normal, middle class children, but attendance in such regular middle class educational programs by the physically, mentally or culturally deprived provides for less than equal educational opportunity.

A fundamental legal question is whether a state's responsibility to provide a child with an opportunity for equal education is successfully discharged where no recognition is given to individual needs and deficiencies. Should a state's constitutional responsibility to the child be elevated from simply providing equal access to dollars, as in the second generation cases, to a level of giving children equal access to educational programs as mandated by the educational needs of children.

The courts to date have dealt only superficially with the pervasive problems of educational needs. The first generation taxpayer suits[43] observed the importance of recognition of educational need variations among school districts, but in no case did the court substitute its judgment for that of the legislature. The courts generally subscribed to the standard that "no requirement of uniformity or of equal protection of the law limits the power of a legislature with respect to allocation and distribution of public funds.[44] With the beginning of the third generation, *McInnis v. Shapiro*,[45] the plaintiffs claimed that the present Illinois finance system created large variations in expenditures per student from district to district, thereby providing some students with a good education and depriving others who have equal or greater educational need. The court concluded that equal educational expenditures are not required by the 14th amendment and that variations created by taxation of property in the school districts do not discriminate. The court said:

> Unequal educational expenditures per student, based upon the variable property values and tax rates of local school districts, do not amount to an invidious discrimination. Moreover, the statutes which permit these unequal expenditures on a district to district basis are neither arbitrary nor unreasonable.[45]

With regard to district wealth variations, the determination of the McInnis court was exactly the opposite of that of *Serrano* and *Rodriguez* and it also declined to establish judicial standards for determining legislative allocations based on educational needs.

490

In *McInnis*[46] which incidentally was decided prior to either *Hargrave* or *Serrano,* the United States District Court for the Northern District of Illinois held that the Illinois state system of school finance was not unconstitutional as violative of the equal protection and due process clauses of the 14th amendment. Since *McInnis* was summarily affirmed by the Supreme Court of the United States,[49] this statement probably represents precedent at this time. This is true in spite of the California Supreme Court's attempt to distinguish *McInnis* solely on the contention that it involved only a plea for equalization in terms of educational needs.[50] The plaintiffs in *McInnis,* however, did not clearly state either the fiscal equalization issue or the educational need issue. With regard to variation in property wealth, the plaintiff was probably intentionally evasive because the four districts involved were not, in fact, property poor. As far as educational needs were concerned the plaintiff districts claimed high incidence of high need children, but did not adequately support their claim with data showing precisely the additional costs of special programs for high need children. In view of the lack of information and standards provided by the plaintiffs, the court held that the Illinois system of financing was not unconstitutional. In so holding, the court quoted Justice Holmes who once said that "the 14th amendment is not a pedagogical requirement of the impractical."[51] The position in *McInnis* was summed by saying that there were no "discoverable and manageable standards by which a court can determine when the Constitution is satisfied and when it is violated."

One may presume, of course, that if the plaintiffs had provided "judicially manageable standards," the outcome of the case might have been different. The court observed that its only possible standard was to provide that "each pupil must receive the same dollar expenditures." In commenting on the detriments of this standard it was pointed out that expenses are not the exclusive yardstick of a child's educational needs—to the contrary, the court maintained that "Deprived pupils need more aid than fortunate ones." It also recognized the problems created by sparsity and cost of living variations throughout the state. In essence, while this court recognized variations in educational need among school districts, it nevertheless would not substitute its judgment for that of the legislature and thereby upheld the present Illinois state school finance system.

The decision in the Illinois case was closely followed by a second "educational need" case in Virginia.[52] In *Burruss*, the plaintiffs instead of being from suburban school districts were from a rural county in western Virginia. Plaintiffs in this suit relied more directly on the educational needs argument than did the plaintiffs in *McInnis*. Bath County, the county in which plaintiffs resided and attended school, had higher than the state average assessed valuation of property per pupil but had a very high incidence of low income families. In terms of property wealth per pupil, Bath County ranked 14th in the state, but when wealth was measured in terms of family income it ranked 55th among counties in the state. With the state aid formula relying almost entirely on property wealth as the chief allocation determinant, Bath consistently received less funds per pupil than it needed to provide adequate educational services for the children from low income families. Specifically, plaintiffs claimed the state formula created and perpetuated substantial disparities in educational opportunities throughout the state of Virginia and failed to relate to any of the variety of educational needs present in the several counties and cities of Virginia.

To the former charge, the court found that the system of finance was not discriminatory as it operated under a uniform and consistent state plan. With regard to educational needs, the court praised the equalization of educational opportunity as worthy and commendable, but refused to interject the wisdom of the court in ascertaining what constituted educational need disparities. In following the hands-off course of *McInnis*, the court said:

> ... the courts have neither the knowledge, nor the means, nor the power to tailor the public moneys to fit the varying needs of these students throughout the state. We can only see to it that the outlays on one group are not invidiously greater or less than that of another. No such arbitrariness is manifest here.[53]

Accordingly, *Burruss* denied relief to plaintiffs under either the "efficiency" provision of the Virginia Constitution or the equal protection clause of the 14th amendment. The United States Supreme Court summarily affirmed this decision.

In neither *McInnis* nor *Burruss* could the school districts in which plaintiffs attended school be classified as fiscally poor if wealth were measured in terms of assessed valuation of property. However, in both instances claims were made that the high inci-

492

dence of deprived children created excessive unmet educational needs which denied children equal access to educational programs. In both instances, the courts recognized the existence of varying educational needs and costs but refused to elevate the disparity to a plane of constitutional discrimination.

The most recent case to acknowledge the problem of educational needs as a possible criterion for measuring the constitutionality of state school finance programs was handed down by a Superior Court in New Jersey.[54] This court viewed approvingly a New Jersey report which stated:

> It is now recognized that children from lower socio-economic level homes require more educational attention if they are to progress normally through school. When the additional compensatory education is provided, it results in *substantially higher costs. The weighting* of the children from the lower income families *compensates in part* for the larger expenditure necessary to provide them with an adequate educational program so they may overcome their lack of educational background. [Emphasis added.][55]

Unfortunately, the New Jersey court's discussion of educational needs did not progress to the point of establishing standards or guidelines, but one could extrapolate from the court's discussion that if educational needs and cost weightings had not been previously included in the state aid formula, the court might quite possibly have imposed them. This is, of course, conjecture, but the decision of this court gave the fullest recognition to varying educational needs and costs of any court to date. It is significant to note that the court gave such credence to educational needs while holding that portions of the state school finance formula of New Jersey violated both the "thorough and efficient" provisions of the state constitution along with the equal protection clause of the 14th amendment. Such judicial acknowledgment of educational needs and costs variations suggests the distinct possibility of a judicial formulation of acceptable standards for legislative identification and funding of special educational needs among children.

Observing the Third Generation

The third generation cases indicate that the court in the future may well establish constitutional standards applicable not only to wealth variations among school districts but also to educational

493

need variations among school children. However, to date, no court has ventured this far into educational policy determination. As courts become more sophisticated in analyzing educational finance programs, they may well begin to realize that wealth as a "suspect classification" holds important implications for the individual needs of children. For example, children from poverty families generally have greater educational needs which are not recognized or ameliorated by simple school district wealth corrections. As the plaintiffs in *Burruss* sought to show, the school district wealth may be average or above, but the high incidence of children with high cost educational needs will create educational disparity. This is not only true of rural counties like Bath County, Virginia, but is also particularly acute in large core cities. Most large cities have higher than average wealth when measured in terms of either property valuations[56] or adjusted gross income, but have high incidence of culturally deprived children. For the courts to enforce wealth equalization among school districts while ignoring the prevalence of high need not only would not help but also would actually hinder the educational programs of cities. Of course, by requiring full wealth equalization among school districts, as is indicated in the second generation cases, the courts do not preclude the legislatures from meeting the areas of special problems through constitutional classifications based on educational needs. However, for the courts to enter the arena of educational finance and attempt to establish constitutional standards governing fiscal ability of school districts while at the same time ignoring the specific educational needs of children would be ludicrous and highly unlikely.

IMPLICATIONS FOR STATE SCHOOL SUPPORT PROGRAMS

In their current state, the court decisions appear to be leaving as many questions unanswered as they are answering. For example, do the decisions apply to school transportation programs, the need for which varies from school district to school district? Do they apply to capital outlay and debt service programs? Within the context of current practice, these two latter programs rely more on the local property tax as a revenue source than do other school programs. In the absence of greater specificity, will the courts permit local districts to have any local "leeway" for enrichment or individuality in financing their school programs? If so, to what degree? Will the courts require an immediate shift in the state school support program to provide for full and complete "equal access," or will states be permitted to enact statutes providing for an orderly transition? Will the courts recognize that certain groups of pupils require different types of educational services and programs, and that the costs for these services and programs are higher than for "normal" programs? Will the concept of "equal access" be extended to include equal access to educational programs and thereby require that educational expenditures per pupil be unequal among school districts within a state?

Reviewing a moment in an evolutionary context, we have viewed the court cases in "three generations." Plaintiffs in the first generation cases sought to provide taxpayer relief by striking down legislation appropriating state aid on a per pupil basis which resulted in a sharing of tax resources among school districts within a state. Through the precedent of this litigation the courts established the constitutionality of using the equalization method in distributing state aid to local school districts; e.g., funds may be distributed in inverse relationship to the wealth of the local school district.

In the second generation cases, the courts established that any child in the state is deprived of "equal protection" if the state school support program does not provide him (or his local school district) with equal access to dollars for the support of the local school program. The second generation court decisions emphasize two basic points: (1) the funding of a child's educational program is to be based on the wealth of the state as a whole rather than the wealth of the district of residence; and (2) the decisions do not require that expenditures throughout a state be uniform or equal. Due to the recency of these decisions, their true impact has not been assessed; however, litigation has been initiated in several states and recent decisions in four states have been essentially consistent.

The most comprehensive pattern has been established through the third generation cases which have added the additional concept that a child cannot be denied equal access to education programs as well as equal access to dollars. Current cases have focused on the relationship between the allocation of revenues and the capacity of local school districts to provide programs with those revenues. The contention has been that certain children have educational needs which result in local districts having to provide high cost educational programs if those needs are to be met. In these third generation cases, the courts have reviewed the dimensions and problems associated with providing revenues on the basis of educational need and have also questioned the *appropriateness of local district educational expenditures being dependent upon the mood or aspirations of the parents or taxpayers of the local district.*

The ultimate extension of this principal of educational need would result in local districts being mandated to provide pupils with access to those educational programs needed by the pupils in the district. State legislative action mandating special education programs are examples of statutory recognition of differing educational needs of pupils and state intervention to assure that those educational programs are being provided.

The research conducted by the National Educational Finance Project[57] (NEFP) provides additional support of the cost differential concept. NEFP researchers have reported that costs for "representative best practice" educational programs varied significantly from a ratio of 1.00 for basic elementary grades 1–6 to a ratio of 2.06 for compensatory education programs, with broad categories of vocational education and special education having a ratio of 1.81. Within special education, the cost differentials for specific categories varied extensively from 1.20 for children in programs for the speech handicapped to 3.25 for children in programs for the physically handicapped. In analyzing the conditions contributing to the differences in costs among programs, the researchers reported that the principal contributing factors were:

1. Pupil-teacher ratio in the particular class.
2. Percentage of pupil's day or week spent in the class.
3. Non-teaching support personnel provided for the class.
4. Equipment and materials provided for the class.
5. Salary level of the teacher.

In addition to those additional costs associated with the incidence of pupils who require or seek educational programs with higher cost ratios, local district per pupil expenditures will also be influenced by transportation requirements. Rather than being a uniform cost in all districts, transportation expenditures will vary in terms of the percent of pupils transported, population density, labor costs in the community, and road conditions.

Even though one might agree that certain groups of pupils require educational programs which are different from those required by others, and that these programs have varying levels of costs, the theory of incorporating cost differentials into state school support computation might be rejected if it were not for the additional research findings that some districts have higher percentages of pupils with need for higher cost programs than other districts. This condition results in the requirement of additional financial resources in those districts with high incidences of pupils with special needs if those districts are to provide pupils with "equal access" to educational programs. The concept of spending different amounts of money on the education of various pupils was supported in *Robinson* when the court recognized that the educational programs required for different groups of pupils dictated different levels of expenditure. The focus was on programs for pupils of low socio-economic status, but the same concept may be applied to vocational education and special education programs.

As a part of the basic research conducted by the National Educational Finance Project, a data bank for a prototype state was developed so that simulated application of various state school programs could be analyzed in terms of their impact on "real world" situations. The data base for the prototype state was developed from a selected number of actual districts whose characteristics are generally representative of typical school districts found throughout the nation. The lone exception is that none of the districts had an average daily membership of less than 1,800 pupils. In Table 13–1, selected data for each of the 32 districts in the prototype state have been presented to illustrate the impact of the cost differentials when the weighted pupil approach is used in determining the incidence of educational needs as contrasted with using an unweighted pupil approach or assuming that there are no differences in the educational programs required by different groups of pupils. The impact of cost differentials is reflected in the increase in the number of program units over the number of ADM (Average Daily Membership) pupil units.

In the following table, district number 24, with the highest incidence of high cost pupils, is rural and agricultural. The district with second highest incidence is the largest city and can be classified as having a core ghetto and a typical large city pupil population. District number 2, with the lowest impact of incidence of high cost pupils, is essentially a high income suburban area.

In making more detailed analysis of the impact of the weighted pupil approach, the NEFP staff found that the incidence of pupils

TABLE 13–1

IMPACT OF COST DIFFERENTIALS ON VARIOUS TYPES OF
SCHOOL DISTRICTS IN A PROTOTYPE STATE
(GRADES 1–12 ONLY)

District	ADM Units[a]	Program Units[b]	Percent of Impact	Type of District[c]
1	8,243	10,700	29.8	City/Suburb
2	12,905	16,174	25.3	City/Suburb
3	28,801	37,318	29.6	City
4	107,024	138,545	29.5	City/Rural
5	4,485	6,670	48.7	Rural/Town
6	6,218	9,659	55.3	Rural/Town
7	9,022	11,450	26.9	City
8	1,624	2,105	29.6	Rural/Town
9	13,246	17,141	29.4	Suburban
10	3,718	4,725	27.1	Town
11	3,534	5,230	48.0	Rural/Town
12	118,514	152,277	28.5	Suburban/Town
13	4,208	6,387	51.8	Rural
14	2,959	3,700	25.0	Suburban/Town
15	137,177	172,194	25.5	City/Rural
16	18,235	26,107	43.2	City/Rural
17	14,430	19,245	33.4	Rural/Town
18	63,561	83,297	31.1	City/Rural
19	21,491	29,622	37.8	City/Rural
20	13,066	18,584	42.2	Rural/Town
21	25,626	33,286	29.9	Rural/Town
22	16,370	23,995	46.6	City/Rural
23	5,305	8,081	52.3	Rural/Town
24	6,364	10,301	61.9	Rural/Town
25	174,927	282,798	61.7	City
26	11,816	16,296	37.9	Rural/Town
27	11,671	16,872	44.6	Rural
28	9,164	14,024	53.0	Rural
29	2,392	2,992	25.1	Suburban
30	5,297	8,010	51.2	Rural
31	4,866	7,256	49.1	Rural
32	4,425	6,181	39.7	Rural
TOTAL	870,684	1,201,222		

[a]Total pupils in average daily membership in grades 1-12.
[b]District entitlement computed by using a weighted pupil approach to recognize incidence of pupils in high cost programs.
[c]In this classification: cities have populations of over 25,000 and towns between 2,500 and 25,000.

with need for high cost programs varied among the types of districts, e.g., rural-small town, suburban, and independent city, as well as among all districts in the prototype state.

The previous discussion illustrates that techniques can be utilized to determine the "educational needs" of different subgroups of pupils and that these pupils are not uniformly distributed among school districts. Through the application of the research techniques discussed above, an individual state can determine its cost differentials, incorporate either the weighted pupil or instruction unit into its state school support computation, and then begin to meet the thrust of the third generation of equal protection cases — that is, providing pupils with equal access to educational programs as well as equal access to dollars.

CONSTITUTIONALLY ACCEPTABLE ALTERNATIVES

The courts have not identified specific operational state school support programs which are considered to be constitutionally acceptable; however, sufficient guidelines have been stated which suggest the following four basic alternatives which have been illustrated in this book in Chapter 9, "Alternative State Finance Plans."

1. Full state funding — fixed level program.
2. Equalization with no leeway — fixed level program.
3. Equalization with minimal leeway — fixed level program.
4. Incentive — variable level program.

In each of the suggested alternatives, cost differentials have been incorporated so that pupils would be provided with "equal access to educational programs" as suggested by the third generation cases. To increase the level of equity, the cost of necessary services such as pupil transportation have also been recognized in the tabular material which accompanies each of the graphical presentations contained in the previous chapter. Additional adjustments could be provided to recognize capital outlay and debt service expenditures. To meet the test of the second generation cases, it does not appear as though the courts would require the inclusion of the cost differentials to recognize the differences in educational need among pupils and among school districts. However, to meet the test of the third generation cases, the courts would require inclusion of the educational needs measures in the state school support program.

Full State Funding

This alternative meets the test of "the wealth being dependent upon the total wealth of the state." In operation, educational programs could be identified with accompanying cost differentials. The allocation for the total program could then be computed by multiplying the program units by the state allocation with whatever additional modifications might be incorporated into the state school support program. The key consideration is that the local district's, and thereby the pupil's, access to wealth is dependent upon the total wealth of the state. Revenue for the program could be obtained completely from the general fund of the state or from state tax earmarked for this purpose.

A graphical presentation of this alternative with supporting tables is shown in Models IV–C and V–C in the chapter entitled "Alternative State Finance Plans." The first model is a flat grant and the second a minimum foundation program, but the net financial impact is the same under either distribution scheme. The critical factor is that all of the funds come from the state sources, thereby meeting the court test of the access to dollars being a function of the total wealth of the entire state rather than the wealth in the individual local school district.

✓ Another alternative under full state funding would be for the legislature to establish a state-level school budget approval agency which would determine the funds to be allocated to each district, with such determination being made after a review of the budget requests of each local district and a consultation with local school district officials. This approach has been referred to as the "negotiated budget." At first glance, the option seems attractive, for it provides an opportunity for recognition of the unique local conditions which may influence the level of local district expenditures, e.g., cost of living, level of teachers' salaries, variations in the type and quantity of educational services, and locally-determined differences in instructional programs provided for pupils.

Operationally, the administration of the "negotiated budget" in allocation of funds to local districts would have several problems. Equity to all parties would require the extensive development of criteria or standards to be used in making the allocations; considerable amounts of time would be consumed in conferring with local school officials in reviewing and approving their budgets; and considerable power would be concentrated in the state agency with review and approval responsibility. Lingering questions of equity and favoritism would inevitably be raised.

If standards and criteria for programs and cost differentials were to be developed and utilized in apportioning state funds, the budget would no longer be "negotiated" and the program would resemble the basic computation method outlined in the previous two alternatives in this section. It would be difficult to develop equitable administrative procedures for this approach, and there would be a tendency to centralize educational budgetary decision-making at the state level rather than to provide opportunity for allocation decisions to be made as close to the point of implementation as possible.

Full state funding obviously meets the "equal access" test and makes the level of expenditures per pupil in the local school district dependent upon the wealth of the entire state rather than on the concentration of wealth in the district. The concept of "equal access to educational programs" can be incorporated through the use of cost differentials. However, full state funding does not provide an opportunity for districts to make higher levels of local effort if they desire to provide or supplement programs or services beyond the level recognized in the computation of the local district's entitlement. Even though considerable support may be found for permitting local school districts to have the option of a "leeway levy" for enrichment, this practice was questioned in *Robinson* when the court emphasized that this practice results in "... control for the wealthy, not for the poor." In other discussion of this issue, the *Robinson* decision further stated that, "Education was too important a function to be left to the mood — and in some cases the low aspirations — of the taxpayers of a given district, even whose children attend schools in the district."

Even in view of the previous discussion, the courts might permit a state to "phase into" a complete "equal access" state school support program. A gradual reduction could be scheduled in the level of reliance on local revenue resources with an accompanying increase in reliance on state revenue sources. Under this arrangement local school districts might retain the "leeway" option temporarily, but it would be "phased out" within a relatively short period of time, e.g., three to five years. However, in the absence of direct precedent, this is pure conjecture, even though the courts have permitted these practices in the area of racial desegregation.

Equalization With No Leeway

This alternative has been referred to as the minimum foundation program and the Strayer-Haig formula as well as the percentage-equalizing, state aid ratio, or guaranteed assessed valuation program for funding state school support programs. Various computational schemes have been devised, but the end result is the same dollar allocation to local school districts if the unit value of the program remains constant for all districts in the state and if the same measures of local fiscal capacity are used for all districts.

Under this alternative, the basic value of units of educational need would have a fixed dollar value for all districts in the state; however, certain modifying factors could be included to permit dollar adjustments for transportation, cost of living, teacher training and experience, and similar items. The allocation of funds per unit of educational need would be uniform whether the distribution be based on a cost differential approach for various programs or on a standard allotment irrespective of the nature of the educational programs provided in the local school districts. In assuring that the local district has funds to support the computed program, the state provides variable amounts of state funds among the districts of a state in inverse relationship to local wealth per unit of need.

A specific example of this alternative is shown in Model II–D in the chapter entitled "Alternative State Finance Plans." Each local district in the state is required to levy a tax on a specified revenue base or bases; the proceeds of this levy are then "charged against" the value of the local school district's computed program and the state then funds the remaining amount. If the yield of the local levy exceeds the dollar amount of the local school district's program, the local district retains the amount required to fund its program and is required to forward the remainder to the state treasury to be used in meeting the revenue needs of the less wealthy districts.

In this alternative, locally available revenues would be dependent upon the wealth of the entire state rather than the wealth of the district; therefore, it would meet the tests established by the courts in the second generation cases. The inclusion of cost differentials in the computation of the fixed value program would enable the alternative to meet the standards implied in the third generation cases.

Equalization with Minimal Leeway

This alternative could be an adaptation of the "full state support" or "equalization with no leeway" programs. In Chapter 9, Models II–C and V–B and their supporting tables illustrate the effect of an equalization program with a 10 mill rate charged against the local district's state school support program, but the district is permitted to levy an additional two mills to supplement or enrich its educational program.

In the absence of the courts' having determined the constitutionality of this alternative or having set standards for leeway, discussion of this alternative might be characterized as pure conjecture. However, *Robinson* did briefly discuss this possibility in reviewing an enacted, but not fully funded, state school support program in New Jersey. The court indicated that the level of that program, if it were fully funded for all districts, might meet the test of providing adequate support for a ". . . thorough and efficient system of public schools. . . ." even though the program might result in disparities in access to revenues among school districts within the state.

If the courts should permit states to operate under a "constitutional plan" of orderly progress toward full and complete "equal access," this alternative might be permissible. In the prototype state, the net effect of this alternative is that the richest school district would have access to approximately ten percent more revenue per pupil than the poorest district. From the richest to the poorest district in the prototype state, the range in wealth per pupil is approximately six to one — a range much less than typically found in states throughout the nation. In other states with greater disparity in per pupil wealth, the inequities of this alternative would be greater.

If the concept of the available revenue being dependent upon the wealth of the state as a whole is accepted and implemented literally, an "equalization with minimal leeway" alternative would not meet the test of the courts. However, the courts have been consistent in stating that their decisions should not be interpreted as mandating uniform expenditures per pupil among districts within the state. Proponents of local control would undoubtedly advocate this alternative, but as *Robinson* has emphasized, ". . . local control is illusory. It is control for wealthy, not for the poor." This alternative provides for a minimal level of disparity and possibly would meet the test of equal access if any variation would be permitted by the courts.

Incentive

Under this alternative, local school district officials are permitted to exercise discretionary judgment in determining the level of local effort (beyond a prescribed minimum) to be made in providing school revenues. The total locally available revenues become a function of the effort rather than the wealth of the school district; therefore, the test of equal access to wealth will be met through this alternative. This plan is also discussed in the chapter entitled "Alternative State Finance Plans." Two critical features characterize the model in the discussion: (1) a fixed level base has been prescribed to assure that all pupils have access to an "adequate" educational program irrespective of their district of residence; and (2) the state's proportional contribution is the same for the last dollar of available revenue as it is for the first dollar.

Various titles have been given to this program from the time it was first proposed by Updegraff[58] until its recent advocacy by Coons et al.[59] under the title of "district power equalizing." In computing the relative state and local share, the amount of the local district's state allocation is determined by multiplying the local revenue which a district raises by that district's state aid ratio as illustrated in the discussion of the incentive plan in Chapter 9. The combination of the state and local funds provides the revenues to support the local district educational program.

The amount of available revenue is dependent upon the "effort" of the district rather than its wealth. As with the previous alternative, this approach meets the court tests of equal access to wealth among districts within a state, but does make the quantity of funds dependent upon the mood and aspirations of the taxpayers — thereby creating a disequalized access to educational programs among the state's districts. However, this choice does provide assurance that pupils will be provided with equal access to a predetermined minimal level of revenues to support local educational programs.

An adaptation of this alternative would be for local district officials to have the opportunity to exercise discretionary judgment in determining their level of local effort and in turn the total amount of available revenues which would be a function of the effort of the district rather than its wealth. This alternative would meet the test of the courts in the area of equal access to wealth, but would be suspect on other grounds in that the amount of funds available to support education in the school district would be left to the mood and aspirations of the taxpayers, thereby opening the possibility of pupils' having unequal access to educational programs among school districts within a state. This latter possibility is of even greater concern when one recognizes that local school officials could set their level of effort, and thereby their level of available revenue, at whatever level they deemed appropriate. A disequalized access to both revenues and educational program would seem to be an inevitable outgrowth of leaving this range of discretion to local school officials; therefore, this adaptation of the incentive model in all likelihood would not stand the test of the courts.

SUMMARY

The "full state support" and "equalization with no leeway" alternatives are the only two which meet the full set of requirements set forth by the courts. The "incentive" program might be permissible, but the problem of educational expenditures in a district being left to the mood and aspirations of the taxpayers would obviously result in some degree of unequal access to educational programs for pupils in districts which chose to make a minimum level of local effort. In absence of more precise guidelines from the courts, the exact status of the incentive program remains undetermined, for it meets the criterion of "equal access to wealth" but fails to guarantee "equal access to educational programs."

The judicial fate of "equalization with minimal leeway" is also somewhat uncertain because of the absence of precise guidelines from the courts. A literal reading of the court decisions would suggest that this alternative would not meet the test of the courts, but some minimal disparity in access to wealth might be permitted.

Under any of the alternatives discussed above, the interest of the third generation cases in the varying "educational need" among districts in a state could be ignored, thereby depriving certain groups of pupils of the ultimate form of "equal protection." The concept that varying educational programs are required to meet the educational needs of different groups of pupils appears to have been accepted, but previously the question of judicially manageable standards has been a barrier which discouraged the courts from entering into this area. The *Robinson* decision, recent research by the National Educational Finance Project, and other studies made in particular states support the basic concept and provide data which indicate that these programs do have different levels of costs and that these pupils are not uniformly distributed among school districts within a state. With this recent research, it is possible that the precedent of *McInnis* and *Burruss* might be reversed by further litigation.

The question of local determination of the level of effort to be made in support of education remains essentially unresolved, for the recent decisions have uniformly stated that their interpretation of equal protection should not be extended to require equal levels of educational expenditure for all pupils in a given state.

If subsequent court action should uphold *Robinson* by holding that "Education is too important a function to leave it also to the mood — in some cases the low aspirations — of the taxpayers of a given district . . ." the result will be a form of fixed level program for all districts in the state. Revenues may be raised at the state level or be a combination of local and state and federal funds, but the wealth base will be that of the state as a whole. The key factor in the further extension of the "equal protection" will be to provide for equal access to educational programs so that the level of expenditures and the range of educational opportunities will be substantially equal for all pupils irrespective of their school district or residence and the incidence of wealth in that district.

FOOTNOTES

1. See: *Tinker* v. *Des Moines School District*, 393 U.S. 503 (1969) and School District of *Abington Township* v. *Schempp*, 374 U.S. 203 (1963).
2. *People* v. *Cohen*, 57 Misc. 2d 366, 392 N.Y.S. 2d 706 (1968) ; *Piazzola* v. *Watkins*, 316 F. Supp. 624, (M.D. Ala. 1970).
3. *Brown* v. *Board of Education of Topeka*, 347 U.S. 483 (1954).
4. In the matter of Gault, 87 S. Ct. 1428 (1967) ; *Madera* v. *Board of Education of the City of New York*, 386 F. 2d 788 (1968).
5. *School District No. 25 of Woods County* v. *Hodge*, 199 Okla. 81, 183 P. 2d 575 (1947).
6. *Bell's Gap Railroad Co.* v. *Pennsylvania*, 134 U.S. 232 (1890).
7. Wade J. Newhouse, *Constitutional Uniformity and Equality in State Taxation* (Ann Arbor: University of Michigan Law School, 1959, p. 602).
8. *Ibid.*, p. 608.
9. *Ibid.*, p. 603.
10. *Bell's Gap Railroad Company* v. *Pennsylvania, supra.*
11. *Sawyer* v. *Gilmore*, 109 Me. 169, 83A 673 (1912).
12. Constitution of Maine, Section 8, Art. 9.
13. *Bell's Gap Railroad Co.* v. *Pennsylvania, supra.*
14. *Dean* v. *Coddington*, 81 S.D. 140, 131 N.W. 2d 700 (1964).
15. *Ibid.*
16. *Miller* v. *Korns*, 107 Ohio St. 287, 140 N.E. 773 (1923).
17. Ohio Constitution, Section 2, Art. 6.
18. See: *Taylor* v. *School District of City of Lincoln*, 128 Neb. 437, 259 N.W. 168 (1935).
19. *Miller* v. *Childers*, 107 Okla. 57, 238 P. 204 (1924).
20. Constitution of Oklahoma, Section 1, Art. 13. See also: *Kennedy* v.

506

Miller, 97 Cal. 429 (1893); *Piper* v. *Big Pine School District,* 193 Cal. 664 (1924).

21. *Hess* v. *Mullaney,* 15 Alaska 40, 213 F. 2d 635 (U.S.C.A. 9th Cir. 1954), Cert. Denied *Hess* v. *Dewey,* 348 U.S. 836, 75 S. Ct. 50 (1954).

22. See: *Cumberland Coal Co.* v. *Board of Revision of Tax Assessments of Green County,* 284 U.S. 23, 52 S. Ct. 48 (1931).

23. See: *Gen. Amer. Tank Car Corp.* v. *Day,* 270 U.S. 367, 46 S. Ct. 234 (1926); *Carmichael* v. *Southern Coal Co.,* 301 U.S. 495, 57 S. Ct. 868 (1937).

24. 79 C.J.S. § 411.

25. *Miller* v. *Childers, supra.*

26. *Miller* v. *Korns, supra.*

27. 347 U.S. 483 (1954).

28. *Tinker* v. *Des Moines School District,* 393 U.S. 503 (1969); *Palmer* v. *Thompson,* 39 U.S. L. Week 4759 (1971); *Griffin* v. *County School Board of Prince Edward County,* 84 S. Ct. 1226 (1964).

29. "Is Denial of Equal Educational Opportunity Constitutional?" *Administrator's Notebook, No. 6.* XIII (University of Chicago, Feb. 1965). See also: Arthur E. Wise, *Rich Schools Poor Schools* (Chicago: The University of Chicago Press, 1968).

30. *Griffin* v. *Illinois,* 351 U.S. 12 (1956).

31. *Baker* v. *Carr,* 369 U.S. 186 (1962); *Gray* v. *Sanders,* 372 U.S. 368 (1963).

32. *Hargrave* v. *Kirk,* 313 F. Supp. 944 (May 7, 1970); *vacated and remanded on other grounds sub. nom., Askew* v. *Hargrave,* 401 U.S. 476, 91 S. Ct. 856 (1971).

33. 377 U.S. 533, 84 S. Ct. 1362 (1964).

34. Equal protection as related to educational needs constitutes the third generation cases discussed later in this paper.

35. *Brown* v. *Board of Education, supra.*

36. *Griffin* v. *Illinois,* 351 U.S. 12, 76 S. Ct. 585 (1956); *Williams* v. *Illinois,* 399 U.S. 235, 90 S. Ct. 2018 (1970); *Douglas* v. *California,* 372 U.S. 353, 83 S. Ct. 814 (1963).

37. *Harper* v. *Virginia State Bd. of Elections,* 383 U.S. 663, 86 S. Ct. 1079 (1966); *Cipriano* v. *City Houma,* 395 U.S. 701, 89 S. Ct. 1897 (1969); *Kramer* v. *Union School District,* 395 U.S. 621, 89 S. Ct. 1886 (1969).

38. *Harper* v. *Virginia State Board of Elections, supra.*

39. *Van Dusartz* v. *Hatfield,* 334 F. Supp. 870 (D. Minn. 1971).

40. Also raised issue of discrimination under Civil Rights Act, 42 U.S.C. § 1983.

41. *Rodriguez* v. *San Antonio Independent School District,* _____ F. Supp. _____ (W.D. Texas, 1971).

42. R. L. Johns, Kern Alexander, Forbis Jordan, *Planning to Finance Education* 3 (Gainesville, Fla.: National Educational Finance Project, 1971).

43. *Miller* v. *Korns, supra.; Miller* v. *Childers, supra.*

44. *Hess* v. *Mullaney, supra.*

45. *McInnis* v. *Shapiro,* p. 336.

46. 293 F. Supp. 327 (N.D. Ill., E.D., Nov. 15, 1968); affirmed mem. 89 S. Ct. 1197 (March 24, 1969).

47. *Supra.*

48. *Supra.*

49. 89 S. Ct. 1197 (March 24, 1969).

50. *Serrano* v. *Priest, supra,* pp. 1263-1265.

51. *Dominion Hotel* v. *Arizona,* 249 U.S. 265, 39 S. Ct. 273 (1919).

52. *Burruss* v. *Wilkerson,* 310 F. Supp. 572 (May 23, 1969) affirmed mem., 397 U.S. 44, 90 S. Ct. 812 (1970).

53. *Burruss* v. *Wilkerson, supra.*

54. *Robinson* v. *Cahill*, Superior Court of New Jersey Law Division-Hudson County Docket No. L-18704-69.

55. *The Bateman Report*, State Aid to School Districts study Commission, N.J., December 19, 1968, p. 48.

56. R. L. Johns, Kern Alexander, Dewey Stollar, *Status and Impact of Educational Finance Programs*, 4 (Gainesville, Fla.; National Educational Finance Project, 1970).

57. *Alternative Programs for Financing Education* 5 (Gainesville, Fla.: National Educational Finance Project, 1971).

58. Harlan Updegraff, *Rural School Survey of New York State: Financial Support* (Ithaca, N.Y.: By the author, 1922).

59. John E. Coons, *et al. Private Wealth and Public Education* (Cambridge, Mass.: The Belknap Press of Harvard University Press, 1970).

ate Due

	Due	Returned